Western North Carolina Since the Civil War

Ina Woestemeyer Van Noppen

John J. Van Noppen

APPALACHIAN CONSORTIUM PRESS

BOONE, NORTH CAROLINA 28607

The Appalachian Consortium was a non-profit educational organization composed of institutions and agencies located in Southern Appalachia. From 1973 to 2004, its members published pioneering works in Appalachian studies documenting the history and cultural heritage of the region. The Appalachian Consortium Press was the first publisher devoted solely to the region and many of the works it published remain seminal in the field to this day.

With funding from the Andrew W. Mellon Foundation and the National Endowment for the Humanities through the Humanities Open Book Program, Appalachian State University has published new paperback and open access digital editions of works from the Appalachian Consortium Press.

www.collections.library.appstate.edu/appconsortiumbooks

This work is licensed under a Creative Commons BY-NC-ND license. To view a copy of the license, visit http://creativecommons.org/licenses.

Original copyright © 1973 by the Appalachian Consortium Press.

ISBN (pbk.: alk. Paper): 978-1-4696-3831-7
ISBN (ebook): 978-1-4696-3833-1

Distributed by the University of North Carolina Press
www.uncpress.org

TABLE OF CONTENTS

AUTHORS' PREFACE	iv
INTRODUCTION BY CRATIS WILLIAMS	vi
PROLOGUE	1
PART ONE: THE PEOPLE AND THEIR HOMELAND	23
1. On Main Traveled Roads	25
2. Off The Beaten Path	59
PART TWO: A CHANGING SOCIETY	69
3. Religion	71
4. The Bar and The Forum	88
5. That All May Live	103
6. Public Education	121
7. Church Related and Private Institutions of Learning	151
8. Teacher Education	166
9. From The Heart, The Hand, and The Head	184
10. Literature	201
11. The Lore of The Folk	223
PART THREE: A DEVELOPING ECONOMY	251
12. Hear That Whistle Blow!	253
13. Agriculture	269
14. Timber!	291
15. From Indian Trails to Broad Highways	323
16. Business and Industry	346
17. In Pursuit of Pleasure	371
SOURCES	414
INDEX	430

AUTHORS' PREFACE

Since its organization in 1952 and even before that time, members of the Western North Carolina Historical Association have searched zealously for history in their communities and in their counties. They researched old letters, records, account books, family histories, historic happenings. They have written county histories and presented papers before the historical association. They have sought the aid of the state Department of Archives and History. They have promoted the preservation of historic sites. Their contributions have been invaluable for a history of the region. Among the leading contributors have been Miss Cordelia Camp, Dean W. E. Bird, Mrs. Mary Jane McCrary, Dean D. J. Whitener, and Professor John A. McLeod. Journalists John Wikle, John Parris, George McCoy and his wife, Lola Love McCoy, and such writers of county histories as Judge Johnson Hayes, Clarence Griffin, Mrs. Sadie Smathers Patton, Mrs. Margaret Freel, Mrs. Nancy Alexander, Horton Cooper, Arthur Fletcher, and Mrs. Lillian Thomasson, provided information sifted out from local annals.

The newspapers of Western North Carolina, especially the Asheville *Citizen-Times*, are to be commended for publishing anniversary editions and encouraging the people to be interested in their history and its preservation. Publisher George M. Stephens has been a promoter of the Carolina Highlands, publishing numerous books and pamphlets dealing with Western North Carolina history.

January 27, 1963, a committee to promote a history of the Western North Carolina Highlands was appointed. It consisted of W. Ernest Bird, Miss Cordelia Camp, John A. McLeod, D. Hiden Ramsey, George M. Stephens, Glenn Tucker, and Daniel J. Whitener, chairman. By late 1964 the present authors had been drafted to write the book. Interested members contributed financially to support the research, most generous of whom was Wendell Williamson of Asheville.

Robert Conway of the North Carolina Department of Archives and History furnished a list of names of persons who were particularly interested in history, one in each county. We called upon the persons named, and they usually guided us around their counties to view the historic sites and distinctive features. Leroy Sossamon took us flying over the Great Smoky Mountains National Park. In Brevard Mrs. Mary Jane McCrary took us into her home, as did Dr. and Mrs. Edward Phifer in Morganton. Several county-wide meetings of local historians were held. Informative ones were arranged by Worth Morgan of Forest City and Frank Rogers of Waynesville. Many members of the association took us to old residents who knew of historic events. They showed us letters, furnished newspaper clippings, some of which were undated and had no sources listed. John Wikle of Bryson City furnished an extensive file of his articles from the Asheville *Citizen* and the Atlanta *Journal*.

Dozens of graduate students researched local topics, contributing useful information. Lawrence Groves, Thomas Corbitt, and Rosalie Sexauer Dorsey deserve special mention.

We are grateful to members of the administration at Appalachian State University for released time for research, to the Office of Development for photographic assistance, and especially to John Dinkins, photographer.

Our sincere appreciation is due Dean Cratis Williams who wrote our introduction, Mrs. Allie Hodgin of the Appalachian State University Library who aided us tirelessly, and Jack Van Noppen who reviewed the manuscript and helped organize it. Our greatest indebtedness is to Miss Myra Champion who encouraged and contributed more than words can tell to the completion of this book.

Ina Van Noppen
John J. Van Noppen

Boone, North Carolina
February 12, 1973

INTRODUCTION

The late Daniel J. Whitener, Chairman of the Department of Social Sciences and Dean of Appalachian State Teachers College, was commissioned in 1948 to prepare a history of Watauga County, North Carolina, for the Centennial Celebration of the formation of the county and the Sesquicentenial Celebration of the founding of Watauga Academy, the parent institution of Appalachian State University. Dean Whitener's experience inspired him to assume leadership in the forming of the Southern Appalachian Historical Association, which set about to build the Daniel Boone Outdoor Theatre in Boone and produce Kermit Hunter's *Horn in the West*, but he also saw the need for a carefully done history of Western North Carolina which he hoped ultimately to be able to write himself.

Encouraged by both the Western North Carolina Historical Association and the Historical Society of North Carolina, Dean Whitener began gathering material and planning a history, but his heavy burden of administrative duties at the rapidly growing college and his wide range of interests and involvements in local and state civic activities did not leave time for him to engage in the field research needed for the kind of history he thought should be written. During the year prior to his scheduled retirement from his administrative position at Appalachian, Dean Whitener realized that the condition of his health was such that he would not be able to write the history he had dreamed of writing. He sought the advice of the members of the Western North Carolina Historical Association and his collegues at the college. He was urged to determine whether Ina Woestemeyer Van Noppen, a productive scholar and professor of history at Appalachian, might be willing to undertake to complete the history.

Ina Van Noppen, who had collected oral history, visited the sites of engagements along the route of Stoneman's Last Raid, and searched for materials in archives and libraries in preparation for her writing of *Stoneman's Last Raid*, had become interested in the history of Western North Carolina and the mountain people who live there. She had already discovered that, aside from a few county histories of uneven quality written for the most part by people little acquainted with the techniques of historical scholarship and often motivated by genealogical interests, little had been done, and no one had attempted a comprehensive history of the entire mountain region of the state since 1914 when John Preston Arthur published his *History of Western North Carolina*. Dr. Van Noppen, reluctant to undertake to do the assignment because of her work in collaboration with her husband, John James Van Noppen, a professor of English at Appalachian, in the preparation of a biography of Daniel Boone, requested time for consideration of the request. Urged by the membership of the Western North Carolina Historical Association and encouraged by promises of such resources as might be available to it in helping to underwrite the publication of the book, Dr. Van Noppen agreed to write it provided she could work in collaboration with her husband.

As the plan for the history developed, the Van Noppens began to see that it ought not to be the usual history of the political and economic progress of a region within a state but, rather a whole history, which would include a treatment of the differentiating qualities of the mountain people as well as their institutions, traditions, customs, folklore, arts and crafts, way of life, and the literature written about them and by them.

Western North Carolina is the state's share of Appalachia, but no history of Appalachia has been written. Much has been written about the folklore of the mountain people, the economic problems which plague the region, and the nature of the people themselves, as well as their social problems, customs, old fashioned religious views, and political conservatism. The Van Noppens thought that a history should treat all facets in the lives of the people about which it is written. Hence, they have produced an economic, political, social, and cultural history which might well be taken as a model for similar histories of western Virginia, eastern Kentucky, and eastern Tennessee, which, when taken together, might provide a base for a comprehensive history of a unique and fascinating people, the Southern Appalachians.

Western North Carolina Since the Civil War is the product of eight years of research and writing. Not content to rely upon such sources as might be found in regional libraries and state archives, the Van Noppens sought out individuals in the mountain region who possessed primary sources, traveled over the mountains from town to town and courthouse to courthouse in search of sources, sought documents and reports stored in state archives and the Library of Congress. John Van Noppen reviewed the literature about the mountain folk, visited living writers, studied the collections of ballads and folk songs, and read theses and dissertations written about the cultural heritage of the area. Together, the Van Noppens attended fairs and festivals and visited museums, libraries, and colleges in the area. They traced out the early roads through the mountains, studied the histories of the railroads, visited the forests and the national and state parks, examined the history and development of tourism, and sought out the seers and craftsmen, the educators and the religious leaders, the politicians and the developers who share in guiding the native mountain folk living in what has come to be known as North Carolina's vacation land through their transition from a highland rural and largely self-subsistent society to what is rapidly becoming an urban society.

Ina Woestemeyer Van Noppen, a native of Bethel, Kansas, was educated at the University of Kansas and Columbia University. Soon after graduating from the University of Kansas, she began teaching history in high schools in Kansas City. After receiving the M.A. degree from Columbia, she taught for a time at the Woman's College of the University of North Carolina at Greensboro. While working toward her doctoral degree at Columbia, she taught history at Penn Hall Junior College, where her husband John J. Van Noppen, was dean and a teacher of English. Later she and her husband taught at Hiram College and at Youngstown College in Ohio before going to Appalachian State Teachers College in Boone, North Carolina, in 1947. She is the author of *The Westward Movement* (1939), *The South: A Documentary History* (1958), and *Stoneman's Last Raid* (1961), for which she received the Thomas Wolfe Memorial Award from the Western North Carolina Historical Association. She and her husband collaborated in the writing of *Daniel Boone, Backwoodsman* (1966). An outstanding teacher of history, Dr. Ina Van Noppen received one of the first distinguished teacher awards presented by Appalachian State University.

John J. Van Noppen grew up in Madison, North Carolina. He holds degrees from the University of North Carolina at Chapel Hill and Columbia University. After years of teaching in secondary schools and preparatory schools, including experience in Italy, where he became personally acquainted with Benito Mussolini, Dr. Van Noppen began a long career as a college teacher and administrator. He was an English teacher and Dean of Penn Hall Junior College and Preparatory School at Chambersburg, Pennsylvania, Head of the Department of Education at Hiram College, and a teacher of English at Youngstown College in Ohio. He joined the English faculty at Appalachian State Teachers College, Boone, North Carolina, in 1947. He has engaged in extensive research on Archibald Henderson and George Bernard Shaw and collaborated with his wife in the writing of *Daniel Boone, Backwoodsman* (1966).

The Van Noppens are world travelers, having conducted summer tours abroad for students and teachers for many years. While researching in England, Scotland, Wales, and Ireland in preparation for their biography of Daniel Boone, they learned much of the ferments which sent English, Scottish, and Scotch-Irish pioneers into Western North Carolina prior to the American Revolution. Among the descendants of these settlers are the Western North Carolina mountain people of today.

Western North Carolina Since the Civil War, though a scholarly work, is published without the extensive footnotes which the authors painstakingly prepared. Aimed primarily at the reading public, particularly of Western North Carolina, the book is none the less of value to the historian and the student of local cultures.

Moving slowly and often painfully out of their dark period of economic and social disintegration following the Civil War, the mountain people living in the isolated and insulated "lost provinces" of Western North Carolina had by 1900 begun their steady march of progress into contemporary times. Uneven at times and faltering as the state and the nation suffered through such social and economic upheavals as war, economic booms and recessions, and drouths, the people of Western North Carolina have made solid progress in improving education, local economy, communication, land use, and natural resources. Most importantly, they have clung to the traditions and nurtured the heritage that is uniquely their own. With pride in themselves and appreciation of the grandeur which lies about them, they have managed to preserve their own culture and conserve their own beautiful homeland so rich in resources that the degree of poverty there is not comparable with that found elsewhere in Appalachia. As the Van Noppens have so aptly observed, Carolina mountain folk are not "yesterday's people" nor is night likely to come to them, for they have become the shapers of their own destiny.

Cratis Williams

Appalachian State University
Boone, North Carolina

PROLOGUE

Extending from Rutherfordton on the south to Mount Airy and Fancy Gap on the north is an elevated region, the foothills, from 1,000 to 2,000 feet above sea level. Beyond are lofty, mist-shrouded and haze-creating mountains, the picturesque barrier of the Blue Ridge on the east, the magnificent Great Smokies and the scenic Unakas on the west. Between the Blue Ridge, which is the eastern Continental Divide, and the Unakas there is a high plateau with altitudes ranging from 3,500 to 4,000 feet. Grandfather Mountain 5,964 feet, is the highest and most spectacular peak in the Blue Ridge, but not as high as the Black Mountains farther south, where Mount Mitchell rears its lofty crest 6,684 feet above sea level.

This elevated tableland encircled by the two great mountain ranges is traversed by cross chains that run directly across the country, from which spurs of greater and lesser height lead off in all directions. Among the transverse groups are the Black, Roan, Yellow, New Found, Pisgah, Balsam, Cowee, Nantahala, Cheoah, and Tusquitee ranges. Between these ranges lie valleys formed by rivers which flow through gorges near their headwaters, then widen out and continue through fertile valleys across the plateau, and narrow again, dividing the rampart into the Unicoi, the Great Smokies, the Iron, the Bald, and the Stone Mountains. Clingman's Dome in the Smokies is 6,642 feet above sea level, almost as high as Mount Mitchell. The Black Mountain range extends for twenty miles, and its sides are covered in places by almost impenetrable forests. Of the transverse chains, next to the Blacks in size and altitude are the Balsams. In general magnitude and length they are the most extensive of the cross ranges. Fifty miles long, this range has numerous peaks which average 6,000 feet.

2 / Prologue

Geographically Western North Carolina, consisting of foothills, valleys, peaks, the crest of the Blue Ridge, the Great Smoky Mountains, and the transverse ridges, is about 250 miles long and up to 150 miles wide. It consists of approximately one-fifth of North Carolina's area but only one-seventh of its population. It has one county with sixteen persons per square mile, three with fewer than thirty per square mile, three with from thirty to thirty-nine per square mile, five with from forty to forty-nine persons, and two with from fifty to fifty-nine, while for the entire state the population density is ninety-seven per square mile.

Since 1739 the subdivisions of the state have been known as counties, each serving as an administrative unit for the colony and later for the state. As new areas were opened they too were designated as counties; some of them were quite large, and later as the population increased other counties were formed by subdividing the existing ones. Rowan County, formed in 1753, was the parent of Western North Carolina although the present-day Rowan County is not in Western North Carolina. In 1771 Surry County was created from Rowan and remained the westernmost one until Burke was also formed from Rowan in 1777 and Wilkes from Surry in 1778. In the southwest Mecklenburg was created from Anson and in 1769 Tryon was formed from the western part of Mecklenburg. In 1779 Tryon was abolished and its land divided between Lincoln and Rutherford counties; the latter is in Western North Carolina.

Meanwhile four additional counties, later part of Tennessee, were formed: Washington in 1777, Sullivan in 1779, Greene and Davidson in 1783. They anticipated cession to the United States and in 1784 tried to create the State of Franklin, which did not survive as a state. Three other counties, Sumner, Hawkins, and Tennessee, were subdivided from the four before cession did take place in 1789. The seven became part of the State of Tennessee which was admitted to the union in 1796.

In 1800 Western North Carolina consisted of Surry, Rutherford, Burke, Wilkes, Buncombe (which had been created from lands ceded by the Cherokees), and Ashe counties. Ashe had been separated from Wilkes. As the Cherokees gave up additional lands Haywood County was established in 1808, Yancey in 1833, and Henderson in 1838. From Rutherford and Burke came McDowell in 1842, and from Buncombe and Yancey was formed Madison in 1851. In 1828 Macon was set apart from Haywood, and in 1851 Jackson County was created from Haywood and Macon, the latter having surrendered the land evacuated by the Cherokees for the county of Cherokee in 1839. Further subdividing created Polk from Henderson in 1855, Transylvania from Henderson and Jackson, and Clay from Cherokee, in 1861, Swain from Jackson and Macon in 1871, and Graham from Cherokee in 1872.

In the northwestern part of the state Caldwell was formed from Burke and Wilkes in 1841, Watauga from Wilkes, Ashe, Caldwell, and Yancey in 1849, Mitchell in 1861 from Yancey, Watauga, Caldwell, Burke, and McDowell. Alleghany was created from the eastern part of Ashe. The last county, Avery, was formed in 1911 from Mitchell, Watauga, and Caldwell.

Upon examination of a map showing the counties of Western North Carolina one must conclude that they have very peculiar shapes. This is due no doubt to the mountainous terrain and to the necessity that people be able to travel from the farthest point to the county seat.

In the eighteenth century immigrants poured through "William Penn's new port of Philadelphia" from the British Isles and Germany. With them they brought their skills, speech, ballads, dances, and folk customs. Many of the second and third generations came southwestward seeking land. Salisbury in the newly-created Rowan County (1753) became the springboard into the West. In the 1750's Salisbury was like the hub of a wagon wheel. Settlers flowed in along the northern, eastern, and southeastern spokes. They paused briefly to rest their horses, repair their wagons (if they had any), and to buy needed supplies of salt, powder, lead, and tools. Many fanned out along the western spokes toward the beckoning beauty of the Blue Ridge. They plunged deeper and ever deeper into the wilderness, lured on by the prospect of cheap and still richer lands on which to build their homes. Soon they had settled all except the most mountainous parts of what are now Surry, Wilkes, Burke, and Rutherford counties. Intrepidly they disregarded the threat of Indian attacks and moved into the uncharted wilderness. Some lost their lives but many survived, the ancestors of present-day mountaineers. Men bearing the names of Alexander, Boone, Bryan, Robertson, Sevier, Shelby, Campbell, Clingman,

Jackson, Davidson, Patton, Rutherford, Councill, Calloway, Howard, Horton, Gudger and Moore were among the advance guard. They cleared land, built primitive cabins, hunted, trapped, and fought the Indians. Their incentive was the passion for land where there were few taxes and no restrictions upon political and religious freedom. The extent of their migration may be seen from the fact that in 1746 there were not one hundred fighting men in the North Carolina foothills; while in 1753 there were three thousand. In 1765 one thousand wagons passed through Salisbury going westward.

During the Revolutionary War the Cherokee Indians made the fatal mistake of siding with the British. They were badly defeated and decimated by frontiersmen led by men like Griffith Rutherford and John Sevier. Their towns were burned, their women and children killed, and they were driven ever westward. During the Revolution many who fought the Cherokees saw the mountains for the first time, admired the beauty of Western North Carolina and were determined to return and settle as soon as the war ended. A law passed by the state legislature in 1777 provided the method of acquiring land. Each claimant took to the entry recorder a statement of location and approximate boundaries of the land he wished. The county surveyor then surveyed the tract and prepared two plots with descriptions of boundaries and acreage, which he transferred along with the warrant of survey to the secretary of state. The claimant paid the entry taker two pounds and ten shillings per one hundred acres. A husband was allowed to take six hundred forty acres for himself and one hundred acres for his wife and each of his children. For purchases in excess of his allotment the purchaser paid five pounds per one hundred acres, or one shilling per acre. Tracts of as many as 1,000,000 acres were laid out and were acquired by speculators who disposed of the land in tracts of 500 or 1000 acres. Among the large landowners in the region before 1800 were Charles Gordon in Wilkes County, Robert and William Tate in Burke, David Allison, John Gray Blount, and William Cathcart in Buncombe. When the war was over the state offered land to servicemen in payment for their having served.

The bold and dauntless pioneers pushed across the great mountain barrier into a natural wonderland with magnificent scenery, a cool climate, clear air, pure water, fertile valleys, and game in plenty. In this region men and women extended a frontier civilization that became Western North Carolina, consisting ultimately of the twenty-four counties that are in the mountains or ascend the eastern slope of the mountains.

Many of the settlers moved into the back country on foot and on horseback, bringing their household goods on pack horses. Among these goods were, in addition to rifle, axe, and hoe, clothing, blankets, bed clothes, bed ticks to be filled with grass, a large pot, pothooks, an oven with a lid, a skillet, a frying pan, a handmill to grind corn, a wooden trencher in which to make bread, pewter plates, spoons, the iron parts of plows, a broadaxe, a froe, a saw, an auger, seed, and a few fruit trees.

The historian John Fiske implied that the settlers of the mountains were descended from poor whites and indentured servants who migrated westward rather than compete with slave labor, that their ancestors had been herded into ships from the slums and jails of England. His opinion was true of only a small minority. He and others who held this opinion ignored the predominant Scotch-Irish and German origin of many settlers. John C. Campbell believed that the early mountain population was recruited chiefly from the poor but vigorous small farmers of the piedmont, few of whom owned slaves.

A study of family names in the Southern Highlands by the Russell Sage Foundation revealed that of 497 names, one-third were English, one-third were Scotch-Irish, and fifteen per-cent were of German origin. Most of the families were descended from those living on the frontiers of Virginia and North Carolina in 1790. They were the same stock that later peopled the Midwest and the Southern states along the Mississippi, except Louisiana. According to S. H. Hobbs, the English in Western North Carolina contributed most to the civilization of the region. "Wherever the Englishman has gone . . . he has carried with him the industrial, political, and intellectual customs of his native land. The English ideal of home life, the English industrial system, the English principles of politics and government, the English language and literature sooner or later became the dominant force wheresoever the Englishman set up his home."

R. D. W. Connor characterized the racial strains of the population as follows: the English were law-abiding, commercially minded, and self reliant; the Scotch-Irish were democratic, liberty loving, and religiously minded; the Germans were shrewd, economical, conservative, lovers of learning and religion. Although Connor was writing about the people of the state as a whole, these national strains made up the population of Western North Carolina and his description is apt.

There has been a tendency to speak of the early settlers as though they were all alike, all of one class. This tendency has created a misconception. They were not a homogeneous group. Three classes came to the mountains: the prosperous settler class that came and bought good bottom land and perhaps thousands of acres of mountain land as well; those who bought land in smaller tracts from the first group or from the state; and those who came on foot or horseback carrying their few possessions, and who squatted on the land. Many of the prosperous people of the area today are descended from the settler class, although their prosperity did not result from agriculture. Their land was their most valuable resource, and scions of pioneer families are still realizing tremendous returns from land sales — land that has grown amazingly valuable. On the other hand poverty for many resulted from the extinction of the game, over crowding, and exhaustion of the soil. As time passed many valleys, ridges, and coves had a population greater than they could support. Large families lived crowded in one or two-room cabins. As late as 1910 eighty per-cent of the population lived outside towns of one thousand population. As the original farms were divided among descendants holdings became smaller and smaller.

The Civil War brought disunion and discord to Western North Carolina. Many people loved their section and their state, but they also revered the Union for which their ancestors had fought. Some favored the South, some the Union. Brother fought against brother and father against son. Neighborhoods split, families divided. Many heroic young men fought for the Confederacy; others fled through Tennessee and Kentucky to join the Union army. Numbers hid out in mountain caves and recesses to avoid conscription. Many of the latter two groups were opposed to slavery; others felt that the Civil War was a war of the planter class and they had no reason to fight for planter dominance of the state.

There was no actual campaign in the mountains of North Carolina until 1865, but the mountain passes were of strategic importance. The Northern strategy was to divide the South into segments, and control of the passes would have contributed.

A number of roads crossed the mountains from east to west: the Western North Carolina Road across the Balsam Mountains; the great highway from South Carolina and Georgia crossing Saluda Gap, passing through Henderson, Buncombe, and Haywood counties; roads from Wilkesboro diverging in three directions: northwest into Virginia, west through Watauga County into Tennessee, and southwest through Morganton, crossing the Blue Ridge at Swannanoa Gap. Turnpikes supplemented the state roads, making it possible for wheeled vehicles to cross through some of the gaps, but there were many little-known mountain paths where only experienced guides could find their way. The great mountain barriers discouraged invasion by hostile forces even though the area was divided in sentiment. Railroads to cross the mountains had been planned, but none had been built.

During the war campaigns were fought all around the mountains but not through them. The salt works at Saltville, Virginia, were a target of several Union raids. Cumberland Gap was in Federal control in 1863; Chattanooga and Knoxville were captured by Union forces and the Shenandoah Valley and the gaps in the Virginia mountains saw considerable action. Braxton Bragg, Kirby Smith, and John Hunt Morgan led Confederate troops through the passes of the Cumberlands, and Union troops fought their way through Georgia's mountains from Chattanooga to Atlanta, yet North Carolina's mountains remained a formidable barrier. General U. S. Grant considered following up the victory at Chattanooga by sending 50,000 men through the mountain country, but after a ride of 175 miles, he abandoned the plan because of the bad roads.

The Confederacy realized the importance of North Carolina mountain passes. Colonel William Holland Thomas of southwestern North Carolina anticipated such a campaign as that planned by Grant. He believed that Lee might wish to use the mountains as a stronghold where he could have an invincible base of operations. Confederate soldiers built roads over the passes through the Great Smoky Mountains, and they controlled the mountain passes toward Tennessee. Early in the war Thomas's Legion of Indians and Highlanders, the Eightieth and Sixty-ninth North Carolina regiments, had guarded the bridges between Bristol and Chattanooga, but after the fall of East Tennessee, they fell back on the Smoky Mountains toward Waynesville and Webster.

After East Tennessee became Union territory, the Fourteenth

North Carolina Battalion (Woodfin's Battalion) was created. Originally three companies, it later had six. Its members were Western North Carolinians and its function was to defend the state's borders against invasion and pillage. After Woodfin's death James L. Henry was made Lieutenant Colonel and commander of the battalion. As Henry had only one eye the command was sometimes referred to as the "One-Eyed Battalion." It made raids into Tennessee and used the guerilla methods necessary in mountain fighting.

In 1864 the defenses of Northwestern North Carolina were very meager. Madison County was patrolled by a cavalry company; while Major Harvey Bingham had two companies in Watauga and a Captain Price had a small company in Ashe. These companies defended the counties against predatory bands from East Tennessee. Yancey and Mitchell counties were virtually undefended.

The mountains sheltered fugitives from both armies, who hid by day and raided by night, often in bands of twenty or more. Many prisoners who had escaped from Confederate prisons made their way to the Union lines in Tennessee. Prisoners from Salisbury followed the Yadkin to Wilkes County, said to be the strongest Union county in North Carolina. The Confederates called it "Old United States." The Unionists sheltered and fed the escapees and guided them to Banner Elk where men like Keith Blalock and Harrison Church guided them to Tennessee. Those escaping from the prison at Columbia made their way across South Carolina, through Saluda Gap to Hendersonville and Asheville, where Dan Ellis guided them to Tennessee. One group of prisoners escaping by this route were hidden for four days by the girls of a family near Flat Rock. The father of the girls was a "rebel," the mother a "home Yankee," and the father never learned of the fugitives. Guides for the prisoners roamed the country "sacking" the fine houses and stealing money, jewelry, and silverware.

In March 1865 the Union army was ready to begin the final campaign of the war. Mobile, the last port in Confederate hands, was being attacked by General E. R. S. Canby. General George Thomas was sending out two powerful expeditions, one under Brevet Major General H. Wilson in Alabama, the other under Major General George Stoneman toward Lynchburg. General Philip H. Sheridan's cavalry had completed its raid through the Shenandoah Valley and had moved to White House on the Pamunkey. The armies of generals William T. Sherman and John M. Schofield were at Goldsboro. General John Pope was preparing for a spring campaign against Generals Kirby Smith and Sterling Price west of the Mississippi. Grant with the armies of the Potomac and the James confronted General Robert E. Lee, who defended Petersburg and Richmond. Very important was General Stoneman's raid through the mountains of Western North Carolina, Southwestern Virginia, and the piedmont of North Carolina in March and April 1865.

General Stoneman, a West Point graduate stationed in Fort Brown, Texas, at the start of the war, refused to surrender to Confederate troops when his immediate superior did. He escaped with his command and continued to serve the Union army as a cavalry commander in West Virginia, under General George B. McClellan, and with the Army of the Potomac. In 1864 as a commander of the cavalry corps in the Atlanta campaign he was captured at Clinton, Georgia. Exchanged, he returned to command under General Thomas in East Tennessee. He conducted a destructive raid against Bristol and Saltville, Virginia, in December 1864. Early in 1865 he was ordered to collect horses and men to destroy the railroad between Bristol and Lynchburg. Participating in Stoneman's raid were three cavalry brigades under Brigadier General Alvan C. Gillem, with brigade commanders Colonel William J. Palmer, Brigadier General Simeon B. Brown, and Colonel John K. Miller.

On March 28 General Stoneman notified General Thomas from Boone that he had captured the place, killing nine, capturing sixty-two, and that the raid was a surprise to those on his route. His raid was a surprise. A few weeks earlier, a few Union men had surprised and captured Camp Mast with one company of Home Guards. The other company of Home Guards were surprised by Stoneman. Colonel George Kirk of the United States Army had gathered a regiment of volunteers from the deserters, bushwhackers, and Union sympathizers. In January Kirk had created a diversion up the French Broad River and cleared the mountain region of deserters. Now Kirk barricaded the passes from Blowing Rock and Boone westward. On the day that Kirk arrived in Boone, Lee was evacuating Petersburg and Richmond and was moving toward Lynchburg following the Confederate defeat at Five Forks, and Grant feared that Lee might escape to North Carolina by way of the Richmond and Danville Railroad. Stoneman was supposed to prevent Lee's retreat to North Carolina by the railroad or his establishment of a bastion of defense in the mountains.

At Boone Stoneman's command separated. Palmer's brigade went by way of Deep Gap to Wilkesboro; Brown's moved by way of Blowing Rock to Patterson's factory on the Yadkin near Lenoir. Here they found an adequate supply of corn and bacon, and Miller's brigade, following, destroyed the factory. The latter brigades joined Palmer's at Wilkesboro where they captured stores and horses and were forced to camp because the Yadkin River was in flood.

On March 30 Stoneman's cavalry moved out of Wilkesboro. James Gwyn, whose plantation was passed, said that the raiders took only cattle and horses and that they did little damage. They went thence to Elkin and used up provisions but did not burn the factory or the cotton. September 1, 1863, Gwyn had written that Union sympathizers had taken over Wilkesboro but that they would rue the day. They had been influenced by Parson Brownlow's Knoxville *Whig* and Holden's *North Carolina Standard*. Now Gwyn pointed out that Stoneman's men did not respect those calling themselves Union men. Gwyn saved some of his cattle by hiding them in the woods.

At last the raid on the Virginia and Tennessee Railroad took place. The Union cavalry passed through Dobson and Mount Airy, crossing the Blue Ridge. It captured and burned a Confederate wagon train. Having reached Virginia the forces were divided. It is sufficient here to say that Stoneman's men destroyed the railroad successfully, then, returning to North Carolina they destroyed the Confederate prison at Salisbury (they did not liberate the prisoners, who had already been removed) and large quantities of supplies. Following this they began their return to Tennessee. We take up their activities again as they reached Lenoir on Easter Sunday, April 15.

Meanwhile a Union scouting party sent to Asheville on April 4 reported that the roads were barricaded and that 2000 men under General R. B. Vance defended it. The Union commander Colonel Isaac M. Kirby had orders not to participate in a battle. He was engaged in a skirmish about four miles from Asheville and retreated.

At Lenoir Stoneman's invasion had long been expected.* March 29 reports had come that Yankees were in the Yadkin Valley, on April 7 that Kirk with 300 men occupied Blowing Rock, and on April 13 that Salisbury had been "bummed." On April 15 Stoneman's men rushed in and camped their prisoners on the grounds of St. James Episcopal Church.† Citizens were invited to feed the prisoners and to move freely among them. Major A. C. Avery of a very prominent Burke County family had been captured by chance in Salisbury. In 1864 he had obtained permission to organize a regiment to protect Northwestern North Carolina. The regiment was never organized, but the local companies did become a battalion, and arms, ammunition, and equipment were sent to them by Governor Vance at the request of Major Avery. Avery had gone to Salisbury to obtain men to join him in an attack on Kirk at Blowing Rock when he was captured. He was taken as a prisoner to Tennessee, but Stoneman did not realize that he had captured Avery. People of Lenoir helped him to conceal his identity by shaving his beard and giving him the clothing of a relative, after which his own men did not recognize him. The Yanks liked the people of Lenoir but called it the "d — est little rebel town."

At Lenoir General Stoneman left the command, returning through Watauga County to Tennessee. He reported that the tithing depots had furnished food and that captured horses had made his command better mounted than when it left Knoxville, and "this after crossing Stone Mountain once and the Blue Ridge three times, and a march made by headquarters since the 20th of last month of 500 miles, and much more by portions of the command."

Colonel Palmer was sent to Lincolnton and General Gillem to Morganton. James Gwyn reported of Morganton: "They tore everything to pieces at Uncle Avery's, held pistols to the ladies' heads, drove them out of the house and took what they liked." After Stoneman left the command the plundering and

---

* In her Diary on March 30 Mrs. Ella (G.W.F.) Harper wrote of rumors that 10,000 Yankees were in the valley, and that they had burned the factory. The next day she expressed fear that Tories would be raiding Lenoir, and that the furniture had been removed from their store for safe keeping.

† Mrs. Ella Harper wrote in her Diary "Everyone cooking as much as possible for our poor famished prisoners."

12 / *Prologue*

sacking of houses and mutilations of furnishings increased greatly.

General James G. Martin with Palmer's Brigade (Confederate) of the 62nd, 64th, and 69th Regiments, a South Carolina battery, and Love's Regiment of Thomas's Legion defended Asheville. On April 24 General Gillem met General Martin under a flag of truce. He promised that if his command were furnished three days' rations it would not molest the country but would peaceably march through and proceed to Tennessee. "The almost starving country" furnished the supplies, but the Yankee army soon returned, terrorized the people, burned houses, and destroyed the armory and all the guns and ammunition they could find. A Negro garrison was left in charge of the town for a year and "burners roamed the countryside for miles around."

General Gillem reported the complete surprise of the rebels at every point, and of the entire campaign he enumerated the captures: "25 pieces of artillery . . . 21 that they were forced to abandon in Southwest Virginia . . . 6000 prisoners and 17 battle flags."

The war was not over yet in Western North Carolina: a part of the "One-eyed Battalion" was in a skirmish as late as May 10. And James Gwyn of Wilkes County wrote in his diary May 4: "We have a quiet time now, our Southern armies are disbanded . . . and terms of peace are said to be agreed upon . . . . All we dread here now is robbers & no doubt there will be plenty of them this summer."

By the time that Gwyn wrote the comment about the robbers, depredations in Wilkes County had become a certainty. Fort Hamby came into being shortly after Stoneman and his army left Wilkes County March 31, 1865. The men who used it and terrorized the surrounding countryside were said to be deserters from Stoneman's forces and "home Yankees" who sympathized with them. Their leader was named Wade, and he was reputed to have been a major under Stoneman. Fort Hamby was not a military fort but a stronghold for the desperate band of criminals who occupied it. The houses belonged to disreputable women named Hamby. After having been occupied by Wade and his men, it was called Fort Hamby.

There were two old-fashioned log buildings. The larger was two stories high and was the one used as a fort. The other, about

Clark's N. C. Regiments cites May 10 as the date of this skirmish
PHOTO BY ASHEVILLE CITIZEN-TIMES CO.

thirty feet from the fort, a single story, was used as a kitchen. These buildings were on the north side of the Yadkin near the mouth of Lewis Fork Creek on the top of a hill which overlooked the two streams. This strategic location gave excellent vision from both sides of the fort and made it easily defensible.

The men of the fort, heavily armed with the latest type of Union rifles, roamed the countryside for miles about, plundering, robbing, terrorizing the people in Alexander, Caldwell, Wilkes, and Watauga counties. Without compunction they killed women and children. Elated by their strong grip on Wilkes, Wade's men made a raid on Caldwell County May 7; on the Sunday following Major Harvey Bingham and a few men surprised the fort. Wade begged for the lives of his men and time for them to dress. While the captors were off guard, the robbers seized their guns which had been concealed near their beds. They killed two of their captors, one the son of General Clark of Caldwell County. The others escaped, leaving the bodies of the two slain men.

On Saturday May 13 Wade and his men went into Alexander County to kill Reverend J. B. Green, a former Confederate lieutenant. Forewarned, the Greens and their former slaves repulsed the raiders. On May 14 the second attack was made on the fort by some twenty men under the command of Colonel Wash Sharpe, Colonel C. W. Flowers, and Captain Ellis. James Polk Linney, sixteen, and James Brown, eighteen, were killed. On Tuesday some forty men from Alexander, Iredell, Caldwell, and Wilkes counties surrounded the fort, constructed breastworks and beseiged it during the night. About daybreak Wallace Sharpe sneaked up to the old kitchen at the rear of the house and set it on fire. Wade and the men in the fort came out in apparent surrender. Suddenly Wade bolted through the surrounding line and escaped. The four men who were captured — Beck, Church, Lockwood, and one other — were executed. The fort was burned. It is believed that Wade's band numbered about thirty, of whom about ten actually stayed at the fort with the other members of the band living nearby. With the destruction of Fort Hamby, Wilkes County saw the end of its Civil War strife.

In Madison County during the Civil War great hostility was felt between those who favored secession and those who supported the Union. Augustus S. Merrimon of Buncombe County was appointed solicitor for the Eighth Judicial District during the war, and his task of maintaining law and order was difficult. Once when some inhabitants (so-called Union sympathizers) seized the town of Marshall, plundered the stores and committed many acts of violence, one thousand Confederate citizens of Buncombe County formed a posse and hurried to Marshall to punish the marauders. Solicitor Merrimon prevailed against this disregard of civil power, and the occasion passed without further incident. Merrimon held his courts throughout the war, and persons who committed depredations were brought to trial, imperiling Merrimon's life. When he ran for election to be a delegate to the constitutional convention of 1865, former members of Kirk's regiments threatened vengeance and Merrimon lost. Later he was elected Judge of the Superior Court for the Eighth Judicial District and upon the convening of court in several counties violence was threatened. In Clay County hundreds of armed men awaited the beginning of an onslaught when the court opened. After a skirmish involving sixty to eighty persons, Judge Merrimon directed the sheriff to select and swear in sixty trusted men from both factions, to see that they were armed, and to tell them to shoot the first man guilty of violence with intent to start a general disturbance. A similar occurrence happened at the court in Cherokee.

As has been pointed out, many of the pre-war Whigs after serving the Confederate government became Democrats, but since the name *Democrat* was repugnant to them the party was called the Conservative Party. A Republican Party organization was formed in North Carolina in 1867. It consisted of some former Whigs, many small farmers who had not favored secession, Northerners who came to the state to participate in political affairs, and freedmen. It controlled North Carolina until 1870. From the beginning it was popular in Western North Carolina. Perhaps it is true, as a historian has remarked, that the Western counties did not suffer as much during the years 1865–1870 as piedmont and eastern counties where there were more Negroes to vote and hold office, but there were trying times. Republicans organized the Union League in the state to campaign for Republicans; and William H. Holden of Raleigh and Tod R. Caldwell of Burke County, Republicans, were elected governor and lieutenant governor respectively in 1868. Terrorist activities of members of such organizations as the Ku Klux Klan and editorial campaigns of newspapers against Holden's administration prompted the governor to call for two regiments of volunteer troops as "detailed militia" to arrest the violence and disturbances which he and his advisers attributed to the Conservatives. George Kirk of Tennessee, leader of Union regiments in Western North Carolina during the Civil War, was chosen to head one regiment. A circular written by Holden was circulated in the western part of the state. It read: "Rally Union Men in defense of your state! Rally soldiers of the old N. Carolina 2d and 3d Federal troops! Rally to the standard of the old commander.... 1000 recruits are wanted immediately, to serve six months unless sooner discharged. These troops will receive the same pay, clothing and rations as United States regulars. Recruits will be received at Asheville, Marshall, and Burnsville, North Carolina."

The so-called "Kirk-Holden war" was part of the political campaign of 1870 which did not include the election of governor, whose term had been fixed at four years by the constitution of 1868. The election resulted in victory for the Conservatives in the legislative offices: five of the seven North Carolina members of Congress and majorities in both houses of the General Assembly. While the Republicans had controlled the General Assembly the issuing of $27,850,000 in bonds for railroad repair and construction was authorized, although only $17,660,000 were issued. The bond issues constituted a fraud participated in by some seventeen legislators led by George Swepson and lobbied for by Milton Littlefield. Most of the proceeds were not used for railroad construction. Of the bonds issued, $6,387,000 was authorized for construction of the Western Division of the Western North Carolina Railroad, Asheville to the Tennessee line, and $613,000 for the Eastern Division, Salisbury to Asheville.

When the Democrats took over the General Assembly in 1870, they authorized a railroad investigation, the findings of which enabled them to impeach Governor Holden and convict him in March 1871 of high crimes and misdemeanors. Tod Caldwell became governor and was reelected in 1872. Upon his death Curtis H. Brogden of Wayne County, Lieutenant Governor, succeeded to the office. Although the Conservatives controlled the General Assembly, Republicans served as governors until 1876.

Ku Klux activities subsided in the piedmont by 1871 but they continued in several mountain counties, Burke, Polk, McDowell, and Rutherford in a very uncontrollable fashion. Meanwhile Congress had passed the Ku Klux acts and more

United States troops were sent into the state. Wholesale arrests were made, and 981 persons were indicted for "Ku Klux depredations" by a federal grand jury in Raleigh. Of the thirty-seven convicted, the most famous Western North Carolinian was Randolph A. Shotwell, Democratic editor of Rutherfordton. J. G. de R. Hamilton, editor of the *Shotwell Papers*, concluded, "Shotwell was the county chief in Rutherford County, having assumed the position at the request of leading men in the hope of checking the movement. He had never been on a raid and never ordered one and had sought to prevent . . . raids. He was convicted on false evidence, fined $5000 and sentenced to six years in Albany." Shotwell was pardoned after two years. Hamilton found that the Klan in Rutherford and Cleveland counties had been used to cover "private vengeance, sheer lawlessness, and in certain cases the activities of certain republicans in violation of the United States Internal Revenue law concerning whiskey."

The Civil War ended, but the bitterness between opposing factions lasted for years. The acrimony over Reconstruction was perhaps not as violent in Western North Carolina as in Eastern North Carolina, but the impact of both the war and the Reconstruction that followed it are still evident in the partisan rivalry that exists between Democrats and Republicans in the mountain counties. Moreover it is believed by many that those constituting the Democratic power structure in the state resented the fact that Western North Carolina was a divided region during the war, and that they have discriminated against those in the mountains by limiting appropriations that would aid the economy.

Much has been written about the mountain people for the last hundred years or more. Perhaps the description by Randolph A. Shotwell of the people in Rutherford County in the late 1860's is as good as any. He saw four different groups: (1) families of wealth, intelligence, and cultivation — they were the ex-slave holders, who educated their children at distant schools, and owned large tracts of land; (2) those who lived in substantial frame or log dwellings and enjoyed "good living" although their members had little education; (3) log cabin dwellers who owned only a few acres and lived in one-room structures, with little furniture, and who had in money no more than twenty dollars in a year, hunting and fishing supplementing the products of the garden patch to provide the family's food; (4) those who owned little or no land and who lived in complete ignorance of the outside world. Shotwell included in this group the illicit distillers who lived in the wildest woodlands and operated three-gallon stills in the most secluded places.

For those who lived on the hills and in the coves, frontier conditions persisted and poverty was widespread, yet many descendants of the first settlers remained. They stayed because of the beautiful scenery and the healthful climate. The rolling hills, the green valleys, and the lofty mountains covered with laurel, rhododendron, hemlock, balsam, pine, oak, and chestnut made Western North Carolina one of nature's wonderlands. They loved their native area, its beauty and its freedom. Julius Caesar was right in writing "Mountaineers are always free."

Life in the villages and towns of Western North Carolina was not very different from that of rural villages in other parts of the state. These people were not mountaineers as the term is usually used; neither were the gentry, those on large valley farms, to be considered mountaineers. Keeping in touch with kinfolk throughout the piedmont they participated in local government and the General Assembly, educated their sons for the professions such as law and medicine, and entertained in the Southern manner. When Arnold Toynbee wrote, ". . . in the heart of our Western Society's 'New World' of North America, there is today a large and widespread population of English and Lowland Scottish origin, with a Protestant Western Christian social heritage, which has been unmistakably and profoundly barbarized by being marooned in the Appalachian backwoods . . . " he could not have been referring to the farmers who developed the holdings at the mouths of the rivers and large streams, who built two-story log houses which as time went on they enlarged or replaced with fine brick homes, many of which are still standing in Caldwell, Burke, McDowell, Rutherford, and Polk counties. These families were large, and marriages were made to preserve the link between the households of mountain valleys and the piedmont.

Most of the prosperous families had owned slaves. Dr. Edward M. Phifer made a study of the slaveholding families in Burke County. He found that in 1860, "921 families engaged in farming, 548 of the families were landowners, 9 were listed

"Magnolia," one of the elegant ante-bellum homes in Burke County

as owning as many as 300 improved acres, 38% of the 548 landowners were slaveholders, 16% of the slaveholders owned only one slave each, 60 family heads owned 100 or more slaves, 26% of the population was slave." He explained, "The Scotch-Irish and German upcountrymen turned to legalism, already a component of their thought process, to justify the institution of slavery." Those who owned slaves were professional people, church officers, farmers, and merchants. A Methodist minister William Fullwood owned as many as nineteen slaves at one time, and in 1850 the Presbyterian minister at Quaker Meadows, John McKamie Wilson, Jr., had ten slaves. Many of the slaveholders had occupations unassociated with agriculture. The slaves worked in shops, engaged in household manufacturing, gold mining and railroad construction as well as agriculture. Slaves were considered a good investment, liquid assets, and some slaveowners are not known to have owned any land. Dr. Phifer's description of slaveholding in Burke County can no doubt be applied to the other counties of Western North Carolina. The Population Table shows how many slaves were held in each county in 1850. The leading families of 1850 were still the dominant element in the population of 1877.

For the persons usually characterized as mountaineers, who

POPULATION TABLE

Counties	1850 White	1850 Free Negro	1850 Slave	1880 White	1880 Colored	1950 Total	1960 Total	1970 Total
Alleghany		Created in 1859		4,967	519	8,155	7,600	8,134
Ashe	8,096	86	595	13,478	958	21,878	19,100	19,571
Avery		Created in 1911				13,352	11,600	12,655
Buncombe	11,601	107	1,717	18,424	3,486	124,403	132,400	145,056
Burke	5,477	163	2,132	10,090	2,721	45,518	54,900	60,364
Caldwell	5,006	108	1,203	8,688	1,600	43,352	51,200	56,699
Cherokee	5,493	8	337	7,796	386	18,294	15,800	16,330
Clay		Created in 1861		3,173	143	6,006	5,300	5,180
Graham		Created in 1872		2,123	212	6,886	6,300	6,562
Haywood	5,931	15	418	9,787	484	37,631	43,300	41,710
Henderson	5,892	37	924	8,895	1,385	30,921	37,700	42,804
Jackson		Created in 1851		6,594	749	19,261	17,300	21,593
Macon	5,613	106	549	7,396	668	16,174	14,500	15,788
Madison		Created in 1851		12,353	457	20,522	16,200	16,003
McDowell	4,777	207	1,262	7,037	1,899	25,720	27,000	30,648
Mitchell		Created in 1861		8,932	503	15,143	13,500	13,447
Polk		Created in 1855		3,920	1,143	11,627	11,300	11,735
Rutherford	10,425	220	2,905	11,925	3,273	46,356	44,810	47,337
Surry	16,171	272	2,000	13,234	2,067	45,593	48,800	51,415
Swain		Created in 1871		3,236	549	9,921	8,000	7,861
Transylvania		Created in 1861		4,823	517	15,194	16,600	19,713
Watauga	3,242	29	129	7,751	409	18,342	17,300	23,404
Wilkes	10,746	211	1,142	17,258	1,923	45,243	45,100	49,524
Yancey	7,908	50	346	7,368	325	16,306	13,300	12,629

lived in the more remote coves and valleys and on the steep hillsides, life did not change much, even after the turn of the century, because new means of transportation did not reach them. Dr. Benjamin Washburn, who grew up in Rutherfordton, and who after completing his medical training practiced medicine in the upper part of Rutherford County early in the twentieth century, in the South Mountains, wrote: "It seemed to me that to go from the lowland section of the county into the South Mountains, although the distance was only about thirty miles, was to pass into a different world — a world which showed stage-by-stage changes in civilization which had been going on in our Appalachian hills since the early years of the nineteenth century.... As I became better acquainted with the people I found it hard to realize that the South Mountain folks and those of the lower part of our county were descended from the same English and Scotch ancestors. This was all the more interesting because I was related to many of these mountain families, one of my grandmothers having come from this section." Washburn called the South Mountains "a picturesque section with simple, loyal, homeloving families."

Cecil Sharp, an Englishman who came to the Appalachians to collect mountain ballads, found the people "leisurely, cheery, ... in their quiet way, ... with a very highly developed social instinct. They dispense hospitality with openhanded generosity and are extremely interested in and friendly toward strangers, communicative and unsuspicious.... They have an unaffected bearing and the unselfconscious manners of the well-bred."

The one other group in the population of Western North Carolina was the Cherokee Indians. Following a treaty with the United States at New Echota in 1835, for a money payment and land in present-day Oklahoma the Indians reluctantly ceded their remaining land in the East, and in 1838 their removal began. Many Cherokees opposed the treaty and some hid out in the mountains; while others stole away from the procession and returned to the mountains with numerous white families befriending them. In 1839 there were about one thousand living in the Smokies. William Holland Thomas, a trader, went to Washington to negotiate permission for them to remain in North Carolina. With their share of the treaty money Thomas bought a tract of land in his own name since North Carolina had passed a law forbidding Indians to own land. The area situated on the Oconaluftee River became known as the Qualla Boundary. It contained about 50,000 acres. Other small tracts including one in present-day Graham County brought the total to about 65,000 acres. When after the Civil War Thomas lost all of his personal fortune, the federal government repurchased the land and in 1875 the Indian Office assumed direct control of the affairs of the band. Formal title to the Qualla Reservation and outlying tracts was granted to the Eastern Cherokees in 1876, and in 1889 they became a corporation under the laws of North Carolina.

The Cherokees have long been known as thrifty, hardworking people. A traveler through the Qualla Reservation wrote in 1892 that the village of Yellow Hills was "beautiful..., neat, orderly, and picturesque. We have gone through the Qualla Cherokee Reservation, down its most populous valley, through its roughest and most picturesque scenery. Coming through, by way of their thoroughfare and by their churches, we have seen most of the population in their Sunday dress and holiday garb, men, women, and children. We have seen their houses and farms, and visited them at home.... This Monday morn, we have seen the native at work — the red man, actually at work — driving oxen, reaping, mowing, one actually running a reaper — shades of McCormick! We have passed by and seen a road-working party. Every Indian we have seen this morning has been at work. They are in their work-a-day attire and even in that they are well dressed."

Chapter One, "On Main Traveled Roads," reveals a county by county view of the more or less normal lives, the places, and the leaders, 1877–1880. Superior Court Judge David Schenck traveled from county to county, met the professional people, the hotel keepers, the leaders of the communities. Interwoven with his account are descriptions of the sports, the churches, the schools, to give a picture of the life of the substantial people of the region.

Chapter Two, "Off the Beaten Path," describes the life and customs of the poorer mountain people who lived in the coves and on the ridges. They are the mountaineers of the stereotype created by the outlanders and writers of fiction. A traveler in the mountains would see a man who was tall, lean, emaciated, poorly dressed, and think that he was seeing a typical mountaineer.

These accounts introduce topics whose histories will be narrated in subsequent chapters.

PART ONE

The People and Their Homeland

CHAPTER ONE

On Main Traveled Roads

To a resident of one of the western counties, the holding of the superior court was of major importance, and the county government seemed more significant than the national one because to it they were more closely related. When a new county was created by the General Assembly that body would appoint a group of commissioners to select a site for the county seat, purchase the land (sometimes it was contributed by an interested landholder) and lay it out in lots, setting aside the amount needed for the courthouse and jail and selling the remaining lots to businessmen and householders. Thus the county seat developed into a service center for the county, with the usual businessmen: general merchants, tanners, millers, distillers, carpenters, cattle dealers, and in some cases a drug store. Churches and schools grew gradually, and one or more hotels were built to accommodate the judge, the lawyers, and the people from the outlying parts of the county during court week.

Burke County, the parent of many western counties, has a rich and interesting history centering around its courthouse. It was the earliest seat of justice and law in Western North Carolina. For a while the Supreme Court of the state held its summer sessions in Morganton, the county seat. Colonel Lusk, an Asheville lawyer, when he was ninety-two in 1928, reminisced that there had been a time when Asheville was jealous of Morganton. Burke County's third courthouse, which is still in use, was begun in 1833 and was under construction for several years. It was made

26 / *Part I: The People and Their Homeland*

Burke County's historic courthouse   ASHEVILLE CITIZEN-TIMES CO.

Aerial view of Burnsville, county seat of Yancey County today
HUGH MORTON PHOTO

of native stone which was later covered with concrete. It served not only as a courthouse but as a center for every kind of gathering. For example, when a group of citizens and their slaves assembled in 1849 to join those who rushed to California to find gold, they met and left from this venerable courthouse.

The English and the Scotch-Irish settlers and their descendants have always been proud of their system of law that was transplanted into the North Carolina mountains in the eighteenth century by their ancestors. This heritage of English common law and legal justice was centered around the courthouses. When highways came they were designed to run from county seat to county seat. The courthouse was to the county seat what the cathedral was to a medieval city: it expressed the hopes and aspirations of the people. It was the heart's core of the western counties, the shaper of human lives and destinies. It was the center of government and authority. It brought order and system to wilderness Carolina. It was the focal point of the social life, the occasion when those from one cove could meet and gossip with their neighbors from other coves and ridges, whom they had not seen for months. It gave to the mountaineer who loved litigation the joy of indicting someone. With the limited opportunities for recreation and social experiences, trials and court cases gave excitement and spice to his life.

Charles Dudley Warner and other writers have described how the people in the mountains would gather in the county seats for court week. They came to meet their friends and relatives, to buy and sell, and to barter their home-grown products for store-bought-goods, needed supplies of salt, coffee, medicines, and tools. As soon as their business was transacted, they gathered in front of the courthouses. They would chew tobacco, spit, dip snuff, and drink liquor. The towns would be full of their buggies, their covered wagons, which were really tents on wheels, used as conveyances and as beds. Often they were loaded with apples, produce, or barrels of hard cider. There were always several wagons near the court. Cider, ginger cakes, maple sugar, and whiskey were sold.*

---

* "The A.S. Merrimon Journal," *North Carolina Historical Review*, VIII, 300–330, gives the best account of court week in Western North Carolina, full of detail, such as the following: "Scores of women attend this court [Madison County] for the sole purpose of drinking and pandering to the lustful passions of dirty men." The judge had to order the whiskey wagons off the court house grounds so that court might proceed.

The administration of the law was not always just, but it was exciting. Spring and fall, court week was the magnet to draw all to the county seats. The judges and lawyers came on horseback or when possible in buggies — those who rode the circuit — "old pettifoggers, young shysters, and brilliant, neat attorneys." Alexis de Toqueville remarked more than a century ago that in the United States every major problem ends in a law suit. The law was so often used to subvert justice that many people doubted its fairness, yet most men believed that the law was good if men used it lawfully. The folklore of the law is that if a murdered man has called the murderer a bastard or a son of a bitch, the jury will often acquit the murderer. If his lawyer or the murderer convinces the jury that the victim brushed his hip or his coattail as if reaching for a weapon, he may be acquitted. If the lawyer can show that the victim has been intimate with the murderer's wife, the accused will be acquitted under the "unwritten law." Mountain people are far more peaceful than writers of fiction would have their readers believe. There have been and still are "pockets of riffraff." But violence was not limited to the "riffraff." Some of the most prominent families in Western North Carolina numbered among their members those who had killed or had died at gun point. Dr. Robert B. Vance of Buncombe County, in 1827, defeated by Samuel P. Carson for election to the United States House of Representatives, remarked that Colonel John Carson, father of Samuel, had been a Tory during the American Revolution. Samuel Carson denounced Vance as a liar, and other bitter remarks led Carson to challenge Vance to a duel, which was fought in Tennessee. Vance was killed by Carson's bullet. William Waightstill Avery of Burke County, the eldest child of Isaac Avery, was a distinguished North Carolinian, but he shot and killed a legal opponent, Sam Fleming, in 1851. Earlier Fleming had horsewhipped Avery, and although Fleming was unarmed Avery shot him in the courtroom from a distance of five feet. Avery was tried and acquitted on grounds of temporary insanity. The jury deliberated only ten minutes. This case illustrates the fact that a man could kill an unarmed man and be acquitted. This incident had little effect upon Avery's subsequent career. In 1852 he was again elected to the legislature and in 1856 to the state Senate and became its speaker. In 1860 he was chairman of the North Carolina delegation to the Democratic convention. In spite of his skill as a public speaker he was defeated as a candidate for Congress

On Main Traveled Roads / 29

Franklin, Macon County seat, surrounded by mountains   HUGH MORTON PHOTO

Brevard, Transylvania County seat   HUGH MORTON PHOTO

by Zebulon Baird Vance in 1858. He was active in organizing the Western North Carolina Railroad and became one of its directors in 1857. In 1860 he was again elected to the state Senate. He later served in the Confederate Provisional Congress. He died July 3, 1864, of a wound received in pursuit of Kirk's raiders.

Judge David Schenck held court between 1877 and 1880 in most of the county seats in Western North Carolina. If we follow him around the circuit, we gain a rare view of a region about which he had experienced much concern. He wrote on December 29, 1879, "Since the 24th of August . . . I have been toiling over the great mountains and the Circuit that I dreaded more than any other in the state has ended, and *ended peacefully*." He commented briefly on social activities, remarked about politics and leading citizens. He shared with his diary the scenic high points and the difficulty of travel in the mountainous areas. His remarks touched upon numerous people and places which will be dealt with at greater length in other chapters.

Schenck was elected on the Democratic ticket — the first Democrat elected by the general public to preside over a superior court in the Western District. The Reconstruction constitution drawn up and adopted in 1868 provided for popular election of judges (formerly they were chosen by the General Assembly). An amendment added in 1875 required their rotation from district to district. In 1876 the Democratic Party won almost complete control of North Carolina.

At the beginning of the 1877 court sessions, Judge Schenck traveled from his home in Lincoln County to Newton by buggy. There he took a train to Morganton, arriving almost simultaneously with the new era since the railroad had been completed beyond Morganton to Old Fort. A county seat and a railroad town, Morganton was one of the centers of growth in Western North Carolina. Burke County had a population of 12,809, about three tenths Negro. It was one-third mountainous, the balance in rolling hills and valleys. W. C. Erwin, lawyer and promoter of the county to northern capitalists, called the area "a country that has fertile soil, hospitable people, magnificent scenery, a perfect climate, vast mineral wealth, abundant water power, great forests of pine and the hard woods, and immunity from droughts and blizzards and unseasonable frosts." Morganton had 861 persons.

On Main Traveled Roads / 31

Upper class travelers in the 1870's shared the road

Asheville was the center of trade for a large area

There were two hotels. Judge Schenck chose the Mountain Hotel, kept by Dr. J. M. Hoppeldt, where the cooking was "equal to any I ever saw — steaks an inch thick, rare and so tender and juicy that it almost melts in your mouth." John Gray Bynum, a popular lawyer, was the judge's host for Sunday dinner — the menu, ham and chicken, all kinds of vegetables, and dessert of peaches, watermelons, and cakes of different kinds. As the Bynums took boarders, there were ten person at dinner.

The judge was looking forward to winning other political honors, and he felt that his charge to the court on Monday made a good impression. The lawyers were Colonel Burgess S. Gaither, A. C. Avery, J. S. Bynum, Alfred Erwin, and S. C. W. Tate. James M. Gudger was solicitor. Cam Pearson, the clerk, was a Radical. Colonel Gaither was the "leader and father" of the Burke County Bar, and Major A. C. Avery was the leader of the Democratic Party there.

Burke County had a number of fine old plantation mansions including Belvedere and Bellevue, both Erwin family homes, and Swan Ponds, built by Waightstill Avery, part of the house dating back to the late eighteenth century, and lived in by generations of Averys. Quaker Meadows is one of the most attractive farming areas in Burke County, and a number of ante-bellum brick houses remained, remnants of prosperous times before the Civil War. Many of these houses are still in a good state of preservation.

If the judge had been interested in the economic life of the region he would have reported that the county had the following businesses: 15 blacksmiths; 3 cattle dealers and 4,410 head of cattle; 2 coopers; 5 distillers (licensed); 3 fertilizer agents; 1 insurance agent; 2 livery stables; 2 lumber dealers; 8 flour and grist mills; 2 millwrights; 1 mine for asbestos; 6 or 7 gold mines; a Democratic newspaper, the *Blue Ridge Blade*; 4 tanners; 2 tobacco manufacturers; 2 watchmakers; 3 boot and shoe manufacturers; and six physicians. On the farms, 752 acres were planted in cotton, 58 acres in tobacco, 22,613 in corn, 8 in rice, 1,654 in rye, and 10,016 in wheat. Of schools there were fifty-two for white children and fifteen for Negroes. In addition there were two academies and one college. Methodist churches predominated, with thirteen Methodist Episcopal South, nine Methodist Episcopal (northern), one African Methodist Episcopal, three Methodist Episcopal Zion, and one Methodist Protestant. The others were one Episcopal, three Presbyterian, and four

Baptist. In a later chapter all of these denominations will be discussed.

In the northern part of Burke County were several tourist attractions: Hawksbill at the top of Jonas Ridge, and Table Rock, both of which attracted excursionists; Linville Falls, formed by a shelf of rock and a drop of ninety feet, from the base of which the Linville Gorge runs south about twelve miles between Jonas Ridge and Linville Mountain. This wild and rugged ravine never failed to charm the energetic souls who rode horseback up its course. At Linville Falls the Franklins, descendants of John, brother of Benjamin Franklin, who have lived for generations at the falls, served as guides and also "took travelers" overnight. The last half mile of the trek to the gorge could be covered only on foot.

The South Mountains fill the southern third of the county, and the Blue Ridge cuts across the northwest corner. The South Mountains create a "thermal belt" where frost is infrequent. They run nearly parallel with the Blue Ridge for about forty-five miles, extending through parts of Burke, McDowell, Rutherford, and Polk counties. They were sparsely settled but in some places were farmed to the very peaks. On a plateau three hundred feet higher than Morganton was Glen Alpine — a glen with four mineral springs — almost surrounded by mountains. Twelve miles from Morganton, seven miles from the railroad but with regular hack service, Glen Alpine Springs had a large hotel which attracted visitors, and for those who wanted to explore some of the peaks of the Blue Ridge it was conveniently located. The waters were believed to be healthful. Piedmont Springs, ten miles north of Morganton, was another resort.

Following his two weeks in Burke County the judge was to hold court in McDowell County, and Major James W. Wilson, president of the Western North Carolina Railroad, furnished an extra train to carry the members of the bar to Marion on Sunday evening, the party consisting of Colonel Gaither, Major Avery, Solicitor Gudger, and Judge Schenck. The judge chose to stay at the Fleming House. Marion was a town of 372 persons, with businesses similar to those of Morganton.

At the old Erwin mansion on the Catawba River three miles from Marion lived Major E. A. M. Erwin and his maiden sisters,

Misses Matilda and Mary Ann Erwin. Schenck wrote, "The ladies are the finest specimen of that splendid race of people who inhabited this luxuriant valley, but whose fortunes have been swept away by the desolation of a war leaving them little else than honor, grace, dignity, intelligence and the love of the Presbyterian faith to solace them in their misfortune. This family however have left them a fine farm and entertain sumptuously and delightfully."

One of the most famous and handsome houses in McDowell County was the Carson House, situated on the banks of Buck Creek near the Catawba River. Built in 1810, for many years it had been a stopping place for Brown's line of stages that ran from Marion to Asheville. Since the Western North Carolina Railroad had been completed beyond Old Fort in 1877, the stage line had been discontinued between Marion and Old Fort, but summer visitors frequently made a night's stop at the Carson House before continuing northward toward North Cove and the Linville Gorge. Advertised rates at the Carson House were as follows: man and horse, $1.50 per day; single person, $7.00 per week; single person, $25 per month. J. L. Carson advertised, "Much attention has been paid to beautifying the grounds and the house has been well fitted up."

Judge Schenck's political ambition was gratified by the interest and approval shown him in each county seat. He wrote of his reception in Marion, "The people as far as I heard were delighted and expressed themselves decidedly for me."

The next stop on the circuit was Henderson County. To reach it the judge traveled by train from Marion to Henry's, the inn near Old Fort at the end of the railroad in 1877, and there he and the solicitor spent the night. The next morning they took the four horse stage coach for Asheville, had dinner there at three P.M., and continued on the same stage to Hendersonville, where they stayed at the Henry Hotel. Judge Schenck was an admirer of the mountain scenery.

In Hendersonville some of the most prominent citizens called on him: William Miller, B. T. Morris, Captain J. M. Toms, and others. As he organized the court he noted that the Democrats were "satisfied." Although the officers of the court were Republican — C. M. Pace, clerk, and Jonathan Williams, sheriff — Schenck was "constrained to say they are very good officers, especially the sheriff, who is a nice clever gentleman.... He is the first Radical I ever had any respect for, and he disclaimed being a full blood, is only tainted enough to get office from the party."

Colonel H. T. Farmer, who operated the famous old inn built in 1853 at Flat Rock (still serving the public in 1972 as the Woodfield Inn) sent for Judge Schenck to spend the night. Colonel Taylor took the judge out in his buggy, and on the way they drove around among the magnificent summer residences, about twenty-five of them, each in a park-like tract of from sixty to one hundred acres, that had been owned and occupied each year during the summer season by prominent South Carolina families. Flat Rock may well claim to be Western North Carolina's first resort center.

The Saluda Mountains are a spur of the Blue Ridge and are the boundary between North and South Carolina. Hendersonville was built on a smooth bench of land about halfway up the Blue Ridge Mountains. Between Hendersonville and Saluda Gap were fine farms and orchards, especially of peaches and apples.

Schenck returned to Asheville September 2, 1877, and registered at the Eagle Hotel, room 35. The Honorable Thomas Lanier Clingman was staying in room 36, just across the hall, and the two men spent hours together daily. Clingman had enjoyed a long political life and knew "most of the distinguished statesmen and politicians of this age." He had practiced law around the whole of the Western Circuit when there were only four lawyers of any prominence in the mountain counties and they all went the rounds with the judge. Beginning with membership in the legislature he went on to serve fourteen years in the United States House of Representatives and three and one-half in the Senate before the state seceded.

The Eagle Hotel was operated by James Patton and was the stopping place for the stage coaches over the Swannanoa Gap and from Greenville, South Carolina. J. H. Gudger's Buck Hotel, in the center of Asheville, was the coach stop for the stage that ran from South Carolina via Saluda Gap and Hendersonville. This route Judge Schenck found not very scenic, but it was nevertheless the most comfortable to travel. A third hotel, the Buncombe, was the choice of many because it was apart from the busiest section of town. There were five other less-known hotels.

Farmer's Inn, now Woodfield Inn ASHEVILLE CITIZEN-TIMES CO.

Asheville, the only city in Western North Carolina, had about 2,100 people and twenty-three attorneys. The sheriff, Levi Plemmons, was a Democrat, but the clerk, J. H. Reed, was a Radical. J. M. Gudger, the solicitor, accompanied Schenck on the circuit. The judge felt even before holding court in Asheville that his prospects there were flattering. Leaders Thomas D. Johnson, H. B. Carter, and C. M. McLoud gave him "every assurance that the bar here are for me and the people evidently are my best friends. If I get through successfully next week, I think all will be well."

As was his custom in each county he served, Schenck made sightseeing trips in Buncombe, socializing with all he met. He wrote, "Beau Catcher, a small mountain which overlooks the little city of Asheville and commands quite a fine view ... is the resort of the 'Beau Catcher' and the 'Beauty lovers' every evening, who drive there, ride there, and walk there and do their courting there. Old Folks are tolerated too, so I went up the other evening and witnessed from it a most glorious sunset. But old as I am, I admired the round limbs and tapering waists and merry faces of the girls more than the grandeur of the mountains in the distance. ... Such is the frailty of poor mankind — a slave to woman, no matter how silly, if she has a pretty face and ankle."

Buncombe County had the largest population of any of the mountain counties, 21,209, of whom 3,487 were Negroes. There were thirty-four post offices and sixty churches, Methodist predominating. There were sixteen Methodist Episcopal South, ten Methodist Episcopal (northern), one African Methodist Episcopal, one African Methodist Episcopal Zion, eight Methodist Protestant, twelve Baptist and three Free Will Baptist, five Presbyterian in the U.S. (southern), one Presbyterian U.S.A. (northern), one Disciples of Christ, two Episcopal, two Missionary Episcopal, and one Roman Catholic, the only Catholic church in the entire area.

Asheville had a public library on the fourth floor of the court house. Private schools were Asheville Female College (sometimes listed as the Female High School), Asheville Male Academy, Montanic Institute. Elsewhere in the county were Black Mountain High School, Weaverville College, Hominy Academy at Hominy Creek, and Leicester Academy. The Asheville Female Academy is said to have attracted students from Maine to Florida with its four year course.

The businesses in Asheville were more specialized than in other towns. Thirty-four general merchants operated stores, but in addition there were two bakers, one restaurant, two booksellers and stationers, two photographers, two banks, one furniture store, three druggists, and three barbers. There were eleven wheelwrights, thirteen grist mills, six sawmills, two woolen mills, three millwrights, and one marble-working establishment, five lumber dealers and eleven carpenters and builders. Asheville had two tobacco warehouses, as in the late seventies most of the mountain counties were having a try at growing tobacco, the bright-leaf variety. The effort was abandoned in a few years and not until the late 1920's was burley tobacco introduced in the region.

The two newspapers, the Asheville *Pioneer* and the Asheville *Citizen*, were weeklies. The Citizen (Democratic) had been published since 1869 with Randolph A. Shotwell as its first editor.

Calvin H. Wiley in his *North Carolina Reader* (1868), said, "Some of you will be surprised to find Asheville a place of much intelligence and refinement." The cosmopolitan air was created by those who had come there for their health. Rebecca Harding Davis, who traveled in the Southern Highlands during the 1870's wrote, "There is a sanatorium in the little town Asheville which

38 / Part I: The People and Their Homeland

View of Asheville from Beaucatcher Mountain, a favorite rendezvous of young lovers

Countless hogs and other animals were driven through Asheville to South Carolina markets. Other traffic had to give way

is becoming a Mecca for consumptives."

In addition to the eight hotels in Asheville there were flourishing inns on all the turnpikes leading into town — Smather's at Turnpike, Alexander's at Alexander, and the Reagan House at Weaverville were all well known. Smather's Inn contained forty rooms. John C. Smathers had started it with ten rooms but his business had flourished. Here he furnished grain and roughage, a fenced enclosure for stock, with pasturage; had a mill, a blacksmith shop, a carpenter shop, and served travelers, drovers, and their livestock. The inn was crowded with "hundreds and thousands of horses, mules, hogs, and cattle" driven on foot, and was a stopping place for stage coaches and private vehicles carrying tourists and business men. Alexander's had been in operation since the Buncombe Turnpike was completed in 1828 when James Mitchell Alexander of Asheville bought and improved a place on the right bank of the French Broad River, ten miles from Asheville, for a hotel and mercantile business. The hotel was in use as long as the turnpike was the highway for interstate travel. Another Alexander's was ten or twelve miles

Hardy travelers stopped here on the ascent of the highest mountain in Eastern America

east of Asheville; it was a long-famed wayside house. This Mr. Alexander was characterized by one visitor as "a hale sprightly young man of eighty, who, like all other farmers in the mountains 'took in' travelers, gave them an excellent supper and comfortable beds, and sent them on the next day."

The resorts Haywood White Sulphur Springs, Warm Springs (now Hot Springs), and Asheville complemented each other, guests stopping at one for a few days, then riding by stage coach to another. A popular horseback excursion route from Asheville ran up Reem's Creek to Weaverville and Elk Mountain. Weaverville had a college, one of the four in Western North Carolina. The Weavers were early comers, and it has been estimated that thirty percent of the early settlers in the valley north of Asheville were related to them.

Adventurous visitors to Asheville made the ascent to Mount Mitchell. Leaving the main road to Marion at Alexander's, up the narrow valley of the North Fork, headwaters of the Swannanoa, the explorer would reach the foot of Mount Mitchell the first day. The night would be spent at Glass's, the roomy cabin of a family that accommodated strangers. The vehicles were left, the rest of the trip being made on horseback. A pack horse would be used to carry supplies for twenty-four hours: blankets, rugs, and food. From Glass's to the summit of Mount Mitchell was a very steep and difficult twelve miles of trail. A rest stop could be made half way up at the ruins of the once famous Mountain House which had been built many years earlier. Above that point were unending forests of balsam and fir, the latter growing in perfect cone shapes, their bases meeting in close thickets, giving the mountains their name, the Black Mountains. Along the trail great boulders and fallen trees heightened the adventure for the mountain climber.

During the course of Judge Schenck's travels on the circuit he was accompanied part of the time by Mrs. Schenck and at other times by his daughter Lucy. They were ecstatic over the mountain scenery. The judge employed the owner of a nice carriage to take Mrs. Schenck and himself from Asheville to Burnsville, where he had a choice of two inns or boarding houses. He chose Sol W. Carter's hotel. The other was owned by the versatile G. D. Ray, who also owned a mica mine, a saw mill

Climbers camped overnight before the descent from Mount Mitchell

at Ivy Gap, and a flour and grist mill in Burnsville. He was a druggist, a tanner, a general merchant, and one of the principal farmers in the county. Eight mica mines were being worked in the county and mica from the mine of G. D. Ray was exhibited at the World's Fair in Vienna. This sparsely settled county of 7,694 persons was a grazing area, and there were eight cattle dealers who bought up cattle from the farmers and had them driven to market in South Carolina or Tennessee, where there were rail connections. The Black Mountains run through the center of Yancey County, and while parts of this range were forested with heavy timber, other parts were in native grasses. About one-half mile from the summit of Mount Mitchell was a piece of tableland one-half mile wide, a natural pasture. The Western North Carolina Land Company which advertised this area for sale boasted, "Hundreds of cattle fatten here in summer. Herbs and flowers abound, as do wild fruits." The company was offering a site about half way up Mount Mitchell as "a terrace ideal for a sanatorium."

The name Boon (as the family in that county spelled it at the time) was constantly in Judge Schenck's mind during the stay in Burnsville. The case of Thomas Boon who had been convicted of murder a year before had been appealed, and while he had not fired the fatal shot, the court found him guilty of aiding and abetting the murderer. Sam Boon, father of Thomas, appeared in court as a witness. Among the nine blacksmiths in Yancy County was Macdaniel Boon. In that family it was and has continued to be traditional for each generation to provide at least one blacksmith.

Court closed in Burnsville in time for the judge to enjoy a fox chase with the Allens. He borrowed a horse from his landlord and with three of the Allens and their six well trained dogs rode to the foot of Green Mountain. The trail was fresh and the dogs were sent in pursuit of "Reynard." The men rode around to an eminence from which they could hear the race. Schenck wrote, "In ten minutes after the trail was struck the pack was in full cry and the music glorious. They ran in a circumference of a mile or two around us where we could hear the 'cry' all the time. The race was 'fast and furious' for forty minutes when the fox was pressed so closely that he put into a cliff of rocks but out of this the Allens soon forced him to retreat by means of poles and as he jumped from [the] cavern the race was renewed with increased noise and speed, and continued for ten minutes longer until Reynard was overtaken and our chase was over."

But a much more exciting hunt was about to occur. The telegraph line to Asheville had just been completed. From Marion Schenck had telegraphed for permission from a Mr. Murchison in Raleigh to have some sport on Murchison's Black Mountain lands, 13,000 acres on the south side of the Black Mountain that had been posted to forbid trespassing. Murchison had bought the land at sheriff's sale that year for $2,200, to use as a timber and game preserve. (In 1909 it was sold for $225,000.)

"Big Tom Wilson" had become a legend in his own day as a guide and hunter. He was now fifty-six years old. He lived nine miles south of Burnsville. Schenck, J. M. Gudger, Schenck's landlord Carter, and Wilson Allen of the preceding hunt, went on horseback to Tom Wilson's, had noonday dinner, and were at the forks of the two Caney rivers two and one-half miles from Big Tom's by two o'clock. Mrs. Schenck and Mrs. Gudger followed to the Wilsons in a buggy and waited for the hunt to be over. The first day the party killed a big stag and had "a keen relish for another day's sport." At 8:30 the next morning Gudger and Schenck stood about 200 yards above the Forks, where they had a clear view as the other hunters climbed the mountain for a drive. Their wait was rewarded, for at ten o'clock a beautiful

Big Tom Wilson, twenty years before Judge Schenck met him, had become famous for his discovery of the body of Elisha Mitchell, scientist and professor

doe came galloping down the stream. After killing the deer, wrote Schenck, "We had a general jollification and gathering up and after the hunters had hoppassed the deer [tied the feet together and suspended it from a pole] the party fished for speckled trout and Wilson Allen killed two beautiful pheasants. Big Tom went to a mountain orchard and filled his hat and pockets with October peaches, large white freestones, and brought them down for the party to feast on". That night appetites were keen and the venison and trout and good corn bread were acceptable to all.

After supper the party sat around the fire while Big Tom told yarns, bear tales, fishing tales, and adventure tales of all kinds. One of the tales was of how on the rugged cliffs of the Black he killed a small bear (125 pounds) and five raccoons. These, with a rifle weighing eleven pounds, he had to carry down the mountain. He "hoppassed" the "coons" on a grape vine and strung them around his shoulders, three on one side and two on the other. Then he tied the fore feet of the bear together and ran his head between, with the bear on his back. With his left hand he held the two hind paws to keep the bear's weight from choking him. In his right hand he carried the gun. Big Tom believed, and most southerners agree, that "coon" meat is the best of all wild game. (Big Tom was the mountain man who found the body of Dr. Elisha Mitchell for whom the mountain had been named.)

At night the party slept "in true mountain fashion." A room with several beds was shared by the Gudgers and the Schencks. A tallow candle was the only light.

After ten days' vacation Judge and Mrs. Schenck started to Bakersville in a "jersey" at seven o'clock in the morning, to hold court in Mitchell County. Heavy showers fell as their vehicle climbed over and around Green Mountain. "The mud was deep and the road slippery, then the clouds rose and the rain stopped." The ford in the Toe River at Peterson's was dangerous because the water was so high. Peterson rowed the Schencks across in his "dugout" twenty feet long and two and one-half feet wide and made another trip for their baggage, while a boy drove the jersey across. Then at the edge of Bakersville the gray horse began to balk and the judge and his lady finished the

Here the Schencks and the Gudgers spent two nights

journey on foot. At the Penland House dinner was eaten, clothes were changed, and at three o'clock the judge was charging the grand jury. The docket was small and the session of court uneventful. The judge was eager to continue his exploration of the mountains.

Mitchell County is much smaller than Yancey and was part of Yancey, Caldwell, and Watauga until 1861. The Nollichucky River forms the boundary between Mitchell and Yancey counties, while on the east is the Blue Ridge and on the west the Toe (Estatoe) River which flows the entire length of the county forming a valley "rich beyond description."

On Saturday, October 25, 1879, Judge and Mrs. Schenck set out with a caravan for Roan Mountain, with a horse and buggy provided by Major Jacob M. Bowman for the first five miles, after which they had to travel five on horseback. General Wilder, an iron capitalist of Chattanooga, Tennessee, a Union army veteran who owned the mountain, had built a twenty room lodge called Cloudland. Only a caretaker and his little daughter were at the lodge, but the nine guests were welcomed with a cheerful fire, coffee, and tea and sugar, to which they added the "snacks" they had brought along. From the Pinnacle

46 / Part I: The People and Their Homeland

The only dry way to cross swollen streams

Roan Mountain in early June is colorful with myriads of purple rhododendrons
U.S. FOREST SERVICE PHOTO

half a mile from the Cloudland Hotel, 6,306 feet high, could be seen ranges of mountains in Virginia, West Virginia, Tennessee, and Georgia, as well as the ridges and peaks of North Carolina. The Bluff, ten feet lower than the Pinnacle, is at the southwest end of the mountain, and from it one looks down on a dreadful abyss below, although in the distance were to be seen thriving farms and villages in Tennessee, and on Big Rock Creek was the "Iron Works" at Cranberry. Charles Dudley Warner, exploring a few years later, wrote about the large variety of flora on Roan Mountain: "There are many [plants] we are told, never or rarely found elsewhere in the United States. . . . The rhododendron [growing there] . . . has a deep red, almost purple color."

About one-fifth of the land in Mitchell County was cultivated. The usual corn, oats, wheat and rye were to be seen, and fifteen acres were in cotton. Seventy-seven acres were planted to tobacco. Bakersville had a stoneware manufactory and a newspaper, the *Republican*. Churches in Mitchell County were chiefly Methodist and Baptist.

Avery County had not been created, and Schenck went next to Watauga County, where Boone, the county seat, was the highest such seat of government east of the Rockies at that time. To Schenck the routine of the court was monotonous in the small village of two stores and two hotels. Colonel Folk from Lenoir conveyed Schenck in a buggy drawn by two good horses. He stayed at Bryan's Hotel, where he was fed speckled trout, buckwheat cakes, sugar tree syrup, and the best milk, "good enough for a king." With a Captain Todd he fished in Howard's Creek. They caught twenty trout, the "most beautiful and gamey of all fishes." The court lasted only from Monday to Thursday, and on Friday the judge wrote, "Lawyers, suitors, and witnesses are gone, leaving the town lonely and uninteresting." A week would intervene before the next court, in Jefferson, and he did not know how he could "make the time interesting."

Charles Dudley Warner commented about the two "taverns" in Boone and concluded that they were necessary to accomodate judges and lawyers when court was in session: "The court is the only excitement and the only amusement. Everybody in the county knows exactly when the court sits and when court breaks. During the session the whole county is practically in Boone, men, women, and children. They camp there, they attend the trials, they take sides; half of them, perhaps, are witnesses, for the region is litigious, and the neighborhood quarrels are entered into with spirit. . . .

"This tavern, one end of which was a store, had a veranda in front, and a back gallery, where there were evidences of female refinement in pots of plants and flowers. . . . The front porch in the morning resembled a carpenter's shop; it was literally covered with the whittlings of the row of natives who had spent the evening there in the sedative occupation of whittling."

On November 12, 1879, Judge Schenck went from Boone to Jefferson, twenty-two miles, in a carriage. He made his headquarters at the old George Bowers House, kept by Martin Harden, in "room no. 3, which was for many years known as the judge's room and had been occupied by almost all the antebellum judiciary."

Ashe County is one-third larger than Watauga in area, and its population was almost twice that of Watauga, but the county seat, Jefferson, was smaller than Boone. There was great interest in mining in Ashe County, and grazing was also important. There were thirty-eight cattle dealers. One brandy distiller and ten whiskey distillers were licensed. There was a Negro population of 966, and the county had three Negro schools, a large number for a mountain county.

Judge Schenck's circuit did not include Alleghany, Wilkes, and Surry counties. While all of Alleghany has an elevation of over 2,500 feet (and the Blue Ridge passes along its eastern and southern border), it has no peaks of over 5,000 feet. Sparta, the county seat, had about 100 residents in 1880. The population of the county was 5,486. Wilkes County lies south of Alleghany, with the crest of the Blue Ridge forming its northwest boundary. It is so large that it is sometimes called the "State of Wilkes." The population of 19,181 seems to have been fairly well distributed in 1880. The county seat, Wilkesboro, had only a few hundred people. One hotel and one boarding house accommodated the court officials and lawyers. The parent county, Surry, once included present-day Stokes and Forsyth and all of the land to the west as well as what came to be seven Tennessee counties. Partitions dated from 1777 to 1850, after which Surry County had its present boundaries. Its mountains are in the northwestern part, the crest of the Blue Ridge just skirting the corner of the county. On the south is the historic Yadkin River, along which lived some distinguished families. Surry County's best known spot was Pilot Mountain, which was in 1970 made a state park. Surry is hilly or mountainous, with swift streams that were utilized for water power. One industry, the Elkin Manufacturing Company, established in 1848 by the Gwyn family for making cotton cloth, was in 1884 employing thirty-five workers and producing daily five hundred yards of sheeting and five hundred pounds of yarn. While Dobson, population 95, was the county seat, Elkin and Mount Airy were the important towns. In the latter there were manufacturers of cotton goods, but the new line of manufacture was tobacco. The county processed almost a million pounds of the weed in 1883, and Mount Airy had five tobacco factories, with four more at other points in the county. Two newspapers were published in Mount Airy: the *National Visitor* and the *Mount Airy Watchman*. The mineral of Surry County was not yet being exploited, but an abundance of granite was to become in later years one of the important resources.

Winter was coming on as Judge Schenck traveled fifty-five miles from Jefferson to Lenoir, over the Blowing Rock Gap. The first thirty-two miles were done in a two horse buggy with Colonel Folk. "The New River, a rapid mountain stream 125 feet wide," Schenck wrote, "was frozen over in many places, and Meat Camp Creek bore the weight of horses, buggy, and passengers. A night was spent at the home of Len. W. Estes, on the Blue Ridge. Mrs. Estes had the finest B.W. [buckwheat] cakes I ever ate. They were about nine inches in diameter, round as a plate and thick as your hand, and very light.... Estes has a beautiful mill pond, full of trout, and I have a special invitation to fish in it, which I hope to accept and enjoy."

On Sunday Colonel Folk and the judge rode on to Lenoir, making the twenty-two miles by four P.M. "I am rejoiced to leave the high elevations and the dangerous roads of the mountains as the cold winter comes on," wrote Schenck.

One civil case on the docket, Freeman v. Sprague, took from Wednesday to Saturday to complete. It dealt with the ownership of the Henry Hotel at Henry Depot on the Western

North Carolina Railroad west of Old Fort, and the lawyers employed for the plaintiff were E. H. Malone, J. C. Bynum, and Romulus Linney; for the defense, Burgess S. Gaither, George N. Folk, and D. P. Cilley. All of these names are those of well known families of the area. Colonel and Mrs. Clinton A. Cilley entertained Judge Schenck, the Joneses, and Colonel Pearson at tea. The Jones, Lenoir, Patterson, and related families were residents of attractive and stately homes on plantations near Lenoir. Kemp Plummer Battle wrote, "I state as a fact that the lovely and fertile country through which flows the upper Yadkin and its tributaries has been for years the home of a prosperous, high toned and harmonious people.... [It is] designated by admiring visitors as Happy Valley."

Lenoir's newspaper, the *Topic*, one dollar per year, advertised that it was "published weekly in the liveliest town in the mountains." Schenck called Lenoir "one of the most literary and cultivated places in the state."

Court ended after almost four months of "toiling over the great mountains," and Schenck went home to rest until March when he was next to travel to Asheville. That trip was made by train to Charlotte, thence to Spartanburg, South Carolina, where he missed his train to Hendersonville. Mr. Anderson, superintendent of the railroad, sent him to Hendersonville on an engine. "It was a grand ride over Tryon Mountain," he wrote.

While holding court in Asheville the judge met Kope Elias, Esquire, of Macon County, his devoted friend. Upon hearing a report that some fine wild turkeys had been in a field nearby, Schenck and Elias borrowed a horse and buggy on Saturday and rode out to shoot turkeys. "It was seven miles, and the roads were desperately bad, and we just got to the 'blind' in time to hear the turkeys fly out of the field." The birds were seen again on Sunday. Monday morning "came wet and foggy, but by 6 o'clock Kope and I were in the 'blind.' I was armed with [a] double barreled breech loader, Kope with a muzzle loader. In about a half hour we heard one fly down from the roost and give a low call or two and in a few minutes we heard the gang, five in all, fly over the fence. I was to 'conduct the shooting,' so I whispered to take a position and keep a keen watch. Directly a large gobbler came running to the bait, and we could see his outlines through the dense fog about twenty-five steps from us, then another joined him, and I gave command to aim, then to fire. At the word I fired both barrels at my gobbler, full and square in the breast, as he had discovered our presence and was peering his keen eyes into the crevices of the 'blind' to see what we were. Kope fired one barrel simultaneously, and both turkeys fell. Kope's turkey, to our surprise and mortification rose up and flew into a thicket and left him feeling 'blank and cheap'." Later Kope's turkey was found dead where he had fallen from a tree. Schenck continued, "My gobbler weighed 17 pounds.... I preserved the 'tails' and 'wings' for fans, and stuffed the head, leaving the full breast of feathers attached. The beard is nine inches long."

Schenck had very little to say about the court at Marshall in Madison County, which he conducted in March 1880. He rode to Marshall in a hack and stayed at Jack Gudger's hotel. He wrote of Madison County, "This county is now wild over tobacco. The raising of this weed has increased very greatly and is proving remarkably profitable. Lands are increasing in value, and labor is greatly in demand."

Marshall had little room for more than the main street, "the mountains rising to a lofty summit, almost from the water's edge of the river." It had about 150 people. Warm Springs to the northwest had hotels and boarding houses and was to become an even more popular resort after the railroad reached there.

We next find Judge Schenck in Brevard. The French Broad River rises in Transylvania County and the judge marveled at "the fertility, wealth, and beauty of the valley." He enjoyed shooting pheasants there. These birds "come to apple orchards in secluded places to eat the tender buds." Court over in Brevard (he had nothing to say about the lawyers or the docket), Mr. B. D. Lankford, Esquire, was "kind enough to furnish me two good mules and drive me to Waynesville without charge." They admired the "magnificent valley of the Mills River" on the way. One night was spent at Turnpike Post Office at the Smathers Inn.

Waynesville was not incorporated until 1871, but to Judge Schenck it appeared "an old dilapidated town, dirty and dingy,

Downtown Marshall today squeezed in between the French Broad and the mountains   HUGH MORTON PHOTO

and in itself without attraction." Hence he chose a room at Major W. W. Stringfield's White Sulphur Springs near Waynesville, of which he wrote, "... one of the lovely spots in this world, and capable of being made a paradise with capital. The mountain scenery is grand, the river or creek running in stone's throw is transparent as crystal, the spring is very fine, and there are no cleverer people in the world than the Major and his wife."

The population of Waynesville was 225. Much interest was shown in agriculture, clubs and societies having been organized including the Haywood Agricultural Society.

From Waynesville Judge Schenck proceeded to Webster, then the county seat of Jackson County, with Walter E. Moore, a young lawyer. The docket was short and court closed in two days; a "horse thief" and a "house thief" were both sentenced to ten years in the penitentiary.

Jackson County as described by William Ernest Bird "is essentially medial within the extremely western subdivision of the mountain region. Its shape is that of an elongated oval bowl with an irregular rim: the Blue Ridge on the southeast, the Smokies to the southwest, the Balsams to the northeast, and the Cowees to the southwest. It is divided for almost its entire length by the Tuckaseigee River."

At the Cherokee town of Stekoa near present-day Whittier, Griffith Rutherford met the Indians in 1776 and drove them into the Smokies. In 1781 John Sevier defeated them a second time near the present town of Sylva. In 1796 the "Meiggs and Freeman Line" was established from the Smokies to South Carolina, limiting the Cherokees to the territory west of the line. Thus part of what later became Jackson County was available to white settlers, and near the Meiggs and Freeman Line certain men were permitted to operate trading stations: Foster's, Love's and East la Porte. In 1819 another treaty gave the State of North Carolina the entire Tuckaseigee Valley, and the land newly available was divided into districts, surveyed, and sold to white settlers. Thereafter the area went through the pattern of home, church, and school building common to each valley in turn.

The most exciting natural landmark in Jackson County was Judaculla Rock, now a state shrine, a large stone on Caney Fork Creek which has inscribed in hieroglyphics a message that no one has ever been able to decipher. Legend tells of a super-human being named Judaculla of prehistoric times who carved the inscription to commemorate his activities in the area.

In the southeast corner of Jackson County Confederate General and later Governor of South Carolina Wade Hampton had an estate at a very scenic point which later became the resort, High Hampton. Whiteside Mountain is one of the most spectacular mountains in the state. One side has a rock precipice 1,800 feet high, giving the mountain its name.

Franklin, with a population of 207, was the county seat of Macon County which had been formed in 1828. It became a cultural center for the southwestern part of the state, had a number of schools and academies, and was the home of the first normal school established in Western North Carolina. In 1875 another town, Highlands, was laid out in the southeastern part of the county as a summer resort. Settled chiefly by newcomers, it boasted a literary society, the Highlands Improvement Association, the Highlands Floral Society, the Highlands Temperance Union, and a newspaper, the *Blue Ridge Enterprise*. Both Franklin and Highlands had high schools.

Waynesville was described in the 1870's as a quaint, old-looking town. Life was simple and rural

After Judge Schenck had finished the court in Franklin, he and his daughter Lucy who had joined him set out with Thomas Slagle as guide to climb the Nantahala Mountain Range. They were able to go by two-horse buggy to the gap, and there "took saddle" for the summit which was three miles farther. Near the summit was the famous "wine spring," which furnished water to drink with their lunch.

On the way to Hayesville in Clay County the judge, Kope Elias, and Lucy stopped at Alexander Munday's at Aynone Post Office at the western foot of the Nantahala Range. Schenck had sent word to the host to have plenty of speckled trout ready, and he had "a most bountiful supply of this most delicate of all fishes." After dinner they crossed "Tusquitcher Mountain" (Tusquitee) to Hayesville. The road followed "cool crystal branches, with gushing streams at every turn, and grand forest of hemlock and wilderness of rhododendron on every side." One night was spent at the "cozy cottage" of one of the Shearer families on Tusquitee Creek. There was a little mill nearby, and water had been piped to the Shearer house and to the mill race.

On Main Traveled Roads / 55

What giant hand carved these mystic inscriptions on Judaculla Rock?

The Schencks followed the Nantahala Gorge between Franklin and Hayesville
ASHEVILLE CITIZEN-TIMES CO.

Only two days were required for the session of court in Clay County, which had been part of Cherokee until 1861. The county's population was only 3,316. After the court closed the judge's party continued to Murphy, the road following the Hiwassee River for part of the way. They had time for sightseeing before the next session in Cherokee, and the judge wrote, "I spent the next week very pleasantly." He was able to take "several fine drives" to explore scenic attractions.

Cherokee County was described by Chataigne's *Directory* as having "marbles of the finest quality and of various colors that compose whole mountains," but at that time marble was not being mined.

Kope Elias accompanied Judge Schenck on this trek on the Western Circuit in 1880, and they next traveled to Robbinsville, Graham County, spending the night at Dr. R. C. Washburn's at the head of Valley River. The docket was finished in a day and a half. Robbinsville was a hamlet of sixty-one persons, the entire county's population numbering 2,335. Graham County was very young at the time of Schenck's visit, having been created in 1872. Some Indian families continued to live there on land purchased for them by William Holland Thomas. They subsisted by farming and hunting. A few white families had straggled in even before the Cherokee removal. The roads were poor, most of them lying at least at a thirty degree angle. Not until the lumbering industry started would people come to Graham County in any great numbers.

The county seat of Swain County (now Bryson City) was then called Charleston. It was thirty-two miles from Franklin, to which the judge had returned after court at Robbinsville. The Little Tennessee River was high, and as the judge crossed it his buggy and valise filled with water.

In Swain County law enforcement had been made a problem by a band of rioters and desperadoes led by members of the "Wiggins family." The judge sentenced about ten to jail for terms of from three to twelve months, and he sent them to the Franklin jail "for safe keeping." Swain County had a total population of 3,784, and its land was assessed at 78¢ per acre. Charleston had 100 people. The main portion of the Cherokee Indian lands, the "Qualla Boundary" was partially in Swain County.

Two other counties not included in Schenck's circuit were Rutherford and Polk. Rutherford was one of the more populous counties, much of its land lying in the piedmont, with a population of 15,208. In part of the county are the South Mountains. Inserted in the southwestern corner is little Polk County — through which run the Saluda Mountains. Chimney Rock in Rutherford County was one of the tourist attractions, and the highest point is Pinnacle Mountain, 3,832 feet. The Broad River and the Second Broad flow through the county. In cultural life Rutherford and Polk had a head start, as they had begun to be settled before the American Revolution and they were always in touch with more highly developed areas. The Speculation Land Company promoted settlement and advertised, attracting purchasers. From 1814–1845 Rutherford was the center of gold production for the nation, and Bechtler's mint north of Rutherfordton was allowed to coin money. The county began the textile industry in 1874 when an old wheat mill was converted to production of cotton goods. It employed fifty people until, within the year, it was destroyed by fire and not until years later were plans made for its successor. Its mill village of fifteen houses was probably the first in Western North Carolina.

Polk County with 5,062 people and an area of only 234 square miles had 1,646 acres devoted to cotton and 931 in tobacco. A fine old home in Polk County was Green River Plantation built by Colonel Joseph McDowell Carson about 1800. Inherited by Carson's granddaughter Mrs. Frank Coxe, it served as a country home, the Coxes spending most of each year in Asheville, where Mr. Coxe built the first charming Battery Park Hotel. Green River Plantation house still stands.

Columbus, the county seat of Polk, had only 71 people in 1880. The southern and eastern portion of the county is a fine fine farming area. Within a few years after 1880, Polk County was to become attractive to both summer and winter residents (not the same groups) when rail connections with South Carolina were made. The route followed had been the Indian Trading Path, later a main traveled road from Kentucky and Tennessee to the South.

CHAPTER TWO

Off the Beaten Path

The distinctive mountain culture as described by visitors, missionaries, social workers, members of study commissions, and residents during the last hundred years, was to be found among the people off the beaten part. Edward King in *The Great South*, 1875, described a visit to a mountain cabin. He saw the housewife smoking a corncob pipe and warming her hands before an open fire. Rain dripped through the roof; the children were huddled together. There were few furnishings, but the barns were full and the family had a few sheep and goats. At that date the mountain people were not destitute, but the public schools were deplorable. He concluded that the people were relatively well off.

A description of mountain life about 1880 by the great psychologist William James is so typical of outlanders' views that it is quoted at length: "Some years ago ... in the mountains of North Carolina, I passed by a large number of 'coves' ... which had been cleared and planted. The impression on my mind was one of unmitigated squalor. The settler had ... cut down the more manageable trees and left their charred stumps standing. The larger trees he had girdled and killed. ... He had then built a log cabin, plastering its chinks with clay, and had set up a tall zigzag rail fence around the scene of his havoc, to keep the pigs and cattle out. ... He had planted the intervals between the stumps with Indian corn ... ; and there he dwelt with his wife and babe — an axe, a gun, a few utensils, and some pigs and chickens . . . being the sum total of his possessions.

"The forest had been destroyed; and what had 'improved' it out of existence was hideous . . . without a single element of nature's beauty, ugly indeed seemed the life of the squatter . . . beginning back where our first ancestors started and . . . hardly better off for . . . the achievements of . . . intervening generations. . . ."

"Then I said to the mountaineer who was driving me, 'What sort of people . . . make these new clearings?' 'All of us,' he replied. 'Why we ain't happy here unless we are getting one of these coves under cultivation.' I instantly felt that I had been losing the whole inward significance of the situation. Because to me the clearing spoke of naught but denudation, I thought that to those whose sturdy arms and obedient axes had made them they could tell no other story. But when they looked on the hideous stumps, what they thought of was personal victory. The chips, the girdled trees, and the vile split rails spoke of honest sweat, persistent toil, and final reward."

James, like many other writers and visitors to the mountains, had deplored the meagerness of the life of those who lived in the coves and on the ridges. The isolated mountaineers that he saw were poor, terribly poor, but they retained their pride, their self-respect, their independence, their individuality, and their zest for life. Many of their children left their mountain homes to "seek their fortunes" in the mill towns, the county seats, or the cities, but they always remembered nostalgically the experiences, the sounds, and the sights of their childhood: crossing streams by footlogs; washing wool in streams; carding, spinning, weaving; boiling clothes in a black iron pot swung from a tripod; salting sheep from a gourd; a mother churning milk and cooking the evening meal by the light of a fat pine stick; the father riding for the doctor by the flare of a burning torch or taking the corn to the mill on foot or on horseback; log-rollings; house-raisings; corn huskings; the crushing of sorghum; the stomping, swinging, shuffling of feet; the voice of the caller and fiddle music at neighborhood square dances. Mountain sounds were those of the howling winds, the singing of birds, the tinkling of cow, horse, and sheep bells, the ringing of axes, the thud of mauls, the crash of falling trees, the sputter and crackle of open fires, the clank of the blacksmith's hammer, the hissing of frying meat and the whir of the spinning wheel and above all the sound of the human voice with all its varying

A log cabin of the type lived in by the earliest settlers and the poorer mountaineers later　　　　　　　　　　　　　　　　ASHEVILLE CITIZEN-TIMES CO.

Going to the Mill — riding is better than walking

intonations in talk and in the singing of hymns and old ballads. Other sounds came from the mass hysteria and jerkings at revival meetings, laughter, obstreperous cursing, crying at trials, kettles singing over a crane. Interesting smells were those of oak, cedar, pine burning, hominy boiling, sassafras steeping, corn bread baking, ham frying, and woolen clothes drying before a fire.

A small mountain settlement of the type that might be found in almost any county of the region was that on the North Fork of the Swannanoa River, described by Fred M. Burnett in *This Was My Valley*. The Burnets (earlier spelling) built their first log cabin there in 1762. In the valley, less than four miles long, closed in by mountains on all sides, lived at least fifty families. Here were "all the crafts — blacksmith shops where they built their own wagons, plows, knives, and tools. They tanned leather, made shoes, harnesses, and saddles. They carded, spun, and wove their own wool and made their clothes." From the peach and apple orchards came the fruit for their brandy. Wheat, corn, and rye were also distilled. Their fields produced corn, and every farm had poultry and domesticated animals. The community was almost entirely self-sufficient. After the crops were harvested in the fall, the men went on the first hunt, which would last from Monday morning until Saturday afternoon. Each man carried a sack of supplies such as corn meal for fritters, flour for gravy, salt, coffee, a slab of bacon, potatoes, and onions. The hunt would provide the meat. To the group of men who had known each other and hunted together all their lives, the hunt was a way of life, a prized experience.

Mountain families have usually been patriarchal. In them the men have been dominant, the women subservient. The men made the decisions, did "men's work"; the women did the chores and the house work and often did not eat at the table with the men, especially if guests were present, but stood to serve men and guests. Women however generally were loyal to their men and not unhappy. They often referred to the husband as "The Mister" or "him." They usually would not go visiting or to town without his permission. The mountain man respected all women but was not chivalrous. He would not tip his hat nor offer his chair to an older woman. He would let his wife carry a child or other burdens. He would walk in front of her down the road or path. But he was scrupulous in teaching manners to his children.

Off the Beaten Path / 63

One of the simplest of grist mills

An old mill that is still in existence ASHEVILLE CITIZEN–TIMES CO.

64 / Part I: The People and Their Homeland

Mountain music for a play-party game

A mountain hunter

The mountain man believed that everyone was equal in the sight of God and man. He resented condescension with fierce pride. There were no marked distinctions in the mountains. He was intolerant of anyone who tried to "get above his raisin'." He would balk at doing a "woman's work." He was ashamed to milk a cow, wash dishes, or make a bed, but he was quite willing to do the "hard work" of plowing, harvesting, felling trees, clearing land, sawing or chopping wood for cabin or fireplace. He was not lazy: he used great energy in his primitive methods of farming, in hauling his produce to market, in walking many miles over the hills hunting animals, birds, ginseng, or other salable herbs.

During the three months of the growing season, men's work was regimented by the demands of their crops. That season was short because of frosts coming late in the spring and early in the fall. After crops were in and the land made ready for spring planting, the men could choose their activities until seed time. The more ambitious cleared land, split rails, cut firewood; others hunted, gambled, pitched horseshoes, attended shooting matches, drank liquor, and swapped yarns. Many made liquor; most drank. The drinking often made them quarrelsome.

The mountain man had poise, self-confidence, versatility, was able to adapt to any kind of job. He was proud, "touchy," a jack-of-all trades, had learned to do almost everything for himself. He took education seriously because he had to work so hard to get it or because he was denied the opportunity. He could stand any amount of hard work, but he chafed at monotonous jobs. He was rash, precipitate, oversensitive, quick-tempered. He usually resented all outlanders.

Although the general level of cultural achievement had dropped because of isolation and the meagerness of opportunity, the mountaineer has been found to be a naturally capable, honest, intelligent, and efficient worker. He had an air of leisure, did not seem to be in a hurry, but he got things done that had to be done.

It has been said that child-bearing, hard work, and hopelessness were the lot of mountain women. Sometimes that was true when a family was crushed by hopeless poverty. But women were the bulwark of mountain society. They held the homes together. They did the household chores, tended the livestock and garden, raised hemp and sheep and made the family clothing from hemp or from wool that they had sheared, thread they had spun, and cloth they had woven. They cooked, cleaned, hoed the garden. Often they plowed; sometimes they even pulled the plow. They hunted herbs for medicine and greens for "sallets." In season the whole family would hunt ginseng, which sold for sixty cents a pound in 1848 (and for $9.68 green or $38.00 dried, in 1969). On Sundays the women often walked behind the horse, mule, or ox while the men rode to church holding what children they could. The women would put on their sunbonnets to work in the fields. They dried beans, corn, apples, peaches, pumpkins, and prepared kraut, pork, venison, and squirrel meat for winter. They made their own soap from the lye of hickory ashes and grease. They made their own candles and they dyed the cloth that they wove — linsey for underwear and dresses, jeans for men's clothing. Their dyes were homemade: indigo (blue), madder (red), maple bark (purple), hulls, roots, and walnut bark (brown). Dyes were also made from sumac berries and laurel leaves. While they worked or during their few leisure moments many dipped snuff. They had tin snuff boxes into which they dipped chewed birch sticks to rub the snuff on their gums. Snuff dipping was not a pretty custom, but it gave them satisfaction, and the women deserved any pleasure they could get. Other women smoked clay or corncob pipes filled with twists of home-cured tobacco.

R. R. Smith, who engaged in mission work north and west of Asheville near the end of the nineteenth century, wrote, "In the summer and fall the women, wise like ants, store up food for winter... drying and canning fruits and vegetables... leather britches [long strands of dried snap beans hanging on the walls of the cabin], dry pumpkin... cut in thin, spiral pieces put on sturdy sticks and hung in dry places.... Gourds were plentiful and made a cheap substitute for tin and earthenware. The small ones were used for drinking cups, the large ones for holding salt, sugar..., the largest size for carrying water from the spring. Each family had a supply of remedies gathered from forest and field: boneset, goldenseal, burvine, catnip...."

These intrepid women had few conveniences and few pleasures. They faded early from hard work and child-bearing. But they took pride in their cooking, preserving, in their weaving and dyeing. A woman could weave five yards of linsey in a day. They liked company and often met for spinning, carding, reeling, knitting, and weaving contests. There was a quilting frame in many a mountain home. It was suspended from the ceiling and was about waist high. Patchwork pieces of brightly colored cloth had been gathered and saved. The quilting consisted of spreading cloth under a filler of cotton or wool, covering it with the patchwork which had been pieced together in intricate designs: sunburst, log cabin, crazy quilt, and others; and with tiny stitches sewing through all three thicknesses following a design that was repeated throughout the entire quilt.

It was never a mountain custom to rely on hired help. When anything needed to be done that required many hands, the neighbors were "right neighborly." They used sickles to harvest small grain. When a man's crop was ripe, neighbors would gather to reap and shock it. A dozen or more men would cut through a field. Then they hung their sickles over their shoulders and bound back. Boys gathered the sheaves and old men shocked them. Corn crops were gathered and thrown in heaps beside the cribs. Neighbors came and husked the crop. Dr. C. D. Smith of Franklin said he had seen eighty to ninety men around his father's corn crib. Neighbors helped also in a barn or house raising or in a "rail mauling." This was a communal splitting of rails for fences. Neighborliness was more than a custom. It was a way of life. Neighbors would help each other at grinding cane stalks, wheat threshings, or making molasses. They attended Methodist camp meetings, Baptist association meetings, community picnics, school commencements, circuses. All helped the sick. Some who were gifted in their knowledge of herbs were called "yarb" doctors. They and the "granny women" did much to maintain health.

Weaving was among the many responsibilities of the mountain woman. The loom is home-made

John C. Campbell wrote entertainingly of mountaineers as horse traders. He wished that he could live to see a horse trade between a Carolina mountaineer and a Connecticut Yankee. He affirmed that to the mountain man every business transaction was a horse trade and that he sought to get the better of his competitor. He gave his opponent credit for knowing as much as he did. Sometimes his shrewdness seemed like dishonesty to those who did not understand him. If one caught up with him he thought more of the trader's shrewdness. If one tried to deceive him, he would find him a shrewd judge of human nature. Horse trading took place anywhere, any time: at county seats on court days, at public speakings, at country stores, blacksmith shops, mills, and crossroads.

The language of the mountain people a century ago has been said to be similar to that of the Elizabethan English. It was archaic, picturesque, figurative. There was too in the language quaintness which set it apart from that used outside the mountains. Not only had the language been preserved but the English and Scottish ballads and folk songs had survived also. Many have been changed greatly; others are remarkably close to the original versions. Their melodies have not only a touching beauty, but they are uniquely expressive of mountain character. They were preserved because of the isolation of the people. The folk speech of the mountain people had its dialectal individuality. Many studies of mountain dialect are available. A few examples are the following: *fotch* for fetch, *ye* for you, *hit* for it, *antic* for a comical person, *preacher-parson, fotched-on furriner, granny woman, neighbor-people, tooth-dentist, play-purties, heer'd* and *afeard, mought, hyar* for here, *right smart* for a considerable amount, *right pert, consentable* for willing, *plague* for tease, *I wouldn't care to* for I do not object, *We got along plain* for we did fairly well, *Hit was thickety* for It was not an easy passage, *after preachin' has broke, sculp* for scalp, *shootin' iron* for fire arm, *skeerd, ourn, franticky* (a combination of frantic and panicky), *endurin'* for whole, *swallow a punkin' seed* for get pregnant, *galackers* for pickers of galax leaves, *sangers* for pickers of ginseng, *settin' up* for courting.

Until the coming of the roads and railroads, life in the mountains remained as it had been. These modes of access made marketing of produce possible; they were the opening wedge to the good life for the mountain people.

PART TWO

A Changing Society

Western North Carolina was never a land apart from the rest of the state, even in the earliest days, in spite of the mountain barrier. One of the first ties that existed was religion. Churches were established in the colony in the wave of protestant evangelical activity that followed John Wesley's lead in England and then in America. Camp meetings sprang up out of the work of orderly smallgroup gatherings, grew and spread ultimately into a "movement whose aspects and practices were completely free affairs of the uninhibited masses" — the Great Revival which reached Western North Carolina by the end of the eighteenth century. At singing-gatherings (which continue to this day) and camp meetings, pioneer people were given to use what may have been their first manufactured and mass-produced article, the folk-hymn or revival song. This article employed as its tune a folk-tune, as its text words composed by a spiritually-minded man, in the words of one of them, taking the "devil's ditties" to do the Lord's work.

What happened to the simple folk-songs of a bye-gone era was symptomatic of change. New ways were built upon the old. They did not supplant the traditions of the past — the agriculturally based social system making prestige the property of the river-bottom gentry; the politics of heredity making power an establishment belonging to the prosperous few. The religious awakening was what first brought isolated men into a great participation with masses of men. Methodist Conferences and Baptist Conventions were loyally attended by delegates from the mountains, who usually rode horseback to an eastern meeting center.

There had been highways of commerce too, tortuous wagon roads on which it was not unusual to see merchants' wagons drawn by as many as eight oxen, taking feathers, eggs, beeswax, medicinal herbs, apples, to the markets of the piedmont and returning with a full line of finished merchandise for the general stores. Travelers might ride in stagecoaches drawn by six beautifully matched horses like those that for a while went from Marion to Asheville. Those who were chosen to represent the area in the General Assembly and the United States Congress traveled thus.

And one must not forget the taste that was developing in people for entertainment. In the smaller towns the only spectacles of importance to draw crowds, in these days before the motion picture, may have been politics and the courts, and it was only to towns that one could go for the latter. North Carolina's most widespread folklore, like the ballad "Tom Dula," has to do with criminal actions and legal proceedings which aroused great interest in the arena of the day, the courts. Tom Dula was defended in several trials by the famous lawyer and former governor Vance, and reporters came to little Wilkesboro from far off New York newspapers, public interest in the case being so great. An earlier trial, that of Frankie Silvers in Burke County and a still earlier one, that of John Lewis for the murder of Naomi Wise (the ballad is "Omie Wise") show the interest of an enduring nature that a great trial can arouse in an eager audience of common citizens.

Not all trials were criminal cases, and not all courts were so well attended, but one must conclude that then the courts were more interesting and exciting than now. Nor were courts so far removed from the other great arena, politics.

Other cultural institutions developed slowly. Only the well-to-do could afford to attend the academies and institutes that were usually located in the county seats, and for the masses the one-room school had to suffice until a state system of education for all developed.

The changing society in Western North Carolina could not have come without the railroads and the highway system. The historian must arbitrarily choose the order in which different topics fall. Part II which follows traces the changing society; Part III will narrate the developing economy. Both took place simultaneously.

CHAPTER THREE

Religion

Many Western North Carolinians are traditionally fundamentalists who believe in a literal interpretation of the Bible, particularly of the Old Testament. Their beliefs are deep, strong, sincere, although not always have the believers transformed their creed into Christian living. It has been said that religion to Western North Carolinians is bred in the bone. It took various forms, depending somewhat on their national orgins but more on the opportunities offered and on evangelism in the particular locality.

The denominational pattern existing in Western North Carolina after the Civil War had been determined many years earlier by the work of the pioneer ministers who had given unstintingly of their time and their lives. We might have expected that at least one-third of the people would be Presbyterians, if family traditions had prevailed, since that proportion were of Scottish descent. But Presbyterians did not engage in missionary work in the mountain area until near the close of the nineteenth century. Meanwhile, Baptist churches were easily established and many potential Presbyterians joined them. Baptist churches outnumber all others in Western North Carolina. Methodists, too, had a system for organizing new congregations and creating new churches, and their results in Western North Carolina were good. For example, a community of Presbyterians living in the Tuckaseigee Valley far away from their church were advised by the Presbyterian minister in Asheville to join the Methodist Church until they could obtain a Presbyterian pastor.

They became staunch Methodists and continued in that denomination.

Baptist churches promoted democracy, and they also tied newly settled areas with the ones from which people had removed, thus helping to unify the population of the area and the state. The method was simple. A group of Baptists who had moved too far from their church to attend services would start a new congregation with the help of the parent church. After a period of recruiting enough members to carry on church discipline, the branch, called an "arm," would petition the parent church asking for the dismission of its members for the purpose of forming a new church. The mother church usually sent helpers to constitute the new one, and the minister of the mother church was responsible for the spiritual welfare of the "arm". A member of the new congregation might be chosen as their minister. He would be examined for his doctrinal views by a "presbytery" of at least two ministers. If they approved him, they would ordain him by "the laying on of hands" and by prayer. Thus new churches sprang up rapidly and at small expense. The minister was a self-supporting man. He was sometimes an illiterate one who would have to teach himself to read the Bible because he felt a "call" to preach or to "exercise his gifts" (of words). Thus a church might be the mother of a number of smaller ones.

Baptist churches formed "associations" whose meetings were attended by the delegates chosen by each congregation. In this way they kept in touch with other communities. Judge Johnson J. Hayes's excellent history of Wilkes County traces the formation of each Baptish church in the county from 1771 to 1960. The earliest churches organized in the county, first part of Rowan, then Surry, and finally Wilkes, became members of the Strawberry Association of Virginia. In 1790 the churches in North Carolina in that association were dismissed to form the Yadkin Association, and in 1799 the churches from the Yadkin Association were permitted to withdraw to form the Mountain Baptist Association. By 1831 the Baptist State Convention was in operation, and it founded schools and colleges, established a religious press, and produced an advanced type of scholarship.

As the denomination grew in numbers and strength, missionary activities multiplied, and the Sunday School was introduced. Church members began to participate financially in support of missions and benevolent societies. A number of the churches objected. The Mountain Association by a majority vote in 1838 declared itself an anti-missionary body hostile to the "institutions of the day" and took the name "Primitive Baptist," a step which had already been taken by the Fisher's River Association in 1832 in Surry County, another former member of the Yadkin Association. The Primitive Baptist churches opposed the new system and refused to sit in conference with those who favored it. They expelled from their numbers members of such secret organizations as the Sons of Temperance and the Masonic order, fearing that these organizations might compete with the church for influence over the members. Primitive Baptists were opposed to a paid ministry or to schools and colleges for the education of men for the ministry, and while they were actually zealous in missionary efforts they disapproved of financial activities of churches in any form. Most of them objected to instrumental music in churches. The Primitive Baptist movement was felt in Surry and Ashe counties and in the portion of Wilkes County that later became Alleghany County. In 1884 there were twenty-one Primitive Baptist churches in that area. The Missionary Baptist churches were expelled from the Mountain Association and formed new associations which supported Sunday schools and educational institutions. The Primitive Baptists seem not to have spread into the southwestern part of the state, but there another offshoot developed, the Free Will Baptists, who were also very rigid in doctrine but extremely anti-Calvinistic (the Primitive Baptists were Calvinists). The Free Will Baptists in Buncombe, Madison, Yancey, and Mitchell counties in 1884 numbered sixteen churches.

The Missionary Baptist churches in the United States split into two conventions over the issue of slavery, and most of the churches in North Carolina have been affiliated with the Southern Baptist Convention since 1845. However, there were numbers of mountain people opposed to slavery, and when after the Civil War the Union League came into existence and Union sympathizers joined it, about one hundred of them in 1867 formed the Mountain View Baptist Association. Its growth was slow. In 1884 there were two of these Union churches in Alleghany County, and today there are four or five small associations in North Carolina and Virginia.

To the south the French Broad Association was organized in 1800 with fourteen churches in North and South Carolina. These churches had been dismissed by Bethel, the mother association, to form the new group. By 1807 there were seven member churches west of the Blue Ridge. Each of these churches sent out arms and organized congregations. When the State Baptist Convention was organized, these churches in the western section found it difficult to keep in touch with its proceedings. Travel by horseback for such long distances to the meetings of the convention was arduous although the delegates were diligent in attending. In 1844 an appeal was made by delegates from the French Broad Association for a new convention. In 1845 at Boiling Springs Camp Ground near Hendersonville, the Western Baptist Convention was organized. Its aims were, "distribution of the Bible among the destitute, employment of Home Missionaries within her bounds, the sustaining of foreign, domestic, and Indian missions; also to educate poor young men called of God to the Ministry of the Gospel who may be approved by their churches." This convention served until 1895, and after 1865 its membership was limited to associations west of the Blue Ridge. It founded Judson College in Hendersonville and authorized the establishment of Mars Hill College in Madison County.

Examination of the history of the Baptist churches in all twenty-four counties would be impossible here. Two counties that illustrate the steady increase in the number of Baptist churches are Wilkes and Cherokee. Records of Baptist churches in Cherokee County are available in Margaret Freel's *Our Heritage: The People of Cherokee County, North Carolina, 1540–1955*. The fifty-eight churches are divided between the West Liberty Baptist Association and the Western North Carolina Baptist Association, and in each association twelve churches have been established in the twentieth century, while sixteen were in existence in each before 1877. In Wilkes County the Baptist churches are listed by Judge Hayes in *The Land of Wilkes*. In the Brushy Mountain Association there are thirty-five churches, thirteen of which were constituted after 1900, indicating that missionary activity has continued and multiplied as the urban area around the Wilkesboros developed. In addition, thirteen Baptist churches in Wilkes County are in the Elkin Baptist Association, only two of which were established after 1900. The Stone Mountain Association had in 1960 twenty-nine churches. The Briar Creek, Elkin, and Stony Fork associations include some churches outside Wilkes County. Many of the churches now occupy modern brick structures with educational classrooms and heat and water facilities, and the minister is usually furnished with a house.

The locating of Methodist Episcopal churches in the mountain counties was begun by English-born Francis Asbury, who became the first Methodist bishop in America in 1784. He crossed the mountains sixty times, carrying religion to the people along his route. He began the system of "itinerancy," and when it became impossible for him to attend all of the congregations he had founded, the office of elder, later presiding elder, was created. A Methodist circuit consisting of a large number of congregations was followed by a "circuit rider" who visited each "appointment" periodically. Often meetings were held in the homes. Because the life was strenuous, a Methodist minister would frequently serve only four or six months as a circuit rider, after which he would "locate," and establish a church. By 1800 almost the entire area of Western North Carolina was divided into circuits in which were numerous "classes" presided over or taught by lay leaders except when the circuit rider was present.

As time went on the churches were organized in "conferences," each conference into districts, and each district into circuits. The Holston Conference began in 1783 with sixty members and one preacher. By 1824 there were 13,444 white members, 1,411 colored ones, and forty-three preachers. It had three districts — Abingdon, Knoxville, and French Broad — and twenty-five circuits with thirty-eight preachers besides the presiding elders. Among the circuits of the Holston Conference was the Waynesville Circuit and Echota Mission, under the leadership of the Reverend Ulrich Keener. It included all of Haywood and parts of Transylvania, Jackson, and Swain counties. Most of the people in the charge were Cherokee Indians. The Black Mountain Circuit included the mountainous region of Buncombe, Yancey, and Burke counties. The French Broad Circuit also was mountainous. The life of the circuit rider has been described thus: "Traveling day after day, preaching in the houses of the people, in school houses, in little log meeting houses, and in the open air, mingling with the people in their homes, . . . visiting the sick, comforting the dying, burying the dead, marrying the young, baptising the children, warning sinners, and reclaiming the backsliders — such was the life of the young preacher as he rode over the rugged hills."

In 1824 a dispute arose in the Methodist Episcopal churches concerning the lack of opportunity for lay members to participate

76 / Part II: A Changing Society

Typical of the hundreds of country churches is this in Jackson County, except that today many are being replaced by brick structures

in church meetings. "Union Societies" were formed by those who wanted more democracy in their church. Starting in Maryland, the agitation spread southward, two conferences being formed in rural North Carolina of circuits of the dissenters who practiced lay representation. They objected to the episcopal form of church government of the main body of Methodists. These societies, which later called themselves the Methodist Protestant Church, multiplied slowly. In 1884 there were eight Methodist Protestant churches in Buncombe County, one in Burke, and one in McDowell.

Another division in the Methodist Episcopal Church occurred in 1846 over the right of a bishop to own slaves, and the Methodist Episcopal Church South was formed. The counties in Western North Carolina were in one of three conferences of the Methodist Episcopal Church South: the Holston Conference, including Asheville, Burnsville, Hendersonville, Waynesville-Echota Mission, and Franklin circuits; the North Carolina Conference, with Surry County, Jonesville, and Wilkes County; and the South Carolina Conference with Rutherfordton, Morganton, and Lenoir. Thus it was that Davenport College at Lenoir, when ready to accept students in 1857, was turned over to the South Carolina Conference.

After the Civil War the Methodist Episcopal Church [North]

started evangelistic activities in the South, forming its own Holston Conference, of which the Asheville District had in 1866 1,007 members. A new conference of the Methodist Episcopal Church was created in 1867, the Virginia and North Carolina Mission Conference, including all of North Carolina except Watauga County and the area west of the Blue Ridge, which remained part of the Holston Conference, Asheville District. Much of the work was among Negroes. In 1876 there were forty churches, thirty-one local preachers, and 3,500 members. In 1880 the Blue Ridge Conference was formed and at first all of North Carolina was included. Later it was reduced to thirteen counties west of the mountains. Branson's *North Carolina Business Directory* for 1884 listed eight northern Methodist churches in Buncombe County and two in each of Clay and Transylvania counties.

In addition there were two types of Negro Methodist churches in the area: the African Methodist Episcopal Church which traced its founding back to Philadelphia in 1816 of which there was one in Buncombe County, one in Burke, and one in Rutherford; the African Methodist Episcopal Church Zion, organized in New York in 1796, of which there were two in Polk and one in Buncombe counties.

Camp meetings played their part in extending the work of the churches. One of the famous locations was Turkey Creek Camp Ground at Leicester in Buncombe County. A tract of land was deeded by the Gudger family in 1826 to be used for meetings and religious services. It evidently had been so used even earlier, as Bishop Asbury wrote in his diary on September 27, 1806, "I rode twelve miles to Turkey Creek to a kind of camp meeting. On the Sabbath I preached to about five hundred souls." For over sixty five years camp meetings were held there. It was a typical camp meeting ground. The camp was laid out like a big square, in the middle of which was the "arbor" where services were held, covering one-fourth acre, with room to seat one thousand to fifteen hundred people, roofed over but with no side walls. The arbor was on a slope with the speakers' stand at the lower side, making it resemble an amphitheater. The rough wooden slabs which served as seats were later replaced with better ones. People who attended the meetings came to stay several days. They lived in "tents," which were really rough wooden sheds, surrounding the arbor and making the square. Some tents had two stories, the floor of the first story being dirt covered with straw. The beds were bunks built around the walls like a long shelf. The meetings usually began on Thursday and lasted until Monday or Tuesday. They were held in August, and Sunday was the big day. They furnished opportunity for people from different communities to get to know each other and for families that were separated to have reunions. Eventually the nature of the meetings changed. Horse traders and merchants invaded the camp ground to engage in their businesses, whence the meetings were discontinued.

Since 1939 when the three large Methodist bodies, Methodist Episcopal, Methodist Episcopal South, and Methodist Protestant, became the Methodist Church, and later the United Methodist Church, laymen have participated in all matters, a victory for the Methodist Protestants. In 1966 the General Conference of the Methodist Church held in Chicago adopted a resolution to do everything possible to eliminate any structural organization based on race at the earliest possible date and not later than the jurisdictional conference in 1972. There had been in North Carolina the Central Jurisdiction which had consisted of Negro churches. In 1968 the Central Jurisdiction was abolished and the Negro Methodist churches became part of the conferences and districts in which they were geographically located. [The Winston-Salem District of the Western North Carolina Conference has been divided into Winston-Salem Forsyth and Winston-Salem Northeast districts. Mr. James C. Peters, a Negro, was appointed by Bishop Hunt as District Superintendent (the office formerly known as the Presiding Elder).] Of the 272,000 members of churches in the Western North Carolina Conference, about 12,000 are Negroes, and of the 750 active ministers, 56 are Negroes.

The Presbyterian family of churches is third in membership in North Carolina, although its communicants number only about one-twelfth of the church membership of the area. There have been Presbyterian churches in Western North Carolina at least since 1786. The first three congregations west of the Blue Ridge are said to have been in Buncombe County: Swannanoa, Rim's Creek (Reem's Creek), and Cane Creek. In 1799

George Newton was called to Buncombe's churches to be minister. Leadership for these churches came from Virginia, where the Abingdon Presbytery was constituted in 1786, to extend west about two hundred miles and eastward to the Blue Ridge. Church government in the Presbyterian church may be compared with civil government in the United States. Local self-government prevails in individual churches through elected elders and congregational meetings. Delegates are sent to the presbytery, a district organization of Presbyterian churches, to which the obligation of missionary work is assigned. The body corresponding to the state government is the synod, and at the top is the assembly, which has jurisdiction over all of the churches of the organization.

The Holston Presbytery, organized in 1827, included what are now Watauga, Mitchell, and Yancey counties. Meanwhile churches east of the Blue Ridge and in southwest North Carolina were members of the Concord Presbytery, far away in those days of slow travel. For a brief period of five years a Morganton Presbytery was in existence, but it was abolished in 1840. Extension of the church into the mountains was not vigorously sought. The Presbyterian Church, too, was split at the time of the Civil War, and the Presbyterian Church of the Confederate States of America was established. In North Carolina it made no gains during the war; in fact, 2000 communicants lost their lives. After the war the southern church was named the Presbyterian Church in the United States, and the Presbytery of Mecklenburg was set off from that of Concord, but still little effort was made to establish churches in the mountain area, although a need to do so was recognized. When the Synod of North Carolina met in Charlotte in 1877 a report was presented, from which the following is quoted: "Scotch-Irish Presbyterians settled in the western part of the State. They rapidly increased, until at the time of the Revolution, they numbered three or four thousand. ... At this time [1877], after a lapse of a hundred years, they numbered 16,544 communicants in 214 churches, with 113 ministers.... We have failed to perform our whole duty. With our educated ministry, our intelligent, influential and wealthy members, we ought to have planted the Presbyterian Church in every corner of the State." In 1880 when the Synod met in Raleigh it was reported that of the ninety-four counties included in the Synod, twenty-nine had no Presbyterian churches, and twenty-four had only one each. In 1884 Branson's *Directory* reported twenty-four Presbyterian churches in the counties of Western North Carolina. At that time there were just two evangelists in the state, and the Synod was spending only $2300 for evangelistic work. In synod meetings frequent discussions of responsibility for missions brought up the argument that mission work was the responsibility of the presbyteries, not of the synod. Finally, however, in 1893 the Reverend R. P. Pell was sent by the Synod as district evangelist to Watauga and Mitchell counties. At that time there was not a Presbyterian church in Mitchell County and there was only a very small one in Watauga County. Mr. Pell's report to the Synod the next year was, "Churches in charge, 4; mission points, 5; communicants 162; Sabbath schools, 4; pupils, 275, with seven teachers." Pell had traveled on horseback, in a buggy, and on foot and had held services in places hitherto unknown to the Presbyterians.

In 1896 the Asheville Presbytery was formed, being set off from the Mecklenburg Presbytery. There were eleven counties, ten ministers, and one thousand communicants. The area lay west of the Blue Ridge and included Buncombe, Clay, Cherokee, Graham, Haywood, Henderson, Jackson, Macon, Madison, Transylvania, and Swain counties. It was almost entirely missionary ground. In four of the counties there was still no Presbyterian church and in four other counties there were only 150 communicants. Two missionaries, Robert F. Campbell, pastor of the First Presbyterian Church in Asheville, and R. P. Smith, were sent out to investigate the destitution within the presbytery. Both men were natives of the mountain area and would be welcomed in the homes. They were directed to leave the railroads and telegraph lines and the larger valleys behind and to penetrate the secluded coves and highlands and report what they found. They spent three months preaching from house to house and in the woods, sharing the rude accommodations and plain fare of the people. They found numbers of houses without a lamp, a candle, a comb, a brush, a looking-glass. Many of the people had never seen a town, and the buggy of the evangelists was a curiosity. They found many families in which not a member could read a syllable and in whose homes there was not a word of print. An area of 150 square miles had 400 children of school age and no school, church, or Sunday school. There were large areas in which there was no physician, and old women and quacks administered herbs and practiced their superstitious arts. Women and children did most of the work in these remote homes, and men were idle except when hunting, fishing, or running illicit distilleries. Campbell wrote, "In some regions a young man has reached the summit of his ambitions when he has learned to pick the banjo, owns a dog, and carries a pistol and a bottle of whiskey."

Many persons told the missionaries that their parents had been Presbyterians, and Campbell concludes, "The Presbyterian Church failed to feed and tend these scattered members of its fold, and the more aggressive Methodist and Baptist churches gathered them into their folds. God bless them for it." R. P. Smith wrote, "They never had a fair chance. Entrenched here for generations and far removed from the thoroughfare of a progressive world, the wonder is that they have done so well.

After the survey of the summer, 1898, work of the Presbytery began in the areas where need was greatest. School conditions in Robbinsville were deplorable. Suitable buildings were lacking and teachers were incompetent. People grasped the opportunity for a good school. A two-room building was built, one room for school, the other for church services. Soon two additional rooms were needed, as the enrollment reached 350; Three teachers were engaged and a library of 300 books was installed. A pastor was employed and church and Sunday school started. People in the county said that this was the greatest influence for good the county had ever experienced. In Haywood County in a district where there had not been a public school in operation for two years, the Snyder Memorial Academy was built and it soon had an enrollment of 295 pupils. In Big Ivy Community in the Black Mountains, two churches were organized and in 1905 there were 150 members. Schools were established in connection with the churches, and an ex-moonshiner said the Presbyterian workers had done more to benefit that section than all the laws of North Carolina.

In Haywood County an orphans' home at Crabtree was opened in 1904, with a day school attached for the benefit of the poor children of the neighborhood. During the first year twenty orphans were cared for and sixty-five children attended the school.

From 1897 until 1904 E. Mac Davis was the pioneer evangelist of Madison County. He preached at thirty-eight points, distributed thousands of tracts and books, organized three or four churches and a large number of Sunday schools and mission summer day schools. A number of women and one man assisted him in the work. When he left the area he had two hundred members in his churches.

Following Mr. Pell in 1895 were Edgar Tufts, L. E. Bostian, and E. D. Brown in Watauga County and L. A. McLaurin in Mitchell County. They were seminary students who worked during the summer months. In 1897 Edgar Tufts came back after completion of his seminary work to spend the rest of his life in Northwestern North Carolina.

Greater than the desire to found churches was the determination to educate the boys and girls, to let them "know the good life." The Presbyterian Church set up a pattern that public schools might follow. It sent in strong personalities, if possible ones well acquainted with mountain life and character, to establish high schools, often in a county seat, with boarding facilities and dormitories. Even after the State of North Carolina authorized the counties to support high schools, many could not because of the lack of funds. The church schools' objectives included that of leadership training for the time when the state would maintain high schools. When that time came a number of the church schools continued to furnish living facilities for students who lived too far away to be day students. After school buses were put into operation, some of the high schools established by the churches were advanced to college level and are still functioning.

At about the same time the Asheville Presbytery was formed, the Presbyterian Church in the U.S.A. (northern) began to dream that it would "make Asheville the center of Scotch-Irish Presbyterianism in the Southern Appalachian mountains." Young men and women were sent all through the mountains as leaders. Schools were attempted for children of all ages. The aim was not to organize Presbyterian churches but to send young people back to their communities to teach and live the Christian faith. The result was that few churches were formed. The schools have dwindled and much of the former school property has been sold. An exception is Warren Wilson College. Today the interest of the young missionaries has been transferred to the cities.

The Protestant Episcopal Church, heir to the Anglican Church of colonial days, had small numbers of communicants in Western

North Carolina congregations, but they were usually leaders in their communities and were often prominent in the state. An antipathy toward the Episcopal Church was evident in many parts of the area. Scholars have concluded that many of the Scotch-Irish had moved westward to avoid paying tithes to the established church and their disapproval has been passed on to their descendants. Perhaps that is the reason that more people did not affiliate with the Episcopal Church. At the end of the Civil War there were few of these churches in Western North Carolina and most of them were in the foothill parts of the counties. Those in the mountainous areas were established by South Carolinians who summered there. In 1836 a chapel was built for Episcopal families at Flat Rock, called St. John's in the Wilderness. In 1859 another church was completed near Fletcher, Calvary Episcopal Church. Miss Fanny Blake contributed thirteen acres and a building in which she conducted a school at Calvary Church from 1859 until her death. Tradition has it that a band of Stoneman's cavalry command during his raid in 1865 camped for a night in the yard of Calvary Church, and Stoneman was so impressed with the beauty of the church's interior that he ordered his men to take special care not to destroy anything in the House of God. Stoneman was not in the Asheville area during the campaign. The account may be true of part of his command. The story is that the next morning the cavalrymen were permitted to use pieces of the red church carpet for saddle blankets, and they rode away with "red carpet fluttering from their horses' backs."

Another chapel was St. Paul's in the Valley which dated from 1856. The first services were held in the carriage shed of F. W. Johnstone at Montlove, his summer home. James Stuart Hankle, of the South Carolina Seminary at Camden, served as pastor. Occasionally he preached on Sunday afternoons at the Baptist church in Cathey's Creek community. After Transylvania County was formed a church was organized in Brevard and services at St. Paul's were discontinued in 1884.

The Diocese of North Carolina was organized in 1817 with the Reverend John Stark Ravenscroft as bishop. He was succeeded by Bishop Levi S. Ives, who visited Morganton, Asheville, and Hot Springs when he journeyed through the mountains to Tennessee to organize a diocese there. His interest in Northwest North Carolina was awakened, and in 1842 he established at Valle Crucis a boarding school for mountain boys and a school of preparation for the ministry. A large farm was acquired and buildings were erected. William West Skiles came from the eastern part of the state to manage the farm and was ordained deacon. Eight candidates for the ministry were educated there. When Bishop Ives resigned Skiles continued his missionary work for ten years although the school stopped. Jarvis Buxton who helped Skiles at Valle Crucis started a school in Asheville. Later another Episcopal school, Ravenscroft, was founded there, and its director, Mr. Hillhouse Buell, established the mission in Brevard that developed into St. Philips Church. St. James Church in Hendersonville was organized in 1840 and consecrated in 1863. The rector, Thomas C. Wetmore, founded Christ School at Arden in 1900. Another St. James grew from a Lutheran church near Lenoir founded by Parson Robert Johnson Miller who later was ordained to the Episcopal priesthood. He had founded Lutheran churches in Lincoln and Burke counties as well. A small group of devoted missionaries held services in Watauga and Ashe counties, and their difficulties were brought home to Bishop Atkinson when he tried to travel from Lenoir to Watauga County on a visitation in 1878. He wrote, "On the afternoon of that day . . . I set off . . . but found the road so washed by the flood resulting from the heavy rains of the previous day and night, as to be impassable. I then attempted a more circuitous route, but the carriage in which I was travelling was overturned in a stream, which was ordinarily very shallow. I escaped with no more consequence than a wetting of myself and baggage, but I found that further progress up the mountain was impracticable, the road that wound its way up its ascent being washed away."

Years earlier, Episcopal churches had been established at Morganton, Rutherfordton, and Wilkesboro through the efforts of Bishop Ives. St. Paul's Church in Wilkesboro had a devoted minister, Reverend Richard Wainwright, who served forty-two years beginning in 1855. He also served as superintendent of schools of the county for twenty years and conducted a private school for young men in his home. His daughter Mary Taylor started a school for girls in Wilkesboro in 1879 and conducted it until 1919, with an average attendance of twenty. Wainwright held services at Wilkesboro once a month, traveling on horseback to other places to hold services on other Sundays.

As the number of Episcopal churches increased, a need was felt for a training school for the ministry, and Ravenscroft

School in Asheville offered such work from the late 1860's until about 1890, during which time fifteen candidates for the ministry studied there. Dr. Buxton of Ravenscroft Mission started holding services for Negroes at Trinity Chapel, now St. Matthias. General and Mrs. James Martin drilled Negro classes in the catechisms and teachings of the church, and a day school was held there. The first Negro priest, S. V. Berry, came in 1874 from Western New York to serve at St. Matthias for eleven years.

Interest in Valle Crucis was revived in 1893 and an associate mission was established. A school for mountain girls held there is discussed elsewhere. With several churches in Asheville, and small ones in Blowing Rock, Beaver Creek near Jefferson, and All Souls Church in Biltmore built by George Vanderbilt, the Episcopal Church was on sound footing by the close of the century.

Other denominations have congregations in Western North Carolina. There are twelve Lutheran churches, five of which are in Watauga County. Two of the latter, Holy Communion and Mount Pleasant, date from 1842 and 1845 respectively. Several Catholic services were held in court houses in various county seats before the first Catholic church was built in Asheville in 1869. As in-migration of the managerial class occurred when industries moved into the area, Catholic churches have been established in the residential areas near the plants as well as in resort communities.

Western North Carolina is now being called the "South's Summer Religious Capital." In the Asheville area in 1951 there were ten assembly grounds and in the entire region twenty-two religious conference grounds. The investments in the grounds and buildings amount to millions of dollars, and it was estimated in 1951 that each year the conferees spend almost $5,000,000. The total of expenditures in the area is larger more than twenty years later.

Montreat, established first, dates back to 1897 when the North Carolina General Assembly chartered the Mountain Retreat Association. In 1905 the Presbyterian Church in the United States bought it as a summer conference ground. Since that time it has been used the year around. In 1913 the Montreat

Normal School was established, the forerunner of Montreat-Anderson College. In 1962 more than twenty-one conferences were held at Montreat in September and October alone. Nineteen different groups use the facilities for conferences.

Ridgecrest is the second oldest. In 1907 an organizing committee for a Southern Baptist assembly bought 850 acres of land selected by James M. Tucker of Asheville. He had been the principal author of the idea; he obtained the charter and sold the idea to the Southern Baptists. The Southern Railroad to Asheville passed through the grounds but there was no station, and the assembly grounds could be reached from the east only by a road up the mountain through Swannanoa Gap, which in rain or snow turned to mud. When a railway station was obtained, the stop was first called Terrell's, later Blue Mont, and finally Ridgecrest. The buildings on the assembly grounds have been built gradually until thousands of delegates may be accommodated at one time. In 1965 twenty-two conferences were held from June 10 to September 16. The grounds are administered by the Baptist Sunday School Board of the Southern Baptist Convention.

Lake Junaluska, the World Methodist Center, was established by a laymen's missionary movement of the Methodist Episcopal Church South in 1908. It now belongs to the Southeastern Jurisdiction of the United Methodist Church. The World Methodist Council established its headquarters there and the World Methodist Building was erected in 1955. The assembly grounds were opened for conferences in 1913. The tract of 2500 acres contains a beautiful lake of 250 acres. Elmer T. Clark wrote that "Across the years the most famous personalities of Methodism have appeared upon its platform."

Another Methodist center is at Hayesville, the Hinton Rural Life Center, dating from 1953 when Mr. and Mrs. Walter Moore deeded four and one-half acres of land and an unfinished hotel building to the Hayesville Methodist Church. With contributions from Mrs. H. H. Hinton, the Duke Foundation, the Annual Conference, and the Waynesville District, and with private gifts, the center was completed to be used by groups in the Southeastern Jurisdiction of the Methodist Church. It is the center for the Appalachian Development program of the Methodist Church, a laboratory school for ministers and students.

Camps for boys and girls in conjunction with the conferences enable families to spend their vacations in the same general area.

Other conference grounds include the following: Lutheridge, near Arden, by the Lutheran Synods in the Southeast; Cragmont, near Black Mountain, for Free Will Baptists of North Carolina, which occupies the old Cragmont Sanitarium; Blue Ridge, near Black Mountain, established by the YMCA of the South in 1906, which serves as headquarters for varied meetings and may be rented by any recognized educational, religious, or social group; Kanuga Lake, in the Hendersonville area, the assembly of the Episcopal Church of the two Carolinas; Bonclarken, established at Flat Rock in 1963 by the Associate Reformed Presbyterian Church for youth and adult programs for eleven southeastern states; Ben Lippen, a short distance from Asheville, owned by the Columbia (South Carolina) Bible College and used as an interdenominational Christian vacation center; Our Lady of the Hills, near Hendersonville, the assembly of the Roman Catholic Diocese of Raleigh, begun in 1956 and now used as a camp, convention site, retreat, and rest site; Christmont, for the Disciples of Christ, near Black Mountain. Others are Blowing Rock Assembly of the Southern Synod of the Evangelical and Reformed Church, started in 1945 by a gift from the family of Abel A. Shuford; Wildacres, near Little Switzerland, an experiment in the betterment of human relations, open to all denominations for conferences and workshops; the Fellowship of Southern Churchmen, in Buckeye Cove, built to serve as a meeting place for ministers and church groups throughout the South who are unable to find space in any of the other conference grounds.

Perhaps the most unusual of the assembly grounds is Fields of the Wood, of the Church of God. On the side of Burger Mountain near Murphy have been constructed a huge concrete cross, the largest altar in the world, a reproduction of the sepulchre from which Christ rose, a stairway with 320 concrete steps, each marked by tablets on which are carved Biblical teachings, and the Ten Commandments laid out in huge stone letters, with each letter five feet tall.

CHAPTER FOUR

The Bar and the Forum*

The law above all other professions offered its followers the opportunity for political power, public office, and prominence. A man often progressed from solicitor to superior court judge and thence to the state supreme court; or he might be elected to the General Assembly or to the United States Congress. Judge Richmond Pearson's law school, Richmond Hill in Yadkin County, which had ended with his death in 1877, was very popular and prepared more than a thousand young men for the legal profession, but many studied under Judge W. H. Battle at the state university, and others attended the schools of Dick and Dillard in Greensboro, Colonel George Folk of Lenoir, Judge John L. Bailey of Asheville, and A. C. Avery of Morganton. There were other lawyers in the West who guided young men in the study of law. In some families it was a tradition that one son would follow his father in the legal profession. Some read law although they had no intention of practicing it. Such was Rufus Lenoir Patterson of the wealthy family of Happy Valley, Caldwell County, who became owner and manager of three manufacturing enterprises and whose cotton mill was burned by Stoneman's troops in the raid through Western North Carolina and Virginia in 1865.

Lawyers still accompanied the judge and the solicitor from

---

* The following chapter is not intended as a comprehensive treatment of lawyers and lawmakers in and from Western North Carolina. Rather, it illustrates the quality of the region's lawyers and lawmakers.

county to county on the circuit, a practice that has been discontinued now when travel is easy. Road conditions during the 1870's made the travel difficult. Colonel Clinton A. Cilley of Lenoir went one day to Morganton for court. His diary entry for that day read, "Left at seven, got beyond the crossroads and turned back by John's River. Went to ferry with Folk and Wakefield, Crossed at three, and walked to Morganton. Paid boy for carrying baggage, 60¢." The distance was about fifteen miles. At another time going from Lenoir to Jefferson he spent two days on the road each way. He wrote, "Left for Boone 7:10 — toll 20¢. Got into Boone at 5:10 P.M. Stay at Coffey's." The following day, "Left for Jefferson at 8 A.M. In at 4:15 — last ten miles it rained a good deal." On his return from Jefferson he had to pay 25¢ to have a log chopped from the road.

The lawyers usually traveled on horseback, stopped at the same hotels in the towns and at the same wayside inns in the country, sometimes as many as ten or fifteen of them together at one of the country stopping places, and there they would try important cases in their discussions before the cases ever came before the court. The wit and humor of certain of the lawyers, the scholarliness of others, became well known. Isaac Avery commented on Romulus Z. Linney of Taylorsville and Watauga County (he had a summer home on a mountain top in the latter): "Most men who read literature hold it in reserve as mere ornate punctuation or emphasis for every day speech, but Mr. Linney breathes composite literature at breakfast. In Congressional halls he has caused laughter by the use of colloquialisms which are his birthright, while in the back rural districts he has combined in furious speech Spencer, the Old Testament, Bill Nye, Blackstone, and the Constitution, and aimed them with telling force at an audience that was moved to weep blind tears."

Many of the great statesmen of Western North Carolina in the Ante-bellum period had been Whigs who worked for roads and railroads to and in their region and for constitutional reform. Gradually most of them became Democrats or later Conservatives. Those who survived in 1877 were still the great lawyers of the area. David Lowry Swain, native of Buncombe County, lawyer, member of the state House of Representatives, governor at the age of thirty-one, and president of the state university for thirty-three years, died in 1868. William Holland Thomas, great benefactor of the Cherokees and organizer of a legion of soldiers in the Civil War, who succeeded in getting laws for the cutting of roads from Jones Gap to Caesar's Head, Bakersville to Burnsville, Patterson to Valle Crucis and on to Jonesboro, Tennessee, Zionville to Mountain City, Cataloochee to Newport, Tennessee, Oconalufty through Soco Gap, from Valleytown over the Snowbird Mountains via Robbinsville, was ill and although he lived until 1893 he was not able to participate in public affairs by 1877. Thomas Lanier Clingman, former United States Senator, who deserted the Whig Party for the Democratic in 1856 over the slavery issue, was living in retirement in Asheville. Augustus S. Merrimon became Judge of the Eight Judicial District in 1865, was elected United States Senator in 1872 and served from 1873 to 1879. Zebulon Baird Vance, the most spectacular and universally popular man born in Western North Carolina, after serving as war governor of the state, practiced law while the Reconstruction government was in power, was elected Governor in 1876, and in 1879 was chosen to succeed Merrimon as United States Senator. Tod R. Caldwell of Burke County did not join the Conservative Party. He was the Republican lieutenant governor who was promoted to the governor's chair when Holden was impeached and removed from office. Caldwell was reelected to succeed himself, but he died in office in 1874. Burgess Sidney Gaither who had practiced law in Morganton since 1829, served in the state Senate, being elected president of that body in 1846, was solicitor of the Seventh Judicial District after 1848, and worked for the election of Bell and Everett of the Constitutional Union Party in 1860. Gaither was pronounced by Judge David Schenck the "leader and father of the Burke County Bar" in 1877. Of Nicholas W. Woodfin of Asheville, who had studied under Michael Francis and Governor Swain, it was said "There is no name in Western North Carolina more identified for the last thirty years — that is beginning with 1845 — with the material, industrial, and educational interests of that part of the State." Allen Turner Davidson also studied under Michael Francis and in 1845 was licensed to practice law in North Carolina. He established his practice in Murphy, seat of the new county of Cherokee, and traveled the circuit as far east as Cleveland County. The Davidson family was one of the best known in the area. They had come from Pennsylvania in 1748, some settling on the Catawba River in present-day Iredell County, others in the Swannanoa Valley. In subsequent generations several had gone westward to Tennessee and to Texas. Allen T. Davidson left the law in 1860 to become president of the Merchants and Miners Bank of Murphy. During the Civil War he served as an agent of the state commissary department, and after the war he practiced law in Asheville until 1885.

Among former Democratic leaders of the area, William Waightstill Avery had been killed during a battle with Kirk's raiders in Burke County in 1864, but his brother, Alfonso Calhoun Avery, had a successful career as a judge and lawyer, living until 1913. Judge John L. Bailey who had been associated with Supreme Court Justice Nash in Raleigh, had moved to Buncombe County and conducted a law school until his death in 1877. Theodore F. Davidson, one of his students wrote, "I think his influence upon the Bar of the Mountain Circuit has been more inspiring and lasting than that of any other member of the profession."

A new, younger group of lawyers was appearing in the courts of Western North Carolina in the 1870's and 1880's. In 1884 in the twenty-three counties there were 162 lawyers, many of whom are well remembered for their ability and wit. James Madison Gudger, Jr., and his brother Hezekiah A. Gudger, born in Madison County, were admitted to the bar, H. A. Gudger in 1871 and James M., Jr., in 1878. The latter served as a member of the United States House of Representatives, and Hezekiah was appointed Assistant Attorney General by President Cleveland in 1893. Jeter C. Pritchard said of James M. Gudger, Jr., "[he] had a splendid legal mind and could prepare a case for trial with as much ease and facility as any lawyer I ever knew.... He was always at his best in a rough and tumble contest.... A lawyer who served in the first Cleveland administration was Edmund Jones, related to the Patterson and Davenport families of Caldwell County. He read law under Colonel George Folk and was licensed by the Supreme Court of North Carolina in 1881. His activity in the Democratic Party led to his appointment to a "responsible position in the Treasury Department." He also served five terms in the General Assembly. Kope Elias, born in South Carolina, studied under the Reverend Laban Abernethy at Rutherford College, then under Richmond Pearson. Admitted to the bar in 1870, he began his practice in Murphy, moving to Franklin two years later. "At one time he enjoyed the largest practice of any lawyer west of Asheville." He was admired by other members of the bar for his story-telling prowess.

Three first cousins, grandsons of Colonel William Moore, pioneer whose homestead is now occupied by the Enka Corporation on Hominy Creek in Buncombe County, became eminent lawyers: Walter E. Moore studied under Dick and Dillard, practiced in Webster, Jackson County, and was made judge of the Twentieth Judicial District in 1926; Charles Augustus Moore studied law with Judge John Bailey in Asheville and practiced in Asheville, serving as Judge of the Buncombe County Criminal Court, 1887–1890; Frederick Moore studied law in Hayesville and at Chapel Hill. He was admitted to the bar in 1892, became a judge at age 29, and served ten years. Frederick's son, a resident of Haywood County, named for his grandfather Daniel Killian Moore, was governor of North Carolina from 1965 to 1969. Locke Craig wrote half a century ago, "For more than a century the Moores have stood in the front rank of the people of Western North Carolina."

Theodore F. Davidson, son of Allen Turner Davidson, served in the Civil War, enlisting at sixteen. After the war he studied law under Judge Bailey and was admitted to the bar in 1867. He practiced law with his father in Asheville until 1882. He had become quite active in the Democratic Party, served in the state Senate, and helped to promote the completion of the Western North Carolina Railroad, of which he was made state director in 1879. He developed a great interest in history and collected a notable library.

The Doughton brothers, Rufus and Robert of Laurel Springs, Alleghany County, wielded great influence in state and nation. Rufus, the elder, studied law at the state university and opened his office in Sparta in 1880. In that year he was elected to the state House of Representatives, serving as chairman of the Finance Committee. Robert Lee Doughton, a farmer, was a member of the State Board of Agriculture from 1903–1910, a member of the State Prison Board, served as president of the Deposit and Savings Bank of Wilkesboro, and in 1910 he was elected to the Sixty-second Congress where he served continuously until January, 1953. He was a member of the Ways and the Means Committee of the House of Representatives and became its chairman in 1933.

Thomas C. (Tam) Bowie was a generation younger than the Doughton brothers but he belongs in the same tradition. Born in Louisiana, he came to Ashe County with his mother after the death of his father. His maternal greatgrandfather Elijah Calloway had served in the General Assembly at the age of twenty-one when there was no road to his plantation. Elijah walked from his home on the South Fork of the New River to Raleigh to assume his seat in the legislature, and he secured a bill to build a road from his home intersecting with the stage line from Jefferson to Wilkesboro. Elijah Calloway had the first brick house in his section, and the first house with glass windows. He was a Whig in politics. His son James studied medicine at Jefferson School of Medicine in Philadelphia and settled in Louisiana. After his father's death Tam attended a school at Moravian Falls in Wilkes County, North Carolina, went to Kentucky to work at coal mining on two occasions. He attended Mars Hill College and the University of North Carolina, receiving an A. B. degree in 1899. After a year of study at Yale University Tam returned to North Carolina and studied law at the state university. He was admitted to the bar in 1901. He served in the legislature in the terms of 1908, 1913, 1915 (when he was Speaker of the House) and in 1921 was chairman of the Committee on Roads when the state highway system was created. Governor McLean appointed him a special emergency superior court judge in 1927. He was called a "man with a golden tongue."

Locke Craig, child prodigy who went to the University of North Carolina at age fifteen, moved to Asheville after completing his study of law, and set up a practice in 1882. He participated actively in Democratic Party politics and in 1898 he campaigned for Aycock. He was in the General Assembly in 1899 and in 1901. In 1908 he ran unsuccessfully for the Democratic nomination for governor, but in 1912 he was elected governor.

Most men were content to leave the legislative halls to those trained in the law. Now and again someone from a mercantile family sought and won political honors. James C. Harper, born in Pennsylvania, who moved to Caldwell County after a residence in Ohio in 1840 when the county was being formed, had laid out the town of Lenoir, practiced civil engineering, surveying, and draftmanship, merchandising and textile manufacturing, served in the state House of Representatives 1865–66, and was elected to the United States House of Representatives in 1871. Almost a century later James T. Broyhill of Lenoir, associated with the Broyhill Industries, probably the largest family-owned furniture manufacturing concern in the world, represents the Tenth Congressional District. Richard Thurmond Chatham was chairman of the board of directors of the large Chatham Manufacturing Company in Elkin when he was elected to the United States Congress in 1949, and he continued to serve in both capacities until in 1955 he resigned from the chairmanship. He died just before his term in the House of Representatives ended in 1957.

The Democratic Party in North Carolina has from 1870 until today had a majority in the legislature with one brief exception — 1895–1901 — the Fusion period. The Fusion period involved the rise of the People's Party or the Populist Party, the fusion of that party with the Republican Party, the temporary overthrow of the Democratic party, and then the restoration of the Democrats to power. Most of the writers concerning the Fusion period have a Democratic bias.

The violent political attitudes in the last third of the nineteenth century were the result of the Civil War and Reconstruction. As has been pointed out there were two parties, the Republican and the Conservative, later called the Democratic. The Conservative Party was composed of white men whose desire was to drive the Northern "foreigners" out and to return control of the state government exclusively to whites. The rivalry of the two parties, the Republican to maintain control and the Conservative to gain it, is the story of Reconstruction in North Carolina.

The Conservatives captured the legislature in 1870 and the governorship in 1876, and North Carolina was Democratic from 1876 to 1894, when the Republican Party and the Negro were again political factors.

The Democrats had chafed under the Reconstruction constitution and had called a constitutional convention that met on September 5, 1875. Instead of drawing up another constitution the convention wrote many amendments, two of which were of great importance: the residence requirement for voting would be ninety days rather than sixty, and any person convicted of a felony could be disfranchised; and the General Assembly was given power to modify, change, or abrogate county governments. The association of the Negro with the Republican Party gave the Democrats the lever by which to control the state. Former Whigs had formed and led the Conservative Party and they refused to use the name Democrat for eight years. But Zebulon Baird Vance and the Democrats defeated the Republicans in 1876 and Vance was hailed as "the redeemeer." The name Democrat became acceptable.

The national issues in the 1880's centered around the regulation of railroads, currency fluctuation, tariffs, control of monopolies and agricultural demands by a vocal West. Prior to 1894 no efforts were made by the Democratic Party to foster social and economic reforms, for these were opposed by the industrial and railroad interests. Men in control of the Democratic Party in North Carolina were in alliance with the railroad and manufacturing interests. Many of these men had used the state between 1876 and 1894 to further their own business interests and were content to rest on their chief accomplishment — redemption of the state from Yankees and Negroes. Democrats thus failed to offer North Carolina a vitalized program. This evasion of issues was made possible by reminding the voters of Negro rule under the Republican Party during Reconstruction.

From 1876 for many years the question of the Negro in politics was the dominant issue in all party affiliations. Democratic election law, Democratic control of county governments gerrymandering, intimidation, manipulation and corruption had kept the party in control from 1876 to 1894.

In 1890 the Democratic Party had two elements: a dominant conservative wing (pro-business, anti-reform) led by a few leaders who controlled the party, and a liberal, agrarian anti-corporation wing with spokesmen like Walter Clark and Leonidas Polk. The liberal agrarian element grew in strength because of agrarian discontent and criticism of the railroads. The two farmers' organizations, the Grange in the early seventies and the Farmers' Alliance, which was organized in 1887, made little impression in the mountains, but that section benefited from their influence. In the election of 1890 the Alliance virtually captured control of the Democratic Party.

"The 'Farmers' Legislature of 1891' ... increased the tax rate for public schools, established a normal college for white girls, and an agricultural college and a normal college for Negroes;

increased the state appropriations to the University and state colleges; [established a School for the Deaf and Dumb in Western North Carolina] and provided state regulation for railways by forbidding rebates and rate discriminations and creating a railroad commission of three members elected by the legislature and empowered to reduce rates and eliminate the special tax exemptions and low assessments enjoyed by the railroads," summarized historian David Holcombe.

Again the conservative Democrats controlled the party in North Carolina in 1894. They stood for *laissez faire* policies, no governmental regulation of railroads, and favoritism to business. It was a large party but it was governed by a few and was interested chiefly in self-preservation.

The geography of North Carolina was significant in the development of the post-Reconstruction Republican Party. A few western counties were centers of Republican strength. Sectional hostility had been incited before the Civil War by a lack of just representation in the legislature and the contempt with which non-slaveholding white farmers were treated by the slave-holding oligarchy of the lowlands. After the Civil War many of the small farmers became Republicans. In gubernatorial elections seven mountain counties voted Republican in each election from 1876 through 1896: Ashe, Cherokee Henderson, Madison, Mitchell, Polk, and Wilkes. Nineteen other counties voted Republican during the same period — in other parts of the state. There were forty-seven counties in other parts of the state with from forty to forty-nine per-cent of the vote being Republican during this same period. This potential strength was often sufficient to challenge the Democratic Party at a given election.

The Republican votes in the western counties were those of adult male whites, since the Negro population in each county was comparatively small. Because of the Republican counties and the small Democratic majority in many other counties, Western North Carolina was an important political region. It was not the sole determinant in state politics, but mountain leaders exercised importance out of proportion to the size, the population, and the wealth of the area.

The resurgence of the Republican Party, 1890–1900, was closely linked with the rise of the Populist Party as a result of agrarian discontent which projected the Farmers' Alliance into politics. The Populist Party was a protest against social and political grievances which the Democratic Party had done little to alleviate. Since the demands of the Alliance were intended to correct outstanding abuses, its entrance into politics was inevitable. Its leaders wanted it to work with both old parties rather than to form a separate political party. More was expected from the Democrats than from the Republicans in North Carolina since they were the party in power. In 1892 the Alliance split. The more conservative members remained loyal to the Democrats because of the fear of the Negroes and the Republicans. The more radical joined the Populist Party of the midwestern farmers.

In 1892 the Populist Party held its first state convention and set forth a progressive platform. W. P. Exum, the party's candidate for governor, received a small vote in the western counties as did James B. Weaver, the Populist candidate for President, but the state as a whole cast a Populist vote which combined with the Republican vote exceeded that for the Democratic candidates. Seven mountain counties voted Republican as usual.

In 1894 the Republican and Populist parties endorsed a cooperative ticket. This fusion ticket carried the election. The Democrats retained only forty-six seats in the House and eight in the Senate. The Populists gained thirty-six seats in the House and twenty-four in the Senate, and together the Fusionists elected their Supreme Court ticket and their State Treasurer, and captured control of both houses by a large majority. In Western North Carolina there were sizeable Republican and Populist gains. The legislature in 1895 set the maximum interest rate at six per-cent and provided for a four-month school term.

The election of 1896 brought into office Daniel Russell, the only Republican governor in North Carolina, 1877–1973. He carried eleven of the mountain counties. Between 1897 and 1899 the Fusionists were in complete control of the executive, legislative, and judicial offices in the state. Local self-government for the counties was vested in boards of three county commissioners elected by the people.

The Fusion period came to North Carolina because economic distress existed and political reforms were needed. The marriage was not permanent. The "white supremacy" campaign of 1898 defeated Fusion and by 1900 the Democrats were again in complete control in North Carolina. They decided to eliminate the Negro as a factor in North Carolina politics by an amendment to the constitution combining a literacy test and a grandfather clause provision to disfranchise the Negroes. Although the amendment carried, in only five of the counties of Western North Carolina did a majority of voters approve the amendment which was submitted to them in 1900: Alleghany, Buncombe, Burke, McDowell, and Rutherford. All except Alleghany had fairly large Negro populations. A law passed in 1899 gave the General Assembly the power again to elect county commissioners.

During the period of Fusionist rule Jeter C. Pritchard, Republican of Madison County, was elected United States Senator to succeed Zebulon B. Vance who had died. In 1897 Pritchard was chosen by the General Assembly to serve a full six-year term, and when he was defeated for the senatorship in 1903 he was given federal offices, in 1903–1904 as Justice of the Supreme Court for the District of Columbia and from 1904 until his death as Judge of the United States Circuit Court of Appeals for the Fourth Judicial District.

The two other United States Senators elected from Western North Carolina since 1903 were Democrats: Robert Rice Reynolds from Asheville, who was elected in 1932 and served until 1945; and Samuel James Ervin, Jr., of Morganton, who served first as a member of the United States House of Representatives to complete the unfinished term of his brother, Joseph William Ervin, who had died, and then in 1954 was elected to the United States Senate to replace Clyde Hoey, deceased. He had been a member of the North Carolina Supreme Court from 1937 to 1943 and again from 1948 to 1950. He still serves in the Senate.

Five Republicans have been elected to the United States House of Representatives from Western North Carolina in the twentieth century. Edmund Spencer Blackburn, with a law office in Jefferson, served from 1901 to 1903 and from 1905 to 1907. Charles Holden Cowles of Wilkesboro, who acted as Blackburn's private secretary during his first term, was elected to the House in 1909. Richmond Pearson, son and namesake of the great Chief Justice and law teacher, served in the North Carolina House of Representatives from Buncombe County from 1885 to 1889, and during the four years 1895 to 1899 he was the Representative from the Ninth Congressional District. He was reelected in 1900 but did not complete his term as Theodore Roosevelt appointed him to a succession of diplomatic posts. From 1907 until Taft's inauguration in 1909 he was minister

The Bar and the Forum / 99

to Greece and Montenegro. Except for the leadership of the Roosevelt forces in North Carolina in the campaign of 1912 he did not participate in public life after 1909. Jeter M. Pritchard, son of Jeter C. Pritchard, was a prominent Republican who served in Congress from 1929 to 1931. James T. Broyhill has represented the Tenth District since 1962.

In 1960 nineteen of the twenty-four western counties voted for Nixon for President, although only four voted for Goldwater in 1964. Madison County voted Democratic for the Presidency in both 1960 and 1964. It seems to be anybody's guess how these counties will go politically.

Even before a Republican governor was elected in 1972, the choice of the Democratic machine was no longer certain of winning the office. Victories of Kerr Scott in 1948, Terry Sanford in 1960, and Dan K. Moore in an election of great turmoil in 1964 indicate that the Democratic organization can no longer handpick its candidate.

No longer is the county courthouse so completely the center of mountain social life but it has remained the center of political life — the seat of power and patronage. Crimes of violence have decreased, more amusements are available, and the coming of the automobile and of good roads has increased social intercourse. County agents, welfare departments, mental health clinics, and county libraries are often centered around the courthouse. The courthouses and the county seats have been the centers of coteries of power, the "courthouse rings," the political machines. Here in these little Tammany Halls the political bosses have dispensed patronage and determined in an autocratic manner the political destinies of the county. In Western North Carolina these political machines were Democratic and were kept in power by friendly Democratic legislatures. In a number of counties Republicans were in the majority but as long as the legislature appointed the county commissioners the county chairman of the Democratic Party had the power, not the Republican representatives in the legislature. He selected the candidates for the office of county commissioner. Often no teacher could obtain or hold a position without his approval. The Democratic legislature appointed the school committees, controlled many of the educational and welfare administrations,

James Holshouser, elected in November 1972 the first Republican Governor in North Carolina in this century and the fifth Western North Carolinian elected to that office since 1865. Holshouser is a native of Boone and has practiced law there except when serving in the General Assembly, since his graduation from the University of North Carolina Law School at Chapel Hill.

PHOTO COURTESY OF WATAUGA DEMOCRAT

and kept a Democratic minority in power. For example, in Republican Madison County for years a Democratic county boss ruled the county as completely as Huey Long ruled Louisiana.

Election of county officials has been restored to the people and recently members of county boards of education have been made elective officers.

Over all the counties west of Asheville the Asheville and Buncombe County political machine had tremendous influence. From the end of the Civil War to the Depression of the thirties many of the counties were traditionally Republican. Because of the social program of Franklin Roosevelt the Democrats gained the ascendency. Weldon Weir, the city manager of Asheville, Coke Candler, chairman of the board of county commissioners, Lawrence Brown, the sheriff, and Don S. Elias wielded great power. The political adroitness of these men was notable. Weldon Weir was credited with masterminding the fortunes of the Democratic Party in Asheville election after election. For decades Sheriff Lawrence Brown was political arbiter of the county. He built a strong political base by helping the needy and by persistently enforcing the law but used his powers dictatorially. Throughout the 1930's, 1940's, 1950's a third political figure allied with Weir and Brown was Don S. Elias, newspaper owner and financier. He was the third leg of political tripod. He was a statewide figure operating powerfully in local politics. As a newspaper man he often held the politicians in check and served as a balance of power. The political dynasty ruled by these men began to crumble in the 1950's. In 1958 Dave Hall of Webster with the backing of Judge Dan Moore defeated Weldon Weir for the congressional nomination, evidence that no longer did "Big Buncombe," dominate politics west of Asheville. Don Elias had supported Weir and the defeat proved that he was not invincible in the Twelfth District. The passing of Buncombe's dominance was further seen in 1966 when Congressman Roy A. Taylor lost Buncombe by 4000 votes but still won reelection. It had been a truism that to win in the district one had to win in Buncombe.

Sheriff Brown's high-handed treatment of Jay Hensley, who had exposed the Democratic toleration of gambling in Buncombe County, and the seizure of liquor bottles at the state convention of the North Carolina Junior Chamber of Commerce after they had condemned Brown's actions aroused such indignation that in 1964 Brown was defeated by Harry Clay and Buncombe had its first Republican sheriff since the 1920's. In 1968 Weldon Weir retired at sixty-two, Coke Candler decided not to run again, Harry Clay was reelected, and the Republicans elected a member of the board of county commissioners. These events are indicative of the resurgence of historic Republican strength in the mountains. The Democratic Party has dominated North Carolina for one hundred years, but the Republican Party is a power to be reckoned with, particularly in Western North Carolina.

The lawyers and the legislators, most of whom were lawyers, have profoundly influenced the laws and the politics of the region. Lawyers often dominate the political destinies of their towns and counties. They are frequently elected to the legislature or to Congress and they influence the laws that affect the region. Formerly the number of lawyers was small and the contributions of each could be evaluated as Arthur did in his *Western North Carolina*. Today the number of lawyers with potential political influence is legion and a full treatment of their history would require a lengthy book.

CHAPTER FIVE

That All May Live

From the time of the first settlement until after the Civil War, most medical needs in the mountains were attended to by granny women, herb doctors, and midwives. There were no railroads, few roads, and the efforts of the occasional doctor on horseback were truly Herculean. During and after the Civil War the movement of troops and the wandering of freedmen was accompanied by epidemic diseases, especially typhoid and smallpox. Out of the memory of the terrible experiences during the war, the state's doctors sought to provide better medical facilities and health measures. The State Medical Society, organized in 1800, given up in 1804, reorganized in 1848, had met annually except during the war. In 1859 it had persuaded the General Assembly to establish the requirement that before a new doctor might start his practice he must be passed by the State Board of Medical Examiners. During the trying years of Reconstruction, health measures were not among the issues considered important, but in 1875 the legislature authorized the building of the Western Insane Asylum of North Carolina (now Broughton Hospital) at Morganton. It was estimated that there were at least seven hundred "insane" persons in the state who were not receiving treatment. The appropriation of $75,000 was made to provide a hospital for four hundred patients. As an economy measure fifty convicts were sent to Morganton to make bricks. The contractor for the bricks was responsible for clothing, feeding, and guarding the prisoners. When the institution was completed, it was already too small to meet the need of the western part of the state, and an additional

$60,000 was appropriated for another wing in 1877. One portion was set aside for those who could pay for their own care.

In 1877 a group from the State Medical Society went to Raleigh to lobby and succeeded in getting created a state board of health (with an annual appropriation of $100!). Another act made the county medical societies county boards of health. Two years later, after an intensive campaign by Dr. Thomas F. Wood, Secretary-Treasurer of the new State Board of Health, who sent out hundreds of letters at his own expense, a more effective public health act was passed. A nine-member board (composed of physicians and others, including one civil engineer) was provided for. The revised law had been backed vigorously by the State Medical Society.

In the counties of Western North Carolina as late as 1883 only twenty doctors were members of the State Medical Society, and consequently there were no county boards of health to function. Typhoid had a serious incidence in the West, and diptheria abounded. New theories about the causes of these diseases — polluted water, insects, and direct contact — were known only by the few doctors who did attend the meetings of the medical societies or read their journals.

In Western North Carolina the doctors had to travel many hours per day (usually on horseback because of the poor mountain roads) to visit the critically sick and to dispense remedies. Some mountain counties had more physicians in 1884 than in 1958; in 1884 Ashe had 8, Clay 4, Graham 5, Mitchell 8, Swain 4, Yancey 6; in 1958 Ashe had 6, Clay 1, Graham 4, Mitchell 6, Swain 4, Yancey 5. But a much smaller number of patients could be seen by a mountain doctor who had to travel to the sick than is possible today. An example was the father of Dr. Gaine Cannon, who practiced medicine in Jackson and Transylvania Counties and in the vicinity of Pickens, South Carolina. Cannon remembered: "Father had to do most of his traveling on horseback, carrying his medicine and instruments in his saddle bags. He rode long distances, and not only were the calls tiring and time-consuming, but he was also often paid poorly. Father could hardly make a call far over into Jackson County and get back the same day. And often he collected not a penny.... Sometimes those who were able to pay him wouldn't do it, even though he charged little.... Most of the time he was paid in things the family could eat — a country ham, potatoes, fresh vegetables, ... produce ... from the farms and orchards.

Father couldn't carry much of that sort of stuff on his horse, along with his bulging saddle bags, so often a patient would bring it down to us, sometimes in a cart pulled by an ox."

Such doctors had neither the time nor the money to attend meetings of medical societies or to buy medical journals. They continued to practice medicine as it had been taught to them years earlier. Meanwhile the moderately ill were cared for by "granny women," some of whom luckily had a surprising knowledge of herbs and their medicinal values; superstitious and injurious treatments were characteristic of many of them.

The majority of the people did not enjoy good health. Chronic ailments were typical. Dr. Benjamin Washburn said that dyspepsia was found in almost all adults and children, caused from "eating thick, soggy corn pone, greasy vegetables, and too much salt pork." Bad sanitary conditions contributed to the typhoid, diarrhea, and other bowel ailments which were common. Other well-known diseases of the area, in the vernacular, were "pneumony fever," "side pleurisy," "joint rheumatism" "jumpin' toothache," the "bloody flux" (dysentery), and "gallopin' consumption." "Dew pizen," it was learned later, was a preliminary stage of hookworm disease. It caused mountain children to have a stunted, anemic condition. "Bold hives" might be scarlet fever or other childhood infections. Babies were usually delivered by ignorant midwives, and as a result many women suffered ill health all their adult lives. Dr. Washburn described medical practice in dealing with the above-named diseases in the South Mountain district in Rutherford County, where he began his practice in 1912. Diphtheria and tuberculosis were the great killers. They were so widespread at times that there were epidemics causing a reign of terror. Many children died of diphtheria and were buried in wooden boxes. Eight children died in one family. The philosophic resignation of the parents was expressed by saying "The Lord giveth and the Lord taketh away." With diphtheria a child would be lumpy, listless, feverish. He might have a sore throat. The breathing would be obstructed by a swollen membrane, the pulse rapid, thready, and uncountable. About the sixth day the child would die of toxemia, the effect of the poison produced by the bacteria. Violent pain was usually followed by death. Fortunately, diphtheria is no longer the great child-killer that it once was. Medical science developed an anti-toxin that has almost wiped out the dread disease.

Another serious epidemic disease, scarlet fever, would sweep through whole neighborhoods. It often affected the kidneys, the brain, the middle-ears, leaving some children deaf mutes. It was less often fatal than diphtheria and would run its course in a week or ten days. It is still dangerous but less prevalent than formerly. Measles was the most highly infectious of the epidemic diseases. It was usually not fatal but often went into pneumonia and complications. Smallpox was the only infectious disease the doctors really knew how to prevent. Vaccinations were used, but so crudely that infections often resulted. A healthy child who had a good "take" was used as the source of vaccine for other children. The doctor scratched a place on the arm until blood began to ooze, then dipped the lancet into the pus on the arm of the inoculated child and rubbed the pus in the scratched arm.

Tuberculosis was the great and universal scourge. People believed that its spread was inevitable, the result of the Divine will, an act of God. Patients had a phthisical cough, a fever flush, an elevation of temperature, and they spat, usually on the floor. Isolation of patients was not usual, as the bacterial cause of the disease was not recognised. There was no effort at prevention by quarantine. Poor housing conditions caused the prevalence and virulence of tuberculosis to increase. Yet an area one hundred miles by fifty miles centering in Asheville was believed to have complete immunity from tuberculosis, and, as has been noted elsewhere, the town became a resort for tubercular patients.

Surgery was practiced sparingly by mountain doctors because of the antipathy of the people to it. Compound fractures resulted in amputations because it was believed that if there was no amputation the patient would die of infection. Anesthesia was seldom used in the mountains, although elsewhere ether had been used since 1842, and chloroform since 1872. Whiskey was often given to dull the pain during an operation.

The mountains were also believed to be safe from yellow fever. During a yellow fever epidemic in Florida in 1888 hundreds of people fled from the state. Both Waynesville and Hendersonville welcomed the refugees, 260 coming to Hendersonville. Eastern towns grew alarmed and quarantined against persons coming from Waynesville and Hendersonville. The State Board of Health then forbade the coming of yellow fever refugees to North Carolina.

Meanwhile, in the world at large between 1890 and 1910 the germ theory of disease was thoroughly established and the science of bacteriology developed. The State Board of Health turned its attention to providing safe water supplies and sewage disposal in towns and cities. Its system of disease control included quarantine, abatement of nuisances, and vaccination. A doctor in each county was employed as county superintendent of health. He was chosen by the county board of health, which consisted of all practicing physicians, the mayor of the county seat, the chairman of the county commissioners, and the city or county surveyor. The county superintendent of health performed post mortems for the coroners, registered vital statistics, and attended persons at jails and poorhouses.

The education of the people of North Carolina for retention of their health really began with the campaign to eradicate hookworm disease. In 1903 Dr. Charles W. Stiles of the United States Public Health Service addressed the State Medical Society at Hot Springs on the prevalence of hookworm disease in the South. In 1905 Dr. W. P. Ivey of Lenoir, a member of the State Board of Health, read a paper to the State Medical Society titled "Uncinariasis (hookworm disease) in the Mountains of North Carolina." He recommended the holding of clinics, to be attended by doctors who did not attend the meetings of the medical societies, in the counties. He found the disease common in Caldwell County and he believed that other Western North Carolina counties "were wormy too." He ended his paper with the following lines: "Hear, gentlemen, my conclusion. Uncinariasis is among us. . . . It is a grievous burden. . . . It is a menace to the neighbors. It kills folks. It makes mental underlings, . . . physical dwarfs. It curtails producing power. It steals dollars from our wealth. What are you going to do about it?"

The Rockefeller Sanitary Commission spent $15,000 annually in North Carolina for a Bureau of Hookworm Eradication which was established in the state in March 1910. Dr. W. P. Jacocks directed the campaign, which lasted five years. A corps of doctors and microscopists worked in one county after another. First a member of Dr. Jacocks' team visited a county to sell the idea to the county commissioners and ask them for an appropriation. About six weeks later a field director arrived to conduct the treatment. The first week was devoted to advertising and education. Handbills were circulated, and posters were placed in public buildings such as post offices and stores inviting people to the lectures and demonstrations. An exhibit consisting of a set of large charts to illustrate the lecture showed the life history of the hookworm and the manner in which infection occurred, showed patients before and after treatment and diagrams of privies which would prevent soil pollution. Hookworm eggs and larvae were shown under the microscope.

About five places in each county were designated for the holding of clinics, and at each a dispensary was held once a week for five weeks. A typical one, at Mill Spring in Polk County, was described by Dr. Washburn, who joined the campaign in 1913. Men, women, and children began arriving at the designated spot at 8 A.M. Approximately two hundred people came: in buggies, on horse back, and in wagons. Activities were varied. People who had been treated previously were examined to determine the extent of improvement, after which a lecture was given explaining how hookworm disease stunted the mental and physical growth of children. Then additional diagnoses were made and medicine (large capsules of thymol mixed with milk sugar) was distributed.

The clinic was like an all-day picinic, and most of those who came in the morning stayed throughout the activities. They examined an exhibit showing how soil pollution, flies, dirty food, and contaminated water could cause hookworm disease. Typhoid, it was explained, was spread in the same way. About half an hour was spent by the crowd in singing, led by a volunteer with a tuning fork, while the microscopist prepared a report on specimens brought in. People had packed picnic lunches and the clinic recessed long enough for the meal. Other families arrived in the afternoon, and the clinic lasted until nearly five o'clock.

One of the lessons taught in all of the counties was that the placing of privies over swift-running streams as was customary in the mountains, when homes boasted privies at all, caused pollution of water that could seep into the springs from which the drinking water was taken. Efforts were made to persuade county boards of education to provide safe drinking water and sanitary privies at each school.

All but one county, Ashe, appropriated funds for the hookworm eradication campaign. Even in counties where the incidence of the disease was small, the educational value of the program was tremendous because through it people learned how to prevent other serious diseases. After the hookworm campaign ended in 1915, public health work was continued with the full-time services of a county doctor in several counties, including two in Western North Carolina, Surry and Buncombe.

Practically all of the 206 physicians in Western North Carolina in 1884 were general practitioners. Many of them were of well-known families that had furnished leaders in other professions as well. Moreover, it was not unusual to find two and even three doctors in a county with the same surname, of whom two were often father and son.* In many families it was a tradition for one son to be a physician. The doctors, in addition to the strenuous obligations of their profession, were often civic leaders: trustees of academies, members of local school boards, and of the county boards of health. Such a leader was Dr. James A. Reagan, physician and surgeon, who served as president of Weaverville College for three years from its incorporation as a college (1873) and who continued after that to serve as a trustee. Dr. H. B. Weaver of Asheville in an obituary to Reagan in 1910 described his public service: "In the heat and in the cold; up the rugged mountain sides . . . ; down the sunless valleys; in dangers seen and unseen he never faltered. . . . No matter from where the cry for relief came, . . . he responded. . . ."

As time passed many of the doctors opened parts of their homes or built special buildings in which they maintained clinics or hospitals. This practice continued in smaller communities until well into the twentieth century. It made possible surgery and more sanitary nursing conditions and saved many lives.

Then there were physicians who were not native to Western North Carolina who came in after completing medical school because of an invitation by the community, such as Dr. W. C. Tate, who came to Banner Elk to conduct a small hospital already established, and Doctors Eustice H. and Mary Martin Sloop,

* For example, there were doctors C. B. Roberts, R. K. Roberts, and Robert Roberts in Haywood County; drs. J. L. Egerton and Thomas Egerton, G. W. Fletcher and M. H. Fletcher, and Josiah Johnson and L. L. Johnson all in Henderson County; Latta Reagan and W. S. Reagan in Madison County, Oliver Hicks and Romeo Hicks in Rutherford County, to name only a few.

who founded a hospital in Crossnore.

An example of Western North Carolina doctors who devoted much of their professional lives to public health work is Dr. Lewis Burgin McBrayer of Buncombe County. He was licensed in 1890 and conducted a surgical practice in Asheville until 1909, when he became city health officer. Sanitation, especially concerning water and milk supply, was emphasized during his administration. Meanwhile the State Medical Society had organized an association to combat tuberculosis, and Dr. McBrayer worked at Raleigh in 1907 with the General Assembly to get the State Sanatorium for Tuberculosis established. In 1914 he left the mountains to serve as superintendent of the Sanatorium for ten years. He played a part in getting another state tuberculosis sanatorium established, in Western North Carolina, and in setting up public health nursing. He was president of the State Medical Society in 1914, and from 1917 to 1937 he was its secretary-treasurer. The resolution passed by the State Medical Society at his death included these words: " . . . his pioneering labors in this field [of fighting tuberculosis] won for him and for his state nation-wide recognition."

When Dr. McBrayer became superintendent of the State Sanatorium for Tuberculosis he replaced Dr. J. E. Brooks, who then (1914) came to Blowing Rock to retire. There was no resident physician in the village at that time, and although at first Dr. Brook's health did not permit him to do more than answer emergency calls, he eventually maintained an office practice in Blowing Rock. He was aghast at the opportunities that the tourist center offered for the spread of contagious diseases. Conditions were no doubt similar in most of the mountain villages, and the crowding in of summer visitors in the resort centers made the danger of epidemics even greater. Dr. Alfred Mordecai described the situation. Within the village the average family had a stable for the horse and one or more cows, a pigpen, a chicken lot, an outdoor privy, a spring, and a garden. No screens were used to keep the flies out of the houses. Garbage was thrown out to the pigs and chickens.

While the larger hotels were situated on hills apart from the village center, they had their stables and "a retinue of stable boys and domestic servants, who were very prone to use the back lots and bushes instead of the surface privies provided for them." Diseases such as typhoid and smallpox were increasing in frequency.

Dr. Brooks began holding "fireside chats" with civic leaders, inviting one or more to visit with him to talk about community affairs. He pointed out the unsanitary conditions and what they might lead to. At "smokers," suppers and other meetings the local citizens were roused to action. Dr. Brooks brought such speakers as Governor Thomas W. Bickett, future governor Cameron Morrison, and James I. Vance, D. D., to speak on the subject of public health. Soon the fly breeding places were eliminated. A chamber of commerce and other civic organizations developed from Dr. Brooks's work. Tuberculosis was very prevalent in Watauga County and that part of the state, and Dr. Brooks launched a drive to control it. He believed that socio-economic conditions caused its spread, and he lectured in schoolhouses throughout the area, asking people to stop their promiscuous visiting with sick people whose illnesses had not yet been diagnosed and to provide their families with less crowded living conditions. An epidemic of smallpox in Watauga County in 1914 followed by one of diphtheria in 1915 caused people at least to heed his advice about visiting. Dr. Brooks's services continued in Blowing Rock until his death in 1921.*

A Philadelphia physician, Dr. Henry Norris, and Mrs. Norris, came several times to Rutherford County for Dr. Norris to hunt. They visited often at the Coxe estate, Green River Plantation. They made friends in Rutherfordton and came to realize that there was no hospital between Charlotte and Asheville at a time when travel was slow and difficult. In 1905 the Norrises decided to found a hospital in Rutherfordton. The buildings of a former military academy were purchased and reconditioned, and the hospital functioned there from 1906 until 1911, by which time Dr. and Mrs. Norris had built and equipped an excellent new facility. In 1907 Mrs. Norris organized a school of nursing at the Rutherford Hospital. Dr. Norris and Dr. Montgomery Biggs, and two nurses, all from Philadelphia, soon won a widespread reputation for excellence. Additional

* Alfred Mordecai, "James Edwin Brooks, M. D.," Part II, *North Carolina Medical Journal* (June, 1958), 238–242, described intimately his association with Dr. Brooks. In a letter to Ina Van Noppen, Dr. Mordecai wrote, "I entered the practice of medicine in 1915 at Blowing Rock and sat in quite often at his [Dr. Brooks'] fireside chats.... I was so impressed by the work of Dr. Brooks that I later entered the field of Public Health in Western North Carolina.... I think he could be called the Father of Modern Sanitation and Health Education in Watauga County."

equipment and space were added from time to time, and after the death of Dr. and Mrs. Norris a Committee of Friends of the Hospital raised funds in 1941 for a Norris Maternity Building. Its construction was delayed by World War II, enabling Rutherford Hospital to acquire a much larger building than had been anticipated. In 1946 Congress passed the Hill-Burton Act to give federal funds to communities to match local funds for the construction of non-profit hospitals. Thereupon the North Carolina Medical Care Commission was created to administer a combination of state and federal aid to counties that wished to build hospitals. Consequently in 1951 a new wing which doubled the bed capacity of the Rutherford Hospital was built and a completely modernized hospital was dedicated. Another new building, the Crawford Memorial Building for the School of Nursing, was dedicated in 1956 and conditions for teaching were improved through a grant from the Ford Foundation in 1957. The nursing education program was transferred to Gardner-Webb College at Boiling Springs, in 1965, with students doing their clinical work at the Rutherford Hospital.

Grace Hospital in Morganton is another excellent institution of the same age as the Rutherford Hospital. Miss Maria P. Allen, a graduate of the Episcopal Hospital in Philadelphia who was serving as a visiting nurse in Burke County, wrote an article, "The Spirit of Missions," in which she explained the need for $3000 for a small hospital. The money was given by a generous woman in New York. The Reverend Walter Hughson, rector of Grace Episcopal Church of Morganton, established the hospital in 1906 in a frame building containing fifteen beds. Dr. E. W. Phifer, who had been in practice in Morganton for four years, generously contributed administrative services, and he and Dr. J. B. Riddle were the hospital staff. In 1918 Dr. W. H. Keller joined the two. In 1920 a new brick hospital was built, and staff and services have grown until in 1950 there were 120 beds and a staff of twenty-five specialists and generalists. A school of nursing was established in 1910 with Miss Maria Allen as its director. By 1950 about 230 nurses had graduated. In addition to their clinical experience in Grace Hospital student nurses were given a twelve week affiliation course in psychiatric nursing at Highland Hospital in Asheville and a twelve week course in pediatric nursing at Duke University Hospital. In 1959 Lenoir Rhyne College in Hickory engaged in a joint program to offer college degrees for Grace Hospital School of

Nursing graduates. Subsequently the School of Nursing was discontinued; now Lenoir Rhyne's nursing students obtain their clinical training at Grace Hospital. Burke County has recently added a splendid new hospital.

Before 1945 there were hospitals with seventy-five or more beds, outside the urban area of Buncombe County, only in Burke, Haywood, and Rutherford counties. Ashe, Macon, McDowell, Caldwell, Transylvania, and Jackson counties had more than forty hospital beds each, while Watauga, Avery, Cherokee, and Swain counties had hospitals with fewer than forty beds. Since then many new hospitals have been built. By 1958 there were 3.2 short-stay hospital beds per one thousand population in Western North Carolina, while for the state as a whole the average was 3.3 beds per one thousand. In addition, new public health centers were constructed between 1948–1958 with federal aid in all of the counties except Buncombe and Henderson.

Nurses' training in the 1960's was largely taken over by the educational institutions, practical nursing courses being given by Wilkes Community College, Asheville-Biltmore Technical Institute, and Caldwell Community College near Lenoir. A two year course in nursing is offered at Western Piedmont Community College in Morganton terminating in the Associate of Applied Science degree, and a four year course in nursing given at Mars Hill College leads to the B.S. degree. The three hospitals in Western North Carolina in 1966 that still had hospital schools of nursing were Martin Memorial at Mt. Airy, Memorial Mission in Asheville, and Mountain at Fletcher.

A very special institution in Western North Carolina is Western Carolina Center, located just outside Morganton. It is one of four state-supported residential centers for mentally handicapped children. A part of the North Carolina Department of Mental Health, it serves thirty-two western counties. In 1959 the legislature appropriated $4,500,000 for its construction, and the first patients were admitted in 1963. The center's director, Dr. J. Iverson Riddle, stated that the Center provides diagnosis, treatment, and care for the mentally handicapped child by the use of the "multi-discipline approach to the total child." Regimentation is avoided and each child is treated as an individual who may return to his community and live a relatively normal life. Two hundred eighty acres of land with rolling hills and the South Mountains in the background form the setting for the sixteen buildings, including residence cottages, academic buildings, diagnostic clinic, hospital for crippled children, infirmary, an additional children's unit of 120 beds, and workshop. The population consists of adults and children with an average age of eighteen. The capacity, 832 in 1970, will be increased constantly as new "cottages" are completed.

Morganton has become one of the four regional health centers in the state. In 1959 the name of the North Carolina Mental Hospital (earlier the Western Insane Asylum of North Carolina) was changed to Broughton Hospital. The School for the Deaf, Broughton Hospital, and the Western Carolina Center are appropriately located in the same community. Many of the techniques used in teaching deaf children can also be used successfully with mentally handicapped children who have communication difficulties, and the psychiatric staffs at Broughton and Western Carolina Center can complement each other. The Mental Health clinics located in a number of the thirty-two mountain and piedmont counties served by the Center and by Broughton Hospital are associated with the two by an administrative staff. Also served is the Western North Carolina Correctional Center in Morganton, a new type of prison where rehabilitation rather than punishment is the aim.

Related to the health of the people are water, air, and noise pollution and contamination of soils and foods from pesticides. There is today a world-wide concern over pollution of the environment. Man pollutes the air, water, and land with noxious fumes, sewage, noise, pesticides, and nuclear radiation. With the population explosion and the proliferation of manufacturing plants, pollution is being highly accelerated. The fouling of the world's land, air and water is the fastest-spreading disease of civilization. It is potentially one of history's greatest dangers to human life on earth. If present trends continue it will make all of the world's cities and most of the countryside uninhabitable. Toxic gases and "killer smogs," suspended over cities, contain sulfur dioxide, nitrogen oxide, ozone, and carbon monoxide, and cause lung cancer and emphysema and can actually asphyxiate respiratory sufferers. These gases emanate from automobile exhausts, smokestacks, and incinerators. They can be reduced by fitting offending smokestacks with filters and electrostatic precipitators and by inducing factories to use low-sulfur fuels.

Automobiles can be equipped with anti-pollution devices.

As early as 1932 Asheville citizens circulated petitions requesting smoke control. June 3, 1932, the town council adopted an anti-smoke ordinance which was not entirely effective. A cooperative study in 1963 by the City of Asheville, the Buncombe County Health Department, and the North Carolina State Board of Health found that Asheville still had a serious smoke and air pollution problem. In 1964 it was found that air pollution was damaging trees and shrubs, and in 1965 a federal grant of $23,945 was made to enable Asheville to study its air pollution problem. January 1, 1965, a two-year study was begun during which many industries installed or began installation of air-control equipment. Recommendations were made for (1) adoption of regulations by four county boards of health, (2) the establishment of air-monitoring stations, (3) education, (4) enforcement, (5) coordination of administration. In 1966 clean-air rules were adopted for the Asheville area. In 1967 the North Carolina General Assembly added air pollution control to the water control program and created the Board of Water and Air Resources to study the problem, to devise means of control, and to supervise local air control programs. The Assembly offered tax benefits for air pollution abatemant facilities. A law was passed, to be administered by the North Carolina Board of Water and Air Resources. This law is not yet effective, as only after July 1, 1974, will industries face fines of $1,000 a day. Even then there will be many loopholes, and it is feared that the state board will be unable to resist pressure from industries.

June 25-26, 1968, upon request of Governor Moore, a conference on Appalachian Development was held at Asheville-Biltmore College (now the University of North Carolina at Asheville). In this conference all forms of pollution and programs of pollution abatement were discussed.

It is evident that cities, towns, and industrial plants in Western North Carolina have air pollution problems. It is a hopeful sign that organized and concerted efforts are being made to ameliorate conditions on local, state, and national levels. If these efforts are to be effective, laws with teeth in them must be enacted and enforced. Penalties must be sufficiently severe to induce compliance by offenders. The magnitude of the air pollution problem may be perceived from the fact that the United States Department of Health, Education, and Welfare estimates that air pollution costs more than $13,000,000,000 annually.

Far older and much more widespread in Western North Carolina than air pollution is the problem of water pollution. The sharp increase in water pollution is alarming. "Every major river in the United States is grossly polluted. Even the lesser streams have been made slimy and foul by factories [and towns] that freely sluice their noxious wastes into any nearby flow.... We are pumping enough poisons into our environment — and into our bone and flesh — to threaten the survival of the species within two or three decades." This water pollution problem can be improved by the treatment and purification of sewage and industrial wastes.

For almost one hundred years doctors in North Carolina have been concerned about water pollution. They organized and served on county boards of health. They worked and educated to eliminate "privies" in thickly settled areas, to get communities to create water and sewer services, and to eliminate unsanitary conditions that might cause epidemics. In 1891 "the State Board of Health was given responsibility for protecting streams used as sources of public water supplies from municipal sewage . . ." but little attention was given to the pollution of other streams by industrial wastes.

On August 10, 1927, a conference was held at Canton, North Carolina, at the request of the State Health Officer of Tennessee. Present were Mr. Reuben Robertson, president of the Champion Paper and Fibre Company, officials of the North Carolina State Board of Health, and the district engineer of the United States Public Health Service. The meeting concerned possible measures for correction of pollution of the Pigeon River in the interest of protecting the water supplies of Tennessee from wastes emitted by the Champion Paper and Fibre Company. Thus as early as 1927 water pollution was recognized as an interstate matter.

In the earlier decades of this century conservationists were concerned about the preservation of the forests. By 1939 the protection of forests and timber was under relative control. Industries were induced to come to the mountains, population increased, and the water pollution problem was magnified. Little effort was made to stop stream pollution by industrial plants until the present stream sanitation law was passed by the General Assembly in 1951. The act created a Stream Sanitation Committee and required it to establish water quality standards in keeping with "best usage," to study pollution of the state's waters, to classify the waters in the public interest, and to develop a stream pollution control program. Articles began to appear in the *Asheville Citizen* under such titles as "Problem of Stream Pollution," (1951), "TVA Claims Three Plants Pollute Streams in Western North Carolina" (1953), "Polluted French Broad Blemish on Western North Carolina Scenery" (1957), "Plan to Abate French Broad Valley Stream Pollution Drafted" (1958), "Fifty Towns and Industries Filed Plan for Pollution Control" (1960), "Good Progress in Cleaning Western North Carolina Streams (Champion Spending $3,000,000, Hendersonville $1,000,000, Enka and Buncombe County $7,500,000)" (1963), "North Carolina Has Spent over $200,000,000 on Water Pollution in Fifteen Years" (1966), "State Water and Air Control Councils Appointed" (1967), "Twenty Projects to Stop Stream Pollution — to Remove Damage of Pesticides" (1968).

The French Broad River Basin encompasses 2825 square miles in North Carolina and it is a major part of the Tennessee River system. The North Carolina portion of the basin contains the French Broad, the Pigeon, and the Nolichucky rivers and their tributaries. Studies were made in the 1950's of the pollution of the streams, under the auspices of the State Stream Sanitation Committee. The 1950 population was 247,290, of which twenty-one percent lived in Asheville. There were eighteen public water systems in the basin serving an estimated population of 149,645 which used 20,000,000 gallons of water daily. There were thirty points of significant water pollution. Total wastes from these points had an estimated domestic sewage population equivalent of 1,096,280. Only a small percentage of the waste load received treatment before it went into the streams. The basin is rich in natural resources and scenic attractions. It has abundant water power and adequate water supplies to sustain an increased population and additional industries if stream pollution can be controlled. The smaller streams were relatively unpolluted; but the French Broad, Hominy Creek, Pigeon River, Nolichucky River, Tucker Creek, Davidson River, and the North and South Toe Rivers received excessive amounts of waste.

The amount of wastes from cities and particularly from industrial plant is frightening, although many communities and the major industrial plants are making efforts to solve their pollution problems. The Ecusta Paper Corporation, a branch of Olin Mathieson, in 1955 emitted wastes equal to those of a city of 249,000. Part of these wastes were treated, part were not. Asheville drained the majority of its wastes into streams untreated or with only primary treatment. In Asheville and its suburbs are twelve sanitary districts. The wastes and sewage from these and from towns, plants, and schools all the way to Mars Hill, Marshall, and Hot Springs were discharged untreated into streams. In Haywood County the wastes of Canton, Clyde, Waynesville, and Lake Junaluska were discharged into the Pigeon River. In 1957 the wastes discharged by the Champion Paper and Fibre Company were equal to those from a population of 624,000. Around Bakersville, Burnsville, Spruce Pine, tremendous amounts of water were used by the mining industry to separate the earth from the minerals. The resultant wastes going into the Nolichucky River extended for a great distance downstream and caused complaints from people living in Tennessee.

In 1959 all agencies of the Department of Conservation and Development were reorganized in a Department of Water Resources. One of this department's four major divisions, that of Stream Sanitation and Hydrology, is responsible for pollution abatement and control. The Department of Water Resources administers policies concerning stream pollution, ground water supplies, and surface water. The seven-man Board of Water Resources and the seven-man Stream Sanitation Committee have parallel responsibilities. The Stream Sanitation Committee has studied all of the state's sixteen major river basins. By 1963 it had adopted "best usage" classifications for all basins and had issued pollution abatement plans for thirteen river basins, ninety-two percent of the state.

In 1957 the Department of Conservation and Development established a Division of Community Planning to help cities and towns with land-use planning. Resource planning is being conducted by the local Area Development Associations. These are beginning to be effective. The Western North Carolina Regional Planning Commission released its first economic study in 1961. Another study was that of Asheville Township which presented a twenty-year plan for physical development. In this plan "conservation easements" were recommended to induce industries to cooperate.

Using a grant from the Appalachian Regional Commission, the State Planning Office employed the firm of Rummel, Klepper, and Kahl (1968) to study selected growth areas along interstate and Appalachian Corridor highways. This company's report contained significant information. There are seventy community water systems in the North Carolina portion of Appalachia. Many are outdated or loaded to capacity. They must be enlarged and improved to provide for increasing population and additional industrial plants. Sixty communities now provide sewer services. Twenty-eight of these have satisfactory facilities, twenty-one have under construction or are preparing to construct the needed facilities, two are having financial difficulties, 117 other unsewered communities need facilities. About $400,000,000 for construction by communities will be needed. Of industries, eighty-one have significant water discharges into streams. Of these, sixty-four are providing adequate treatment, seventeen are not.

Tourism, present and future, is the lifeblood of the economy of Western North Carolina. The area has the Great Smoky Mountains National Park, the Blue Ridge Parkway, extensive fishing and wildlife, recreation facilities, and many summer camps. With its beautiful scenery and its enticing climate, the region has the greatest tourist and vacation attractions in Eastern America. But if tourists are to continue to come to the mountains, towns and plants must study their problems and provide waste treatment facilities.

Daily in newspapers and on television there are articles and comments by public men about pollution control. A crusade against pollution was well begun by 1970. Pollution is often an interstate problem. Rivers rising in Western North Carolina flow into Tennessee, Virginia, South Carolina, and Georgia. It was the complaint of Tennessee authorities in 1927 that first caused North Carolina health authorities and the Champion Paper and Fibre Company in Canton to become concerned about pollution control. Nevertheless, progress was negligible for many years. Currently the people of Ashe and Alleghany counties are being asked to have acres of their richest farm lands inundated so that pollution wastes can be flushed from the New, the Kanawha, and the Ohio rivers in West Virginia. Local and state agencies must do their parts. The state must pass effective statutes and enforce them effectively. Strong federal laws must be enacted to control the major polluters: automobiles, factories, cities, and towns. A good example was the Water Quality Act of 1965, which provided for the adoption of water quality standards for interstate and costal waters by all the states. The federal government has the power through its control of interstate commerce, interstate relations, and its taxing powers. Penalties should be sufficiently high to induce compliance, and the statutes should be firmly enforced. Again it must be a uniformly applicable federal program; otherwise states that stringently enforce pollution control might find industries moving to states with less expensive programs of regulation. Furthermore federal funds must be made available, for many communities lack the needed finances to meet their needs. If the federal government will do its part, the State of North Carolina can cooperate through its Department of Conservation and Development, and its Boards of Water and Air Resources with their Sanitation Committees. Local communities and industries must cooperate and expend their own funds to meet their individual responsibilities.

CHAPTER SIX

Public Education

The great cultural progress made in Western North Carolina since 1900 is due largely to the improvement in its schools. The change was statewide and must be seen within the framework of state legislation and judicial opinion. Over half of the General Fund of North Carolina annually now is spent for public education.

"I have visited several places in this Western North Carolina — and have found a kind and hospitable people wherever I have gone. Truly there seems a wide field open ready for the laborer in this portion of our State. Good teachers are wanted. . . . I am satisfied to cast my lot among this people and if my impressions remain what they are and my school flourishes — this will probably be my home for some time to come." So wrote George F. Dixon to his friend Calvin Wiley, past General Superintendent of Common Schools, indicating that Dixon was opening a subscription school in Watauga County in the year following the end of the Civil War. Such schools were springing up in the mountain region and across the state. The office of General Superintendent of Common Schools had just been abolished by the General Assembly. The county courts were authorized to apply any school taxes collected to subscription schools, which were to be permitted to occupy public schoolhouses to prevent the buildings from falling into decay from nonuse. Private (i.e. subscription) schools did spring up everywhere, but they

An early school, no windows, no stove, only a hearth for light and heat

School terms were short, and boys and girls attended until well along in their teens

served only a limited number of children. This was a sad climax to the movement which had been hailed as the first effort of a Southern state to give serious attention to providing a system of public schools for the education of all of its white children. The Literary Fund, founded in 1826, which had been the state's contribution to the support of the schools, had been all but wiped out by the worthlessness of state and Confederate securities, and the Assembly ruled that any moneys remaining be placed in the State Treasury for general expenses.

During the remainder of the century the state followed an exploratory pattern, revising the public school law each biennium. The groundwork was laid by the Constitutional Convention of 1868, which consisted of eighteen Northern men, fifteen Negroes, sixty-four Radicals (Republicans), and thirteen Conservatives (Democrats). The convention adopted a resolution stating that "... the interest and happiness of the two races would be best promoted by the establishment of separate schools." The most significant educational provisions of the constitution they wrote were these: "The General Assembly at its first session under this Constitution shall provide by taxation and otherwise for a general and uniform system of public schools, wherein tuition shall be free of charge to all children of the State between the ages of six and twenty-one years. Each county shall be divided into a convenient number of districts in which one or more Public schools shall be taught at least four months in every year; and if the county commissioners of any county shall fail to comply with the aforesaid requirements of this section they be liable to indictment."

One of the Northern members of the Constitutional Convention, Samuel S. Ashley of Massachusetts, was elected Superintendent of Public Instruction in 1868. He had been in the state only three years, having been sent by the American Missionary Association to conduct a Negro school in Wilmington. It was his responsibility to rebuild the public school system, and he wrote the school law of 1869 to implement the provisions of the constitution. The townships, new subdivisions of the counties provided for by the constitution, were to play an important part in his plan for the operation of the schools. The township board of trustees, elected annually by the registered voters, would receive yearly from the township school committee an estimate of the financial requirements for supporting a four-month term for all of its schools each year, and at the annual township meeting would submit it for a vote. If the township voters failed to levy the tax, the committee would forward the estimate to the county commissioners, who were to levy the required taxes under penalty of indictment.

The constitutional provision and the law to implement it were excellent, but in 1871 the State Supreme Court ruled that such a levy by the county commissioners was not constitutional on the theory that schools were not a necessary expense. While the General Assembly could levy a tax without the consent of the people, so ruled the court, the county commissioners could not do so without the approval of the people. And so the plan failed before it ever got into operation. While the communities could vote a tax, the compulsory aspect of the law was annulled.

Lacking the tax monies that were to have been levied by the communities under the constitution, funds provided for the support of public schools by the General Assembly were woefully inadequate. The school law of 1867 provided that seventy-five percent of a poll tax of $1.05 would be used for schools and that an additional appropriation of $100,000 from the state treasury would be apportioned among the counties. The appropriation was not made in 1868–1869, but by 1870 a special tax of eight and one-third cents on one hundred dollars valuation was levied to pay the $100,000. Other sources of school funds were taxes on retailers and auctioneers, fines, penalties, forfeitures, and entries of vacant lands and swamp lands. Instead of providing for free public schools the General Assembly in 1871 levied a new statewide tax of six and two-thirds cents on one hundred dollars valuation and a twenty cent poll tax, to supplement the revenue from the existing provision that seventy-five percent of all county and state poll taxes, be allocated to the counties for the support of schools.

The funds from these several sources were to provide fifty cents per month for each scholar in any "free school" that might be established. In communities where taxes to support schools were not voted, the "free schools" were often subscription schools. All children who could afford to pay tuition were expected to do so in such a union of private with public schools, and only students unable to pay were admitted free of tuition. Neighborhoods that took the initiative to start a school would receive the state aid, and those that did not would lose their share of the school money, although an amendment in 1873 gave such districts the right to acquire credit for their share of the school money, to be used later.

Ashley resigned as superintendent in 1871 and was followed in office by a quick succession of other men, but the situation did not change. The incumbent superintendent in 1874 reported the policy thus: "The State does not go into the school districts and establish a school without any effort on the part of the people of the district. It rather aids the people to establish their own school." What the state's policy had created was a voluntary system in which each community could determine the kind of schools and the amount of schooling it wanted to have.

Supervision of public schools was practically nonexistent from 1865–1881, as there was no local official charged with their operation. An *ex officio* state board of education was provided for by the constitution of 1868. It consisted of the governor, lieutenant governor, secretary of state, state treasurer, auditor, superintendent of public works, superintendent of public instruction, and attorney general. The county board of education was also *ex officio*, consisting of the county commissioners, with the chairman of the board of county commissioners as chairman of the board of education. This board was to supervise the public schools and to appoint one resident of the county of good moral character and of suitable attainments to be styled the "county examiner." He would examine all applicants for teachers' certificates at the county court house and issue certificates of three grades, to be valid only in the county where issued. Later each county was provided with a board of three examiners. In 1881 county superintendents were provided for, to be elected by joint meetings of the county commissioners and the county boards of magistrates. A law in 1885 required that separate county boards of education be elected by the two above-mentioned boards.

In spite of their lack of professional education, some of the teachers in the 1870's were engaging in professional activities. In 1872 a State Educational Association was formed at Wilmington. It met in Raleigh for three days in 1873, "organized permanently," and adopted a resolution recommending the establishment of permanent county educational organizations. This organizational movement began to be felt even in the western counties, as in Henderson County, where an educational association was formed in 1874. The members at the Raleigh meeting in 1873 prepared a "memorial" to present to the General

Assembly stating the improvements needed in the public schools. In 1877 Governor Vance presented such a memorial to the General Assembly, asking that body to give its attention to education.

The school law of 1877 included two significant provisions. One was to create two normal schools, the first at the state university for white students and the second at Fayetteville, for Negroes (the normal schools will be discussed later). The other provision was to permit any township containing a city of 5,000 or more inhabitants, upon the petition of one hundred "respectable citizens," to vote upon the levying of an annual tax for support of one or more graded schools in such township. Greensboro and Charlotte already had graded schools which had been established under clauses in their charters, but there was no township in Western North Carolina that could qualify in population for a graded school district under this law. In 1879, however, the General Assembly passed a law directing the commissioners of Buncombe County, upon the petition of one hundred "respectable citizens" who were freeholders of the city of Asheville, to submit to the voters the question of a special school tax. Not until 1887 did Asheville approve the plan, and even then "the opposition was keen and the proposal carried by one vote." The town had some excellent private schools and some of the most influential citizens disapproved of public schools.

In 1879 Governor Vance became a United States Senator and Thomas Jordan Jarvis, Lieutenant Governor, succeeded to the office of Governor, to which he was reelected two years later. His six years were to be felt in Western North Carolina in the completion of the Western North Carolina Railroad, the establishment of the State Geological Survey, the Agricultural Experiment Station, and some improvement of the public schools. In 1881 he described to the legislature the current condition of the state's schools, stressing the need for additional normal schools and increased taxation. The assembly increased the tax rate to twelve and one-half cents per one hundred dollars valuation and the poll tax to thirty-seven and one-half cents.

Until uniform schooling and compulsory attendance grew out of the state's increasing awareness of its responsibility for education, the development of schools was not systematic. The opportunities for an education depended on many things: local initiative in providing the funds and buildings; efforts of individuals in founding academies and institutes, and of philanthropists and religious denominations as well; concern of teachers in supplementing the meager terms of the public schools; and ambition of parents which made them support local institutions where they existed and send their children away to school where they did not.

In the mountain counties where money had always been scarce, the people of most districts made little effort to provide adequate schools. I. N. Benners, County Treasurer of Haywood County, in 1875 reported, "Our school system is a failure.... The people are too poor for more taxes, and will not vote to tax themselves; consequently there can be little more than a two months' school taught with the money provided by law." And from Rutherford County came the complaint, "If the people would submit to be taxed to aid the school fund our schools would soon be built up, teachers would be encouraged to prepare for teaching, and the whole community would take an interest in the work of education."

The responsibility to provide separate schools for Negroes created two problems. Mitchell County was like several other mountain counties in that it had too few Negro children in any district to make a school; consequently it used its share of the money assigned by the state for the education of Negro children to provide one Negro school centrally taught. The other problem was the statewide opposition of many prominent persons to public support for education, persons who held that it was "robbery to tax one man to educate another man's children" and that the burden of educating the Negroes who paid such a small portion of the taxes was too heavy for the improverished South to bear.

In contrast to the few schools maintained for Negroes, more and more schools for white children began eventually to operate, and, owing partly to the poor facilities for transportation, in Western North Carolina more than eight hundred public schools of the one-room variety opened their doors for an average term of from six to ten weeks. The township boards submitted to local demand for more schools. From Unaka Township, Cherokee County, came the complaint, "We find that every patron would like to have the school kept near his door." Thus the school term was necessarily shortened to make the available funds stretch to pay all of the teachers.

In most of the public schools the term was brief. Often the regular term was held during the "dormant season" when there was the least amount of farm work to be done. It ended by or before Christmas. Following the free term, a subscription school was often offered to supplement the work already completed. Sometimes the same teacher would conduct the public school and the subscription school. As parents were required to pay the teachers in the latter, a limited number of children attended, and the teaching could be made much more effective than in the public school. Even adults sometimes attended the subscription schools. Another supplemental school sometimes held was the writing school, which lasted approximately ten days, during which teacher and pupils concentrated on penmanship.

In Western North Carolina during the eighteen-seventies one of the greatest incentives to the establishment of better schools was the Peabody Fund, created in 1867 by George Peabody, American millionaire with a banking house in London. He gave $1,000,000 to assist educational effort in the impoverished South, to which he added another $1,000,000 in 1869. A later gift of almost $1,500,000 in Florida and Mississippi bonds was lost because those states repudiated their bonds. The fund was kept intact for thirty years by a board of trustees which decided how the income should be spent. No money was appropriated as charity aid to the indigent. It was "used for the promotion and encouragement of intellectual, moral, or industrial education among the young of the more destitute portions of the Southern and Southeastern states" of both races. The board gave only about twenty-five percent in any instance; the rest had to be raised locally. The purpose was to promote community responsibility for education and for the training of teachers. The two general agents of the board, the Reverend Dr. Barnas Sears, and after Sears' death, J.L.M. Curry, became well-known figures in the educational world of the South.

Only a subscription school could qualify for aid from this fund because of the high standards. A Peabody School was required to conform to the following criteria: to have at least one hundred students, two teachers, a ten-month term, and an average attendance of eighty-five percent. In 1871 Mars Hill College, then a secondary school, received three hundred dollars, and Montanic Institute in Buncombe County was allowed a like amount in 1874. Franklin and South Hominy schools each received $450 in 1874, and Asheville, Hayesville, Marshall, and Pigeon Valley $300 each. The following year Webster School, Roan Mountain, Pisgah, Waynesville, Reems Creek, Laurel Fork, Laurel Hill (Clay County), and Cheoah were allotted $300 each. By 1879 the Peabody Fund was distributing funds only to graded schools, of which Western North Carolina had none. But, in those days when state funds were inadequate, the incentive offered by the Peabody Fund had encouraged the operation of some excellent schools in the mountain area.

Buncombe County in the 1880's had better than average schools, because of the availability of capable young women, residents of the districts who had studied in the good private schools. Children paid the usual fifty cents monthly tuition. The county had seventy-two districts for white children and sixteen for colored. In about two-thirds of the schools only the first four grades were offered, while most of the remainder provided seven grades. The Asheville *Democrat* in 1889 commented: "By now every district in the county has some sort of a house. Several of these ... are not comfortable, while a large majority, if they were furnished with desks and other school furniture, would be considered very good school buildings. The popular size for building them at this time is 24 feet wide and 40 feet long by 12 feet high ... from floor to overhead ceiling.... This house requires six windows with twelve lights each 12 x 18, three windows on a side. In the back of the room [is] ... a stage. Here the teacher examines his classes.... This house will hold, on the main floor, 40 desks and leave room for one three foot center aisle and two narrow aisles next to the wall....

"Plain desks made of dressed boards cost 75 cents each.... The entire cost of the building [including desks] may be met with $330.00." Thirteen new county schools had been built that year. The county board furnished $1.25 per child, and the monthly tuition of not more than fifty cents sufficed.

Mrs. Lillian Thomasson made a study of the records of J. S. Smiley of Swain County who was first a teacher in a subscription school, then county school examiner, and finally county superintendent for eight years. As superintendent he visited each school in the county and was paid for the number of days he worked. In 1881 he traveled two hundred miles in his visiting and spent seven days examining teachers and writing reports of which the following is typical: "First school visited was De Hart's District No. 4 of Swain County August 10th 1881. Framed house, but no blackboard. Teacher found sitting during exercises. 'Seraglio,' 'intaglio,' 'biliary' mispronounced by the teacher. No. of pupils in the district was no. present on the day visited — 31. Seats in school house in district No. 4 very inferior slab benches not low enough to be comfortable." One of Smiley's earlier reports written when he was a teacher illustrates the split term necessitated by the farm season: "The Charleston [now Bryson City] School District No. 1 in Charleston Township began August 14, 1876, with a very promising attendance. We had forty before we stopped for fodder, and what added to the beauty of the school was the average age of the pupils which was only a fraction over ten years. . . . Since fodder our largest attendance was 25. All the children learned well." [signed] J. S. Smiley. Swain County had seventeen school districts for white children and one for Negroes during the eighteen-eighties.

In the 1883 session only thirteen schools were taught, owing to the shortage of teachers. About seventy percent of the children were enrolled, but the average attendance was only twenty-five percent, chiefly because of a whooping cough epidemic. In that year the tuition, $1.10 per scholar, plus the apportionment of school funds provided for a term of four and one-half months.

An interesting contrast of a public school and a "subscription school" in Wilkes county was written by Lawrence D. Washington in his *Confessions of a Schoolmaster*. In the former, girls sat on the right, boys on the left, separated by a narrow aisle. Some had slates on which they "ciphered." Books in use had been in the families for perhaps two generations so that there was no uniformity of texts except for several of Webster's "Blue-backed Spellers." Children were dressed in homespun and their shoes were home-made of cowhide. A roaring fire was of little help because the door had to be left open to provide light. The room was windowless, with here and there a log sawed out for light. A plank hung to the wall with leather hinges was used as a writing desk by fire or six pupils at a time. No classes were held in arithmetic or reading. Instead, each child would go to the schoolmaster for help and recitation. At the close of the day came the only real class, a spelling match when the children stood in a row and "spelled down," competing for a "head mark." Some who could not read could spell by heart every word in the "Blue-backed Speller." In comparison, at Edgewood Academy Washington found double desks, blackboards, a large stove in the center of the room, and a carefully worked out course of study. The tap of a bell brought an orderly group of young people into the room in double file. Opening exercises consisted of a hymn, reading of a psalm, roll call, and then recitation by classes. There was instruction in penmanship, geography, reading, spelling, map drawing, and English grammar.

The first state-managed educational institution in Western North Carolina was the School for the Deaf and Dumb in Morganton, created in a mood of social concern by the General Assembly in 1891. The School for the Deaf, Dumb, and Blind at Raleigh which had been in operation since 1846 was too crowded to accept all who applied and was too far from the western counties to serve them adequately. The school at Morganton included dormitory, school building, and cottages for those who operated the farm and dairy. The course of study was that of the public schools of the state. The Oral Department was established for those who could acquire speech and speech reading; others were taught in the Manual Department: for boys, art and free-hand drawing, industrial training, printing and typesetting, wood-working, shoemaking, and farm and garden; girls were taught household work, sewing and dressmaking, and cooking. All were taught the academic subjects. The Report of the Board of Directors in 1900 included an appeal for the establishment of a school for the feeble-minded: "Many of the children could be treated and their conditions much improved, and some of them could be trained and to some extent educated, under suitable surroundings." In the 1960's such an institution was created in Morganton by the state — the Western Carolina Center.

The state did not have a school system; the opportunities for schooling varied from county to county and from district to district. Near the turn of the century a new era began, when the Legislature (in 1899) appropriated $100,000 to be apportioned among the counties on the basis of population. The next session of the Legislature (1901) appropriated the $100,000 plus a second $100,000 known as the "Equalizing Fund," to be distributed to the counties where it was needed in order to extend the school term to four months, as nearly as might be. An act was passed to allow cities and towns and special tax districts outside towns and even whole counties to vote taxes to extend the term to four months.

The farmers' legislature of 1891 and the fusion (Populist and Republican) legislature of 1895 had established state responsibility for higher education for women, for teachers, and for Negroes, and had created the School for the Deaf and Dumb at Morganton. In 1898 the Democrats regained control of the legislature as a result of an intensive campaign against Negro suffrage. Active in the canvass were a group of young men including Charles B. Aycock and Locke Craig of Asheville, two future governors. Aycock became a party leader. The legislature in 1899 approved a constitutional amendment similar to those passed by Mississippi and eventually by eight Southern states. It made literacy a qualification for voting, with the provision that persons whose direct ancestors had been entitled to vote on or before 1867 would be permitted to register to vote at any time within the next eight years (the Grandfather Clause), and to vote, provided they paid their poll taxes on time. Aycock worked closely with the legislature of 1899 that appropriated the aforementioned $100,000 to be distributed among the counties for school support. In the election of August 2, 1900, North Carolina's voters approved the literacy test amendment and elected Aycock governor.

Fortunately for the cause of educational progress, Governor Charles B. Aycock (1901–1905) promised during his campaign in 1900: "If you vote for me, ... I shall devote the four years of my official term to the upbuilding of the public schools of North Carolina. I shall endeavor for every child in the State to get an education." He began his educational crusade immediately, offering his services as a speaker to groups of people who were promoting a local tax levy for schools. Meanwhile other forces were at work in North Carolina and the entire South to provide better educational opportunities.

Beginning in 1898 with a gathering at Capon Springs, West Virginia, composed chiefly of ministers, the Conference for Southern Education was held annually with John Ogden, Northern philanthropist, as president. A number of wealthy Northerners expressed interest chiefly in Negro education. In 1901 the Conference met at Winston-Salem, and Aycock welcomed the guests. The decision to wage a campaign for free schools for all the people in the South led to the formation of an executive committee called the Southern Education Board. It would be largely a publicity and propraganda agency and would not have large sums at its disposal. John D. Rockefeller, Jr., who attended the Winston-Salem meeting, persuaded his father to make large gifts to Southern education (a total of $53,000,000) and another board, called the General Education Board, was created to disburse the funds. Many of the same men served on both boards. Three North Carolinians on the Southern Education Board were Edwin A. Alderman, Charles D. McIver, and Walter Hines Page.

The work of Alderman and McIver had attracted the interest of John Ogden, and in 1901 he invited the two to visit him at his summer home at Kennebunkport, Maine. As a result of this visit, the campaign of the Southern Education Board in North Carolina was launched with McIver as chairman. Forty-three educational workers of the state gathered at Raleigh in February, 1902, to launch the campaign. Governor Aycock presided and organized the drive for better schools. The program included local taxation, consolidation of school districts, building and equipping better schoolhouses, longer school terms, and better salaries for teachers. Members of committees formed at the Raleigh meeting were to send weekly articles to newspapers of the state advocating the above program, and ministers were asked to preach one sermon per year on public school education. The public campaign was carried on by speakers who were provided funds by the Southern Education Board, and especially by the governor and the state superintendent of public instruction, who served in the campaign without extra pay. Superintendent Thomas F. Toon died in 1902 as a result of over-exertion in the campaign, and Aycock appointed J. Y. Joyner, professor at the State Normal and Industrial School, to the position, which he held until 1919. The private campaign, as described by Joyner in his *Biennial Report* for 1902–1903, 1903–1904, was carried by friends of education into their communities as they moved about among the people, around the church door, and on the public highway.

When Aycock began his campaign, he believed that the only way to improve rural schools was by local taxes voted into effect by the people. The executive campaign committee consisting of the governor, McIver, Toon, and later Joyner,

A multiple teacher school, vintage 1906

concentrated its efforts on communities that seemed eager to take action for better schools. As Aycock traveled and lectured he came to realize how great the need was for better schoolhouses. He had asked the legislature in 1901 to allow the principal of the Literary Fund to be loaned for the schools if the $200,000 appropriation were not paid in full. The request was not allowed; however, in 1903 the Literary Fund of approximately $200,000 was made a loan fund to finance the construction of school buildings. This fund had been provided for in the Constitution of 1868; worthlessness of the securities held in the original fund was known. The new fund consisted of the investment of proceeds from sources such as sale of swamp lands and of grants of land from the federal government, and grants and bequests from individuals. Until 1903 only the interest had been used. Under the new provision as much as one half of the cost of new buildings would be lent to any district, although no loan would be made to a district with fewer than sixty-five children of school age unless the size of the district was necessarily limited by scarcity of population or other unsurmountable barriers — an inducement toward consolidation.

Some Western North Carolina districts experimented with consolidation. When Granite Falls in Caldwell County consolidated two districts, the average attendance of the two districts increased from fifty-four to one hundred-thirty. Six teachers were required where three had sufficed before, and the school term was extended from fourteen to twenty-eight weeks. The county superintendent wrote, "Consolidation has been a great blessing for this community. The effort has also been good for local taxation. Gradation and classification have been improved and a greater number of grades added." Wilkes County reported consolidating two schools, increasing enrollment from thirty-five to sixty-two and average attendance from eighteen to forty-six. One of the two teachers was eliminated, thus enabling the school term to be extended from twelve to sixteen weeks. Wilkes County had great need for consolidation, as it had seventy-four schools for white children and forty for Negroes in 1904, with fifteen additional districts that had no school houses.

Compulsory attendance was experimented with under a law of 1903 for Macon County. In the one year of its operation the average attendance at public schools in the county increased twenty per cent and enrollment increased 34.4 percent. This was four times the statewide increase in enrollment and twice the increase in average attendance. Not until 1913, however, did the legislature pass a compulsory attendance law for the entire state.

Joyner wrote in one of his biennial reports concerning teachers' salaries: "As long as the annual salary paid the teacher who works with the immortal stuff of mind and soul is less than that paid the rudest workers in wood and iron, less than that paid the man that shoes your horse or plows your corn or paints your house or keeps your jail, the best talent can not be secured and kept in the teaching profession — the teaching profession must continue to be made in many instances but a stepping-stone to more profitable employments or a means of pensioning inefficient and needy mediocrity."

In 1904 the average white teacher's salary in North Carolina was $29.05 per month and that of Negro teachers was $22.27, the average term for white children was seventeen weeks and for Negroes sixteen weeks. An examination of the table of teachers salaries and terms in Western North Carolina shows that while the schools in the western countries were keeping pace with others in the state in extending their terms, the average salaries were below those for rural schools in the state as a whole. It will also be noticed that salaries of Negro teachers were much lower than those of white teachers. Joyner believed that this differential was justified. He wrote: "... their teachers are not so well qualified and have not spent so much money on their education, their expenses of living are much less, and therefore, they do not need and ought not to have as much per capita for the education of their children. [He continued, however] There is more real danger of doing the Negro an injustice in the apportionment of the school fund, even after considering all these things, by withholding his equitable part, than of doing the white race any injustice by giving him too much."

Comparison of the education of Negro children in Western North Carolina with that in other parts of the state shows that a Negro child in Western North Carolina was as likely to be enrolled in school as one in other parts of the state but not as regular in attendance — due to the long distance he would have to travel, since there were fewer Negro schools. A study of the results of the two educational crusades, that begun in 1889 and the one of Aycock's administration, shows that they were effective in reaching the school population. Only four and six-tenths percent of white children of school age and thirteen and

TEACHERS' SALARIES AND TERMS IN 1904 IN SOME WESTERN NORTH CAROLINA COUNTIES

Counties	White		Colored		City		Term in Weeks	
	Male	Female	Male	Female	White	Colored	White	Colored
Alleghany	$23.50	$22.27	$20.00	—	—	—	*	*
Buncombe	35.00	32.30	25.35	$25.00	$36.00	$36.00	20	20
Caldwell	28.63	23.78	22.14	19.37	—	—	17.66	15
Cherokee	30.38	30.38	26.25	—	24.00	24.00	16	*
Graham	28.94	19.16	—	—	—	—	16	—
Haywood	28.75	28.00	25.00	20.00	—	—	16.80	14.86
Jackson	28.52	23.93	21.00	22.50	—	—	15.72	16.00
Macon	25.96	23.17	21.00	23.66	—	—	18.72	16
Madison	28.42	25.25	22.00	23.66	—	—	17	15
Polk	27.53	25.00	20.00	19.50	—	—	15.20	15.20
Surry	24.00	23.90	22.50	20.00	—	—	16.48	13.33
Watauga	24.16	20.83	15.00	15.00	—	—	16	16
Yancey	24.79	18.64	15.66	12.50	—	—	20	20

* not available
SOURCE: *Biennial Report*, 1904

two-tenths percent of Negro children of the Western North Carolina counties were classed as illiterate in 1904. In 1922 Edgar W. Knight wrote an article concerning education in the Southern mountains for *School and Society*. He said that forty-five percent of the population was illiterate. This was not true of the young people who had benefited from the recently improved schools. He said that less than forty percent were in attendance, which was true only when applied to the entire school census, persons six through twenty-one years old.

In 1907 the General Assembly passed a law permitting any county board of education to establish and maintain for a term of not less than five months per school year one or more high schools. An appropriation of $40,785 was made to aid in establishing such schools. In Western North Carolina dormitories and mess halls were essential to the plan because of the long distances students must travel. Credit toward room and board was given to those bringing raw provisions from home, and private donations were invited from members of the communities because the state appropriaton was so small. By 1911 there were thirty-six rural high schools in the twenty-four counties of Western North Carolina (Avery County was created in 1911). Most of the high schools had a thirty-two week term, although one was in operation only seventeen weeks. Most of them offered only a two-year course, and just five had more than one teacher, four others utilizing a teacher from the elementary grades on a part-time basis. Enrollment ranged from a low of seventeen to one hundred three at Hendersonville, which had a three-year course, three teachers, and a thirty-five week term. In 1917 the North Carolina Supreme Court ruled that high schools were part of the public school system and were subject to the requirements of the constitution, thus reversing the 1871 decision of the court that schools were not necessary and that county commissioners could not levy taxes to support them. In 1921 there were only six counties in Western North Carolina that did not have at least one accredited high school, Yancey, Mitchell, Graham, Clay, Ashe, and Avery. In the following year two high schools were accredited in Ashe County, one in Avery, and one in Yancey. A good many of the accredited high schools were private ones, but there were sixteen graded schools in the

Hayesville High School. Public high schools began with the law of 1907

area, all publicly supported. City and town high schools were superior to rural ones. Of the eight in the twenty-four county area in 1922 five had four year courses and five had thirty-six week terms.

Among the unusual schools founded by dedicated individuals for the improvement of mountain living, two examples are the Stearns schools of Columbus, Polk County, and Crossnore School, Avery County. A wholesome combination of state and private support was to be found in Polk County beginning in 1891. Mr. Frank Stearns of Cleveland, Ohio, spent some time in Columbus, North Carolina. Charmed with the scenery and impressed with the native intelligence of the people and the lack of educational opportunity, he provided a two-story building for an elementary school. He purchased modern desks and supplemented the public school fund to extend the term to six months, with no tuition charge. A year later he built another two-room building for kindergarten and library. Four years later he bought land for a campus and had a new building erected to house a secondary school which was named the Central Industrial Institute. A board of trustees directed its affairs under a charter from the General Assembly. Thus all grades from kindergarten through high school were offered. A small tuition fee was required of students in the upper grades. Dormitories for boys and girls, a music department, and a library were all provided by Mr. Stearns. In 1916 the school district assumed responsibility for the school and voted bonds to build a new high school building which was named Stearns High School. A consolidated high school later replaced it, and the former school plant houses an elementary school.

Dr. Mary Martin Sloop's work in Avery County began in the year that the county was formed, 1911. Daughter of a Davidson College professor, Mary Martin attended the Woman's Medical College of Philadelphia and hoped to go to Africa as a missionary. Instead, in 1908 she married Dr. Eustice H. Sloop, and in 1911 they began their career of social and medical work, first at Plumtree and then at Crossnore. Mrs. Sloop got a new one-room school built. Gradually additional rooms were added and boarding students were accepted. Money derived from the sale of old clothes contributed by people from all over the nation helped to finance the plant and the social work. At first, girls who were far enough along in their studies were sent to Edgar Tufts' school in Banner Elk, but eventually high school work was offered at Crossnore. In 1917 Crossnore School was chartered as a non-profit organization. Weaving was a major handicraft. Dr. Sloop said, "Our aim is to keep alive an almost forgotten art; to cherish in the young people of the mountains a reverence for the art; to provide a means of livelihood for women and girls as well as to furnish homes with beautiful and symbolic material." The weaving department operated under the Smith-Hughes Law. Crossnore is a public school as well as a craft school. The school property consists of 250 acres, some thirty buildings, living accommodations for some two hundred children and other buildings necessary for elementary and high school; the new Avery County Consolidated High School has absorbed the high school at Crossnore. The county, the state, and the school provide elementary education for the children of the community and the boarding children. School busses bring in those who do not live at the school. The Garrett Memorial Hospital is at the edge of the school grounds.

By 1913 the Equalizing Fund was earmarked to lengthen all school terms in the state to six months or as long as the increased funds from a statewide property tax of five cents on the hundred dollar valuation would permit, and from that time on, efforts were made to establish the six months' term. In 1919 a new equalization plan based on the comparative wealth of the counties was adopted. A statewide revaluation of property was made in 1920, but the effects were undone by a special session of the legislature which ruled that county commissioners might readjust valuations. During that decade constant readjustment of the amount of the fund was necessary because of changes in property values, at the same time that school costs were rising rapidly; from $800,000 in 1919 the fund was increased to $5,250,000 in 1929. In 1925 the county tax rates varied from twenty-one cents per hundred dollars valuation to $1.06 for the counties' part of the current operating expense. Twenty-two of the twenty-four western counties benefited from the Equalizing Fund. McDowell and Buncombe Counties, being industrialized, had increased their wealth and could have low tax rates, while agricultural property fell in value during the prolonged agricultural depression of the 1920's.

By 1929 a number of rural high schools which had been built with funds from bond issues were threatened with having to reduce the length of their terms because revenues were not sufficient. In that year a "Tax Reduction Fund" of $1,250,000 was appropriated for these high schools. Blanford Dougherty, president of the Appalachian State Normal School as it was then called, is credited with having influenced the creation of the state funds for schools. In an address that he gave at the Lansing School in Ashe County he said: "I am one of those that believe that every child from the crest of the Blue Ridge, the Tennessee line, down through piedmont North Carolina, down ... to the sands of the sea, should have as good a chance as any other child, whether he lives in the city or in the country, whether he lives in the mountains or on the plains.... I submit ... that it is not right for this State to allow an 85¢ tax in Watauga County and a 29¢ tax in Forsyth County to run a six month's school if we claim, and are sincere in our claim, that we have a State system of education."

This was not an unusual statement for Dougherty to make, as he had worked for what he called the "Gospel of Equalization" since 1912 and was a member of the State Equalization Board established in 1927.

In 1931 the state abandoned equalization and put into use complete state support of public schools for a six months' term. This meant that North Carolina would have two school systems, a state six months' system and one of local control in counties where there was an extended term which varied from one to three months. The extended term was supported by local levies and the Tax Reduction Fund, which was continued and increased by the General Assembly of 1931. By that time the nationwide depression was causing greater difficulty in the support of schools. Counties were in default on their obligations and teachers were unpaid. Then in 1933 in North Carolina by increasing state school funds and decreasing costs, the principle of complete state support for an eight month term was established. Teacher loads were increased, salaries were reduced, fewer principals were allotted, and bus routes were redirected for economy's sake. Schools were to be supported completely by the state. All special tax districts, special charter or otherwise, were declared nonexistent and no taxes could be levied in said districts for school operating purposes except for courses in home economics, agriculture, and vocational subjects where such taxes were already being levied. (These courses were partially supported by the federal government under the Smith-Hughes Law.) City units with one thousand or more school population were allowed to continue as administrative units under a superintendent. Counties were to serve as administrative units under county superintendents, and they were to be redistricted with consolidation for convenience and economy. Administrative units were permitted by an approved election to improve the standards of the schools for a term of no more than 180 days. Management and control of school buses was to be by the state. Salaries for all personnel were lowered and rural supervisors were eliminated. All school expenditures were to be standardized by the state. Later as conditions improved permissive legislation allowed administrative units to vote special taxes. By 1943 the school term for the entire state was extended to nine months.

The school law of 1933 was of tremendous benefit to the rural schools of Western North Carolina. Nevertheless, its effect on a city such as that of Asheville was catastrophic. From 1920 to 1924 during the city superintendence of W. L. Brooker great progress had been made by the schools of Asheville. Four new buildings were built after a bond issue of $550,000 was voted in 1920, and a new levy of ten cents on a hundred dollar valuation was approved by the voters. West Asheville was annexed and Asheville enjoyed a "boom". Again in 1924 a bond issue was voted, this one also for $550,000, and in 1926 still another of $1,500,000 was approved. The superintendent of schools recommended that a new high school plant and a separate junior college building be erected. In 1929 when the high school was completed with the junior college housed in the same building, Asheville's schools were among the best in the state. Music and creative art, home economics, manual training, and physical education were offered in all of the school grades, and the high school had a commercial department. An administrative staff numbering eighteen persons served the system. Then came the failure of the Central Bank and Trust Company and other banks in the area, and the depression became acute. The junior college was discontinued and several school buildings were closed. The law of 1933 reduced the budget for the city school system from the $763,628 figure of 1929–1930 to $183,761 in 1934–1935. Such courses as manual training, music, and physical education which had been offered since 1905 were eliminated.

Consolidation of the Public schools, an objective of the Board of Equalization established in 1927 and of subsequent legislation, was facilitated by the building of the "Scott Roads,"

HOW THE TAX EQUALIZATION PROGRAM HELPED TWENTY-TWO OF THE COUNTIES OF WESTERN NORTH CAROLINA TO MAINTAIN A SIX MONTH SCHOOL TERM

County	Necessary Rate Without Fund	Actual 1925 Rate	Total Reduction
Alleghany	.75	.47	.28
Ashe	.78	.54	.24
Avery	1.42	.91	.51
Burke	.58	.54	.04
Caldwell	.81	.70	.11
Cherokee	.93	.60	.33
Clay	1.51	1.06	.45
Graham	1.02	.90	.12
Haywood	.79	.70	.09
Henderson	.76	.65	.11
Jackson	.97	.73	.24
Macon	1.19	.64	.55
Madison	.96	.72	.24
Mitchell	.80	.70	.10
Polk	1.20	.90	.30
Rutherford	.68	.60	.08
Surry	.61	.53	.08
Swain	.62	.55	.07
Transylvania	.82	.62	.21
Watauga	1.02	.80	.23
Wilkes	1.15	.66	.49
Yancey	.75	.55	.20

Source: *Biennial Report, 1924–1925, 1925–1926.*

paved secondary roads, during the administration of Governor Kerr Scott in the early 1950's. Subsequently most of the one to four-teacher schools passed out of use. School buses could then carry children to institutions having in most cases a teacher to a grade. The newest development is in the building of mammoth rural high schools serving from a half to a full county. An example is Tuscola Senior High School, which had 1,045 pupils and fifty-four staff members when it opened in 1966. Located on a hilltop overlooking Lake Junaluska in Haywood County, it was named for the one-room school that was once located near by. It replaced three high schools and received students from two additional schools as it serves the entire western half of the county. Its campus of forty-two acres is large enough to accommodate all of the activities associated with a modern secondary school, and it offers "rich programs suited to students with diverse interests, backgrounds, and abilities."

Equalization did not apply to Negro schools as it did to those for white children. It is appalling that as late as 1924 there were in Western North Carolina only two graded schools for Negroes which included high school grades: Asheville, with 217 students, and Hendersonville, with 19. A beginning was being made in Jackson and Wilkes counties with county training schools. The "county training school movement" for Negro youth began in 1911 throughout the South in an effort to provide one good school in each county, to which capable students might go after finishing the work at a one-teacher rural school. The Slater Fund paid $500 to any county that would match it with $750 and run the school for ten months. While the schools were not high schools, their offerings were eventually extended to a four year term. By the 1933–1934 term there were ten Negro high schools in the twenty-four counties of Western North Carolina, but most of them were inadequate. There were thirteen teachers in the Negro high schools of Buncombe County, but most of the other counties had only one or two teachers in their Negro high schools. In 1921 the state set up schedules for teacher certification and salaries, but the Negro schedule provided salaries for Negro teachers that were much lower than for white teachers with equal preparation. Both Negro and white teachers were in most cases paid below the scale for some time to come. During the 1943–1944 term, equalization of salaries for Negro and white teachers was achieved, depending on certificates

144 / *Part II: A Changing Society*

Architect's drawing of a new consolidated high school — one of several modern educational plants in Jackson County

held. In counties where the number of Negro children was insufficient to justify operating a high school, provisions were made by the boards of education to send Negro students to nearby counties where high schools were in existence.

Integration was the solution to the problem of the small number of Negroes in most of the counties. As new rural consolidated high schools were built after the U.S. Supreme Court's decision in 1954 in the case of Brown v. Topeka Board of Education, integration of the races took place. In Buncombe County a gradual program of desegregation was adopted from the first through the eighth grade, and Asheville schools were largely integrated. In January 1970 the Asheville system established "busing" of students to achieve complete integration. Graham County, which has no Negroes, integrated Indian and white school populations in 1960. Yancey abolished its one Negro school in 1962, Jackson County its one Negro school and Madison County its three in 1964. In 1965 twelve counties closed the doors of their Negro schools and sent the students to other public institutions in the counties; Burke eliminated all of its six Negro schools in that year. Other counties followed until in 1970 there was only one all-Negro school, New Hope Elementary School, which was integrated in September, 1970.

Since 1880 education has been provided for Cherokee Indian children. In that year the Friends Meeting of Indiana agreed to establish schools for the Eastern Cherokees, including an industrial school, and to operate them for ten years. In 1892 the federal government took direct charge of the schools and has operated them since that time. An elementary day school was eventually established in each of the townships, with an elementary and a high school at the Cherokee Agency. The last named included both boarding and day students. Although the Cherokees have a written language of their own, their alphabet having been invented by Sequoyah, a member of the tribe, during the 1820's, the English language is used in the schools. Cherokee children may go to public schools if they choose, and a scholarship fund enables many to go to college.

During the 1950's the Board of Higher Education was created to coordinate the work of tax-supported colleges in the state. This board helped to establish a series of junior colleges and at the same time the State Board of Education founded a number of industrial education centers. In 1961 Governor Sanford appointed the Carlyle Commission on Education beyond the High School, with Irving Carlyle of Winston-Salem as chairman. Its recommendations were adopted by the General Assembly in 1963. The law provided for a system of community colleges, technical institutes, and industrial education centers under the State Board of Education but with local boards of trustees. This was just what was needed in Western North Carolina. The area had colleges and junior colleges, but they reached only a minority of the young people. There was no institution designed to teach the skills needed in the developing technological society. Because of the difficulties of travel, high schools had not been consolidated sufficiently to enable them to have the latest expensive equipment needed for effective vocational training. The new institutions were to operate on an open-door policy, admitting any adult and providing whatever training he needed.

An epoch-making decision of the General Assembly in 1967 made four of the senior state-supported colleges "universities." Among these were Appalachian and Western Carolina colleges. East Carolina College, which had grown phenomenally since World War II, had asked the legislature for independent university status. The consolidated university consisted of institutions at Chapel Hill, Raleigh, Greensboro, and Charlotte. Governor Moore and the State Board of Higher Education opposed the granting of university status to East Carolina College and the alternate proposal that the three former teachers colleges be made regional universities. When the latter proposal came up for a vote the Senate added an amendment including the predominately Negro Agricultural and Technical College at Greensboro, and the measure passed. Now that Western North Carolina has two universities that will through the years develop liberal arts and professional training other than for teachers, the bright young people with the potential to become leaders

146 / Part II: A Changing Society

Aerial view of a portion of the Appalachian State University campus
HUGH MORTON PHOTO

This view of a portion of the Western Carolina University campus shows its magnificent setting

will have the opportunity to complete their educations near home, at less expense and with less likelihood of their out-migration afterward.

The regional universities are surveying their community service capability and are extending their programs, graduate and undergraduate, to meet the needs of the region. For instance, both Appalachian State University and Western Carolina University have established various colleges. Their colleges of business will each operate a Bureau of Business Research to supply information to industries and businessmen in Western North Carolina. Appalachian is creating a "Continuing Education Center," a laboratory for learning and living. It is expected to draw and hold persons seeking recreation and vacation programs of educational nature which will greatly extend the usefulness of the university to the region. It will emphasize folk culture, arts and crafts, music and drama. It will enable the university to serve creatively. Western Carolina University will have excellent highway facilities. It will be connected with the roads of the Appalachian Regional Development program and the Interstate system by a new four-lane "limited access" highway. As new industry has moved into the region the university has added two major in-service programs providing bachelors' degrees in business administration and health services. The university has been active for twenty years in regional planning and development of Western North Carolina.

The University of North Carolina at Asheville is the newest state-supported liberal arts institution in the area. It has gone through a process of change since 1927 when a junior college was established by the Buncombe County Board of Education as a part of the public school system, the first public, tuition-free junior college in the state. County students were enrolled free of charge. Such courses as German, Greek, and creative writing were offered in addition to the curriculum usually found in a two-year college, and the student body grew to about three hundred. Meanwhile the College of the City of Asheville was established in 1928. Both operated until 1930 when the North Carolina Supreme Court ruled that a junior college might be supported by the city only if no increase in tax was necessary for that specific purpose and if it could be operated without "impairing the efficiency of the elementary and high schools, and of the kindergarten schools . . . forming a part of the public school system." The depression and the above ruling made necessary the closing of the College of the City of Asheville. The Kiwanis Club of Asheville urged in vain the consolidation of the two colleges. In the 1930's the county's junior college had to institute a tuition charge of $100, and the name of the school was changed to Biltmore Junior College. A literary magazine called *Bluets* with Virginia Bryan Scheiber as adviser offered inspiration to students in creative writing, and it won frequent awards in the annual Columbia Scholastic Press Association contest at Columbia University. Works of such writers as Wilma Dykeman, John Ehle, Patty Sebartle, and Robert Campbell, Jr., appeared in *Bluets*. The dramatic groups won awards in the drama contests at Chapel Hill. The name of the college was changed again in 1936 to Asheville-Biltmore when the city began giving financial support. World War II caused the student body to dwindle. Fortunately the United States Navy set up a program that helped finance the college during those trying years. After the war the Seely estate was obtained for a scenic and spacious campus. In 1955 the North Carolina General Assembly voted an appropriation for Asheville-Biltmore College, which was increased two years later when it was decided to make it a state-supported community college. Asheville-Biltmore was the first institution to qualify under the community college act and state funds were made available for a long-range building program. A campus located nearer Asheville was deemed necessary, and the present site was acquired. A bond issue of $500,000 was approved by the people of Asheville and Buncombe County in 1958 and the state allocated funds to build five buildings on a 161.9 acre tract in North Asheville. An additional bond issue of $750,000 and a tax levy were approved in 1961, which were matched by state funds. The General Assembly in 1963 changed Asheville-Biltmore to a senior state-supported college. The legislature of 1969 made it a unit of the Consolidated University of North Carolina.

Still educational levels in Western North Carolina are well below those of the state. Only 30.6 percent of adults 25 years and over in Western North Carolina have completed high school, compared with 40.8 percent for urban places and 32.3 percent for the state. College graduation was 9.8 percent in urban North Carolina, 7.6 in metropolitan Asheville, and only 5.5 percent in Western North Carolina. Interest in education is gaining momentum in Western North Carolina but the percentage of high school graduates attending college has declined. There is a steady increase in those enrolling in technical institutes, business and nursing schools.

In June, 1968, the State Planning Task Force submitted a report, *Manpower Education in the North Carolina Appalachian Region*. Conclusions drawn were these: "1. Public education must be re-oriented to the world of work and occupational preparation, which enhances traditional general and vocational education . . . ; 2. Teacher education must be improved and more teachers provided in the schools . . . ; 3. Guidance education must be improved and more counselors provided . . . ; 4. Non-curriculum services such as food, clothing, medical and dental care, psychological and social workers, must be increased and extended into new areas."

The high schools that have vocational programs are revamping their offerings in view of the employment needs of the area. New buildings are being funded by grants under the Appalachian Program. Among the courses being given are carpentry, auto mechanics, brick masonry, electronics, blueprint reading and drafting, mechanical drawing, poultry and livestock, and horticulture. Cosmetology and a number of homemaking courses are offered especially for girls. Arrangements are being made for the students to work in industry, agriculture, construction, or services during the summer months at the skills they have been developing during the academic year.

Under Governor Terry Sanford the North Carolina Fund was created with grants from the Ford Foundation, the Z. Smith Reynolds Foundation, and the Mary Reynolds Babcock Foundation. Project areas of the state were outlined and each was invited to organize and construct a plan for community action. For example, four counties, Watauga, Avery, Mitchell, and Yancey created WAMY and sent a program to the Fund authorities. Meanwhile the Economic Opportunity Act was passed and liberal federal funds were available. In this state the North Carolina Fund was designated to administer the program of the Office of Economic Opportunity. There were many facets to the program. One of the most significant was the Neighborhood Youth Corps, to help economically deprived youth of 16 to 21 years of age, to give them educational and vocational training and cultural enrichment. Fifty-three and two-tenths of the population of Western North Carolina have completed eight years or less of public schooling. These "dropouts" constitute one of the most serious problems, as most of them will never be anything but unskilled workers unless they receive special training. The technical institutes have cooperated with the Neighborhood Youth Corps to provide instruction in such skills as bricklaying, upholstering, drapery, basket-making, and other handicrafts.

An optimistic report published by the Western North Carolina Regional Planning Commission in 1962 ended with these words: "If the people of the region work to clear away the obstacles to growth, make the best use of the region's resources, and take advantage of the outside forces working in their favor, they can look forward to a bright future for Western North Carolina."

CHAPTER SEVEN

Church Related and Private Institutions of Learning

Before 1900 only private schools and colleges offered the "higher branches" of learning. They continued to exist after the passage of the law of 1907 providing that counties might establish public high schools, and many people favored them over the public high schools. Some of the private institutions had been designed to make secondary school available to mountain youth, and others were fashionable schools that appealed partly because of their location in scenic resort areas. The private schools were invaluable in supplementing the work of the infant high schools. Almost all of both types were for white students. Two exceptions were Allen Industrial Home and School for Negro girls at Asheville and Western Union Academy in Rutherford County. Many of these schools did not pass out of existence when the trend turned to public high schools. They exist in various forms today.

Among people of Clay County there are still those who talk of a master teacher, John O. Hicks, who organized and conducted the Hicksville High School, a private school, in 1850. He is credited with improving the quality of public school teaching in Hayesville and all of Clay County by his inspirational example. It is said in Clay County that its chief product has been people, and all in the county are proud of the products of Hicksville Academy. Perhaps they are proudest of all of one graduate, George Truett, born in Cherokee County in 1867. His father moved the family to a farm near Hayesville so the children could attend the so-called "Hicksville High School." George Truett went on to study at nearby Young Harris College in Georgia and became a great Baptist minister. For years he was pastor of the First Baptist Church of Dallas, Texas. Among the honors that he won was that of serving as president of the World Baptist Alliance.

Another of the best private schools in Western North Carolina during the 1870's was the East La Porte Male and Female Academy in Jackson County. There were three teachers headed by A. M. Dawson, a famous educator of that area, and the curriculum included arithmetic, natural philosophy, algebra, Euclid (geometry), grammar, geography, Latin composition, and reading. The catalogue for 1878–1879 promised that although criticism and explanation would be furnished by the faculty, judicious care would be exercised lest "explanation may be made to stand in the vacancy occasioned by the student's want of study...." Room and board, including fuel, lighting, and washing, cost five dollars per month and tuition varied from five dollars to twelve and one-half dollars per term of five months, to be determined by the course chosen.

Some families sent their sons and daughters away to other states to be educated. Emory and Henry College, near Abingdon, Virginia, was a manual labor school where boys might earn most of their expenses. The Stonewall Jackson Institute at Abingdon was praised by Charles Dudley Warner. He visited at Worth's, a trading center in northern Watauga County where he spent the night. The daughters had attended the Stonewall Jackson Institute. The home had two pianos and "a bevy of young leadies whose clothes were certainly not made on Cut Laurel Gap. Books were scattered around the house — evidences of the finishing schools with which our country is blessed."

It is a truism that each school was as good or as bad as its teachers. One great teacher who made his influence felt widely was Robert Logan Patton. A Western North Carolina boy, he earned his way through Phillips Academy at Exeter, New Hampshire, and Amherst College, spending ten years on his education after he was seventeen years old. He was well qualified to assume leadership on a state or national level in either education or the ministry, but he chose to preach chiefly at rural churches and to found academies. When he returned from Amherst in 1876, he was probably the best educated man in Western North

Carolina, and people in different communities urged him to come to them and found academies. He opened his first school at Table Rock in Burke County in August, 1876, and taught there three years, opened his Globe Academy in Caldwell County in 1882, one at Glen Alpine in 1889, another at Morganton in 1890, one at Moravian Falls in Wilkes County in 1891, then returned to Morganton to remain from 1892 to 1901. There were internals when he accepted other appointments, such as the pastorate of the First Baptist Church of High Point, but he always returned to his mountains. From 1910 to 1912 he served as superintendent of schools in Morganton, after which his health failed and he was obliged to retire.

Even earlier than these academies were five so-called colleges in Western North Carolina, three of which were in operation or were being built when the Civil War started. Davenport College was founded in Lenoir, Caldwell County, by a group of far-sighted and prosperous men who wished to make their town a cultural center. They talked about a college for women, first approaching the Concord Presbytery, with which the Presbyterian churches in the county were affiliated, but it decided to locate its college at Statesville (Mitchell College). The Lenoir community had become so enthusiastic that the people would not let the college idea die. The South Carolina Conference of the Methodist Episcopal Church South accepted the proposal of the Lenoir group. William Davenport, James C. Harper, W. A. Lenoir, Jas. Harper, E. W. Jones, and Uriah Cloyd were the most generous givers, although the list of donors was long. Named for the largest contributor, the college was completed in 1857 and was given to the South Carolina Conference, which kept it in operation until the last year of the Civil War. When General George Stoneman's United States Cavalry raid approached Lenoir after attacking Salisbury, the president, the Reverend A. G. Stacy, disbanded the school and moved the girls toward South Carolina. The troops occupied the college premises, plundered the library, destroyed the furniture, and "the place was left a wreck, despoiled of everything except that the buildings were not burned." The friends of the college, although improverished by the war, refurbished the buildings cheaply and classes were resumed. With a preparatory department and a college department it continued in operation until 1936 under the Western North Carolina Conference to which it had been transferred in 1870 when the new conference was set up. After 1893 both men and women were in the student body. In 1938 it was merged with Greensboro College.

Two other colleges originated as private schools but were turned over later to the Methodist Episcopal Church South. Rutherford College, founded in Burke County in 1853 by Dr. Robert Laban Abernethy, was first an academy called Owl Hollow School. Five years later it received its charter as Rutherford Academy, named in honor of John Rutherford, who contributed the land, and in 1861 the name was changed to Rutherford Seminary. In 1870 it became Rutherford College. In 1900 it passed into the possession of the Methodist Church. A number of Methodist ministers were educated at Rutherford College. Soon after it began granting degrees Brantley York became a professor, remaining for five years. York had the distinction of having been the first teacher and the moving spirit of Union Institute, later Trinity College, now Duke University. Rutherford in its later years experienced financial problems, and in 1933 it was merged with Weaver College to form Brevard College. For a while a public school was housed in the Rutherford College buildings, after which the property was sold to persons establishing the Valdese General Hospital.

Weaver College, which was chartered in 1873, occupied grounds that had long been used by schools, the Salem Camp Ground. A building erected in 1836 to entertain the Holston Conference served as a neighborhood school until 1854 when the Sons of Temperance built a larger house. A boarding school, the Masonic and Temperance High School housed there, served a large area until 1862, reopening in 1866. A fire destroyed the building in 1872, and the community rebuilt and expanded the school. Dr. James A. Reagan, physician and surgeon, was one of the founders and served during the first three years as president of the college, after which he continued to serve as a trustee. The college was chartered in 1873 with a local board of trustees as Weaverville College. A later president, W. C. McCarthy (1876–1880), is said to have procured sheep hides from neighboring farmers, which he tanned and used as diplomas. McCarthy wrote each diploma with a quill pen, in Latin. In 1883 the property was deeded to the Methodist Episcopal Church South, and the Western North Carolina Conference supervised the college work from that time. The educator who served longest at the school was Marion A. Yost, who taught Latin, Greek, and other subjects for thirty-five years and was for ten years, 1888–1898, both a teacher and president of the college. Three degrees, Bachelor of Arts, Bachelor of Science, and Master of Arts, were offered until 1896 when the last was dropped. From 1912–1934 the school was a junior college, and the name was shortened to Weaver College in 1912. Literary societies constituted the leading student activity. They were still flourishing in 1934 and were transferred with the college to Brevard College. Summer schools at Weaver had attracted teachers, tourists, and parents as well as regular students.

When the transfer to Brevard was consummated thirty members of the student body and five faculty members made the move. Alumni of both Rutherford College and Weaver College are ardent supporters of Brevard College. It occupies the site of the Brevard Epworth School started at Brevard in 1895 by the Revered Fitch Taylor, aided by the Sunday schools and Epworth Leagues of the Western North Carolina Conference of the Methodist Episcopal Church South. After his death in 1909 the Woman's Home Missionary Society took over the work, and the school, which then became the Brevard Institute, was accredited by the North Carolina State Board of Education. It served a worthy purpose in making high school available to mountain boys and girls when public schools were not in existence. After operating thirty-eight years, however, Brevard Institute was no longer needed; with new trends in education and the availability of public schools, a junior college was needed. Effects of the depression had been hard on Rutherford College and Weaver College, and the North Carolina Conference decided to merge the two in one new institution. The women's organization that had sponsored Brevard Institute offered its school plant, free of debt, to the conference, and the offer was accepted. Brevard College continued the tradition of Methodist aid to education in Western North Carolina. Citizens of Brevard and Transylvania County donated hundreds of acres of land and reconditioned the buildings of the former institute. The institution opened in the fall of 1934 as a self-help junior college with the students doing practically all of the work on the campus and on the college farm and dairy.

Two Baptist associations started colleges in the southwestern part of the state before the Civil War: Mars Hill College in Madison County, first called the French Broad Institute and established in 1856 by the French Broad Association, was chartered as Mars Hill College by the General Assembly in 1859; and Judson College in Hendersonville was founded by the Salem Association and approved by the Western Baptist Convention in 1858. Mars Hill was coeducational and played an important part in its community, a crossroads center on what for many travelers was the favorite passage through the Southern Appalachians. Because of the location the spot was of strategic importance during the Civil War and was held by the Confederacy in spite of the Unionist sentiments of many of the people of the county. The college closed in 1863 because of a lack of male students, and while Confederate soldiers were quartered there fire destroyed two buildings. Additional destruction almost brought ruin to the college and forty years went by before the equipment equalled that enjoyed by Mars Hill before the war.

In spite of poverty, apathy, and the bitterness of the Reconstruction period, the buildings were used for some type of educational activity after 1865. College work was reinstated in 1865 but the next few years were a time of struggle to obtain funds, to repair the one remaining building, and to keep a president. In 1871 and 1872 a "Peabody school" was run, after which the college was dormant until 1878. For a few years an orphanage occupied the buildings, and for two years L. B. Lunsford conducted a private school there. In 1878 the institution was reinstated as a high school, its work beginning with a primary department. The frequent changes of presidents ended with the coming of Robert L. Moore in 1897 to serve forty-one years.

During that time the institution became an accredited junior college. Enrollment grew from 183 students, mostly local residents, to 970 from twenty-four states and three foreign countries. By 1964 it had become a senior college. Accreditation by the Southern Association of Colleges and Schools was granted in 1967. The music department was given membership as a senior college in the National Association of Schools of Music in 1960, and the department of business administration was made a member of the American Association of Collegiate Schools of Business in the same year.

The Building of Judson College was an ambitious undertaking, and it would have been completed on schedule if the war had not come. The structure was of hand-hewn stone with handsome stone columns. The walls were finished by 1861 but the roof was not completed until 1871. The trustees had to take a mortgage to pay the existing debt and continue construction. When the debt fell due a joint-stock company, the Western North Carolina Education Company headed by Pinckney Rollins, purchased the unfinished structure to keep it from falling into the hands of some other denomination. In 1878 work was resumed, one room was floored, and the free school of the township was taught there. In 1879 the coeducational Judson High School was held in the finished part of the building.

The house was completed in October 1882, and the college began its session with five teachers. The name was changed several times during the construction period, from Hendersonville Female College to Western North Carolina Female College, to Judson Female College, and finally to Judson College. Although planned for women, it operated for twelve years as a coeducational college and graduated outstanding citizens. In 1892, the debt on the building never having been paid off, the company had to sell the property. The purchasers continued to operate a college there for two years, after which it was used as a high school. In 1903 Judson College was sold to the town of Hendersonville to be used as graded school building.

A partial list of Baptist schools in Western North Carolina, compiled by John Preston Arthur, includes the following: Mars Hill College, Mars Hill; Yancey Institute, Burnsville; Mitchell Institute, Bakersville; Fruitland Institute, Hendersonville; Round Hill Academy, Union Mills; Haywood Institute, Clyde; Sylva Institute, Sylva; Murphy Institute, Murphy.

All of these schools except Mars Hill College and Fruitland Institute have passed out of existence. Occupying the site of Round Hill Academy at Union Mills is Alexander Schools, Incorporated, a child-caring institution founded in 1925 by J. F. Alexander. Open the year round, it is licensed to accept 178 children. Since 1932 its academic work has been consolidated with the public school at Union Mills. Children in residence are ones who have been deprived of their homes by death or other circumstances. Modern and up-to-date buildings have been built by contributions from churches, laymen, and the Duke Foundation. Fruitland Institute is owned by the Baptist State Convention and is used during the academic year as a school for young ministerial students who do not have college training, and in the summers for assemblies and conferences.

Methodists were always concerned about education in Western North Carolina before the public schools became effective. A list of some of their schools follows. Methodist Episcopal Church South: Asheville Female College, developed in 1856 from the Holston Methodist Female College established in 1842; Hayesville College, Clay County, opened in 1890 and in operation only one year, after which its assets were transferred to Trinity College; Tuscola Institute, Haywood County, founded in 1855 by the Reverend William Hicks, followed by the Richland Institute (its site is now Lake Junaluska); Secondary School at Jefferson, established by the Mount Airy District, 1910–1929; Brevard Institute, 1895, given to the Woman's Board of Home Missions in 1905.

Methodist Episcopal Church (North): Brown Seminary at Leicester, on Turkey Creek Camp Ground; Aaron Seminary, Montezuma, now Avery County, 1890–1911; Fairview College, Traphill, Wilkes County, a private school accepted by the Conference in 1886; Etowah Institute near Brevard; Eagle Mills School at Eagle Mills, Wilkes County; Oberlin Home and School, near Lenoir, founded by Miss Emily Pruden in 1885, name changed in 1903 to Ebenezer Mitchell Home and School, moved to Misenheimer in 1909 and named Pfeiffer College, now a senior liberal arts college (Miss Pruden established fifteen schools in North and South Carolina.); Allen High School, started by Mr. and Mrs. Louis M. Pease, given to the Woman's Home Missionary Society of the Methodist Episcopal Church.

The Allen Industrial and Home School was established for mountain Negro girls about 1875 by Mr. and Mrs. Louis M. Pease, social workers from New York who had come to Asheville to retire. The couple purchased land, including an old livery stable which they converted into a home and school. After conducting the school for twelve years they gave the property to the Woman's Missionary Society of the Methodist Episcopal Church (Northern) to be carried on as a mission school. In 1897 it was made a boarding school called the Allen Home School, now known as the Allen High School. It has become an example of excellence in secondary education for Negroes. For many years the curriculum included grades one through twelve, but as responsibility for the work of the grammar grades was assumed by the public schools, Allen High School limited its offerings to grades eight through twelve. The present buildings were built in the 1950's, the school is accredited, and the graduates are accepted by colleges and professional schools.

Two Presbyterian assemblies have participated in the educational progress of Western North Carolina. The Asheville Normal and Associated Schools represent the work of the Presbyterian Church in the U.S.A. (Northern), now the United Presbyterian Church. Mr. and Mrs. Pease, who founded the Allen Industrial and Home School, were closely associated with the founding of the excellent Asheville Normal which functioned from 1892 until 1940. Their first school for white girls developed from the boarding house which they maintained in their home. Vacationing guests observed that the girls employed for household work were capable but uneducated, and through the influence of a guest, Dr. Thomas Lawrence, the Board of Home Missions purchased the thirty acre tract owned by Mr. and Mrs. Pease and employed the Peases to help conduct a school, to be called the Home Industrial School. It opened in 1887 and was soon filled to capacity with seventy boarding students and forty day students, ranging in age from five to twenty. The Asheville Normal and Collegiate Institute was established in 1892 on the same property, to educate rural school teachers. Thus it antedated both the Cullowhee and Boone training schools.

The Home Industrial School and the Normal and Collegiate Institute were among twenty-five day and boarding schools throughout Western North Carolina established by the Woman's Home Mission Board of the Presbyterian Church in the U.S.A. In 1920 all of these schools in and around Asheville were organized into a system called Asheville Normal and Associated Schools with Dr. John E. Calfee as president. Two other schools of the twenty-five mentioned above were Dorland-Bell School for Girls at Hot Springs and the Asheville Farm School for boys. Dorland originated in the home of Dr. and Mrs. Luke Dorland, who had been working since 1867 at Scotia Seminary, which he founded, a Presbyterian school for Negro girls at Concord. Coming to Hot Springs in 1887 to rest, the Dorlands invited some children into their dining room to learn to read and write. Soon a school developed, which in 1893 the Woman's Board of the Presbyterian Church U.S.A. sponsored. Two miles away at a farm called the Willows a home for boys was established by the same group. The Bell Institute, a third school, merged with Dorland in 1918 to form Dorland-Bell. Eventually housed in a campus of eight buildings, the school was accredited as a high school, but the work was always broader in scope than that of the usual high school. Mrs. Maud Gentry Long of Hot Springs, an alumna of Dorland-Bell, wrote, "The friends of this school are investing their money not at 4 or 6 per cent but in the lives of the womanhood of our mountains." The school's stated purpose was as follows: " . . . to help girls from remote mountain districts who are not within reach of a good school; to lead those to a vision of the possibilities of a rich, happy life in the country; to send back into the mountain homes young women who will know how to make healthy, happy Christian homes. . . . Our main interest is in the girl who will have no schooling after she leaves here."

Meanwhile in 1894 the Asheville Farm School was established at Swannanoa. The first students were young men, rather than boys, who had had no opportunity for schooling. As the years passed and the elementary schools improved, the Farm School was able to advance its work and to be a high school. Its campus was to be the home of Warren Wilson College.

Warren Wilson College dates from 1942 when the Presbyterian Board of National Missions combined the Dorland-Bell School and the Asheville Farm School on the campus of the latter. At first it offered four years of high school work and two years of college studies. Each student continued his academic program and also majored in a vocational field, such as agriculture, auto mechanics, business, construction engineering, homemaking, journalism, woodworking, carpentry, printing, and weaving. Each student contributed half of each day to his vocational program. When high school work became readily available, it was dropped at Warren Wilson and two additional years of college work were added, the first class graduating with the A.B. degree in 1969. Since its founding the college has been concerned chiefly with young people of limited financial means and superior promise. Every student works part of each day, and thus the college is maintained and the student cost is reduced.

In Asheville the Normal and Collegiate Institute was discontinued in 1940 as the Presbyterian Church U.S.A. changed its emphasis in the Southern highlands and especially in Western North Carolina to the liberal arts concept. But it had played a mighty part in the drama of education in the mountains. The normal in 1925 began offering work to the four-year college level, leading to a degree, the Bachelor of Education, later the Bachelor of Science in Education. Asheville citizens supported the college by making contributions for new buildings. The normal was approved by the American Association of Teachers' Colleges. In 1930 the Home Industrial School was dropped. It was no longer needed. By 1936 the summer school of the normal enrolled 1500 students. President Calfee was able to influence numbers of noted professors to offer instruction in the summer school, and for several years Columbia University accepted credit earned at the Asheville summer school toward degrees at the former. This enabled Southern teachers to earn degrees at Columbia by doing much of their work in Asheville. Faculty members came from Harvard, Yale, Columbia, Pennsylvania, the United States Naval Academy, Virginia, Duke, Tulane, South Carolina, North Carolina, and many other universities of the highest prestige in the nation. Students from as many as thirty-four states attended in a single season. The summer school grew to be the second largest one in the South with a faculty of ninety-nine. Merchants and business firms, the Chamber of Commerce, and the people of the community cooperated with the normal, all of them recognizing it as a definite asset in advertising Asheville. But with Dr. Calfee's retirement in 1937 after 21 years, the conditions changed. The Board of Missions ended its support of the Asheville Normal and Teachers College as it was finally called. Asheville citizens attempted to keep it operating under the name Asheville College, but available funds were not sufficient, and it closed after the summer school of 1944. It had served its purpose.

The Presbyterian Church in the U.S. (Southern) began at about the turn of the twentieth century to found some schools, largely through the initiative of interested people in the communities served. Such was the Westminster School in Rutherford County, established by some of the old families of the neighborhood, especially for boys, although a few girls were admitted. It was in operation from 1902 until 1923, offering work in twelve grades. Even the best of North Carolina's public schools at that time offered only eleven grades. Glade Valley School, near Sparta, was organized in 1910 as a coeducational boarding school. It is still in operation and is accredited by the Southern Association of Secondary Schools and Colleges and by the State Board of Education.

In the northwestern part of the state the Southern Presbyterian Church in 1897 acquired the services of Edgar Tufts. George McCoy, Asheville journalist titled an article describing Tufts' projects "What God and Edgar Tufts Did." Tufts had just completed his work at Union Seminary in Virginia when he came to Banner Elk to be pastor of a small church. Two years earlier during the summer Tufts and two other seminary students had worked in Northwestern North Carolina where two ladies were holding a small summer mission school. In 1897 Tufts invited some of the more advanced students to continue their studies in his home. In 1899 a two-room building was erected with contributions of work and materials by members of the community and aid from Tufts' friends to whom he had appealed for help. That school has grown into Lees McRae College, a junior college named for the two ladies who started the mission school, Mrs. Elizabeth McRae and Mrs. S. P. Lees. Tufts persuaded Dr. W. C. Tate to come to Banner Elk where he already had a small hospital in operation. In 1922 Grace Hospital was built, and in 1933 a new and larger one replaced it, to serve twelve mountain counties. The latest hospital, built in the 1960's, is named the Charles Cannon Memorial Hospital. With money contributed by friends Tufts bought Lybrook Farm, a mile from the school, for an orphanage. It is named Grandfather Home because of its view of Grandfather Mountain. In 1924 after Tufts' death, the three institutions were incorporated as the Edgar Tufts Memorial Association, and the young Edgar Hall Tufts continued the work his father had started.

Montreat-Anderson Junior College began in 1913 at the invitation of the Mountain Retreat Association to the General Assembly of the Presbyterian Church, U.S., to use its conference ground and buildings in Buncombe County for educational purposes. Nine synods participated in establishing the Montreat Normal School, which received contributions from the synods until 1931. Dr. R. C. Anderson, President of the Mountain Retreat Association, served as president of the normal. Gradually the college department developed and was accredited by the Southern Association of Colleges and Secondary Schools. In the early 1940's Montreat became a senior college, although it was not accredited as such. In the 1950's the high school department was dropped and in 1960 the college, which had been renamed Montreat-Anderson, retrenched, becoming a junior college again. Throughout its history it had been a girls' college, but is now coeducational.

Four schools were established by the Episcopal Church for the education of mountain youth. They were Christ School at Arden in Buncombe County, Patterson School at Legerwood in Caldwell County, Valle Crucis School in Watauga County, and Appalachian School at Penland, Mitchell County. Christ School and Patterson School are strong institutions today. Christ School was at first primarily an industrial, coeducational institution. The tuition could be paid in work. Carpentry, printing, telegraphy, bookeeping, and typewriting were taught along with academic courses. Some students walked as many as ten miles each way to and from school. The General Education Fund of the diocese and private donations supported it. Within a few years the student body was limited to boys, and as the public schools of the state improved, boys from other states were accepted, and gradually accommodations were increased. The school won accreditation as a first class school for boys. Patterson School was founded by Mr. Samuel Patterson, who gave the old Patterson family home near Lenoir to the Episcopal Church, Jurisdiction of Asheville. Patterson was interested in agriculture and improved farming methods, and agriculture as well as academic courses were taught. Income came chiefly from donations of friends and a diocesan loan fund. As time passed the purpose of the school was enlarged to prepare boys for college and business as well as for hometown industries.

Appalachian School was founded by Dr. Rufus Morgan, one of the most notable characters who ever walked the mountains. When he was a mere boy he wished his parents to use the money that they would spend for Christmas presents for him to buy food for a needy family. Quite early he resolved to devote his life to helping the people of the mountains. During the summers he spent his time tramping and getting to know mountain people. When Morgan graduated from the General Theological Seminary in New York, Bishop Horner of the Episcopal Church purchased the Penland property in Mitchell County so that Rufus Morgan could start a school there. When he and his bride arrived at Penland in 1914 there were two buildings on the site which had been used earlier by Mr. Wesley Conley for his "Seven Springs Baptist Industrial School." Morgan began his program of erecting buildings, making roads, establishing water systems, planting crops, administering to the physical needs of the people, molding character, and raising the level of spiritual life of the people and giving himself to the community. This work established, Morgan left Penland in 1918. He was succeeded by Miss Amy Burt, who was joined in 1920 by Miss Lucy Morgan, whose name became nearly synonymous with the later Penland School.* Bishop Ives' interest in Valle Crucis and his establishment of a school for boys there in 1842 has been mentioned. Bishop Cheshire revived interest in Valle Crucis in the 1890's, and a school for girls was built, although boys were admitted as day students. Fire destroyed one of the buildings in 1919 and two teachers lost their lives. During World War II the school was permanently closed, and the campus and buildings are used for conferences.

The John C. Campbell Folk School was named for the author of *The Southern Highlander and His Homeland*. Campbell believed that the folk schools of Denmark had much to offer as models for the mountain people of North Carolina. The school is a noble and continuing experiment in adult education, a workshop for creative living. Its 366 acres of peaceful, rolling dairyland in Clay County, eight miles southeast of Murphy, its craft school, its folk music and dancing are the fulfillment of a dream of John C. Campbell. Its purpose is to help people to "do beautiful things with hands and minds, to be a workshop for life." Campbell died in 1919 before his school had materialized, but his wife made his dream come true. She went to Denmark to study. She sought to answer the question: how to keep an enlightened, progressive, and contented farming population on the land. Mrs. Campbell realized that agricultural improvement had to go hand in hand with enlightenment. Therefore the John C. Campbell School has taught its students improved methods of dairying and farming. They farm the 366 acres scientifically. The school has sought to make the farmers in its area self-sufficient and contented, to make them prosperous and creative, to give them "economic independence based on self-help." In 1925 the school was incorporated with the approval of the Conference of Southern Mountain Workers. The American Missionary Association (Congregational), the Board of National Missions of the Presbyterian church in the U.S.A., and the National Council of the Protestant Episcopal Church contributed toward

---

* The Penland School was started as a handicraft department run in conjunction with the Appalachian School but with many adults participating. When the Appalachian School was discontinued Penland School continued to operate, and it purchased the land and buildings of Appalachian School.

its support. The first classes were held in the winter of 1927–1928. Subjects were simple field surveying, construction of model farm equipment, cooking and sewing, grammar, reading, writing, arithmetic of the most practical kind, lectures in history, literature, economic geography, health, daily music, agricultural science, bookkeeping, forestry, wood carving, weaving. The school did not give credits, but it sought to help young people to utilize fully their natural abilities and to make life in the country more interesting and rewarding. Students laughed, sang, danced, discussed, as well as worked. The philosophy of the school was to get students of the school to think and read and to let them work the rest for themselves. Annual dance courses were taught. Mrs. Campbell went to Massachusetts to see Cecil Sharp, the great English collector of songs and dances. He and she went through the country collecting folk tunes, songs, and ballads. The John C. Campbell Folk School still operates on the pattern of the Danish Folk School. It has some fifteen buildings used for school purposes, faculty homes, and dairying and farm outbuildings. The great part of the acreage is used for demonstration of scientific farming and forestry.

An experimental school that does not fit into any pattern was Black Mountain College, founded in 1933 by a small group of faculty and administrators from Rollins College at Winter Park, Florida. They hoped to develop students who were able to "creatively meet the demands of our century." Major emphasis was placed on music, drama, creative writing, and the visual arts, painting, drawing, graphics, and architecture. Josef Albers, a former Bauhaus teacher, and his wife Anni were hired as the Visual Arts Department, and a place was won by their students of Black Mountain College that was significant in the world of modern art. With the resignation of Josef and Anni Albers the major emphasis of study changed to creative writing, and a literary review was produced. The college ceased to function in 1956, but the people who had studied there were reaching a stage of great influence in art and writing. While no degrees or credits had been offered, those students who had chosen to do further work were admitted to important graduate schools.

CHAPTER EIGHT

Teacher Education
"And gladly would they learn and gladly teach."

In the last fourth of the nineteenth century the General Assembly sought to improve teacher education by supporting normal schools and institutes. In 1893 and 1903 it began the support of the Cullowhee Normal and the Appalachian Training schools. As these schools evolved to become regional universities in 1967, they provided most of the teacher training for Western North Carolina.

Legislation in 1876–1877 provided for two normal schools, one at the state university and one for Negroes. President Kemp Plummer Battle of the university held summer normal schools until 1885. Although the plan of the General Assembly had been that only men would be accepted at the normal school in Chapel Hill, both men and women were enrolled. Some of the young men who were in attendance during the academic year, particularly Edwin A. Alderman and Charles Duncan McIver, were persuaded to remain for the normal school where they were permanently won to the profession. Their work was to revolutionize the schools of the state. Teacher training as provided for by the Act of 1887 was carried on for Negroes at Fayetteville. To each of the two normal schools the state paid $2000 and the Peabody Fund added $500. Many books were contributed by publishers for use in the normal schools. The State Educational Association of 1872 formed at Wilmington must have passed out of existence, as in 1878 in Chapel Hill a North Carolina Teachers Association was formed, and again the organization of county associations was encouraged.

Chapel Hill was a long way from the westernmost counties, and in 1879 only three Western North Carolina counties were represented in the student body of the normal. It was good news for the western counties when in 1881 the legislature provided for eight additional normal schools, four for white teachers and four for Negroes. To finance these, the state paid $500 to each and the Peabody Fund furnished $250 each. The one normal school in the mountains was at Franklin. Throughout the years that it was held, the majority of the members were from Macon County, and the county's schools came to be recognized as superior.

When the normal in Chapel Hill was discontinued in 1885, four additional ones were created for white teachers, including schools at Boone and Asheville. The Boone Normal School was offered only two summers, after which it was transferred to Sparta, where in 1887 it was held from July 6 to 28. Charles Duncan McIver, a young graduate of the state university who had attended the normal school at Chapel Hill, served as superintendent of the Sparta Normal, for which he received $125. His report of the Sparta school reveals some of the values and deficiencies of the normals: "Of the teachers who attended the Boone normal last year, not more than ten were at the Sparta normal. In fact there was only one teacher from Watauga County. Furthermore, from 80 to 90 per cent of the attendant teachers at Sparta had never seen any Normal School before. This indicates that the majority of teachers do not (often they cannot) go a great distance to attend normal schools. Small salaries and short terms render it, in many cases, impossible. Generally, too, these cases need Normal instruction more than any others. Normal Schools, or efficient County Institutes, should be brought within the reach of every teacher in the State. The locating of the school at Sparta this year is a move in that direction." The superintendent of the Asheville Normal School in the summer of 1887 was another of the bright young men who had attended the University Normal School, Edwin A. Alderman.

Teaching arithmetic and reading in the Asheville Normal in 1887 was Philander P. Claxton. In that year Asheville voted to be a special charter school district with a graded school, and Philander Claxton was elected superintendent of the Asheville schools. A native of Tennessee, Claxton had studied at Johns Hopkins University, after which he had spent six months in Germany studying the school system. His biographer says that he brought enthusiasm and new methods and that he and his teachers indoctrinated Asheville for support of better schools. At teachers' meetings papers on Froebel, Rousseau, and Pestalozzi were read, and interest ranged from kindergartens and Greek education to psychology and methods of teaching special subjects.

McIver had referred to county institutes, which were being conducted in a number of the western counties. As early as 1878 Dr. Alexander Graham, superintendent of the Charlotte schools, conducted such institutes, with the aid of the Peabody Fund, and in 1881 the General Assembly passed a law permitting counties to hold institutes, really short normal schools, toward the support of each of which the state would pay $100. In 1883 Rutherford County held two such institutes, one for white teachers attended by thirty-five persons, and one the week following for Negro teachers. Polk County held a four-week-long institute and Henderson County had a two-week one. The *North Carolina Teacher*, a magazine published privately in Raleigh, commented: "From these brief points you will observe that the mountains are alive to the great educational movement of the State."

President Battle of the State University delivered two lectures at an institute in Sparta which caused him to write: "I have always been favorably impressed with the mountain people. The ordinary notion of their want of culture is a mistake. Some may lack the refined manners of the low counties but they are kind and hospitable and many are shrewd. Some of our ablest and most attractive orators were reared in the mountains."

In 1883 a North Carolina teachers' chautauqua was suggested by the *North Carolina Teacher*. Again in 1884 in the February issue the idea was explored. The proprietor of White Sulphur Springs at Waynesville invited the teachers to spend a month there, and the Western North Carolina Railroad, newly completed to that point, offered low fares. The chautauqua was held beginning on June 16, 1884, and lasting two weeks. It differed from the normal schools in that there were no textbooks and no assignments. Colonel Francis W. Parker, who later became famous as founder and principal of the Chicago Institute, an experimental school of the University of Chicago, was one of the speakers. The railroad offered a ticket that would permit teachers to attend the Franklin Normal School at the close of the chautauqua. Room and board for this vacation in the mountains cost six dollars per week at the hotel and from three to five dollars at homes in Waynesville. The *North Carolina Teacher* carried the appeal, "We want to give the pupils in our schools some idea of the State's gigantic system of internal improvements, as seen in the completion of the Western North Carolina Railroad, and the extension of the Ducktown Branch. The ride across the Blue Ridge Mountains reveals one of the most remarkable feats of engineering skill on earth.... As the train climbs up and winds around those great mountains, rising *one hundred and sixteen feet to each mile* traveled, often shooting through a dark and rocky tunnel and over the steepest of trestles the grandeur of the view far exceeds the expectation of the most brilliant imagination."

Perhaps this was the first convention held in Western North Carolina by any group, and the enthusiasm of the members was great. Railroad officials cooperated, providing a special train for the group of one hundred teachers who boarded at Goldsboro and the additional one hundred who joined them at Raleigh. By the time the train reached White Sulphur Springs there were three hundred aboard. The train was divided into two sections to cross the mountains, and at one time the first section was passing over a portion of the road one thousand feet above the other section, causing much applause as the passengers experienced this wonderful sight. Both sections stopped for breakfast at the new Round Knob Hotel, and the party enjoyed the Round Knob Fountain which threw water nearly three hundred feet in the air. During the chautauqua provisions were made for recreation, and on the fourth day about seventy-five teachers rode horseback to the peak of Lickstone Mountain, with Wid Medford, celebrated bear hunter and mountain guide, to lead them. The next two annual sessions of the teachers' chautauqua were held at Black Mountain, after which a permanent building was erected at Morehead City, where subsequent chautauquas were offered.

The county institutes had been held during the months of July and August, and attendance was optional. As many of the rural teachers had no education except what they received in the district schools, further training was essential. The State

170 / *Part II: A Changing Society*

Round Knob, where the trains stopped for passengers to eat. Note the winding track
ASHEVILLE CITIZEN-TIMES CO.

The fountain (geyser) at Round Knob

Board of Education in 1889 decided to select two competent men as institute conductors to carry on the work throughout the entire year, requiring the dismissal of school at the time of the institute in any county and making teacher attendance compulsory. The four thousand dollars hitherto appropriated for normal schools annually was now assigned to the support of institutes and other work for the instruction of teachers. The rules for holding institutes were made by the State Board of Education, while the board of education in each county was expected to provide a suitable place and to defray all local expenses, including the room and board of the conductor of the institute. The county superintendent was to assist the conductor and to help administer a permissive examination at the end of the institute. Those who passed would receive three-year first-grade teachers' certificates which could be used in any county in the state. Edwin A. Alderman and Charles D. McIver, both of whom had been superintendents of normal schools, were selected as institute conductors. They felt that "the logical approach to the southern educational problem was through the teacher and his training." Perhaps it was because of the influence of the two that the normals were discontinued and the state institutes were started. Not only were the institutes to serve as a pedagogical shortcut, reaching every teacher in the state, but Alderman and McIver believed that "the gospel of education" must be taken to everyone: parents, committeemen, and the public at large. It was impossible for two men to hold an institute in every county, and Dr. J. L. M. Curry, agent of the Peabody Fund, gave money to enable the State Board of Education to employ M. C. S. Noble, J. Y. Joyner, and E. P. Moses during July and August of 1889, and the same men plus Alexander Graham, John J. Blair, and E. L. Hughes in July and August 1890. In the western counties Negro teachers attended the same institutes as whites, the Negroes sitting apart in a place assigned to them.

McIver and Alderman divided the state, McIver holding institutes from the foothills to the western boundary the first year, staying a week or two in each county. After working with teachers and trustees of schools he would hold at last a "Peoples' Day" in which he addressed the public in churches, warehouses, schoolhouses, on local problems and on public education. Emphasis was placed on "lack of uniformity in textbooks, want of interest on the part of parents and committeemen, the perpetual change of teachers and the inadequacy of records they left behind them, and the want of general supervisory power, . . . the work of the county superintendent being largely clerical." The following year Alderman held institutes in the west. He outlined his and McIver's purposes in these categories: 1. To carry to the people definite knowledge of the educational work resting on the public schools; 2. To carry to the doors of the public school teachers, who could not seek it, definite instruction as to the meaning of teaching and the teacher's office, and training in scientific methods of teaching; 3. To make suggestions that would tend to perfect and increase the efficiency of the system.

Among the points of concern emphasized by Alderman and McIver in their reports concerning the institutes were the use of Webster's spelling book by about half of the schools, which produced children who could not read but who "spelled through" the speller; children who knew more or less grammar but could not write simple English decently; children who had "been over" arithmetic but "had no grasp upon the simple essentials of that science." The two criticized the bad schoolhouses and poorly trained teachers. Alderman wrote, "I find that only a small fraction of the teachers have had the advantages of any ampler training than that offered by the public schools . . . [;] professional training for their difficult work they have had but little. About twelve per cent of them have read a technical work on teaching."

Alexander Graham who conducted institutes in the summer of 1890 gave in his report a glimpse of educational progress in the counties that he visited. He was pleased with the interest shown in education in Madison County. Thirty-seven schoolhouses had been constructed during the past six years, ten of them costing $1200 apiece, twenty-five costing $500 each; only two were built of logs. Yet only twelve teachers attended the institute. In contrast was the one held in Waynesville, where seventy teachers attended and visitors occupied all of the remaining space in the room. In Graham County the message of the institute, that "Every child has the same right to be educated as he has to be free; the one right is as sacred as the other," was opposed by some, one person being heard to remark, "Men who talk like that ought to be lynched." Thirty teachers attended the institute at Robbinsville in Graham County, and a group of four or five hundred Republicans and Democrats listened to Graham, but he was dissatisfied with the reception of his address.

Later when he visited Franklin he attributed his success there to the influence of the splendid normal schools that had been held in the town for so many years, and he lamented, "Oh, Franklin! if the mighty educational work which had been done for thee had been done in Robbinsville, it would have repented long ago." At Hayesville he addressed the Farmers' Alliance. The crowd was large and the interest was great. He called Clay "the banner county on education" and complimented the county on the establishment of Hayesville College and its influence, concluding, "I think they will have four more schools of high grade in Clay in the near future." [The college had 190 students, but it lasted only one year.] Clay County had a small population, and there were only eighteen white teachers, six of whom received three-year certificates during the course of the institute, an unusually large percentage to qualify for that honor. At Webster, Jackson County, eight certificates were issued and at Waynesville nine certificates were earned. Graham wrote, "I never met a nicer people or more earnest teachers, and I was struck with the absence of old teachers. I examined not more than three gray heads." In eight counties he addressed over four thousand people on education and free schools and issued fifty-three certificates.

The institutes were almost like a great religious revival, and their influence was inestimable for the inspiration they gave in the movement for educated teachers in the mountainous portion of the state. In 1889 the county board of education of Jackson County held an institute at Webster, followed by a state institute in charge of Edward P. Moses, one of North Carolina's most dynamic educational leaders, superintendent of the Raleigh schools, who had taught at the summer normal school at Chapel Hill and had won some great disciples for the teaching profession. Among the teachers attending the institutes at Webster was Robert Lee Madison, who was to found a future state university in the mountains.

A youth from Lexington, Virginia, Madison had come to Jackson County in December 1885 at the age of nineteen to teach in the Qualla community. By 1889 he was serving in two capacities, editor of the newly-established *Tuckaseigee Democrat* in the new town of Sylva on the Ducktown Branch of the

Western North Carolina Railroad, and teacher for the second year in the school at Sylva. This was a subscription school, the public money having been spent for "patent desks." The forty-odd students ranged in age from six to twenty-three, and the subject matter, from the ABC's to algebra, rhetoric, and French. Madison's stay in Sylva, he looked upon as "marking time," although he had abandoned his plan to study medicine and had decided that teaching was to be his profession. To prepare for his profession he had accumulated eight or ten first class books on the subject. A small group of his students volunteered for a class in practice-teaching which he had organized, and he dreamed of a permanent school for educating teachers. In July when Madison attended both of the institutes in Webster he was won by Moses as McIver and Alderman had been. Madison later reminisced: "As never before I became inspired. The effects of his [Moses'] mastery of the principles of education and of his stirring style and contagious enthusiasm for the sacred vocation of teaching were irresistible and convinced me more than ever that . . . I must devote myself to teaching . . . and find my work here in these delectable mountains." As the institute closed Moses was impressed with young Madison's examination paper, and after a talk with him offered him the principalship of a high school in Raleigh, but the offer was declined as the young man chose to stay in the mountains.

Later that year Madison accepted an invitation to teach the rural Cullowhee High School in Jackson County. With forty public school children it drew only forty dollars a year from county funds and a few cents a year per capita from the state treasury, totaling just enough to pay a teacher $22.50 a month for a two-month term. Yet the patrons of the school guaranteed a salary of $400 for a ten-month year. The public-spirited community intended to have a good school. Boarding students from other districts were welcomed and were housed in the neighborhood at prices ranging from four to six dollars a month. Some of the "school-minded men" even put up little houses or "shacks" or allowed students to build such houses on their land, so they might "batch" and keep the cost at "the vanishing point." Enrollment grew rapidly to approximately one hundred and the school was obviously a success. The following year Cullowhee High School attracted students from neighboring South Carolina as well as from other counties and had a staff of three teachers including the principal, Madison, a music and art instructor, and a primary teacher. Commencement in 1890 was colorful, lasting three days. A sermon was preached by D. B. Nelson of Asheville and an address was given by Kope Elias, prominent lawyer of Franklin. Madison recalled: "Music for the occasion was furnished by the Cherokee Indian brass band of sixteen instruments played by Indian boys in uniform. Large crowds attended all the exercises and basket-dinner in abundance was served each day. Such was the lavish hospitality of the community that for three days, all visitors from a distance were housed and fed — and their horses too — without charge. Some near-by homes had as many as fifty for a single meal; and when the beds were all full, pallets of quilts were spread upon the floors, so that if accommodations could not be palatial they could at least be palletable."

In 1893 Madison saw an opportunity to make his dream come true. The state was experiencing a momentum toward practical education as a part of a movement of the farmers in North Carolina as in many other states to organize for their common interest. In 1887 an influential Farmers' Alliance was fostered in the state by Colonel L. L. Polk and his periodical, *The Progressive Farmer*. Farmers had serious financial problems during the eighties and nineties and they were convinced of the benefits to be enjoyed from better public schools and from colleges that could provide a practical education. Under the influence of a crusade for agricultural education the State Agricultural and Mechanical College was established near Raleigh in 1887. In 1890 a large number of farmers were elected to the legislature, and in 1891 the "farmers' legislature" established the Normal and Industrial School for White Girls and the Agricultural and Technical College for Negroes, both at Greensboro, and the School for the Deaf and Dumb at Morganton.

In this rash of legislation for schools, Madison perceived an opportunity for an appropriation for a normal department at Cullowhee. He first proposed to Walter E. Moore, member of the General Assembly from his district, that he introduce a bill to establish a normal department in connection with some existing high school in each of the nine congressional districts in the state, providing $3000 to each, a total of $27,000. The state would have no capital outlay and all of the public schools in the state would benefit from improvement of teachers. When Moore replied that such a bill would have no chance to pass at that session, Madison asked him to introduce a bill providing $3000 for a normal department at Cullowhee. The measure passed with an annual appropriation of $1500, as one act in a decade of legislation for higher education.

In 1895 a fusion legislature dominated by Republicans and Populists established a normal department at Slater Industrial Academy at Winston, for Negroes, which had been in operation for three years as a private institution named for John F. Slater, philanthropist. The school grew into Winston-Salem State Teachers College, and in 1969 the General Assembly designated it Winston-Salem State University. It and the Salisbury Normal School established in 1881 and abolished in 1903 were the only ones in the western half of the state for training Negro teachers, and they were too far away from the mountain counties to help the Negro teachers there. As salaries of Negro teachers were less than those of white teachers, the Negroes in Western North Carolina were almost invariably men or women with no preparation for the work. Biddle University at Charlotte, now Johnson C. Smith University, offered normal school work, but graduates of the university found employment in the cities where pay and living conditions were better than the rural schools offered.

The law that created the appropriation for Cullowhee placed its normal department under the care and supervision of the State Superintendent of Public Instruction, who had power to regulate it and to discontinue it if he found the department inefficient or unnecessary. The principal of the high school was authorized to confer three-year first-grade certificates valid throughout the state to graduates. Students preparing to teach were not required to pay tuition. By 1894 the appropriation began to pay dividends when twelve normal-course graduates went out to teach. The next year sixteen first-grade certificates were granted.

In 1899 Principal Madison reported that seventy-six students representing seven counties were attending the normal school and that eighty had been granted scholarships for the 1900–1901 term. The department had furnished more than two hundred public school teachers, most of them teaching in the rural schools. He characterized the work of the department as a "unique and very necessary one." He admitted that the work of the Normal and Industrial College and of the Department of Pedagogy at the state university was of a much higher order than the

QUALIFICATIONS OF WHITE AND COLORED TEACHERS IN WESTERN NORTH CAROLINA, 1911–1912, IN SOME COUNTIES

County	1st Grade	2nd Grade	3rd Grade	Normal Training	College Diploma
White					
Ashe	774	36	—	4	5
Buncombe	132	4	—	86	53
Rural	132	4	—	44	16
Asheville	—	—	—	42	37
Burke	15	50	—	16	7
Clay	14	6	—	3	3
Henderson					
Rural	54	17	—	14	9
Hendersonville	—	—	—	3	6
Macon	41	25	—	14	4
Madison	46	32	—	28	12
Mitchell	55	30	5	55	6
Wilkes					
Rural	120	40	—	48	5
N. Wilkesboro	—	—	—	5	4
Jackson	69	5	—	69	10
Watauga	43	38	—	81	2
PER CENT OF TOTAL	44%	20%	.4%	25%	11%
Colored					
Ashe	—	10	—	—	—
Buncome					
Rural	10	8	—	11	3
Asheville	—	—	—	17	1
Burke	1	9	—	2	—
Clay	—	1	—	—	—
Henderson					
Rural	5	5	—	—	—
Hendersonville	—	—	—	—	2
Macon	—	4	—	—	—
Madison	—	4	—	2	1
Mitchell	—	4	—	2	—
Wilkes					
Rural	6	16	—	10	—
N. Wilkesboro	—	—	—	—	—
Jackson	2	—	—	2	—
Watauga	—	3	—	—	—
PER CENT OF TOTAL	20%	52%	—	9%	4%

Source: *Biennial Report, 1910–1912.*

Cullowhee institution was able to offer; but the two former were preparing teachers for academies, city schools, and some of the colleges. He wrote: "Our sphere, while an humbler one, most largely affects the great body of public school children outside of the towns. Our specific work is to prepare teachers for the rural and village elementary schools, and there is no other State institution, so far as we know, that is doing this to any appreciable extent. . . . It is just as necessary that normal instruction of teachers be provided for as that the term of rural public schools should be lengthened. 'As is the teacher, so is the school.'"

The curriculum was that of the secondary school with teacher training courses added. The academic instruction included spelling and defining, arithmetic, grammar, composition, English literature, elementary algebra, United States history, North Carolina history, civil government, political and physical geography, physiology and hygiene, physics, and elementary Latin. The professional work consisted of theory and practice of teaching, principles of education, history of education, psychology applied to teaching, lectures, and professional reading. From this beginning the school grew to be Western Carolina University, discussed earlier.

A new building was completed at Cullowhee for the Normal department in 1904, most of the $7,500 required having been subscribed by private individuals. It was located in a wooded tract of about three and one-fourth acres contributed by David Rogers and named in his honor "Rogers Park." The demand for graduates was so great that it could not be met. A summer school was held in the summer of 1904 with a faculty of seven, including E. P. Moses. Teachers from Graham, Clay, Macon, Haywood, and Transylvania counties as well as from Jackson attended and Madison hoped to make the summer school a permanent feature of the school's work. He asked that the annual appropriation for succeeding years include funds for summer schools on a larger scale. He ended his report for 1904 with the assurance that the "patriotic legislators" would encourage in every way the work which "means so much in this promising, yet long-neglected section of our State."

Madison remarked in the 1904 report that there were "demands for the establishment of similar institutions in other parts of the state," and he encouraged the legislature to continue and to enlarge provisions for training young men and women for teaching in the rural and village elementary schools. This advice had already been acted upon by the General Assembly in 1903. In 1902 Principal Madison had met Blanford Barnard Dougherty, co-principal with his brother, Dauphin Disco, of the Watauga Academy in Boone. The two brothers had built the academy, 1899–1900, furnishing half the money from their own assets and cash. The rest was contributed by citizens in the area as a result of a fund-raising campaign that reached across the county, the gifts ranging from twenty-five cents to the $500 from Moses H. Cone, industrialist, who had a summer home in Blowing Rock. The total of the contributions was said to be near $1100. B. B. Dougherty had degrees from Carson-Newman College and from the state university, while Dauphin Disco Dougherty had his bachelor's degree from Wake Forest College, which the younger brother had also attended for one year. Both brothers had been teachers in academies and in Holly Springs College. Edwin A. Alderman had been president of the state university when Blanford Dougherty was a student there, and M. C. S. Noble had been Professor of Pedagogy. Both no doubt influenced the young man's interest in teacher training, as did his employment in the summer of 1899 holding institutes in eight counties along the Blue Ridge. Blanford Dougherty was county superintendent of Watauga County at the time the new academy was built, and from the beginning some of Watauga Academy's graduates became teachers. So when he met Robert Lee Madison in the summer of 1902 while both were serving as instructors in the summer school at Mars Hill College, he learned about Cullowhee's appropriation from the state for the support of a normal department. He plied Madison with questions about how to get state aid for teacher training, and by the end of the summer he had fixed his determination on turning Watauga Academy into a teacher-training school with state support. Captain Edward F. Lovill wrote a bill and Dougherty himself went to Raleigh to present his case — his first visit to the state legislature. He later told about his harrowing experiences. Governor Aycock, President McIver of the Normal and Industrial College, the president of the state university, and the State Superintendent of Public Instruction were all against starting a new training school. Perhaps they remembered how ineffective the eight normal schools of the 1880's had been. After William Newland of Lenoir agreed to present the bill, he and Dougherty waited three weeks to get a hearing before the Committee on Education. That committee reported unfavorably, but a favorable minority report made it possible to place the Newland Bill before the General Assembly. Dougherty made an hour-long speech to a joint session, and the House passed the bill, but the Senate vote was a tie. Clyde Hoey, a senator from Cleveland County, the presiding officer in the Senate at the time, voted in favor of the measure and thus it passed. Henceforth Blanford Dougherty was to visit Raleigh during the sessions of every General Assembly until his retirement as president of Appalachian State Teachers College in 1954. The school, to be called the Appalachian Training School, would receive an appropriation of $1500 for a building, when a like amount had been paid by private individuals, and an annual payment of $2000 for teachers' salaries and maintenance. Tuition was to be free to all who would sign a pledge to teach two years in the public schools of North Carolina. Nowhere in the act was Watauga Academy mentioned. The board of trustees for Appalachian Training School, members of which were appointed in the law, were to open books for subscriptions to the building fund and to choose a site for the training school. Several communities in three counties competed for the new school and made offers of land, money, and buildings. Boone offered $1000 and the use of Watauga Academy, and the board of trustees voted to make Boone the permanent location of the school, with Watauga Academy serving as its first home. This school became Appalachian State University in 1967.

Friends of Cullowhee in the General Assembly favored the passage of the Newland Act, and from 1903 until 1912 when Madison's first administration ended, he and Dougherty cooperated in winning support for the two training schools. (Cullowhee's name was changed in 1905 to Cullowhee Normal and Industrial School.) In 1908 the legislature voted to establish a third training school for teachers in the eastern part of the state at Greenville. A number of efforts were made from time to time to abolish both of the western schools and to establish one more centrally located in or near Asheville. The greatest threat came in 1911 when Dr. George T. Winston, former president of the state university and the State Agricultural and Mechanical College, upon his retirement to Asheville became a spokesman for a training school in Asheville and introduced a bill in the General Assembly to establish in Asheville a western training school. Both Dougherty and Madison were in Raleigh working against Winston's measure and it was rejected by the Appropriations Committee. Again an effort was made in 1915 when Governor Locke Craig, a resident of Asheville, in his gubernatorial address asked the General Assembly to establish in the western part of the state a school similar to the one at Greenville. Craig completely ignored the two existing training schools, but it was understood that he would have the new institution absorb the ones at Cullowhee and Boone. The lawmakers rejected the proposal by a slight majority.

The trustees of the Appalachian Training School elected B. B. Dougherty Superintendent and D. D. Dougherty Principal. There were at the beginning four other faculty members, one of whom was Mrs. D. D. Dougherty. Three terms were held, a three-month fall term, a spring one of four months, and one in the summer of two months. The public school of Boone was incorporated in the training school and all between the ages of six and twenty-one could attend the free term in the fall. They might attend the other terms by paying a small fee. Students from a distance were given room and board at twenty-five cents per day.

In the suburbs of Boone near the Watauga Academy a tract of four and one-half acres was purchased for $212.50, and a brick building (which continued in use until it was demolished in 1967 to make way for a new administration building) was erected at the cost of $7000, of which $3000 was contributed by three hundred people, many of them poor. The building consisted of four classrooms, a library, office, music room, art room, and auditorium. Three hundred twenty-four students attended during the first year, one hundred ninety being public school teachers. Fifty-one came from a distance and paid tuition.

In 1907 the General Assembly provided for rural public high schools, but it was many years before such were established in Western North Carolina and the two training schools continued to offer high school subjects with the teacher training superimposed. In 1917 a State Educational Commission was created by law to investigate various features of public education. The commission was authorized by the statute to call upon any source for aid, and the General Education Board was asked for advice. The study of North Carolina's schools was placed in the hands of Dr. Frank P. Bachman, working in cooperation with Dr. Wallace Buttruch, president, and Dr. Abraham Flexner, secretary of the General Education Board. Concerning Cullowhee

Boys and girls were segregated at Appalachian Training School. The building on the left was the original Watauga Academy

Normal and Appalachian Training School, the report concluded that these were "of non-standard type which must for the present necessarily be of lower grade, that is, admit students who have less than a standard four-year high school course." This, the commission believed necessary because, they said, "only three counties in the western part of the state, Cherokee, Buncombe, and Haywood, had standard high schools." The recommendation of the commission was that henceforth both training schools leave all high school instruction to such high schools as should be established in the mountain sections and concentrate on normal school work for elementary teachers. The commission urged, "[These schools] should admit students who have completed the seventh grade of elementary schools and graduates of non-standard high schools, and give them a two, three, or four year course planned to meet the needs of elementary teachers. No graduates from standard high schools should be admitted; such graduates would go to Chapel Hill, to Greensboro, or to Greenville, or to private colleges offering courses in education. . . . Both schools are well located to serve their respective sections, and if properly developed and equipped should graduate at least 100 elementary teachers a year."

During the next decade the histories of the two schools were roughly parallel, because legislative action applied to both of them. Cullowhee State Normal and Industrial School had been upgrading its curriculum for several years, and by the academic year 1917–1918 it was offering two years of college work. In 1921–1922 the high school had separated from the college, although it remained on the same campus. Two years later a plan was inaugurated to have the high school absorbed by the local school system under the joint sponsorship of the normal school and the county board of education. The local public school after that time served as a laboratory and practice center for the college.

Governor Cameron Morrison showed an interest in the two western schools and pledged his support for an increased appropriation and expansion of their programs. In 1921 the General Assembly made Appalachian a standard two-year normal. There, as at Cullowhee, the elementary and secondary schools would be sponsored jointly by the county board of education and the normal school. Physical plants and enrollments grew, and in 1925 the legislature granted new charters to both institutions and changed their names to Appalachian State Normal School and Cullowhee State Normal School. Enrollment continued to increase and the administrations of both began to plan ways to expand the usefulness of the normal schools to the areas they served. The tendency of normal schools in the nation was to expand to four-year college programs, as state requirements for the education of teachers were advanced. Consequently the General Assembly in 1929 again changed the names of the schools, to Appalachian State Teachers College and Western Carolina Teachers College. The two were now qualified to educate teachers for high schools and were admitted to membership in the American Association of Teachers Colleges, later renamed the American Association of Colleges for Teacher Education. Eventually both were accredited by the Southern Association of Colleges and Schools. Their further development into multi-purpose universities was discussed in a preceeding chapter.

CHAPTER NINE

From the Heart, the Hand, and the Head

To create handicrafts that are beautiful satisfies a basic human need. Handicrafts are creative, often emotionally pleasurable. They are popular, cherished by their collectors and purchasers. They recreate artifacts of the past and they become the art works of the present and the future. They are usually the product of the leisure time of their crafters. They are wonderful as an avocation. Their sale brings added money, like surplus value, to their creators, but it seldom brings in an income sufficient to enable their makers to lead a good life. Handicrafts are, however, the products of the heart, the hand, and the head.

When people moved into the mountains, "took up land," built their cabins, made their homes, they had to be self-sufficient. For their necessities and to satisfy their creative urges they fostered and developed their handicrafts. They had to furnish their mountain homes or log cabins with wooden articles and furniture hand crafted from the native forest. They had to make their beds, tables, chairs — all of their furniture. These articles of wooden furniture were necessary, useful, and often artistic. Corn had many uses. Cornmeal was a useful food for people; corn fed livestock; corn shucks were used for bed ticks, to braid collars for mules and horses, to make mats for the cabin door-way and floor, and to make dolls for girls and toys for children. Chair covers were made from corn shucks, pipes from corncobs and reeds.

Basket making required skill and ingenuity. Baskets were made of oak splits, willow switches, or wild honeysuckle vine. They were used for barter, and the art of basket making was passed on from father to son.

Many mountain craftsmen made musical instruments: banjos, fiddles, guitars, dulcimers, recorders, and shepherds' pipes. The instruments were necessary for the square dances or "play party games" or to accompany the singing of old ballads and carols.

Potters' clay or kaolin was plentiful and there were a number of potteries in which churns, crocks, jugs, plates, pitchers, and dishes were made. Moist clay was held against the potter's kick-wheel and clay was shaped into the desired piece. These shaped pieces were then baked in kilns.

There were iron mines and forges called bloomeries. In 1788 the North Carolina legislature passed a law granting three thousand acres of cultivable land to anyone who would build a forge and carry on iron making. These bloomeries were necessary for making iron for horse shoes, kettles, plows, the metal parts of wagons. Three early forges were in Buncombe County, and in 1820 mining began at Cranberry. The crude iron was processed at the mine into bars. The bars were then bound together and hauled by oxcarts to blacksmiths. The pioneer blacksmiths made kettles, cranes, and irons for fireplaces, axes, knives, nails, rifle barrels, and many farm tools. For generations members of the same families were famous blacksmiths and gunsmiths, like the members of the Boone family of Burnsville who have made artistic pieces of wrought iron. Daniel Boone VI of Burnsville did wrought iron work for the Williamsburg restoration and ornamental iron work for the Hound Ears Lodge.

Many mountaineers raised sheep, and most women carded and spun the wool and wove the cloth for use in the house and for clothing for all members of the family. Many of them took pride in the beautiful bedspreads that they wove, and every woman wanted at least one fancy quilt. Pieces of colored cloth were woven, saved, and then pieced into the designs of these quilts, which were and still are made in many pretty patterns. The bedspreads or coverlets often called "kiverlids" were made of wool woven on to a flax or cotton warp. They were dyed into lovely soft colors with home-made vegetable dyes.

With the coming of the railroads and the highways the mountain handicrafts declined. Cheap cotton cloth largely supplanted handwoven materials; and metal tools, utensils, and objects could be bought from hardware stores more cheaply and in greater variety than they could be made by village blacksmiths. Although mountain families had little cash, they bartered eggs, chickens, dried fruit, herbs, furs, cordwood, galax leaves for these "storebought" articles. Only a few women continued to weave. The old women forgot how to read "drafts" (pattern drawings) and to make the old familiar patterns.

The art, the craft, the skill requisite for weaving cloth and designing quilts and coverlets were disappearing and being lost in North Carolina when in 1895 Miss Frances Goodrich was presented a forty-year-old coverlet as a gift. With the coverlet was a "draft" for the "Double Bowknot" pattern. Miss Goodrich, an Ohioan, and a woman companion were living in Brittain's Cove twelve miles north of Asheville and running a school there. These women were interested in the social and cultural welfare of the mountain people. Miss Goodrich was much impressed by the beauty of the coverlet. She sent it to friends in the North and asked if there would be a market for artistic handicrafts like coverlets, quilts, and hand-woven materials. When she learned that there was an avid market, particularly for woven items, she organized the women in the neighborhood. They located old looms and experienced weavers, especially the ones who knew how to do vegetable dyeing. Younger women began to learn to weave from the older ones, and the coverlets woven in the mountain homes and cabins found a ready sale.

Miss Goodrich set up a roadside market near Marshall on the main highway leading from Tennessee to South Carolina. Here a man named Allan had had a stand for drovers during the turnpike days. He had pens for the stock and accommodations for the drovers. As a result Miss Goodrich chose the name the Allanstand Cottage Industries. An annual exhibit of Allanstand Crafts was held in Asheville, and in 1917 a permanent salesroom was opened in that city to show these products, particularly to the well-to-do visitors who were interested in creative crafts. This venture was so successful that the Allanstand Cottage Industries were incorporated. Except for a small dividend to the stockholders, the profits were to go to the craftswomen and craftsmen of the mountains. In 1931 Miss Goodrich gave the Allanstand Industries to the Southern Highlands Handicraft Guild.

Miss Goodrich thus was a pioneer in popularizing and preserving mountain crafts. Her aims were to give paying work to women whose homes were too isolated to enable them to market their wares; to give these mountain women a new hope and a new interest; to save from extinction the old crafts and to produce artifacts of beauty and value. In addition to coverlets, bedspreads, quilts, the Allanstand Industries produced and sold table runners, mats, pillow and dresser covers.

Mrs. George W. Vanderbilt was interested in mountain people. To aid some of them to secure economic competence, she established a school in Biltmore Village shortly after 1900. She employed Miss Eleanor P. Vance and Miss Charlotte Yale to teach the people carding, spinning, weaving, dyeing fabrics suitable for men's suits. The original intent was to secure the wool from the sheep on Biltmore Estate and to have the wool prepared for weaving in the mountain homes. The woven product was rough. Misses Vance and Yale went to the British Isles to study the production processes used there. As a result the wool for the Biltmore Homespun cloth was imported, and the Biltmore suiting fabrics, exceptional in beauty and wearing quality, were woven locally and with pride. The weaving department of the industries grew rapidly. It was under Mrs. Vanderbilt's personal care until it grew to such size that commercialization was needed. Mr. Fred L. Seely of Asheville bought the industries and moved the establishment and personnel to the site on Sunset Mountain near Grove Park Inn where it has remained. This weaving industry became the largest project of its kind in the world.

In the summer of 1914 Rufus Morgan founded the Appalachian School. During the summer of 1913 he had visited every home in the neighborhood. In those homes he found rare old coverlets, blankets, linsey-woolsey, and jeans — all hand woven. In the smoke houses and outbuildings were the relics of handhewn looms and spinning wheels. These had been discarded when "store-bought" cloth became readily available. In the home of Aunt Susan Phillips he found a spinning wheel and a loom still being used for weaving. There were many pattern coverlets which she had woven before her eyes had given out. Because of Aunt Susan Phillips and Aunt Cumi Woody, Morgan decided to include hand work in his program of instruction. He wished to train the heart, the hand, and the head, and hand weaving fitted admirably into his scheme. On

Demonstration of spinning and weaving at the Brinegar cabin on the Blue Ridge Parkway   NATIONAL PARK SERVICE PHOTOS

one of his trips to Valle Crucis he found a comparatively young woman who was weaving the patterns and designs of her ancestors but was adapting them to the needs of the present day. This young woman, Mrs. Finley Mast, promised to teach Rufus Morgan's sister Lucy Morgan to weave. Miss Lucy was then a student in a Michigan teachers' college. Rufus Morgan urged his sister to come, to learn weaving from Mrs. Mast, and to teach it at Penland at the institution Morgan had named Appalachian School. Miss Lucy came. In 1923 she learned weaving and began to teach it, both to the girls in the school and to the older women in the community. There was a two-fold purpose in teaching the people to weave: to perpetuate this native craft and to provide for the people a more abundant living. New efficient looms were taken to the homes of the mountain women and they soon wove "log cabin" rugs. Miss Lucy had to walk to each home to teach the women to warp, beam, and "thread up." By 1925 roads had been built and she could drive in her truck to the homes of the weavers. Next a weaving house was established, and it was difficult to furnish work for all who applied for it. Then Miss Morgan and Miss Burt (who had succeeded Rufus Morgan) had to market and sell the woven products. In 1924 there was a booth at the State Fair in which Miss Morgan sat weaving. The State Department of Vocational Education became interested and employed her as a vocational education teacher. She received federal assistance for vocational training for women and girls. Also $1400 worth of woven goods was sold at the Episcopal Church convention in New Orleans. She went to Chicago and studied for nine weeks under Mr. Edward F. Worst, learning very complicated weaving. Shortly afterward, in 1928, a pottery department was added to the Weaving Institute. "Proff" Koch of Chapel Hill (director of the North Carolina Playmakers) christened the organization "the Penland Weavers and Potters." In 1928, $2400 worth of goods was sold at the Episcopal convention and $18,000 worth during the year 1929.

The Penland School was incorporated in 1929 as a non-profit educational institution. It has six large buildings and a number of smaller ones valued years ago at $240,000. In 1930 Miss Morgan learned to make pewter plates and acquired a set of molds. Next she exhibited these mountain products at the Chicago World's Fair in 1933 and 1934. Here were sold all of the craft products that had accumulated during the depression years. The school course now includes weaving, ceramics, metal work, enameling, woodworking, and design. Students have come to Penland from every state in the Union and from sixty foreign countries.

In Tryon the Mountain Industries operated by Mrs. George Stone, the "little lady of mountain industries," produce beautiful rugs, splint baskets, chairs, porch furniture, and homespun textiles. Mrs. Stone rendered a valuable service in creating a demand for the products of the crude looms and tools of mountain craftsmen. George Stone is manager of the Appalachian Hand Weavers. In 1915 Miss Eleanor Vance and Miss Charlotte Yale left Biltmore to start the Toy House in Tryon. They trained boys and girls to make toys from native wood: turning, carving, and painting them by hand. Miniature soldiers, animals, and groups were among their products. The Blue Ridge Weavers Shop was started by Mr. and Mrs. George Cathey. A hand weavers' shop sells the popular homespuns woven in Tryon.

Another interesting handicraft industry was the Spinning Wheel founded by Miss Clementine Douglas, a native of Florida and a graduate of Pratt Institute in New York. Miss Douglas had taught in Wellesley, Massachusetts, in New York City, and for three summers had worked at a settlement school in Harlan County, Kentucky. In 1927 she came to Saluda, then to Asheville and set up at Beaver Lake a weaving industry which was appropriately named the Spinning Wheel. Work was done in

190 / Part II: A Changing Society

The insignia of the Southern Highland Handicraft Guild

The old draft of the "Lover's Knot" pattern discovered by John Goodwin. Here it is called "Summer and Winter." This kind of draft, preserved in a few family archives has made possible the recreation of old weaving patterns.
Draft for Lover's Knot Coverlet (Instructions to the weaver)
"The two forward Shafts carries half the yarn, to put in your binding thread you mustt tread the two forward shafts, and the fourth back ones, and the blue to be put in by the draft it ought to be slaid low hang your treaddles, one after the other beginning with the forward shaft and wright hand treaddles."

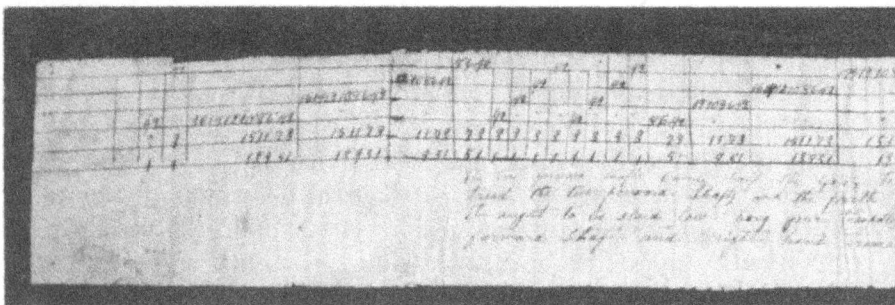

The Lover's Knot, that has been traced to Scotland in the 1750's, is John Goodwin's most popular pattern

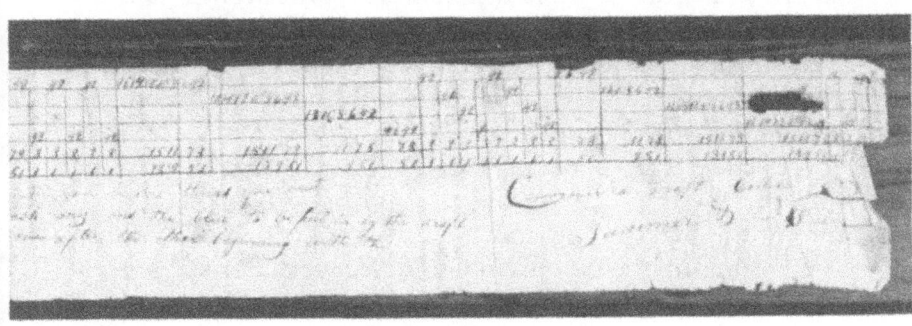

her loom room and in homes in the area. She visited the homes, superivising the work, taking materials and picking up finished pieces, and encouraging the weavers. She purchased an old log cabin in the Reems Creek community, had it moved, and made an attractive place for a salesroom. Subsequently she moved the Spinning Wheel industry to the Hendersonville Road a few miles south of Asheville, where a log house was used for Miss Douglas' home and attached salesroom. Later she sold the industry, and the new owners discontinued the weaving and ran the Spinning Wheel as a sales center for handicrafts.

Today handcrafted articles from Western North Carolina are nationally known and handicrafts are flourishing. Penland, the John C. Campbell Folk School, and the Crossnore School still teach weaving. The fame of the Penland School is worldwide. Visitors come from many states and countries and all are inspired by the excellence, the variety, and the creativity of the craftsmen. Particularly noteworthy has been the woodcarving at the John C. Campbell Folk School. Mrs. Campbell and Mrs. Muriel Martin, director of handicrafts for twenty-five years, taught those in the neighborhood and at the school to "whittle with a purpose": to carve crowing roosters, laughing mules, flying birds, soaring angels, a four-foot high St. Francis, and the figures for Christmas creches. Penland and the John C. Campbell Folk School are production centers as well as schools. They offer short courses in crafts as well as year-round craft programs.

In 1928 Mrs. John C. Campbell took the lead in organizing the Southern Highlands Handicraft Guild. More than twenty mountain schools and community centers interested in crafts were included among the charter members. This guild established standards for handicrafts and markets the products in selected craft centers.

The Vanderbilts are gone, but the Biltmore Homespun shops continue to weave beautiful fabrics for men's and women's suits. The Valhalla Weavers of Tryon weave cloth for suits and for neckties. At Penland Ronald Cruikshank directs the weaving of tapestries, knee blankets, and baby blankets.

Among the outstanding and successful craftsmen of Western North Carolina are the Goodwin Guild Weavers. For six generations members of the family have been weavers of hand crafted designs and materials. In 1951 Mr. John O. Goodwin, the head of the family, moved from Virginia to Blowing Rock. Mr. Goodwin has done field work in collecting 527 different hand-loom drafts since 1907. He sets up the looms to weave these designs that have been popular throughout American history and that are still prized by interior decorators. The looms are power operated, but skilled craftsmen are required to use the techniques of the operators of hand looms. Much of the weaving is done by hand and the weavers have to have hand loom weaving skill in order to maintain high quality and authenticity. Four hours are required to make a single-weave coverlet. The most popular product is a double-woven design, "Lover's Knot," which takes sixteen hours to weave. Mr. Goodwin copied the pattern and created his own "draft" before he became the possessor of a "draft" on yellowed paper that was over one hundred years old. Other creations are shawls, afghans, place mats, table cloths, and drapery materials. These are sold nationally and are cited by *American Heritage* for their authenticity.

Under the North Carolina Fund for Watauga, Avery, Mitchell, and Yancey counties a program has been organized to encourage craftsmen of all four counties to make handcrafted products: toys, dolls, wood carvings, quilts, coverlets, furniture, wrought iron, and hand woven articles. The products of these craftsmen are ingenious and often beautiful. One of their most famous products is the Bader-Hofecker grandfather clock. Made of Honduran mohagany, it is lavishly inlaid. Both Glen Hofecker and William Bader are distinguished artists in wood. The Blue Ridge Hearthside Crafts Association, a cooperative, was organized to sell the products. It purchased two prestige shops, and operates as Creative Crafts.

Special orders come to the various agencies for materials for historical restorations such as that of the Vance birthplace. Homespun and woven curtains were needed. There were draftsmen who could produce them — replicas of those in use 150 years ago. President and Mrs. Woodrow Wilson had spent their honeymoon at Arden, North Carolina. They became interested in mountain folk — in their welfare and in their crafts. In 1913 Mrs. Wilson ordered coverlet fabrics for the Mountain Room in the White House, which she was redecorating. Mrs. Elmeda Walker, who lived near Marshall, was chosen to weave the fabrics.

194 / *Part II: A Changing Society*

A member of the Blue Ridge Hearthside Crafts Association makes fringe for a bedspread   ASHEVILLE CHAMBER OF COMMERCE PHOTO

Independence Hall in Philadelphia was being restored, and a request came to Penland School to weave many yards of green baize material for covering fifteen tables. The material requested was green homespun dyed with vegetable dyes. Since Penland did not have the equipment to produce material in such a quantity, Mrs. John Littlewood of Ashe County dyed and carded the wool. It was necessary that the cloth be forty-five inches wide. The Penland looms were made for thirty-six inch cloth. Therefore the Macomber Company in Massachusetts built a loom for forty-five inch material. Colonel John Fishback, Penland weaver, then wove the cloth on the wide loom. Mr.

The Woodrow Wilson honeymoon cottage at Arden
ASHEVILLE CITIZEN-TIMES CO.

John Mulcahy, specialist in charge of the restoration of Independence Hall, praised the material as being a true reproduction of that used when the Declaration of Independence was signed.

The making of hooked and braided rugs is another profitable mountain craft. The rugs are made in the homes of individuals and groups and also in the handicraft centers like that in Boone. Rugs are often braided from loopers, by-products bought at the hosiery mills. Hooked rugs are made at Crossnore and by the Valhalla Weavers in Tryon. Block prints, silk screens, hand-knitted, hand-crocheted, and hand-fringed artifacts are made in many mountain homes.

Richard Chase, the famous folklorist, collector of folk ballads and tales, author of the *Grandfather Tales* and the *Jack Tales*, rendered an invaluable service to the mountain folk of Watauga County. He taught them folk songs, folk dances, folk tales. Also he induced them to make folk toys and hand-crafted articles. The money earned by Beech Creek folk for these toys and creations enabled many Watauga County people to lead richer, more creative lives and to enjoy greater economic well-being. Richard Chase has left the mountains but Jack Guy has taken the lead in continuing his work.

There are more than two hundred small woodworking shops in Western North Carolina and in East Tennessee. In

196 / Part II: A Changing Society

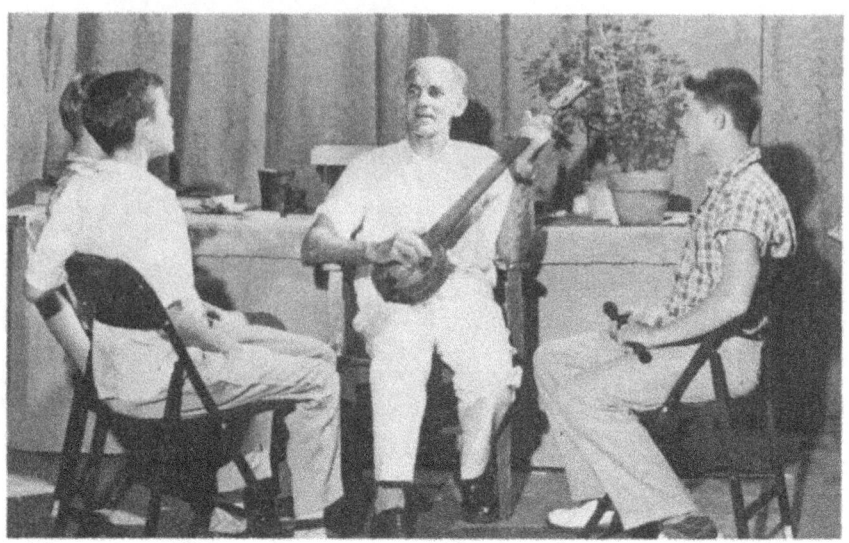

Richard Chase, story teller, folk singer, author, plays a fretless banjo
ASHEVILLE CHAMBER OF COMMERCE PHOTO

Wood carvers illustrate their work at the Asheville Crafts Fair
ASHEVILLE CHAMBER OF COMMERCE PHOTO

1961 they were organized into the Appalachian Woodworkers. They make chairs, desks, bookcases, clocks, bedsteads, tables, bowls, rolling pins, candleholders, and whittled or carved items. Ed Purdom of Macon County and B. H. Moody of Blowing Rock made all kinds of furniture and refinished wood furniture. They designed and made pieces to the customers' demands. They also made items that they believed would challenge their creative talents. Ralph Smith of Bryson City makes pleasing coffee tables. The Woody family near Spruce Pine have made chairs for 150 years. They specialize in ladder-back chairs. S. P. Mace of Mars Hill and John Barnes of Franklin also make ladder-back and other types of chairs. A retired Baptist minister of Spruce Pine, H. M. Stroup, makes the cabinets for traditional grandfather and grandmother clocks of cherry, walnut, or mahogany. He imports the works from Germany. Many craftsmen specialize in making doll furniture. The miniature pieces are exquisite in both design and workmanship. John Councill has a woodworking shop at Sands near Boone. His craftsmen make small wooden items. Bowls, lamp bases, book ends, gavels are turned out on many a mountain lathe. Fruit such as grapes, apples, bananas are carved from poplar, pine, apple, buckeye, cherry, walnut, and birch — all native woods. Many carvers specialize in carving one item: a pig, a duck, a squirrel.

Dulcimers, violins, banjos, guitars are still made by mountain craftsmen. Famous makers of dulcimers are Ed Presnell and the late Frank Proffitt. Odd S. White of Asheville has made violins for many years.

When the village blacksmiths were no longer needed to make guns, tires, axles, hubs for wagons, most of them sought other occupations. In very few towns can one now find a blacksmith shop. In many a town, however, there is a machine shop like Gunter's in Spruce Pine. These machine shops can make or repair almost anything made of metal. Other smiths or families in which there have been smiths began to forge wrought iron objects like those used by the pioneers.

Pewter pieces, plates, bowls, trays, candlesticks are made at Penland and by Dr. and Mrs. Ralph Morgan of Dillsboro. A number of artisans do beautiful work with copper and brass. Enameling is an antique art, and the products are popular. The enamel is applied to a copper base. The copper is worked into the desired shape, then finely powdered glass is sprinkled on the piece, after which it is fired in an electric kiln at 1500 degrees fahrenheit. Mrs. Joe Godfrey of Hildebran, who learned the art at Penland, is one of the gifted enamelists in Western North Carolina.

Many of the mountain craftsmen make jewelry of silver, copper, wood, ceramics. Often these jewelers or gemologists work with the semi-precious stones that are found in the mountains. They cut and polish the stones and design gold, silver, copper settings for them. Stuart Nye of Asheville became famous for designing and making silver and copper jewelry in a dogwood pattern. He designed the first piece in 1933. Now the craftsmen in the industry he started continue to use this design and other flower shapes in metal.

Pottery making is one of the oldest crafts known to man. Pots, pitchers, plates, dishes have been useful, well-nigh essential to man from the beginning of time. Quite early man learned to work with damp clay. Eventually he learned to shape it on a potter's wheel and harden it by heating, ultimately baking it in kilns. Fine clay from Macon County was shipped to Josiah Wedgewood in England in 1767. The Penland Pottery existed in Buncombe County near Candler from 1831 until 1952. The Pisgah Forest Pottery near the old Penland Pottery makes pitchers, mugs and other pieces, specializing in a "cameo" design that looks somewhat like Wedgewood pottery. It was founded about 1900 by W. B. Stephen and his mother. Today it is operated by J. T. Case, the grandson of the founder, and by G. C. Ledbetter. The beautiful coloring, the delicate glazing, the decorating are all done by hand. Wood from the native forests is used for all the firing. Another highly successful pottery is that of Davis P. Brown, called the Brown Pottery, at Arden. Since long before the advent of the white man, the Cherokees have made pottery. They make and sell many kinds of dishes, pots, pitchers, vases that they have made. Lynn Gault is a noted potter of Brasstown. He and eleven other artists have banded together and commercially market their products in Gatlinburg, Tennessee. Just a few miles from the North Carolina line at Laurel Bloomery in Tennessee is the Iron Mountain Pottery. This is highly successful and its products are prized by those who buy them. The industry has provided much needed employment to people of the area.

Dolls have always been popular and doll makers in the mountains are often artistic. Mrs. Orus Sutton of Boone makes dolls

Indian potters at Oconaluftee Village
ASHEVILLE CHAMBER OF COMMERCE PHOTO

Note the variety of shapes achieved by gifted mountain potters
ASHEVILLE CHAMBER OF COMMERCE PHOTO

to resemble their little girl owners. Many mountain craftsmen make dolls of corn shucks to represent the mountaineers as caricatured in fiction: long, lean, emaciated. Others make dolls with bodies of stuffed cloth, and heads and feet of dried apples. A lovely doll fourteen inches high and called the Mary Crossnore doll for Dr. Mary Martin Sloop is made by Miss Marian Brown of Crossnore. These dolls are exquisitely dressed and wear shoes made from kid gloves.

A number of different kinds of hearth brooms are made and sold at various gift shops in the mountains. Other mountaineers make leather belts, purses, moccasins. Quite popular and widely sold all over the mountains at gift shops and fruit stands are wild fruit delicacies: jars of jellies, jams made of wild strawberries, raspberries, crabapples, wild grapes, and a conserve from pumpkin.

The value of handicraft products made in North Carolina annually is over a million dollars. Above and beyond the money, the creation of these handcrafted articles gives unmeasurable joy and satisfaction, for who does not enjoy making things that are beautiful that he and others can enjoy?

CHAPTER TEN

Literature

Until shortly before the Civil War the literature about Western North Carolina was not different from that of the frontier. About 1858 there began the discovery of the region; and Western North Carolina became a rich field for journalists, writers of local color, folklorists, fictionists. These writers began to exploit the peculiar language, customs, manners, and humor of the mountain people.

Visitors were impressed by the contrasts with low-country life and manners. Writers and tourists spread superficial accounts of mountain life. People seeing a run-down mountain cabin still say, "Look, there's a typical mountain home." By far the majority of the mountain people, however, live in comfortable homes. The minority live in shacks and suffer from penury and lack of opportunity. What is the hope for the "poor mountaineers"? Some advocates urge that the younger people leave the mountains and seek jobs in industrial plants in the lowlands. If so, they may well become badly adjusted slum dwellers and renters, and will often be recipients of welfare aid. Others advocate that industry be brought to the mountains so that hill people can live on their own land, drive into a neighboring town, work in a local factory, and operate their farms after working hours. This crisis of the spirit for the mountaineer in the face of the modern world has been largely neglected by the literature of the region to the present day. Our local literature, the subject of this chapter, is largely concerned with the past and the picturesque, with some mixture of the grotesque. Some of the best is strictly personal.

It is illuminating to consider the mountaineer as he has been treated by writers of fiction. Notable authors have written about Western North Carolina and mountain life, and foremost among them is Thomas Wolfe. Wolfe was both a Western North Carolina writer and a writer about his region. No one has written more graphically and more intimately about his land and his people, and no writer from North Carolina has ever achieved the fame and the respect accorded to Wolfe. Born October 3, 1900, he ever afterwards celebrated the beauty of October in "Old Catawba." His father, William Oliver Wolfe, was originally a Pennsylvanian, but his mother, Julia Westall Wolfe, was a mountaineer of mountaineers. She was related to the Westall, Penland, and Patton families whose members lived all over the mountains.

Wolfe had an abnormally prolonged infantile relationship dominated by his mother. He was not weaned until he was almost four, and he had beautiful curls to his shoulder. His mother would not let them be cut until he was nine. In addition to being overly protective, she must have had an almost "insane nigardliness" and an insatiate love of property. Her stinginess warped the social attitudes of the sensitive boy. He was self-conscious also about the lower middle class status of his family. He lived with his mother at the Old Kentucky Home boarding house at 48 Spruce Street. His father, a stonecutter, lived in another house. W. O. Wolfe had his faults, but he was a man with gargantuan appetites and a generous soul. There must have been a great contrast between the parsimony of Mrs. Wolfe and the open-handedness of her husband. This dichotomy in the family possibly caused Tom to begin his search for a spiritual father whom he found in Maxwell Perkins. Tom's best writing is about Asheville and its people. They are seen through the tortured eyes of a sensitive boy. Wolfe's major works are *Look Homeward, Angel* (1929), *Of Time and The River* (1935), *From Death to Morning* (1935), *The Story of a Novel* (1936), *The Web and the Rock* (1939), *You Can't Go Home Again* (1940), and *The Hills Beyond* (1941).

Only a part of Wolfe's work is about the mountains and his people, but he has given the most graphic account extant of family life and relationships among Asheville people. In *Look Homeward, Angel* and *The Web and the Rock* he described his boyhood, but perhaps the most complete account of mountain life appears in the fragment of a novel, *The Hills Beyond*, that

"My Old Kentucky Home," where Thomas Wolfe lived
ASHEVILLE CHAMBER OF COMMERCE PHOTO

was to be a history of North Carolina and of his family. The family is fictional, of course, but it resembles a mountain family. The narrative stops in 1880, twenty years before Wolfe's birth. He was revolted by the bleakness of his environment, and he was enthralled by trains because the sound of a train whistle was a symbol of escape. He had contempt for his mother's people, the mountaineers, because they were the familiar and the known, but he sympathized with their loneliness, the barrenness of their lives, and like them, he saw both the loneliness and the grandeur of mountain life, its beauty and its sordidness. His writings about the hillmen contain both romance and realism. He admired their courage and their independence, but he lamented the fact that they were old and worn out by middle age by their hopeless struggle against their environment. He objected to the romantic stories of mountain life by writers like John Fox, Jr. The great mountain barrier that "rimmed in life" was the determining influence upon the destiny of the people. Wolfe was a rebel against the superstition and romanticism of the South, but he admired the people for their courage and their proud history.

His descriptions of his father, his mother, his brothers and his sisters are so real that the reader feels like one of the family sitting before the fire and hearing tales of birth, death, ghosts, superstitions, and gossip — such tales as epitomize the literature and history of the mountain people. To Wolfe the mountain man was racially pure, clannish, isolated, a hard drinker, quick to fight, prone to violence, cruel, eager to engage in lawsuits, and a sharp, conniving trader.

Wolfe remembered his mother's talk and her tales. He used with unerring skill the dialect formerly spoken by mountain people but now largely archaic. He described satirically the fundamentalism, Calvinism, puritanism, and primitive fatalism of their religion: their belief in a jealous and a wrathful God, in Hell-fire and damnation. They believed also that fiddle music and dancing were sinful. They had a false morality. A woman made her relatives swear not to let the undertaker see her unclothed; another said she would rather see her daughter dead than married to a drunkard. Divorced women were virtually outcasts.

Wolfe believed that hill people should not become out-migrants, that those who left the hills were destroyed by the degeneracy, the immorality, the prostitution, and the poverty of life in the slums of cities. Not only were they exploited but they lost the freedom and the healthy amusements of the hillmen. Yet he described them unfalteringly as the "poor white litter of the hills"; as tall, gaunt, slatternly, with snuff juice rolling down their chins. They might be filthy, degraded, incestuous, infested with rickets and pellagra; but they had a pride, an independence, a virility, a zest for life. In his tales he recreated the life of a folk.

Critics said that Wolfe was too verbose, too incoherent, too autobiographical, that his words burst like a pent up flood, but William Faulkner said he might have become the greatest of Southern writers. Certainly he was a man to "match the mountains," the greatest writer produced by North Carolina. He felt that literature was a transcript of life, and he sought to transcribe the life of his people: his family with their weaknesses and peculiarities, his Asheville neighbors with all their selfishness and materialism. He described the slatternly people gaping at strangers, the gaunt farmer, the dawdling Negroes, the fire and brimstone preachers, the resort-town cupidity of the citizens of Asheville, famed for its loveliness but ruined by pettiness and greed. He described the frenzy of the "boom" as a result of which everyone was going to get rich. But alas after the "boom" there was the "bust" and a desert of frustrated hopes and ambitions. He lamented the commercialization, the unsightly billboards, the fencing in of natural attractions, the cheap tourist honky-tonks, the bank president who became a convict, the mayor who misused city funds and committed suicide.

Wolfe was called a "Judas Iscariot, a Benedict Arnold, ... Caesar's Brutus, the bird that fouls its own nest, ... a viper that an innocent populace had nurtured, ... an unnatural ghoul to whom nothing is sacred, not even the tombs of the honored dead, ... a vulture, ... a jackass, ... a baboon." Yet Thomas Wolfe did return to Asheville seven years after the publication of *Look Homeward, Angel*, and he was welcomed with adulation. Today when his name is mentioned in Asheville, faces become rapt, eyes glow, shoulders straighten, for Thomas Wolfe was one of their own.

The most distinguished figure ever to come out of Western North Carolina was Zebulon Baird Vance — governor, senator, fabulist. Thomas Wolfe created a character and family remarkably similar to Vance and his family. This character was Zachariah Joyner. Wolfe gave a realistic, tongue-in-cheek account of the settlement of the West and the political conflict between the East and the West. Old Catawba was of course North Carolina. *The Hills Beyond* is a fictional-historical analogy. Wolfe satirized the selfish control of state appropriations by the East, its claim to superiority on the grounds of birth, breeding, family, and its descent from the "lost colonists," pointing out that the state was more distinguished for its homespun quality than for its aristocratic ancestry. Zachariah Joyner, a country lawyer from the West, was elected governor in 1858. He attacked the "humbug aristocracy" of the East, asserting that most early settlers had come to eastern North Carolina because the English jails were full and to keep from being hanged. Wolfe asserted that under Joyner (Vance) the "representatives of privilege" had to bow before the rights of humanity, that they should stop thinking about where they came from and think about where they were going. He described the Joyner family, their ancestry, the patriarchal Bear Joyner, quoting myths, legends, stories about "Bear" and Zach. These anecdotes are typical of mountain humor that Wolfe learned in his youth. Many of them are in the folklore about Vance. Wolfe said that to the hillmen Joyner (Vance) was not only their Lincoln but their Paul Bunyan and

Davy Crockett in one. He was a "living prophecy of all that they might wish to be," of what they might become.

Wolfe satirized the mountain attitude toward liquor — that none was bad, that some was just better — and also the fundamentalist attitude that "gettin' drunk" was a cardinal sin — worse than murder. Bear Joyner said that one man had killed another. Zach was relieved; he had believed that the man had done something really bad like "gettin' drunk." He took a dig at mountain honesty and morality when Bear asked young Zach if he had watered the milk, sanded the sugar, fixed the scales. When Zach answered in the affirmative, his father said that they would then have family prayers.

Speaking through Joyner, Wolfe wrote with great indignation of the desecration of the mountains by lumbermen, saying that "some vast destructive 'suck' . . . some compulsive greed had been at work: the whole region had been sucked and gutted . . . denuded of its primeval treasures." Then he showed his resentment of the disparaging treatment of the mountain people by "exultant Ph.D.'s," tourists, "consecrated school marms from the North," social service workers. He did not feel that the hill people should be subjected to the condescending efforts of uplifters and dogooders.

Wolfe criticized lawyers and the law. Bear Joyner said that he would make a lawyer out of his son because he wouldn't work. Wolfe asserted that the lawyers and the courts were not used to uphold the law but to subvert it for "personal advantage and private profit." This is perhaps a nearly justified criticism of our legal system. Equally he despised the materialism of business men who devoted their lives to the pursuit of the almighty dollar and who objected to spending money for education because of resultant higher taxes.

Wolfe admired the courage of mountain people but he felt that the veneration of the Civil War was useless and excessive. Finally in "the Battle of Hogwart Heights" he made fun of aristocratic pretensions. *The Hills Beyond* reveals Wolfe's great gifts as a satirist and a mountain humorist.

There is much travel literature about Western North Carolina. Colonel William Byrd in 1728 described the beauty of the mountains. Colonel Henry Timberlake wrote his memoirs in 1765; William Bartram (1773), Andre Michaux (1792), and the Reverend Francis Asbury (1821) gave detailed accounts of their travels. James K. Paulding wrote *Letters from the South* (1817); J. W. McClung, *Sketches of Western Adventure* (1832), Joseph Pratt, *Incidents of Border Life* (1839). J. G. M. Ramsey in his *Annals of Tennessee* (1853) wrote also of Western North Carolina. William Gilmore Simms, the famous South Carolina historical novelist, set parts of three books in Western North Carolina locales. James Weir's novels are also set in this region. Robert Strange in *Eoneguski* (1839) wrote a novel of the Cherokees. This was the first novel written by a North Carolinian with scenes within the state. He felt that the history, customs, people of North Carolina could provide scenes and episodes, exciting, interesting, and suitable for fiction. This novel deals with the crossing of the mountains, the conflict with the Cherokees, and Andrew Jackson's fight with the Creeks. Calvin H. Wiley, first state superintendent of schools, planned three novels: *Alamance*, about the Regulation; *Roanoke*, about Eastern North Carolina; and *Buncombe*, about Western North Carolina, and he compiled a series of *North Carolina Readers* which were used in the state. Other early writers about Western North Carolina were Frances Hodgson Burnett with her *Esmeralda* and *Lodusky*; Constance Fenimore Woolson with her *Up in the Blue Ridge* and *For the Mayor*; and Mary Greenway McClelland, author of *Oblivion*. John Cairns, Jr., son of the proprietor of the Reems Creek Woolen Mills, was one of the nation's most eminent ornithologists. His articles were published in the best known scientific journals of the nineteenth century.

The *Fisher River Sketches* of Harden E. Taliaferro preserve the way of life and the dialect used by the first settlers of Surry County and their descendants. These stories were enacted and told in the 1820's, written down in 1859. The "musters" were among the interesting occurrences described. Musters were semiannual, in May and November, and the old "Revolutionaries" were present: the "capting," "leftenant," "sarjent," and all the "ossifers." "They knowed a thing or two about military tacktucks." At the musters there was always plenty of "knockem-stiff" whiskey. On one occasion Hamp Hudson was supposed to supply the refreshments, but while he was distilling the brew his dog Famus fell into the mash tub and was distilled. When Hamp reported this to the musterers their faces fell, but after drilling they became so thirsty that they drank all of Hamp's "knock-em-stiff" — Famus or no Famus.

Taliaferro described the picturesque dresss: the rawhide, stitched-down shoes, a "linsey" tow and cotton shirt to the knees, the dressed buckskin pants. People walked to meetin'; courtin' boys and girls would walk side by side, the girls carrying their shoes in a "redicule" until they got in sight of the meetin' house. The boys were barefoot.

The young folks got together for grubbings, log-rollings, reapings, corn-huskings, wheat-threshings. The girls would have sewings and quiltings. On these occasions as soon as the work was done, the fiddle sounded and they danced and courted all night. For one young man to get the better of another in "sparkin'" was considered legitimate and was called "cuttin' out."

Dick Snow wouldn't give up his courting Sally Tucker and said, "I never gins up a thing as long as there's a pea in the gourd." Sally's folks were "Methodises" and kept "arter" him to "git ligion." At the quarterly meeting he determined to "make his jack" and he went up with the mourners. The "circus rider" prayed over him "like he was beatin' tanbark off 'un trees in the daid of winter." Dick tried gettin' ligion a whole week, but then he backslid. Mountain youth married young. They married first and "scuffed for their fortuns" later. Fighting was a common occurrence. They "knocked with their fists, butted, gouged, kicked with their feet." Bullies kept their thumbnails long to "feel a fellow's eyestrings. . . ." In similar vein Taliferro described many customs of the frontier society.

Rebecca Harding Davis gave personal and intimate descriptions of mountain life as she saw it in the late 1870's. She described Morganton as "caught on the shelving side of a hill." She traveled on the Western North Carolina Railroad from Morganton to the end of the completed line "in a chasm between two precipices." Later in 1880 this railroad reached Asheville. At the end of the line there was a rough, temporary hotel where her party spent the night. She wrote: " . . . the gorge swarmed with hundreds of wretched blacks in the striped yellow convict garb. After their supper was cooked (over campfires) and eaten, they were driven into a row of prison cars, where they were tightly boxed for the night, with no possible chance to obtain either air or light." The convicts lived in the most squalid condition, their labor was Herculean, and hundreds of them died that the railroad might be built and a gateway opened to the west. Mrs. Davis and her party spent the next night at Alexander's, twelve miles from Asheville. Alexander's was a noted stage stop. Mr. Alexander, "like all other farmers in the mountains 'took in' travelers, gave them an excellent supper and comfortable beds and sent them on the next day with a team of mules and a shackly old cart up the steep trail to the house of the guide, William Glass." They were on their way to ascend Mount Mitchell. Later they visited Waynesville, of which she wrote that they " . . . found many such picturesque little villages as this hidden in these interminable ranges, perched on sunny peaks above the clouds, or nestling in gorges. . . . Half of their unpainted, weather-beaten houses are always empty, the inmates having apparently died, or gone farther into these sleepy wildernesses and then forgotten to come back. . . . There are always one or two families of educated, well-bred people. They have little money, but they feel the need of it less here than anywhere else in the States. They live in roomy wooden houses, the walls, ceilings, and floors frequently made of purplish fine-grained poplar; which no Persian carpet or tapestry could rival in beauty; they have no new books but they have read the old ones until they are live friends . . . ; they dress in homespun, and sit on wooden benches, but knowing nothing of fashions or bric-a-brac their souls sit at ease and are quiet, and they never feel the void of an empty pocket." As Mrs. Davis's party approached Qualla their road "had been a cartway roughly cut along the sides of the mountains for about fifteen miles along the Tuckaseigee River, but the spring torrents year after year had washed it away, and neither white man nor Indian had ever laid a log to repair it." It was then called a bridle-road, and from the description one can see the need for roads in Western North Carolina: "[The] 'Nation' (the Cherokees) was hidden in isolated huts in the thickets among the ravines of the Soco and Oconoluftee hills. The 1500 Cherokees had 10,000 acres under cultivation, no village, no school, no gathering place of any kind. Grass knee deep before the door of the little church. They were wretchedly poor. Only in 1875 were they given possession of the land on which they had lived for more than 500 years. After the party left the Indians, they came to a cabin: " . . . built on the slope of the little river. It was a sample of the better class of mountain huts. The log walls gaped open in many places. Inside, they were pasted over with newspapers, the ceiling hung with hanks of blue yarn, red peppers, bunches of herbs, and Indian baskets filled with the family clothing. The hut was divided by an open passage into chamber and kitchen. One side of the latter was given up to a roaring fire of logs." Mrs. Davis quoted the woman of the house: " . . . it's two months since I've seen the face of women, white or red. That's what ails the mountings — the awful loneliness. Whar I was brought up, five miles from hyar, it would be a year that we'd not see a living face. But times is mendin' now. They hev Sunday school an' pra'r some'ars every two months. Us folks goes twenty miles to 'em. Go in the mornin', an' stay all day. Exercises lasts till noon; then we have dinner, an' in the afternoon we can see each other, and hear the news. Last pra'r was powerful big; they was nigh onto twenty folks thar."

Mrs. Polly (their hostess) told them of conditions in the mountains. The people were pitifully poor and ignorant. There were some men of seventy who had never seen a wheeled vehicle. Mrs. Davis summed up conditions thus: "Near the Tennessee line their huts are often merely sheds. They cook in a pot, and sitting around it, eat out of it with wooden spoons. At night a couple of boards are lifted in the floor, and disclose a hollow in the earth beneath filled with straw, in which the whole family kennel together. In the morning the boards are replaced, and all cares of housekeeping are over . . . They are hospitable, honest, and, in their ignorant way, God-fearing. Their sole recreation is goin' to preachin' or pra'r two or three times a year when some itinerant missionary penetrates the mountains. Nothing could be falser than the sketches which have been given of them that confound these uncouth but decent people with the Pikes or swaggering ruffians of the West."

Sidney Lanier, esteemed Southern poet, musician, writer of prose, stayed at Richmond Hill near Asheville, visited at Rugby Grange, Henderson County, the home of George Gustav Westfeldt, and spent his last days in the Wilcox house at Lynn, near Tryon, where he died of tuberculosis in 1881. There are memorials to him in Tryon and at Calvary Episcopal Church in Fletcher. His last poem, "Sunrise," was written in Lynn and dedicated to Westfeldt. Vivian Yeiser Laramore, poet laureate of Florida, spent many summers in Western North Carolina and wrote the "Ballad of the Silver Flute," praising Lanier as the "great poet of the South enriching the folklore of his land."

Azure-Lure — a Romance of the Mountains, was a souvenir of Asheville and Western North Carolina edited by Idyl Dial Gray. In it one finds this excellent travel-poster description of the region: "In Asheville an azure sky and a brilliant horizon meet. Nature's artistry presents sparkling waterfalls, precipitous cliffsides, the colors of thousands of flowers, singing rivers, limpid lakes, bottomless pools, cloud-banked mountain-rimmed peaks and the bluest skies under heaven in this land of perpetual vacation."

O. Henry (William Sydney Porter) is associated with Asheville and Weaverville. He married Sara Coleman from Weaverville, an author, and he spent the winter of 1909 in the home of Mrs. Porter's brother, John S. Coleman. He died in Asheville June 10, 1910.

Mrs. Frances Fisher Tiernan (Christian Reid) the popular novelist, wrote a book about Western North Carolina which she called *The Land of the Sky*. In this book she described the lovely mountains, the blueness of the skies, the beautiful, fertile valleys, the glorious sunlight, the cloud-shadowed ranges of mountains which reached the sky. As a result of her book the whole region has been aptly named "the Land of the Sky."

Shepherd Dugger wrote *War Trails of the Blue Ridge* and *The Balsam Groves of Grandfather Mountain*. In the introduction to the latter he included a poem "The Land of the Sky":

> Will you come to Grandfather, "The Land of the Sky,"
> Where a banquet of glory is spread for the eye . . .
> Where the mountains do rear their summits above
> The storm and the cloud to the regions of love. . . .
> Ye ones that are feeble, why linger and die,
> Come up to the beautiful "Land of the Sky. . . . "

In 1904 Horace Kephart came to Hazel Creek to write of the Southern highlands. He had been able to find little written about them, although he probably knew the novels of Charles Egbert Craddock, pen name for Mary Noailles Murphree, and those of Constance Fenimore Woolsen. He became the Dean

Illustration from "Christian Reid's" Land of the Sky, the book that gave the name to the mountain area

of American Campers and wrote *The Book of Camping and Woodcraft*, which had its twentieth printing in 1960. He wrote for *Adventure Magazine, Field and Stream, Sports Afield, Outing,* and the Asheville *Citizen.*

In 1913 Kephart's *Our Southern Highlanders* was published. Ten thousand copies were sold of the first edition; in 1957 the seventh edition was published. The book contains authentic portraits of mountain life. Kephart described real mountain people, not caricatures; he wrote down the language and expressions really used by the people. In Bryson City on the old Bryson place there is a marker: "On this spot Horace Kephart, Dean of American Campers and one of the principal founders of the Great Smoky Mountains National Park pitched his last permanent camp. Erected May 30, 1931, by Horace Kephart Troop, Boy Scouts of America, Bryson City, North Carolina." The tribute was justified because Kephart had fought valiantly for conservation, writing article after article urging the preservation of the forests. He wrote: "When I first came into the Smokies, the whole region was one superb forest primeval.... My sylvan studio spread over mountain after mountain ... and it was always clean and fragrant, always vital, growing new shapes of beauty from day to day. The vast trees met overhead like cathedral roofs.... Not long ago I went to the same place again. It was wrecked, ruined, desecrated, turned into a thousand rubbish heaps, utterly vile and mean. Did anyone ever thank God for a lumberman's slashing?" There was an editorial in the Asheville *Times*: "His eloquent appeal should be the textbook of those who are interested in securing a national park for this mountain empire."

John C. Campbell's *The Southern Highlander and His Homeland* (1921), published two years after his death by the Russell Sage Foundation, was prepared for publication by his wife, Mrs. Olive Dame Campbell. This book aroused national interest in the problems existing in the Southern mountains.

Wilma Dykeman Stokely, born in Asheville in May 1920, is descended from old New York and North Carolina families. Bernadette Hoyle wrote in *Tar Heel Writers I Know*: "Being from the Middle South and the author of non-fictional studies of the region, she is thoroughly at home with both her setting and her characters" in *The French Broad*. Her novels are *The Tall Woman, Look to this Day*, and *The Far Family*. With James Stokely she wrote *Neither Black nor White*. *The Tall Woman* tells the story of the Southern mountain people. "It is neither quaint nor satiric, but it deals seriously with a community caught in eternal change and post-Civil War problems." Lydia McQueen is the tall woman. She was tall, not so much in stature as in character and influence. "The writing is skillful, and the lilt of the mountain speech of the time is musical to read." The novel is rich in detail and in atmosphere and at times has the flavor of some of the old ballads. Its theme is the erosion of both land and character by greed. The characters emerge "breathing, talking, living." *The French Broad* is a book that moves like a river. "It has the continuous, ceaseless, smooth-flowing style that moves relentlessly toward the sounding sea."

Wilma Dykeman's *Prophet of Plenty* is a biography of Dr. Willis Weatherford. A fund-raiser extraordinary, he brought the nation's conscience to bear on the problems of the mountain people. In 1900 he was one of the few prophets of a new and hopeful South, which was "bogged down in poverty, dominated by Northern capital, suffering under discriminatory freight rates, plagued by demagogues, and fighting for its life after Reconstruction. There was one hope — education, education for leadership, for jobs, for citizenship." Weatherford gave inspiration and hope to Southern youth. He told them that regional competance depended upon industrial competence, that the human resources were the heart of the region's hopes.

Weatherford built the Blue Ridge Assembly near Black Mountain and brought in brilliant leaders to meet the many eager young students. He became a leader of a region which had been bypassed by American life. His work, his faith, his ideas caught the imagination of governmental leaders and philanthropists and made those in state and nation see that this land of poverty could become a land of opportunity. His message to those in the mountains was to look to the young people, give them quality education and the region would grow great. He was a champion of all races, and he pioneered in the formation of the Commission on Interracial Cooperation. For decades he was a leader on this commission and did much for race relations in the South. He obtained the money, selected the staff, and took the lead in gathering information for and publishing *The Southern Appalachian Region: A Survey* (1962), financed by the Ford Foundation. This survey revealed conditions in the mountains and made recommendations for their amelioration.

John Ehle, author of seven novels and three books of nonfiction by the time of this writing, winner of the Sir Walter Award and the Mayflower Cup, is one of the ablest portrayers of mountain life and character. *The Landbreakers* (1964) was quite popular. *The Road* (1967) created a sensation and was included in *Reader's Digest Condensed Books. The Road* is almost a mountain epic. It tells the story of the struggle, the drama, the conflict, the almost superhuman efforts required to build the Western North Carolina Railroad from Old Fort to Asheville. The tribute to the convicts is deserved. Most exciting was the pulling of the engine over the mountain so that the 2,000-foot tunnel could be attacked from both ends. The completion of this link of the railroad was of vital importance to all in Western North Carolina.

Fred Chappell wrote two novels, *It Is Time, Lord* and *The Inkling*. He described Canton, called it Withers, and the Champion Paper and Fiber Company he called the Defender Paper and Fiber Company. He says the stench of the paper mill can be smelled for miles. He asks, "What would the town do without the paper company?" and answers with "What is it doing with it?" His "Prodigious Words" appeared in *Southern Writing in the Sixties*. John Yount, born in Boone, wrote a novel, *Wolf at the Door*. A selection, "The Store," appeared in *Southern Writing in the Sixties*. It contains a good description of a boy going to a country store and peering at the candy through the greasy, flyspecked glass.

"These are my mountains," said John Parris, who through *Roaming the Mountains* and *My Mountaineers, My People* showed his love for and appreciation of the people of Western North Carolina. He continues: "If you are born in the mountains, you can't put them out of your heart and soul. There is a peace and quiet that makes you feel closer to God...." Parris was born in Sylva, November 23, 1914. He became a successful newspaper man and a notable author. Nothing in the mountains is an old or jaded story to him. *Roaming the Mountains* (1955) originated around the firesides and homelife of his family and his neighbors. Many of his tales he learned from his grandfather William Riley Tallent, who had a great zest for life. The titles of his chapters are indigenous to mountain life: "Hot Biscuits and Sourwood Honey," "The French Broad Is a Gypsy," and "In Huckleberry Time Courtin's a Pleasure." Parris does not write in dialect but he uses idioms and descriptive terms which create a colloquial feeling such as "He's a distiller of corn' likker, and brother, hold on to your hat," "He's the overlord of a one-room log cabin with a dozen mouths to feed and a passel of hound dogs in the yard," and "In the Carolina Highlands, June is a whip-poor-will."

One of the significant writers born in Western North Carolina was Rebecca Cushman. She was an editor of the *Southern Review* and a special contributor to the *Christian Science Monitor*. She wrote *Swing Your Mountain Gal, Sketches of Life in the Southern Highlands* in 1934. This book is not fiction; it contains a series of sketches taken from mountain life. Each short narrative is a deft character portrait of the rugged but dignified mountaineer. The book makes a real contribution in that it is a spiritual interpretation of mountain life. Her mountaineer Guy Norman is a man who leaves one with a quickened consciousness of life. He is hospitable, unaffected, natural. He says: "We live jest plain.... Life's jest the way you hold it up.... If you've done that you're all right when you come to take your pillow...."

Margaret Morley wrote the challenging *The Carolina Mountains* in 1913. Muriel Sheppards's *Cabins in the Laurel* created quite a stir when it was published in 1935, many people in Mitchell County feeling that she exaggerated conditions there.

216 / *Part II: A Changing Society*

One of the most authentic accounts of mountain life, people, customs, and fiction appeared in the 1,500 page doctoral dissertation of Dean Cratis Williams, "The Southern Mountaineer in Fiction." Dean Williams asserted that in the decades following the Civil War the mountaineer became a caricature in fiction. He became a type — uncouth, ignorant, violent, poor, a fundamentalist, a moonshiner, but hospitable and with feudal courtesy. Stock characters in mountain fiction are the feudist, the witch crone, a jealous mountain youth, an outlaw, a benevolent but illiterate landowner, an idealistic teacher, a hardshell preacher, a demagogue, a rich, heroic outsider, a beautiful but ignorant mountain girl, the corrupt and stingy justice of the peace or sheriff. The preacher and the sheriff find the teacher and education threats to the power structure or to their personal positions.

Perhaps the greatest poet of Western North Carolina has been Olive Tilford Dargan. Born in Kentucky, she moved to North Carolina in 1906. She wrote five books of poetry: *Semiramis* (1906), a closet drama in iambic pentameter; *Pathfinder* (1914), lyrics about the North Carolina mountains; *The Cycle's Rim* (1916), fifty-three sonnets on the death of her husband, the prize-winning book as the best book of poetry of the year by a Southern writer; *Lute and Farrow* (1922), lyrics of the mountains; *The Spotted Hawk* (1958), which won the Roanoke-Chowan poetry award. In addition to her poetry she wrote two volumes of short narratives: *Highland Annals* (1925), and *From My Highest Hill* (1941). Under the pen name of Fielding Burke she wrote the novels *Call Home the Heart* (1932) and *A Stone Came Rolling* (1935). In 1962 her fifteenth book, a collection of short stories, *Innocent Bigamy*, was published. She lived most of her life in Swain County, but in her old age she resided at the Blue Bonnet Lodge in West Asheville. She wrote chiefly of the mountains and mountain people.

James Larkin Pearson was born in the Moravian Falls section of Wilkes County, September 13, 1879. His people were very poor. There were few books in the home: a cheap Bible, a small almanac, a dictionary, and an old Methodist hymnal. Off and on he would attend the one-teacher free school. He taught himself the alphabet by reading circus posters and studying Webster's blue-back spelling book. When he was four years old he began reciting poetry. One cold winter day he and his father were riding in an old wagon. The father asked if he were cold. He answered: "My fingers and my toes — my feet and my hands — are just as cold as you ever seed a man's." His first poem was "The Vision" (1895). In 1897 he composed "The Song of the Star of Bethlehem" while he was clearing new ground. This poem was printed in the New York *Independent* and for it he received eight dollars. He became a typesetter and the editor of several small papers. In 1910 he began to publish a humorous paper, *The Fool Killer*, which he built up until at one time it had a circulation of fifty thousand copies a month.

Pearson was admired by Upton Sinclair, who printed one of his poems in the New York *Times*. Later Sinclair printed "Fifty Acres," Pearson's best known poem. In 1953 Pearson was named Poet Laureate of North Carolina. He is the author of five books of poetry printed on his own press: *Castle Gates* (1908), *Pearson's Poems* (1924), *Fifty Acres* (1937), *Plowed Ground* (1949), and *Early Harvest* (1952). An anthology, *Selected Poems of James Larkin Pearson*, was published in 1960. Pearson wrote simply of "homey" things in a deeply lyrical vein. His poetry has quaintness, local color. One can get the flavor of Pearson from the following lines:

from "Fifty Acres"

I've never been to London,
I've never been to Rome;
But on my fifty acres
I travel here at home.

from "Here is Wisdom"

Old Andy never went to school
And never read a book.
But he who takes him for a fool
Will need a second look. . . .

from "A Night in June"

The June-bug roosted under a leaf,
And the firefly winked at the cricket
The bull-frog sang from the lily-pond
To the owl in the ivy thicket.

There have been a number of anthologies and collections of North Carolina poetry. In these anthologies many poems were by Western North Carolinians about Western North Carolina. The first such anthology, *Woodnotes, or Carolina*

Carols, was compiled by Tenella (Mrs. Mary Bayard Clark). In this anthology was an anonymous poem, "Swannanoa." In 1883 John Henry Boner published a selection of poetry under the title *Whispering Pines*. This included "Hunting Muscadines on the Yadkin" and "The Cliff" about Pilot Mountain. In 1894 Hight C. Moore published *Selected Poetry of North Carolina* and in 1912 E.C. Brooks an anthology, *North Carolina Poems*. In 1941 Richard Walser edited *North Carolina Poetry* and in 1948 *North Carolina in the Short Story*, in 1953 *The Enigma of Thomas Wolfe*, in 1957 *The Picture Book of Tar Heel Authors*, in 1959 *Nematodes in My Garden of Verse* and in 1963 *North Carolina Poets*.

Carl Sandburg, the poet and Lincoln biographer, bought a 240 acre farm at Flat Rock, "Connemara," the former home of Christopher Memminger, Confederate Secretary of the Treasury. Sandburg was also a folklorist and a song collector.

One of the versatile men in Western North Carolina is Leroy Sossamon. He is pilot, poet, bulldozer operator, newspaper publisher, owner of furniture stores, accredited teacher, owner of a steel construction business, a theater, Ford dealer, operator of a mercy airlift and commercial planes. Having graduated from Appalachian State Teachers College *cum laude* in 1934, he taught English and French at the Presbyterian orphanage at Barium Springs. He bought one business after another, including the Bryson City *Times*, which he publishes. He is connected with the Sossamon Steel Company. He wrote *Backside of Heaven*, a book of poetry, and sold an edition of 11,000 copies.

Henry Alexander Sieber, born in New York in 1931, spent his boyhood in the North Carolina mountains. Influenced by Ezra Pound and T. S. Eliot, his poems carry a message of hope. He assumes that man because of his religion and poetry must not be defeated by life. Two of his books are *This the Marian Year* (1954) and *Something the West Will Remember* (1956). Lovers of Thomas Wolfe like the following lines:

> What right have you to say
> That Tom Wolfe of Asheville
> And Brooklyn, New York
> Didn't talk all the time
> All the time with God
> In Asheville
>   and
> Brooklyn, New York.

A unique Western North Carolina poet is Jonathan Williams. Born in Asheville in 1929, he operates an apple orchard near Highlands. He is a book designer, lecturer, publisher, poet, and operator of the Jorgon press. His broadsides and book titles include the following: *Garbage Letters*; *The Iron Face of the Sun's Child* (1951); *Red/Gray* (1952); *Four Stoppages* (1953); *The Empire Finals at Verona* (1959); *Amen/Huzza/Selah* (1960); *In England's Green* (1962). Williams's poems are included in "beat" anthologies because they are "way out."

Miscellaneous poems about Western North Carolina and by Western North Carolinians were Zebulon Baird Vance's "The Little Patched Trousers," Martin V. Moore's "The Rivers of North Carolina," Reuben J. Holmes's poem "The Valley of the Ashe," and "Tom and Mollie" by the anonymous poet laureate of Mitchell County. Struthers Burt was a novelist, but he wrote a book of poetry, *In the High Hills* (1914). He felt that poetry should touch the intelligent heart. Elliott Coleman came to the Asheville School in 1928. He had published two books of poetry: *Poems of Elliott Coleman* (1936) and *An American in Augustland* (1940).

Among dramatists associated with Western North Carolina are the following: Hatcher Hughes, *Hell Bent for Heaven*, and *Ruint* (Pulitzer prize winner); Lula Vollmer, *Sun Up*; Thomas Wolfe, *The Return of Buck Gavin*; George Tedd, Jr., *King Cotton's Children*; Hubert Hayes and John Taintor Foote, *Tight Britches*; Hubert Hayes, *The Red Spider*, *Blackberry Winter*, and *Smoky Joe*; Mrs. Bertha Herter, *The Harp of a Thousand Strings*; Edward Richardson, *Black Mountain*, a play based on the ballad "Barbara Allen"; Anne Bridgers, co-author of *Coquette*, who had a summer home in the Reems Creek section; Cleves Kinnard, *Common Clay*. Kermit Hunter wrote *Unto These Hills* and *Horn in the West*.

Ellis Credle wrote *Down Down the Mountains* (1934). He is a writer and illustrator for children. This was the first picture book of the Blue Ridge country. Lois Lenski wrote children's books like *Blue Ridge Billy*, which depicts mountain life and customs. Mary Hancock wrote *Menace on the Mountain* (1968), the gripping story of a boy who becomes a man while his father is away during the Civil War. Included is a fictional account of the capture of Fort Hamby from the Bushwhackers. This book was filmed for television by Walt Disney Productions. Miss Hancock's work has appeared in *The Progressive Farmer, Extension, Saturday Evening Post, Sports Illustrated, Pageant, Catholic Digest*, and the *VFW Magazine*. Richard Chase is a distinguished writer, ballad singer, and folklorist. For years he taught songs, dances, and traditional games to mountain children. He sang and collected folklore. He wrote widely and well: *Old Songs and Singing Games* (1938), *The Jack Tales* (1943), *Grandfather Tales* (1948), *American Folk Tales* (1948), *Wicked John and the Devil* (1951), and *Songs As Preserved in the Appalachian Mountains* (1956). Croyden Bell and Thelma Harrington Bell wrote about animals and characters from Western North Carolina: *Snow* (1954), *John's Rattling Gourd of Big Cove* (1955), *The Wonders of Snow* (1957). Ruth and Latrobe Carroll moved to Asheville in 1950. They wrote and illustrated fascinating books for children: *Peanut* (1951), *Salt and Pepper* (1952), *Beanie* (1953), *Tough Enough* (1954), and later, *Tough Enough's Trip, Digby the Only Dog* (1955).

The history of Western North Carolina has been the theme of only one previous book, by John Preston Arthur (1913). He also wrote an interesting history of Watauga County. Foster Sondley wrote a two volume history of Buncombe County. Other county histories are Clark Medford's accounts of Haywood County; Sadie Smathers Patton's writings on Flat Rock and Henderson County; Clarence Griffin's books on Old Tryon County and Rutherford County; Horton Cooper's Avery County history: Margaret Freel's work on Cherokee County and Lilian Thomasson's on Swain County, Judge Johnson Hayes' *The Land of Wilkes*; Nancy Alexander's *Here Will I Dwell* (Caldwell County); T. F. Hickerson's *Happy Valley* and *Echoes of Happy Valley*, which deal with life along the Yadkin from Lenoir to Elkin; and Arthur L. Fletcher, *Ashe County: a History*. Histories of colleges are John McLeod's *From These Stones* (Mars Hill College) and William E. Bird's *Western Carolina College*. O. L. Brown's *Blanford Bernard Dougherty* contains much of the history of Appalachian State University. Dr. Edward Phifer has written scholarly articles about ante-bellum life and conditions in Burke County. Glenn Tucker wrote *High Tide at Gettysburg*;

Tecumseh; *Vision of Glory*; and *Zeb Vance, Champion of Freedom*. Works of Cordelia Camp include *David Lowry Swain, Governor and University President*; *The Influence of Geography Upon Early North Carolina*; and *Governor Vance: a Life for Young People*. She edited *Some Pioneer Women Teachers in North Carolina*. Ina Woestemeyer Van Noppen is the author of four published books in addition to the present one: *The Westward Movement*; *The South: A Documentary History*; *Stoneman's Last Raid*; and, with John J. Van Noppen, *Daniel Boone, Backwoodsman: The Green Woods Were His Portion*. Harley Jolley had published in 1969 *The Blue Ridge Parkway*. George B. Watts wrote *The Waldenses of Valdese*. Pamphlets by Fred B. Cranford, *The Waldenses of Burke County*, and by Ruth Royal Poovey, *The Burke County Gold Rush*, were prepared in conjunction with the Burke County Cultural Heritage Project, pursuant to a grant from the United States Office of Education. Con Bryan's *Confederate Georgia*, has passed through several printings.

A number of other writers about this region are worthy of mention. Bill Sharpe's *North Carolina: a Description by Counties and a New Geography of North Carolina* contains much valuable information about Western North Carolina. *The North Carolina Gazetteer* by William S. Powell is indispensable in locating quaint-sounding places and the sources of their names. Julia Montgomery Street's *Fiddler's Fancy* (1955) is about the folk of the Toe River in Mitchell County. It contains a true rendition of mountain speech, folklore, and customs. Legette Blythe wrote *Miracle in the Hills*, the inspiring story of Dr. Mary Martin Sloop of Crossnore, and with Miss Lucy Morgan he wrote *Gift from the Hills*, the story of Penland School. He also wrote *James W. Davis, North Carolina Surgeon*. Davis spent his youth in Wilkes County.

Jacob Carpenter of Three Mile Creek kept an interesting diary. Horton Cooper discusses it in his history of Avery County. Opie Percival Read, humorist, wrote *The Captain's Romance* (1896), *The Jucklins* (1896), *Odd Folks* (1897), and a number of other novels. *The Jucklins* is a romance about a schoolteacher in Western North Carolina. Maria Poole describes the pervasive superstitions that affected the lives of mountain people. Her novels, such as *In Buncombe County*, give a most damaging account of mountain character. She gives a graphic account of a revival meeting near Asheville. Rosser Taylor wrote *Carolina Crossroads*. Logan B. Logan produced *Ladies of the White House*. Mrs. Edith Erskine of Weaverville and Mrs Charlotte Young wrote several volumes of poetry. Martha Norburn Mead wrote *Asheville the Land of the Sky*. Bill Nye, the humorist, lived in Asheville, and his syndicated column appeared in the Asheville papers. Helen Topping Miller wrote *The Splendor of Eagles*, and George Bledsoe, *The Shadows Point North*, about the impact of summer tourists upon the mountains.

Lewis W. Green has written a first novel, *And Scatter the Proud*, integrating six short stories about life in the Blue Ridge Mountains. The setting is on the crest of Big Lonesome, a mountain traversed by the Blue Ridge Parkway. The characters search for meaning in life. Green says: "The mountaineers asked of the outlanders only that their pride be unmolested, their self-respect honored, their dignity left intact. This courtesy they extended to all others." Alberta Pierson Hannum, (*Look Back With Love*) is full of sympathetic understanding and love of the mountain people and their lore of bygone days. Each chapter begins with an entry from the diary of Jacob Carpenter of Three Mile Creek. She also wrote *The Gods and One, April Thursday, Avery County*, and *The Hills Step Lightly*. The author is an Ohioan, but long a resident of the North Carolina Hills.

Mrs. T. Henry Wilson (Dell B. Wilson) had published in 1969 *The Grandfather and the Globe* based on the Civil War exploits of Keith Blalock and his wife in the Globe-Grandfather Mountain area. Romulus Linney, a descendant of the "Bull of the Brushies," the noted lawyer whose namesake he is, wrote the novels *Heathen Valley*, about Valle Crucis, (1962); *Slowly by Hand Unfurled* (1965); and a play, *The Sorrows of Frederick* (1966).

CHAPTER ELEVEN

The Lore of the Folk

> Booted and spurred and bridled rode he,
> A plume in his saddle and a sword at his knee.
>
> Back come his saddle all bloody to see;
> Back come his steed but never come he.
>
> Riding on the highlands, steep was the way
> Riding in the lowlands, hard by the Tay.
>
> Out come his old mother with feet all so bare;
> Out come his bonnie bride riving of her hair.
>
> The meadows all a-falling and the sheep all unshorn;
> The house is a-leaking and the baby's unborn.
>
> But Bonnie James Campbell nowhere can you see
> With a plume in his saddle and a sword at his knee.
>
> For to home came his saddle all bloody to see;
> Home came the steed, but never came he.

The song that tells this sad story can today be heard and enjoyed by many people who have no idea of life in the country, let alone of life centuries ago in Scotland, because in some localities and in some families there have been men, and women, like Frank Proffitt, who like to sing old songs, and men and women who have wanted to preserve their songs or stories, or legends, or superstitions, so that many people might enjoy and profit from them.

But what importance is there in a song that laments a Bonnie James Campbell that nobody can recall, except in this song, aside from the possibility that he may have been the James Campbell who died in 1594 in the battle of Genlivet? There is no easy answer to this question. Frank Proffitt's answer may be as good as any when he explained the value of a traditional life in a letter quoted in the *Carolina Farmer*: "My folks was of the poorest but they was of the highest moral standards. Not knowing about books or letters, they stored in their memory all of the best of the old proven ways and was forever busy making things for useful and entertaining purposes." Proffitt's tradition was one of people who did not depend on others for values but who made their own standards out of what they had inherited and what they had.

Ballads like "Bonnie James Campbell" were a part of the way of life of the people who came to Western North Carolina around the time of the Revolutionary War, and, depending on the locality, in the decades before and after. But they were not by any means the chief cultural tradition that evolved there. Religious activities came to play a very important part in the life of rural America, including Western North Carolina, and the region became the nearly exclusive domain of pentacostal and fundamentalist sects. As a result one of the chief cultural traditions that developed was the singing of religious folksongs in homes, churches, and at gatherings such as the camp meetings.

But there was for everybody the necessity of living not just on Sunday but on all the other days of the week. The religious leaders were often interested in stamping out the "Devil's ditties" that were the abundant heritage of rural people from Medieval times, but the influences of this-wordly necessities and interests have helped preserve the secular materials to the present day, through the use of some excellent subterfuges, as well as out-right rebellion, on the part of the pleasure-loving, the hunting and drinking men, and the spirited and fun-loving youths. The austere fatalism and the visions of glory of many fundamentalist churches were not able to uproot the traditions of living pleasurably and vigorously.

There seem to have developed separate traditions of entertainment. In addition to listening to old songs in the solitude of the home at a father's knee, in a mother's lap or at her side, or at the foot of a grandmother's rocker, there was also the music making, which as often as not involved either drinking or dancing or both. The oldest instrument whose use among the rural folk we may be sure of is the fiddle, and fiddle playing evolved traditions of its own, styles of performance that included the when and the where, and one of the most interesting *wheres* was perhaps the fiddlers' conventions, where champion fiddlers of several localities competed for recognition and sometimes prizes, after long spells of practicing on their neighbors at dances. When and how other instruments came to be added, in addition to the fiddles, to make the musical ensembles that are still nearly ubiquitous in the mountains is not certain.

To the fiddlers' contests and conventions may be added singing conventions, where the singers of religious folk songs are known to have assembled, sometimes for the awarding of prizes for the best performances. Also rural customs in many places were annual hunting expeditions and shooting contests. The mountain folk are a sociable lot to this day, and while old customs fade, new ones are added. For the most part, the camp meetings are gone without a trace, but the "Singing on the Mountain" is reminiscent of the older religious singin' gatherin's. The modern mountaineer may go to the Asheville Folk Festival, to the crafts fairs held in Gatlinburg and Hiwassee, to the fiddlers' conventions that today are gaining in popularity and in the attention paid them such as the ones at Galax, Virginia, and Union Grove and at different times of the year in a host of communities. The annual hunts seem to be less prevalent, but the sportsman may go only short distance from his home to the nearest stock car race to be with a great enthusiastic crowd. Still, many people have the feeling that something has been lost, that nothing like the past will be seen again.

Certainly the nature of community activities has changed. The Appalachian natives, like other pioneer groups, engaged in communal labor sharing, such as quilting, house-raising, and harvesting, and these customs have almost passed away. Just as important, perhaps, were the community entertainments, the play-parties and dances. The play-parties, even in communities where dancing was prohibited, were the harmless and hilarious gatherings of young people, and many of the games were ancient. The dances employed by the older folks were different from those observed in England by Cecil Sharp. These activities seem to have been superseded by institutions centering on the school, the church, and the chamber of commerce.

Finally, some of the most perishable forms of folklore, the oral tales, the superstitions, the legends and fables have been subjected to the eroding influence of the media — printing, schooling, and electronic devices. But some very interesting tales whose progress from India over long centuries of oral transmission has been traced are still to be heard in the highlands.

During the heroic age of Northern Europe there lived poets, in Scandinavia called scalds, in Anglo-Saxon England called scops and gleemen, who entertained and edified courts and kings with their songs. The inhabitants of England before the arrival of the Anglo-Saxons were the Celts, and Celts also inhabited Ireland, Wales, and Brittany in France. Their poets, the bards, also sang heroic songs and at times had the gift of prophecy.

The modern folksingers, in their tragic ballads, may be continuing a tradition that is descended from the influence of these early poets. The lyric songs and love songs of the Appalachian singer seem more closely related to the poets of Medieval Europe, its troubadours, minnesingers, and jongleurs. Since no one knows the origin of a song that is truly folk (by one widely accepted definition, folk songs are anonymous), some of the anonymous authors of folk songs might have been medieval poets.

After centuries had passed since the earliest English ballad (in the thirteenth century) was written down, in 1917 Cecil Sharp, an English folklorist, and Mrs. John C. Campbell toured the mountains and were the first to make an important collection of both the music and the words of the ballads there. They visited White Rock, Allanstand, Alleghany, Carmen, Big Laurel, and Hot Springs in Western North Carolina — the Laurel country. They found that the mountaineers were direct descendants of original settlers from England and Scotland who had left their native lands in the eighteenth century and migrated to America. Members of their families had lived in this secluded region, some of them since the time of the Revolution. Because of the difficulty of keeping in contact with the outside world until the twentieth century, their language and customs had remained in some ways much the same as those of their ancestors in England and Scotland. Even in 1917 some of them had no markets, no surplus produce, and barter was their chief medium of exchange. Sharp and Campbell found that most of those in whom they were interested lived in log cabins and had few material comforts, but they were independent and self-sufficient. They were a leisurely, cheery people in whom the social instinct was highly developed. Sharp described them as physically strong and of good stature, usually spare in figure, their features as clean-cut and handsome, their complexions those of people with out-of-doors habits, with superb carriages and a swinging, easy gait.

Mrs. Campbell and Sharp collected 450 tunes. Sharp commented that in England only the older people sang ballads but in the Appalachian Mountains ballads were sung by nearly everyone — young and old, that singing was as common and universal a practice as speaking. The fact has been forgotten that singing is the one form of artistic expression that can be practiced without any preliminary study or special training. Sharp believed that it was as natural for children to sing as it is to speak the native tongue. He found that mountain people had the "delightful habit of making beautiful music at all times and in all places." They were courteous and cooperative, and he had little difficulty in getting them to sing for recording. He learned to ask for "love-songs," which was their name for ballads.

He found that mountain singers sang in very much the same way as English folk singers, "without any conscious effort at expression and with the even tone and clarity of enunciation with which all folk-song collectors are familiar." One peculiarity that he noticed was their dwelling "upon certain notes of the melody, generally the weaker accents." Most ballad singers sang without accompaniment, but occasionally they accompanied themselves on the guitar or the dulcimer. Many singers had extensive repertoires and none used printed song sheets. Some few, however, had written copies, usually made by children, which they called "ballets," a term used in England to apply to the printed broadsides.

The Sharp-Campbell collection included fifty-five ballads, the first thirty-seven of which were in the Francis James Child collection of 305 ballads; the last eighteen were not known or were not included by Child. Sharp and Campbell included also sixty-seven other folk songs.

The major forms of entertainment — song and story — are combined in the ballad, which is a narrative song. It tells a story without characterization and without comment or moralizing. The mood is merely suggested; the story is stripped to its bare essentials. Although any stage of a culture may produce ballads, they are most characteristic of primitive or isolated societies like the mountains of Western North Carolina in the eighteenth and nineteenth centuries or that of the English-Scottish border in the late middle ages. The difference between ballads and other forms of poetry is in the way they have been preserved in the memories of generations of common people who have learned them, sung them, and passed them on orally to others.

The themes of ballads are those which appealed most to the common people, most of them concerned with universal human experiences: love and marriage, family relationships, struggle, death, and the supernatural. Usually ballad stories end tragically. Stories of domestic tragedies and ill-fated love affairs are common. A great many older ballads deal with the supernatural, particularly with stories of witchcraft, enchantment, demon lovers, and the return of the dead. In most American versions the supernatural elements are left out. Many ballads chronicle the raids along the English-Scottish border during the late middle ages. Others recount sympathetically the exploits of outlaws, notably those of Robin Hood and Jesse James. Some ballads are based on riddles, telling the story of someone who saved himself from imminent peril by answering riddles correctly, usually through his folk wisdom. A number of ballads are on religious themes, and many make frequent reference to religious tradition and ritual.

North Carolina's distinctive contribution to American ballads is a series of brutal murder ballads which establish the standard form for that kind of ballad in America. A famous Western North Carolina ballad is about Frankie Silvers. Frances Stewart Silvers (Frankie) murdered her husband Charles Silvers at the site of the present Black Mountain Station on the Carolina, Clinchfield, and Ohio Railroad, the mouth of the South Toe River, on the night of December 22, 1831. She cut off her husband's head with an axe, dismembered the body, and tried to burn portions of it in the fireplace. The crime was discovered. She was tried, convicted, and executed (the first North Carolina woman to be so executed) at Morganton July 12, 1833. Before her execution she left a poem lamenting her fate. Her crime and her execution have become the subject of a ballad.

Another famous Western North Carolina ballad was that about the murder of Laura Foster by Tom Dula in January 1866. Zeb Vance defended Dula, but he was convicted. Charlie

Davenport is reported to be the author of the following ballad, which enjoyed great popularity in 1959. This song's popularity was the kickoff of the modern "Folk revival."

> Hang down your head Tom Dula, hang Down your head and cry;
> You Killed poor Laura Foster and now you're bound to die.
> You met her on the hill side, God Almighty knows;
> You met her on the hill side and there you hid her clothes.
> You met her on the hill side there to be your wife;
> You met her on the hill side and there you took her life.

Phillip Houston Kennedy's study of the printed collections of ballads found in North Carolina has revealed that in several ways Western North Carolina is distinctive in the repertoire of its singers (ballad collectors have found English ballads sung in every state) and also in the amount of collecting that has been done here. In the *Frank C. Brown Collection of North Carolina Folklore* appear 399 mountain variants of ballads gathered by six collectors (the number of piedmont variants is 267, by three collectors; from the coastal region, 137 ballad variants, by three collectors). Twenty-five of the twenty-seven mountain counties in his study were visited by collectors. He found the southwestern counties the most sparsely collected, but found Watauga county the foremost locality in the state for the number of songs collected there, and in general the northwestern section is the best represented.

A further distinctive feature of the northwest is that the most unusual ballads in the *Brown Collection* came from there, including these examples: "Katherine Jaffray" (Avery), "Robin Hood Rescuing Three Squires" (Watauga), "Queen Eleanor's Confession" (Avery), and "The Suffolk Miracle" (Yadkin). One unusual ballad from the southwestern section is "The Boony Earl of Murray" (Henderson). The rare ballads in the Cecil Sharp Collection were from the singing of a Mrs. Gentry in Madison County who was noted for her extensive repertoire of old songs.

Fifty years ago ballad singers wandered through the mountains singing ballads for bed and board. Most people loved the ballads, but the Hardshell Baptists condemned them as "devil's ditties." They declared: "The devil rides on a fiddlestick." Many ghost tales were told and many ballads were sung before the winter fires of the mountaineers. The love-song ballads were also an inspiration for the love act.

In Western North Carolina "the primitive melodic tradition of the ballads was preserved also in the strange chants and long-drawn funeral songs." The tunes, "mournful and beautiful," embodied the spirit of loneliness, sorrow, and resignation of the isolated mountaineers. The "infare," a heritage from the remote past described sometimes in the tragic love ballads of tradition, was a social event accompanying weddings. A couple married in the morning, had breakfast at the home of the bride. Then came the "infare" at the home of the groom. The frolicking included folk dances, and the groom supplied the whiskey, food, and sweets. In the evening after the bride and groom had retired came the "chivaree." The young people of the neighborhood, fun-bent, would come with outlandish noises, hoping to surprise and embarrass the newlyweds. Usually dancing and drinking followed, with the groom again furnishing the whiskey.

Extensive study has been given to the musical traditions that include the tunes of the ballads and folk songs and of the instrumental music, which also reveals a kinship with old-world traditions. This study has revealed a melodic process traceable before the sixteenth century and bearing evidence of "the uninterrupted continuation of a long-lived and downright archaic tradition of music making among the unschooled people." The melodies of the folk can be shown to belong to some forty tune "families," consisting of melodic ideas which "have been subjected to conscious and unconscious variation, adapted to various uses, extended or contracted, but can be identified if a tune is examined completely...." It is only a music scholar who is capable of revealing the basic melodic ideas in the countless variants and versions of the thousands of songs and the multitude of styles that exist in the American folksong tradition.

The *Frank C. Brown Collection of North Carolina Folklore, III, Folk Songs*, contains many of the popular mountain folk songs. This book has interesting illustrations, pictures of herb gatherers, and of sorghum boiling. Folk songs have merely an expression of sentiment rather than the action implied in a ballad. Included are the following: Courting Songs such as "A Paper of Pins;" Drinking and Gambling Songs like "The Lips that Touch Liquor Must Never Touch Mine;" Homiletic Songs: "The Wicked Girl" and "A Poor Sinner"; Play-party and Dance Songs such as "Oh, Pretty Polly," "Peg in the Parlor," "Turkey Buzzard," "Wish I had a Needle and Thread," "Too Young to Marry," "Pop Goes the Weasel"; Lullabies and Nursery

Rhymes like "Bye Baby Bunting," "The Frog's Courtship," "McDonald's Farm," "Scotland's Burning," "Go Tell Aunt Patsy"; Jingles about Animals: "Possum up a Simmon Tree" "The Old Gray Mare,"; Folk Lyrics: "Sourwood Mountain," "Pretty Saro," "Old Smokey," "Kitty Kline," "Charming Betsy"; Work Songs: "The Corn Shucking Song," and "Old Blue." Religious Songs included are "The Cumberland Traveler," "Rock of Ages," "Pharoah's Army," and "Jacob's Ladder." Songs sung by Indians are "Ah, Poor Sinner," and "Cherokee Hymn."

Among Western North Carolina collectors and singers have been Dr. I. G. Greer, Bascom Lamar Lunsford, Frank Proffitt, "Doc" Watson, Dean Cratis Williams, Edith Walker, Pearl Webb, and Dr. Amos Abrams. Dr. Greer collected over three hundred ballads. At fourteen he could sing more than forty ballads. Lunsford and Proffitt could sing over three hundred from memory. At eighty Lunsford sang for ninety hours for recordings by the Encyclopaedia Britannica Corporation. These singers and ballad collectors awakened the pride of the people in their traditional music. Alan Lomax wrote, "The first function of music, especially of folk music, is to produce a feeling of security for the listener by voicing the particular quality of a land or of the life of the people. To the traveller, a line from a familiar song may bring back all the familiar emotions of home, for music is a magical summing up of the patterns of family, of love, of conflict, and of words which gave a community its special quality and which shape the personalities of its members. Folk song calls the native back to his roots and prepares him emotionally to dance, worship, work, fight, or make love normal to his place. . . . On the American frontier men worked and sang together on terms of amity and equality impossible in the Old World. . . . The common man, the individual, is everything in American folk song. . . ."

Professor George Pullen Jackson has advocated the thesis that the white spirituals of the mountain people are the progenitors of the Negro spirituals. He believes that followers of John Wesley and other revivalists, seeking inspiring revival hymns, took popular folk tunes, wrote religious words for them, and used them in their revival meetings. This activity

A family sings together

constituted an American religious folksong movement. It began in New England and spread southward, until the whole South became the province of these songs. As the practice of singing these songs died out elsewhere, it survived in folk communities in the South. Only the fact of a wide-spread movement was new; in very early times singers had sung songs to folk tunes. Singing hymns to secular tunes has been prevalent for thirteen centuries.

When Cecil Sharp asked mountain people for songs, they thought he wanted hymns. He had to ask for love songs to hear ballads. Nevertheless, a few religious songs, "The Cherry Tree Carol," and "Hicks' Farewell," are in Sharp's collection. Professor Jackson feels that Sharp missed the opportunity to be the discoverer of religious folk songs, that revival and camp meeting hymns used catchy folk tunes, and that many came from Baptist, Methodist, and Presbyterian hymnals. There are thousands of these songs. Many religious mountain folk believe these folk hymns to be the most beautiful music on earth. Thus the white spirituals are an important phase of mountain culture.

Artus Moser wrote in 1969 that group singing of hymns from shaped note song books still occurs in many rural churches of Western North Carolina: "Singing conventions meet in the different communities, and go by such names as the North Buncombe Singing Convention, the Haywood Singing Convention, the Dutch Cove Old Time Singing, the Old Harp Singing in Transylvania County near Brevard." He also reports that singing schools, conducted by itinerant music masters, are still held in some communities. The singing school practice is intended to teach the rudiments of musical knowledge, and then all are encouraged to do as their elders do, to sing and enjoy.

Professor Jackson believed that "the chief source of spiritual nourishment of any nation must be in its own past perpetually rediscovered and renewed" and that there is a national unity in the American folk song tradition. Jackson was a great pioneer in the field of folk studies in his *rediscovery* of early America's little known hymnals and tunebooks and the historical forces that produced them. They were first used by the Baptists, but the Methodists soon made the revival songs their own and became the great spreaders of white spirituals. These white spirituals are a much neglected body of folk music. They are far more numerous and their use was far more wide spread than the singing of ballads. Yet ballad collecting and singing have attracted the efforts of hundreds, while the collecting of gospel hymns based on folk tunes has been largely neglected. Southern country singing inspired Jackson, and he began to study the subject.

"Fasola" (the name of three notes of the scale as the singing schools taught them) singing was based on the shape-note hymnals. These shape notes were musical helps that enabled the musically illiterate to read the notes and to sing. There were singing schools and normal schools for training singers. *The Sacred Harp* (1844), one of the most famous hymnals, went through many editions, twenty-one by compilers in the Southern states. "Singing Billy" Walker's *Southern Harmony* had universal appeal in the South. It channeled the living stream of white spiritual songs into the present and preserved it. There are still Southern Harmony singings like the annual "Singing on the Mountain" on Grandfather Mountain.

At the "sings," the leader holds the book in his left hand, beats time with his right: down, left, up, right. Sometimes he calls the beat audibly. If stanzas not in the book are sung, the leader "lines out" the hymns. *The Christian Harmony* (1805) was probably the first hymnal to record revival tunes; the *Olive Leaf* (1878) was among the last.

Among the widely used hymnals were William Hauser's *Hesperian Harp*, the *Social Harp* by John Gordon McCurry, the *Sacred Harp* with B. F. White as chief compiler and E. J. King as co-author. There were many editions of the *Sacred Harp* from 1844 to 1879 and even two editions in 1911. The *Original Sacred Harp*, a later version, contained 609 tunes and 1226 names of authors and composers, 861 of whom were from the Southern states. Of these tunes "The Romish Lady," "Wicked Polly," "The Little Family," and other songs were based on old ballads. Millions of the shape note song books were sold.

Many of the Scotch Irish elements in the "Fasola" folk songs and hymns were secular; many recalled historical events; many dealt with religious experience: bad men, bad women, biblical events, anti-drinking songs. Many of the spiritual songs were born in camp meetings. Watts and John and Charles Wesley brought religious hymnody nearer to the masses by endowing it with "personal emotion, spiritual spontaneity, and evangelism." The village, town, and city church folk slowly abandoned the South's indigenous songs. But the rural songs met the people's tastes, and they felt that "God's music" was sung in the country churches. This congregational singing used songs handed down by oral transmission. They were often derived from ballads, were "dressed-up folklore." The phrases, rhythms, harmonies, stereotypes of expression, whole melodies often passed from one channel to another. An ancient folk ballad might become a hymn tune and then the hymn tune might be the origin of a bawdy song. Hymns and camp meeting songs were often robbed from fiddlers, fifers, harpers, and frolickers. Over nine hundred published religious folk tunes sprang up in the mid-eighteenth century. The tunes were mainly secular folk airs used in hymns in the *New Light* and the *Great Awakening*.

Many religious ballads are found in the old manuals of country singers. They are for individual singers, not groups. The sung story is the thing. The singer tells the story in the first person: the poor wayfaring stranger going over Jordan. They are similar to the old-world ballads in form. More significant than the ballads are the revival spiritual songs, for where *one* could sing by himself to secular words *all* could sing in a gathering to religious words. "Mountain songs," secular tunes with religious words, have persisted in the Southern Appalachians, but have generally passed out of existence elsewhere.

Folk music is a constantly flowing stream. There are eddies and currents, survivals intact of ancient lore, and new modes of creation. Legends, yarns, folk tales, folk songs, ballads are as much a part of the life of a folk community as are its laws, customs, and ways of making a living. They tell a good deal about what the people admire and about what kind of people they really are.

"And it came to pass, when the evil spirit from God was upon Saul, that David took an harp, and played with his hand: so Saul was refreshed and was well, and the evil spirit departed from him." The harp or lyre was an ancient instrument of widespread use. In Israel the young shepherd soothed the savage beasts with a harp. Representing the ancient traditions of the Celtic people, the harp is the symbol of the Irish people.

The Appalachian mountains are the home of another primitive form of harp, a folk instrument that seems distinctive. The Appalachian dulcimer may be taken, not as the most wide-spread folk instrument, which it is not, but as a symbol of a folk tradition that has its roots in antiquity, but which has developed distinctive forms. It is properly a symbol, like the Irish harp to the Irish, of the best of a traditional culture.

Attempts have been made to trace the mountain dulcimer to origins beyond the seas, with imperfect success. Some writers have even thought the instrument to be descended from the Harp of David. This conclusion seems hardly justified. Among many people who have voiced opinions on the subject, Jean Ritchie of the Kentucky mountains has been one of the most eloquent in the support of its native origin. In her *The Dulcimer Book* she makes detailed comparisons of the dulcimer with the Norwegian *langeleik*, the Swedish *humle*, and the French *epignette des Vosges*, all somewhat related to the medieval German instrument, the *scheitholtz*. She concludes that the instrument found in the Appalachians was "born" after years of experimentation, that it is "adequate, eloquent, refined, a complete statement of the mountaineer's life — its simplicity, sorrows, gaiety, beauty."

An enthusiast about the instrument, Julia Montgomery Street describes the instrument thus: "The mountain dulcimer, with two to eight strings, most commonly three, big tuning pegs, fretted fingerboard, and curved neck [all these fitted to an oblong box played flat on the lap or on a table] has been known and cherished for generations throughout the Southern Appalachians, and nowhere else...." She described the use to which it was put: "... for a solitary singer or intimate family song fest, the preferred music was the melody of a sweet-singing, plaintive dulcimer. The tune-box was generally swept [played] by a girl or woman...," and it was either homemade or handed down.

The relationship of the instrumental music of the Southern Appalachians to the custom of singing ballads is uncertain. The British ballads and the dulcimer both seem to be rarer than the native songs and the other instruments. Both seem to belong to the home. But many experts on the folksong tradition say it has been one of unaccompanied singing.

Certainly, the instruments that are numerous and widely played are the fiddle, the banjo, the mandolin, the guitar, and today, the bass fiddle and electric guitar. The history of these instuments in Western North Carolina is an unwritten story, as much so as that of the dulcimer. There is of course no question about the fiddle. This is a nearly universal instrument throughout areas where Europeans live or have settled. Negro slaves in colonial times provided the music for the stately dances of eighteenth century planters, playing tunes they learned from the English. These tunes are still current in Western North Carolina, and many of them can easily be recognized as directly descended from songs heard in Ireland, Scotland, Wales, England, and even Germany, Scandinavia. The ages of the tunes suggest that the history of instrumental music parallels that of the ballads and folksongs. Further, the instrumental tradition was retained by the same cultural groups as was the rest of North Carolina and Appalachian folklore. The instrumentalists did not live in separate communities.

How extensive, and how important is this music? These tunes are not limited to a couple of dozen only, "and they do not all sound the same, as some people have commented to me [Joan Moser] upon first hearing. Instead, it appears that there are as many as two hundred distinctly separate fiddle tunes along with many variants." But this music has yet to be given the attention of people who have an interest in preserving folklore. "There remains a vital body of material, yet to be explored, more alive today than ballad singing or any other oral folk art. . . . Published editions of this music are practically nonexistent." Cecil Sharp included only half a dozen "jig" tunes in his Appalachian collection. "Yet, if popular usage by the folk of today is any measure of the vitality of this material, then one must note that in North Carolina alone, for every festival or program of ballad singing produced today, there are half-a-dozen fiddlers' contests, at least." In fact, for a century these gatherings have been a traditional local event in many communities.

Miss Moser believes that the instrumental music of Western North Carolina is part of a heritage that belongs to general European folk culture. The tunes themselves are part of a tune heritage that belongs especially to the ethnic groups that settled the region. These tunes are part of more than forty families of tunes, including song, dance, and instrumental music. "Though tunes show stylistic variations in certain areas, similar variations of widespread tunes turn up in area after area. The lack of localized versions may attest the age of the tune families (one of which goes back at least to the tenth century) or their small number. . . ." But the tradition is not just an inherited one. It is perpetually creative of new materials along traditional lines: "This music is part of a cultural heritage which extends back as far as the ancient Morris dances and forward as far as modern ragtime and jazz. The tunes the fiddlers play include sword dance tunes which have been adapted to square dances, Scottish marches inherited from bagpipe melodies, waltzes of a more recent vintage, and tunes with a definite ragtime beat and tonal organization."

The introduction of new instruments into the folk tradition was an important event in the development of a regional style of music. The fiddle, the one folk instrument that came to America with the ballads, was played to accompany dancing and for its own sake. At some point, probably after the introduction of the banjo and guitar, the fiddle became applied as an accompaniment to the voice, at the same time applying rhythms developed to make dance steps. At first exclusively a lead instrument among other instruments, in modern bluegrass, which developed from the "old timey" string ensemble, the fiddle is used as an accompanying instrument, and the banjo, guitar or mandolin take the lead part (or the singer).

The banjo, an American invention in its five-string form, has in the mountain tradition developed distinctive styles. One feature of this distinctive style is the use of the short, fifth string, as a drone, sounded throughout the music, not always in harmony with the music. Another characteristic feature of the mountain banjo style is a system of changing the tuning to achieve different keys without moving the hand from the first position, and to play specific melodies. (This technique is also used with the fiddle, in which case it is called scordature, and has an old history.) Some authorities date the development as having been complete as early as the 1880's. The oldest method of picking the strings is variously named, but many people know it as "frailing." There are a variety of other styles of picking. In ensemble practice, the banjo was not known as a solo lead instrument until the bluegrass era launched it into national prominence as a solo instrument.

The history of the guitar in America is not well recorded, but its popularity in Europe in the eighteenth century spread to this country in the nineteenth. However this may be, most mountain people say there were no guitars around until around 1910. The guitar in the "old timey" string bands was a background instrument until the recording era, when the possibility of melody playing was introduced from outside. Although the guitar is still used as an accompanying instrument, many individuals have become prominent as masters of a special, complicated style, also their varied influences can be heard in bluegrass styles.

The bluegrass band is the modern version of the rural string band that developed into ensemble practice through the introduction of new instruments, the touring medicine show, political campaigning, the commercial possibilities of accompanying dances, playing on the radio, and making recordings. This tradition was at its heyday in the 1920's. The depression drove the practice back into the mountains, as the Nashville music industry developed the "star" tradition. In the recent decades, the advent of bluegrass music as a modernized version of this older string band tradition signalized a rebellion against the commercialization that threatened to take country music away from its origin and into the city.

The amazing feature of the mountain music tradition is that it embodies all the periods of its development, from the unaccompanied singing of ballads and the solo use of the fiddle

A banjo picker   ASHEVILLE CITIZEN-TIMES CO.

for dance music, through its modern manifestations. One of the best places for one who is not acquainted with the mountain traditions to encounter a great deal of what is still to be found of them is at one of the music conventions that have developed, mainly from the old fiddlers' contests, in Galax, Virginia (in August), in Union Grove, North Carolina (at Easter), and at Asheville, North Carolina (in July).

Each of these large gatherings has over forty years of its own history, but the custom of holding such gatherings is much older. An interesting account of the earlier, less enormous fiddlers' contests, was written by Louis Rand Bascom early in the century: "The convention is essentially an affair of the people, and is usually held in a stuffy little schoolhouse, lighted by one or two evil-smelling lamps, and provided with a rude, temporary stage. On this the fiddlers and 'follerers of banjo pickin'' sit, their coats and hats hung conveniently on pegs above their heads, their faces inscrutable. To all appearances they do not care to whom the prize is awarded, for the winner will undoubtedly treat. Also they are not bothered by the note taking of zealous judges, as these gentlemen are not appointed until after each contestant has finished his allotted "three pieces."

240 / Part II: A Changing Society

The 1955 Mountain Dance and Folk Festival held annually in Asheville, directed by Bascom Lamar Lunsford   ASHEVILLE CHAMBER OF COMMERCE PHOTO

At the Old Fiddlers Conventions at Union Grove about as much interest was shown in extemporaneous performances on the grounds as under the big tent. This is a scene from Union Grove in the 1960's

PHOTO BY ROUNDER RECORDS

The modern super convention has to some extent replaced these smaller and more local affairs, and blue grass has made inroads (but not the crooner style of commercial country music). At each of these the variety of entertainment is great, and it is greatest at the Asheville Dance and Folk Festival, where rank amateurs, commercial artists, dancing groups, solo ballad singers, and bands are all to be seen and heard. At the Union Grove Old Time Fiddlers' Convention, at Asheville, and at Galax Virginia's Old Time Fiddlers' Convention, the number of bands is in the hundreds, and the time which is consumed including all-night festivities is several days. Joan Moser recommends them to the interested: "The commercial exploitation of these is far less than that of the ordinary folk festival. The proceeds, for instance, usually go to local non-profit educational or charitable funds, and for this reason the music is less likely to be dressed up for audience appeal. It is performed in more traditional styles than is the case with more commercial and sensation seeking festivals. This is not to say that showmanship and artistic virtuosity are missing, by any means, but they do remain within the bound of traditional practice." Although each of the three festivals named draws crowds in the thousands and from far away, there are a multitude of the smaller, local schoolhouse variety of fiddlers' contests.

To a city dweller or a resident of the suburbia of which so many Americans are a part, a remarkable feature of the mountain culture is the extent to which work and recreation coincide. Artus Moser describes the trait of community sharing this way: "They learned to cooperate and work together, sing together, dance together, as neighbors and friends. Some of the very old people will tell you with much conviction that they had more fun and pleasure when they were young than the modern young generation, . . ."

The square dance is the recognized dance of the mountain people. With it goes the mountain music of the fiddle, guitar, and the banjo. This music bears within itself its own unique musical form with its rapid jump from key to key and its expression of emotion. The square dance is the descendant of the minuet, the Virginia Reel, and English and Scottish folk dances.

242 / Part II: A Changing Society

Square dance groups meet outdoors in the summer
ASHEVILLE CHAMBER OF COMMERCE PHOTO

The majority of the people were fundamentalists and puritanical. They thought that dancing where there was bodily contact was sinful. They condoned "play-party" games. The square dance was an exuberant amusement at these play-parties. It gave the energetic young people a means of enjoying their healthful animal spirits. Many years ago Bascom Lamar Lunsford of Turkey Creek (Buncombe County) organized the Mountain Dance and Folk Festival in Asheville. It has been held every summer since that time. Ballad singers and musicians and square dance groups perform and compete. This competition has helped to maintain and to spread the popularity of square dancing.

Then, too, there is music making for its own sake. These get-togethers might be at several typical places: at someone's house, out doors (often in the summer months), or at a store or filling station. These musical get-togethers involve considerable ritual: reverence for old players or listeners and deference to their tastes, tuning up (an endless and hair-raising process), taking turns at playing the lead (unless the fiddle player is elderly and august, in which case he may always play the lead), and usually drinking (depending on the presence of women). The drinking ritual might impose a different role on the fiddle player (who needs more concentration) than on the guitar player (who needs to loosen up and steady his rhythm). Under some circumstances drinking is always done covertly, behind the house or in a car. The rules are strict.

Folk beliefs and superstitions have evolved from the folk wisdom of an isolated people who had to make-do with what they had and where they were. They used their herb remedies for illnesses, the omens and signs for planting and harvesting crops. They used practices that had worked, based upon their actual experiences. They believed in luck, magic, nature, witchcraft. These beliefs rooted in common sense needed to have added to them the results of scientific knowledge and investigation. When such results were unavailable, they relied upon themselves.

Folklore is the seed, the plant, the natural growth by which legends turn into myths. It has long been an integral part of the lives of the mountain people. It was a product of their primitive lives, their simple pleasures, and their struggle to survive and make their lives as creatively rich and as pleasurable as possible. The folklore of Western North Carolina is rich with the stories, legends, ballads, games, songs, amusements, and occupations of the mountain people. Lacking books, theaters, amusements, they created an imaginative and indigenous way of life for themselves.

Many of the folktales are based on pagan beliefs of other millenia, which have survived as oral literature. When primitive man could not understand death, sickness, lightning, and other nautral phenomena, he attributed them to malignant deities, such as witches and devils. To protect himself from these malignant forces he created benevolent spirits to save him from the forces of evil. Eventually these spirits became his gods. Finally the one-God concept evolved and the gods became God. Then even though man wished with all his might to believe in the benevolence of God, he still feared the devil, forces of evil, malignant spirits, and the consequences of a remorseles destiny. He blamed certain undesirable happenings upon fate, luck, chance, the influence of witches and other malignant spirits. Folklore is a characteristic of man's cultural heritage. Everyone is affected by it, but quite possibly the more simple, ignorant, isolated,

244 / *Part II: A Changing Society*

Bascom Lamar Lunsford and Obray Ramsey make mountain music. They are representative of numerous groups of banjo, fiddle, and guitar players who travel miles to enjoy their favorite pastime

PHOTO BY AMERICAN MUSIC CONFERENCE

and illiterate a person is, the more greatly he is influenced by folk beliefs.

Folk tales like the ballads were handed down by oral communication and transmission. Like the ballad singer, the folk teller of tales "adopted not only the vocabulary and language but also the technique of high-pitched and nasal speech of the people, . . . their soft drawl." These tales were a part of spoken culture until a literary man like Richard Chase came along, collected them, wrote them down, and thus made them available to a wider audience than could have heard the native fabulists.

In the mountains of Western North Carolina there are many folk tales and legends. Concerning these one must ask the following questions: how interesting are they? how significant? how widely are they told? to what extent are they believed in Western North Carolina? One would say that the belief that if a corpse were touched by a murderer it would bleed afresh would be absurd. Yet a suspected murderer was given this test in Ashe County, North Carolina, and the legend is that the corpse bled. There are many legends about witchcraft. There was a witchcraft trial in North Carolina in 1920. Belief in ghosts was once involved to explain North Carolina's most widely advertised natural mystery, the Brown Mountain lights. These lights that can be seen over Brown Mountain from the Blowing Rock highway and elsewhere have been investigated by scientists and have been written about time and again. They were the subject of a mystery novel, *Kill One, Kill Two* by W. W. Anderson in 1940. The lights were investigated by the U.S. Geological Survey in 1913 and 1921. They have also been investigated by the National Geographic Society. The report of the Geological Survey scientists stated that they were reflections of automobile and train headlights. H. C. Martin asserted in the Lenoir *Topic* that they were reflections of the lights of Lenoir, Morganton, and Granite Falls. Hobart Whitman said the lights were really over Hickory, Morganton, and Valdese and that they merely appeared to be over Brown Mountain. Others have asserted that the lights were swamp fire or will-o-the-wisp, luminous reflections from phosphorescent substances. Many people have explored Brown Mountain and have found no cause of the lights. One evidence that the lights are reflections is that there was no legend concerning them before the twentieth century.

There is a legend that the man in the moon is there for burning trash on Sunday. Many are the legends about forlorn lovers. The most appealing of these is about the beautiful Indian princess who, after the death of her lover, leaped from a cliff into the river. Thus the Estatoe River received its name.

An interesting legend tells how the Indians obtained fire. They had no fire. Three old witches over the hill did. The Indians and their animal friends stole a firebrand from the witches. The animals passed it from one to another until it reached the Indian village. Henceforth the Indians guarded the precious fire day and night. This is reminiscent of the Greek myth about Prometheus.

The story of the origin of the woodpecker concerns a stingy old woman. One day a wizard disguised as an old man came by as she was baking cakes. He asked for a cake. She promised him one but then decided each was too large to give to him. Because of her stinginess he changed her into a woodpecker. A flower legend is about a little girl who liked to look at the sun so much that she was changed into a sunflower. The fuchsia is supposed to belong to the devil. The purple bell that drops down is his bell, the red petals that turn up are hell flames. The trees bowed before Jesus, the aspen refused. Ever since, it has trembled in fear. The mistletoe was once a large tree. Its wood was used for the cross of Jesus. Now it is a parasite. At Clifton, Ashe County, legend has it that a witch woman, Lyla Weaver, bewitched a rooster and made a snake appear on the counter in the store, so terrifying the merchant that he gave her a bolt of cloth. In Watauga County Old Henry, supposedly a male witch, put a spell on his daughter-in-law. Her family kept a stoppered bottle hanging from the loft to obviate the curse. There is the belief that the only way to kill witches is to shoot them with silver bullets.

It was believed in Todd, N.C., that under the spell of a witch crops will not mature or will wilt and dry up, that a witch could bewitch horses so that they would die after trying to climb trees and walk logs and fences, that when horses' manes and tails are tangled, they've been ridden by witches, that witches can't abide lye soap, that if you don't want soap bewitched stir it with a sassafras stick, that if butter won't congeal you should put a coin in the churn to attract the witch's attention so the butter will come.

There are legends of famous ghosts in the mountains. Among the most widely believed are those about the Lineback ghost near Cranberry and the Polly-Place ghost near Haunted Spring, one mile east of the Watauga River. This ghost is like a soldier with brass buttons on his coat. In Watauga County a headless dog was seen near the Cove Creek schoolhouse. There is a legend that a traveler and his dog were murdered and buried under the schoolhouse. Ghostly lights have been seen from Big Laurel in Watauga County. Aunt Sally Simms of Pineola had a vision in which she saw the devil, his wife, and four children come into Billy's house. They danced, had music, and one of the hellcats sat on the forelog in the fire. She threw boiling water on it but it was not hurt. Then she saw a hand with a knife. Shortly afterwards Betty and a boy named Ralph were running away. Bill, Betty's brother, knifed and shot Ralph. In Wilkes County strangers are told of Guy-scoot-er sky, the wonderful steer with hind legs longer than his front ones for mountain climbing.

Olive Tilford Dargan in *From My Highest Hill* quoted many sayings such as the following: "You can't raise a child that never falls out of bed. They die shure." "Fodder that has never been wet when made into a tea will cure fever." "A writin' spider means good luck." "To cure a baby's thrash get a strange man to lift his shoe to the baby's mouth, blow in the baby's mouth, say the three highest words in the Bible, or get a black-eyed man to give the baby a drink from his right shoe." "One must have a calm spirit if she puts up beans that will not spoil." She wrote of "yarb" medicines: mullein and shumake for a swelled throat, boneset for "agu," pokeweed for "rheumatiz" and spignet for consumption. For earache the remedy was warm rabbit oil poured into the ear.

John Foster West recalled from his childhood in the Appalachians of North Carolina a lullaby:
"Whatcha gonna do with the baby?
Whatcha gonna do with the baby?
Wrope it up in the tablecloth
And throw it up in the stable loft.
Whatcha gonna do with the baby?

West recalled a toe game that the children liked:
"Big toe: "This old sow say 'Let's go steal wheat.'"
Second toe: "Where we git hit at?"
The Third toe says: "Massa's barn"
The little toe, when twisted, would say: "This little pig say, "Wee! wee! wee! I can't get over the doorsill.'"

Many of our children's games had their origin in antiquity. "Jacks" was mentioned by Aristophanes. The Romans played "How many fingers?". "Blindman's Buff" and "odd and even" were Greek. "Prisoner's base," "Oats, Peas, Beans, and Barley" were played in the Middle Ages. "Leapfrog" was mentioned by both Shakespeare and Ben Jonson. "Anthony over," "Skip to my Lou," "Scissors-Paper-Stone," "Crack the Whip," "Upset the Fruit Basket," "Hide and Seek" have long been popular in the mountains.

A rhyme about "hide and seek" is Bucket of wheat, bucket of clover, All not hid can't hide over. All eyes open, here I come.

Many games involve practical jokes. In "Barnyard Chorus" only the one uninitiated gave the sound of the farm animals. In "Barber" a girl would tie a scarf around a boy's neck, invite him to be shaved and blindfold him. Then a little boy would kiss him. The blindfold would be removed, and the boy would be asked if that were not the quickest shave he had ever had. There were a number of battle games like "Capture the Flag" and many dramatic singing games like "Jenny Jones," "Old Crony," "Old Grumble," "Old Crummle," "Old Grumly" with onomatopoeic refrains like "chicky my chick my crany crow." A witch would catch all the children and send them home. An amusing guessing game was "Grunt, Pig, Grunt." A child would be blindfolded and then would have to identify which other child had grunted. Another guessing game was "Hackety hack on your back, how many fingers do I hold up?" In "Blindman's Buff" the blindfolded one had to catch and identify one of the players. In "Horns" a player would lose when he called the name of an animal that had no horns; in the "Twelve Days of Christmas" the player had to repeat all the gifts — the first one to omit any dropped out of the game. "Prisoners Base," "Fox in the Morning," "Rover, Red Rover, All come over," "Drop the Handkerchief," "Jacks," and "Mumble Peg" were widely played.

There were so many hog drovers passing through the mountains that the children made up a "Hog Drover" game: Hog drovers, hog drovers, hog drovers, we air, A courtin' your darter so neat and so fair, Can we get lodgin' here, oh, here? Can we get lodgin' here?" The child playing the father would answer: "No ugly hog drover gets her for a bride."

Riddles were a popular form of humor: On which side does a sheep have the most wool? The outside. The mountain people were fond of proverbs and picturesque sayings. They are part of the folk wisdom and imagination: for every fog in August there'll be a snow in winter; his wife threw more out the back door than he could tote in the front; as quare as a biddy hatched in a thunder storm. Superstitions represent the primal stage of folklore. One superstition is about a white horse, an omen of good luck. If you see a white horse, kiss the right hand and stamp it twice on the left hand. Thus the white horse, like the first star of evening, is a wishing horse or a magic horse;

one who eats a bear's heart will have supernatural strength; if you carry a lock of hair of a person you can control that person. Some superstitions concerning domestic pursuits are these: set bread to rise before sunrise; soap should be made in the dark of the moon; a seventh son of a seventh son has miraculous healing powers. Death and funeral customs include the following: if a pregnant woman drinks too much water, she may drown the baby; turn the bed tick before nine days and the mother will die; a ringing in the ears is the tolling of the death bell. There are many good luck omens, fetishes charms. Spittle, a rabbit's foot, a small piece of corn, a buckeye, knocking on wood, stump water are good luck charms. Folk ideas about bees are interesting: swarm in May, worth a load of hay. The principal sports, hunting and fishing, were subjects of folk beliefs: fish will not bite when the wind blows; hunting is good when the moon is in the south, when the air is still. "When the wind is in the east, the fish bite least; When the wind is in the west, the fish bite best; When the wind is in the south, the fish bite in the mouth."

A folk hero is Junior Johnson, stock car racer and chicken farmer. The legend of Junior Johnson has developed in Wilkes County. Junior, the "charger," was the idol of the 17,000 people who would drive out Route 421 to the stock car races near Wilkesboro. On such a day the "good ole mountain boys" could hear gospel preaching and shouting on the radio. According to Tom Wolfe the South has preaching, shouting, grits, country music, old memories, traditions, clay dust, old bigots, new liberals, and the lust for racing. Junior was a "hillbilly" who learned to drive by running whiskey for his father, a copper still operator in Ingle Hollow. Junior grossed over $100,000 in 1963. Still the Wilkes boys in the apple shacks wake up in the night, hear a supercharged car roar, and say, "Listen at him — there he goes!" Junior became famous for his "bootleg turn" to avoid roadblocks, a 180° turn made by throwing the car into second, stepping on the accelerator, and skidding the rear end around. He was never caught in a car. Once he got through a road block by using a police siren and a red light in his grill. His admirers are usually in their twenties and wear mod clothes. Very few are clodhoppers. Junior has a huge income, 42,000 chickens, a road-grading business, and a good job with Holly Farms. He is a hero a whole class can identify with. He stirs their imagination. What he is they would like to be.

PART THREE

A Developing Economy

March 11, 1879, Major James W. Wilson, the engineer in charge, wired the Governor: "Daylight has entered Buncombe County today: grade and center met exactly." The last shovelful of earth had been lifted, the rails were laid through the Swannanoa tunnel, and trains from Old Fort and the west met. The place they promptly named Terrell's.

The year 1880 marked the passing of an era and the ferment of a new one for the mountain counties. As the rails reached a county seat it experienced a little "boom." Lumber and tanning companies moved in, new uses were found for wood, wide-eyed tourists converged to experience the wonders that a few daring travelers had been describing for years. Small aggregations of local capital were thereupon invested here and there in furniture factories and textile mills. Telegraph had preceded the railroad by just a few months. The telegraph was the nerve system and the railroad the arteries carrying materials essential to the integration with national life that was beginning to evolve.

The forests in 1880 were great unbroken stretches of never-cut timber, and the timber stands were interrupted only by the island places where men in farms, valleys, and towns made their stands against the wilderness sea of trees. As the fisherman is an intruder on the seas, so then men were invaders of the forests. To make a field or pasture it was necessary to kill trees, so men adopted the practice of burning or stripping a stand of trees to clear land — treating the forest as an enemy to be conquered. Of course most of the houses of men and their contents were won by toil from the forest. Still it was the enemy that was everywhere and eternal. With the railroads came the first lumbering concerns, and the forests were transformed into a marketable commodity, only awaiting the axe.

But the farmer was not so immediately affected by the railroad in the 1880's, except that things probably got somewhat better for him with gradually improving markets and new markets for new crops, such as the tobacco crop, then in its infancy as an industry in Western North Carolina. A change in the weaving of people together into society was surely taking place. County seats grew as centers of influence only if railroads reached them, and in some cases towns were created by the arrival of railroads, the town-maker *par excellence* in America. North Wilkesboro eclipsed Wilkesboro, the county seat, because of the railroad. The railroad now visits West Jefferson, not Jefferson, the county seat. West Jefferson did not exist in 1880.

The growth of towns brought change to everyone within convenient reach of one of these centers of culture. Branson's *Business Directory* for the year 1884 reveals the extent to which business and manufacturing, which today are concentrated, were diffused throughout the counties. Creston, which today is merely a community, was the largest town in Ashe County in 1884, while West Jefferson is today's largest town. Canton in Haywood County was wholly created by the arrival of the railroad in 1883.

And while tourism had been practiced on a small scale and the area had been opened to the imaginations of outsiders by explorers like Francois Andre Michaux and his father Andre Michaux, with the arrival of the excursion train (still a phenomenon in the annual excursions run from West Jefferson to Abingdon, Virginia) a new era in entertainment opened up.

In 1880 there were old men who had lived out their lives never seeing a wheeled vehicle. Of course a great gulf would continue to exist between what were to remain the stern, uncompromising terms of rural life and the possibilities opened up by the arrival on the scene of means of making men closer together — mass communication, mass transportation, mass production.

CHAPTER TWELVE

Hear That Whistle Blow!

The building of the Western North Carolina Railroad to Asheville opened a window to the outside world. The previously secluded mountaineers looked through "charmed magic casements" upon what was to them a "brave new world." As they sat in their cabins, with the winter wind blowing through the cracks, their fingers plucking banjo strings, they could hear the long shrill wail of the locomotive's whistle as the train passed Terrell's, now Ridgecrest, and started on the down grade to Old Fort. The mountain man with the banjo would pick up the tempo of his plucking until the rhythm of the strings matched the rhythm of the wheels. His voice would run into a melodic moan: "hear that whistle blow a hundred miles." The man and banjo, train whistle and wheels were like one being: racing, roaring, speeding, pulsating, vibrating on their way to the wonders of the world outside the mountains. The men would dream of getting out to Morganton, Raleigh, Washington, and New York.

To the people of the mountains the railroad was more than just engine, passenger and freight cars. It was their means of escape, their ticket to adventure, to a new life, to opportunity and excitement. It became a way of life, breathing, walking, making love, dreaming. It became a symbol of freedom, of hope, of escape from bondage, the bondage of loneliness. It opened the door to the affluence of the outside world. It allured men with the bright and shining promises symbolized by the bright and shining rails. It represented romance as well as being an arterial system for carrying goods and services to market. The railroad made both transportation and communication easier. It carried the people and it brought the mail.

Before the days of the railroad and rural free delivery, post offices were numerous, Buncombe County having thirty-four. The United States government contracted with individuals to carry the mail from town to town, and frequently the carriers combined hauling the mail with the operation of a stage coach line, sometimes even keeping a tavern at some place along the route for lunch stops or overnight accommodations for the passengers. Sherrill Inn, a saddle-bag type of house of logs at Hickory Nut Gap, was operated until after 1900. Bedford Sherill carried the mail from Salisbury to Asheville via Lincolnton and Rutherfordton. His four horse Albany type coach carried many notable passengers. Drovers also used the inn, often paying for the services in kind: turkeys, a hog, or a steer. After the Western North Carolina Railroad reached Marion in 1870, a number of stage coach lines furnished regular services to points in the mountains such as the Cloudland Hotel on Roan Mountain, and to Asheville, crossing the Swannanoa Gap and following the Swannanoa River. Stage lines also fanned out from Asheville in almost all directions. Tourists enjoyed the travel by stage coach and the bountiful board and rural accommodations along the various routes.

As early as 1827, when railroads in America were just plans on paper, Joel Poinsett of Charleston is said to have dreamed of a railroad to be built across the Blue Ridge Mountains, down the French Broad River, and on to the Ohio Valley. In 1833 he published a pamphlet advocating such a road. Meetings were held in Asheville, Charlotte, and Knoxville. Judge Mitchell King of the resort at Flat Rock was a staunch promoter, and through his influence some preliminary surveys were made by engineers, one of whom was connected with the College of Charleston. An enthusiastic engineer wrote: "On the table land of Buncombe, the very spirit of health will smile upon the enterprise, and it will be hailed with joy by a flood of migration from the south, which even now sends thousands to make a painful journey to this delightful region."

More than fifty years passed before a railroad was ever built across the Blue Ridge. In 1852 the General Assembly of North Carolina, the railroad having been completed to Salisbury, chartered a Western North Carolina Railroad to have a capital

Hear That Whistle Blow! | 255

Hauling wood to build the Western North Carolina Railroad. The engine at the front is the little Salisbury that was hauled over the mountain to expedite the digging of the Swannanoa tunnel ASHEVILLE CITIZEN-TIMES CO.

of $3,000,000, financed two-thirds by state funds and the remaining third by counties and individuals, to run from Salisbury to the Tennessee line. This was one of the many abortive plans of the next forty years to build a railroad through every western county.

In 1853 Tennessee chartered a railroad to run from Cincinnati to Paint Rock, expecting that North Carolina would build its link across to the South Carolina border. A second charter was issued in 1855 for a Western North Carolina railroad, from Salisbury to some point on the French Broad River beyond the Blue Ridge, and further legislation provided for construction west through the valley of the Pigeon and Tuckaseigee rivers to connect with a point on a projected Blue Ridge Railroad on the Tennessee River. Another provision was for an extension through Madison County to Paint Rock, Tennessee. Surveys were made and the construction began. The road from Salisbury was completed to within a few miles of Morganton when the work was halted by the Civil War. Soon after the war the line was built to Morganton, in 1870 it reached Marion, and by 1873 it was at Old Fort.

In 1870 East Tennessee achieved railroad connections with Atlanta and Mobile, and Buncombe County's lucrative trade from the passage of Tennessee livestock over the turnpikes was lost. Asheville needed a railroad desperately, but the odds were

256 / *Part III: A Developing Economy*

against her. The Western North Carolina Railroad now became a victim of financial difficulties. State aid through the sale of bonds was voted by the General Assembly, but the bonds did not sell for the expected amount because of lack of faith in the state's ability to repay the money. In 1871 the Assembly split the Western North Carolina Railroad into the Eastern Division and the Western Division. Corruption in politics swept onto the scene. George W. Swepson, president of the Western Division, paid Milton S. Littlefield, a carpetbag lobbyist in Raleigh, to use his influence in getting votes in favor of the bonds. Littlefield was to have ten per cent of the money raised from their sale, and he spent money lavishly on the members of the Assembly. When an investigation revealed the fraud, Swepson and Littlefield fled the state. Later the Western Division was merged with the Eastern Division.

Samuel McDowell Tate, Democratic businessman of Morganton, served as president of the Western North Carolina Railroad intermittently after the Civil War, being the choice of the stockholders but not of W. W. Holden, Republican governor in 1866, 1869–1871. Tate continued to act as director and as financial agent of the Eastern Division after 1871, and in 1873 he was appointed by the United States Circuit Court as temporary receiver, but after two months he was replaced by William A. Smith, Republican. The troubles of the road were subjects of political maneuvering by both Republican and Democratic parties in 1874, and in that year Tate was elected to the state House of Representatives from Burke County. In 1875 a coalition was formed between eastern and western Democrats. Tate submitted a bill by which the Western North Carolina Railroad would be purchased by the state and completed as planned. In return the western representatives would support the calling of a constitutional convention to abolish the local election of county commissioners and justices of the peace, the method that was brought into operation by the carpetbag constitution of 1868. Henceforth the holders of these offices were to be chosen by the General Assembly. Thus officeholding by Negroes in the eastern counties could be controlled. Tate's bill was a clever device for getting the East to pay for the railroad. The western members were determined to have their railroad bill passed first. Objections were raised that the western congressional district included 1/7 of the area of the state, 1/8 of its population, but paid only 1/13 of the taxes. They were answered by the argument that until people could sell their products and develop their resources they could not pay more taxes and that when rail communications were established with Georgia and Tennessee outside capital would be attracted to the western part of the state. The bill passed the Senate in 1875, and the state issued $850,000 worth of new mortgage bonds to be prorated among the various creditors. Western Democrats then supported the bill calling for a constitutional convention.

Construction was resumed in 1877 and the General Assembly approved the expenditure of $70,000 annually for the work, provided the money was available. Five hundred convicts, most of them Negroes, were assigned to complete the construction. Utilization of convict labor was common in the Southern states at this time, and in North Carolina they had been used in making the cuts for the Spartanburg-Asheville Railroad under a law passed in 1872. Upon completion of the Western North Carolina Railroad to Asheville the prisoners were to be employed in building the lines to Paint Rock and Murphy.

In 1877 the road was completed to Henry Station at the foot of the Blue Ridge. Grading had been done beyond that point and some tunnels had been worked on, but little progress had been made. From Old Fort to Swannanoa Gap was a rise of 891.5 feet between two points only three and four-tenths miles apart. Six tunnels ranging from 7 feet to 1,832 feet were needed, and the road was laid out to curve 2,776 degrees, the equivalent of eight complete circles. All of the work was done by hand by unskilled convicts using pick, shovel, and mule-drawn scrapes and carts.

The story of the completion of the road from Henry Station to Asheville is dramatic. For the first time in the South nitroglycerine was used for blasting cuts and tunnels. One cut 450 feet long became known as "Mud Cut." The convicts went down each day to dig the mud out with picks and shovels, but each night it filled with mud again. A dinky engine was used to carry the mud out of the cut. Finally the men and engine won. Another challenge came when the decision was reached that the Swannanoa tunnel must be dug from the western as well as the eastern end and that an engine would be necessary to take the mud and rocks from the tunnel. W. P. Terell, engineer of the little engine "Salisbury" directed the dragging of the engine over the mountain on wooden planks using block and tackle. Mules, oxen, and convicts dragged the engine three miles, lifting it 900 feet in the process. The men laid planks, strained up the mountain over the planks, relaid the planks ahead of the engine, and started again. By taking the engine to the western end of the projected tunnel they cut in half the time required to dig it. The road had been surveyed to follow the courses of streams and thus secure a gradual rise. For an air line distance of three and four-tenths miles the road bed is nine miles.

Major James W. Wilson, an original contractor for the work and after 1877 president of the Western North Carolina Railroad, completed the track to Asheville in October 1880. In that year A. B. Andrews became president of the line. By 1880 the Democratic Party in North Carolina had come to regret having supported purchase of the Western North Carolina by the state. Construction of the line between Henry Station and Swannanoa Gap had been slow, and "Mud Cut" had been the butt of criticism by eastern newspapers that were preaching economy. Completion of the two extensions to Tennessee would require an increase in state taxes for years to come. Zebulon B. Vance, elected Governor in 1876, had been elevated to the United States Senate in 1879 and Lieutenant Governor Thomas J. Jarvis, promoted to the governorship, hoped to be re-elected in 1880 on a platform of economy and of increased state support for public education. When William J. Best, head of a northern financial group, offered to buy the road, pay the state for the $850,000 mortgage, and pay $550,000 in first mortgage bonds plus compensation to private stockholders, Governor Jarvis called a special session of the General Assembly for March 15. There was little opposition to the proposal, the bill being passed March 27. Best pledged that the road would be completed to Paint Rock on or before July 1, 1881, and to Murphy on or before January 1, 1885. The new owners were to pay the state an annual rent for each convict employed on the project. Best's associates turned over their interests to the Richmond and Danville Railroad Company, a procedure which had been turned down by the General Assembly in 1875. Thus the Western North Carolina Railroad became part of an important trunk line which in 1894 was reorganized as the Southern Railway Company, but the dream that the mountain area would share a railroad to the state's Atlantic seaports was blasted.

The building of the Western North Carolina Railroad from Old Fort to the crest of the Blue Ridge brought a new life and

The first Battery Park Hotel, luxurious in its day, on the site of Battery Porter, Civil War fortification   ASHEVILLE CITIZEN-TIMES CO.

new hope to the people of the mountains but at a staggering cost: $2,000,000 for eleven miles of track and the loss of some four hundred lives, almost all of whom were convicts, many having been convicted of such minor crimes as vagrancy and loitering because they had no means of support. Thus this epochal railroad building was yet another example of minority exploitation so prevalent in American History.

Construction of the road to Paint Rock was completed in 1882 and through service to Morristown, Tennessee, was opened. The North Carolina part followed the French Broad, and vast amounts of rock had to be moved to provide a road bed. Nitro-glycerine was again used in blasting. It was manufactured near the mouth of Reems Creek and transported in one-gallon jugs in one-horse wagons driven by Negroes along the Buncombe Turnpike to the places needed.

After the railroad reached Asheville, many wealthy Northerners came to the resort to spend a few days or weeks, and among the new hotels built for their accommodation was the Battery Park, occupying the site of Battery Porter, the Civil War fortification erected near Asheville. The Battery Park was luxurious, and the view from its many verandas was magnificent as the town was rimmed with mountains. Gay young people residing at the hotel took horseback excursions into the mountains.

Hotel at Warm Springs, later renamed Hot Springs. The hotel was enlarged to accomodate the crowds after the railroad reached the town

ASHEVILLE CITIZEN-TIMES CO.

The railway station at Hot Springs, typical of the depots along the line

Shortly after the completion of the road to the Tennessee line, the management of the hotel at Warm Springs enlarged the establishment, adding one hundred new rooms. "This improvement comprises a western extension, six hundred and fifty feet long, three stories high, verandas to every floor, extending the entire length of the new building, . . . presenting a hotel outfit, for accommodation of such a throng of guests, unsurpassed by any Summer and Winter resort in the country." The hotel accommodated one thousand guests and was said to be not infrequently full to overflowing.

Next the Murphy branch was constructed. When the railroad reached Pigeon Ford, now Canton, in 1881 the station there became the shipping point for livestock and a town developed. In 1884 when the road reached Waynesville a great celebration was held on April 4. People, many of whom had never seen a train, flocked into town as the first official passenger train came in. New settlements grew up along the line as the road pushed west. Waynesville became a famous resort. In 1879 a large hotel had been built, one-half mile from town, at White Sulphur Springs.

Meanwhile a much talked-of road from Spartanburg to Asheville to connect with the one to Tennessee was progressing without state financial support. The legislature of 1855 had been railroad conscious. A charter was granted to the Greenville and French Broad Railroad Company to join a road in the course of construction in South Carolina. Not until 1873 was work on the line in North Carolina begun in Polk County. This was to be the first railroad to cross the Blue Ridge in North Carolina. The line reached Tryon in 1877, but the route planned proved to be too expensive, necessitating a change, and the next few miles went slowly. It reached Saluda by a climb of six hundred feet in three miles at a maximum grade of more than 220 feet per mile in some places. The "Big Cut" about half way up the mountain was seventy feet in the center and even deeper on the upper side. Convict labor was used on the heavy grades. The town of Saluda was founded while the railroad was under construction and in 1881 it was chartered. It covered a square mile with the railroad in the center. The first train passed through Saluda in 1878. The town became a summer resort, principally for people from Columbia, South Carolina. They were charmed with the wide variety of wild flowers and other plant life afforded by the thermal belt in Polk County and by the mountain scenery.

In 1885 the town of Tryon was incorporated to extend one-half mile in every direction from the intersection of Pacolet Street with the railroad. A hotel now known as Oak Hall had been built in 1881 and the town had already become a winter resort. These two towns in the same county had such different average temperatures that Tryon attracted winter residents and Saluda served as a summer retreat. The county began to attract more year-round residents.

In 1874 the planned consolidation of the two railroads was consummated under the name Asheville and Spartanburg Railroad Company, and it finally reached Asheville in 1886. Construction to Hendersonville had been completed by July 4, 1879. On that day notables from Charleston and Columbia were in Hendersonville. Crowds thronged the streets and people opened their homes to the visitors who had come by stage, horseback, buggy, carriage, oxcarts, and on foot. As one train approached from Charlotte and a special came from Spartanburg a cannon was fired and the crowd cheered. Speeches were made by famous men and the local band played. In the oak grove near the station barbecued meat and other foods were served, followed by more speeches.

In 1894 the Hendersonville and Brevard Railroad was built. The engines were wood-burning, and fuel was obtained from place to place along the track. After three years' operation the company failed and the road was purchased by J. F. Hayes and associates at a receiver's sale and later was leased to the Southern Railroad. About 1895 Joseph H. Silverstein came to Transylvania County, and in 1901 he and a group of associates built the Toxaway Tanning Company, organized the Gloucester Lumber Company, leased a boundary of several thousand acres of valuable timberlands, and built a large band sawmill. Meanwhile J. F. Hayes, millionaire who came to the "Sapphire country" because of poor health, founded the Brevard Tanning Company, manufacturers of tannic acid, at Pisgah Forest. The tanneries made contracts with owners of tracts of chestnut trees to furnish chestnut wood and tanbark to be made into tannic acid, providing a new source of income from the forested land. However, these contracts were a source of great hardship to those furnishing the bark because the buyer's scales did the weighing and because the bark had to be free from mold and defects. It could be peeled easily only during the spring when rains were frequent and at that time mold was hard to avoid.

Other lumber companies followed, and Brevard with three hundred people began to have its first boom. Town lots were selling for three hundred dollars, land in the French Broad Valley was bringing from $25 to $100 per acre, and mountain land from three to ten dollars. There were two trains daily into the village. In 1900 J. F. Hayes built the beautiful Franklin Hotel in Brevard. In 1901 he built 540 acre Lake Toxaway in Transylvania County. Soon he erected a 150-room luxury hotel with electric lights, elevators, steam heat, and a power launch to carry guests around the lake. In Jackson County he built the Sapphire and Fairfield Hotels. He catered to the wealthy and it was said that 200 millionaires were guests during the first year of operation. Some of them invested in Western North Carolina developments. Among distinguished guests were the rubber magnate Edward Baccus, Henry Ford, Harvey Firestone, John Burroughs, Thomas Edison, R. J. Reynolds, the Dukes, and the Nunnally family from Atlanta. A band, dancing, boating, study classes for children were provided, and there was an electric car line to connect the resorts of Fairfield and Toxaway. By 1905 there were six trains a day through Brevard during the season, for a few years. By 1907 business was falling off. The Toxaway Company failed in 1911, Fairfield Inn burned, and the 1916 flood destroyed the dam, the hotel closed, and the wealthy guests went elsewhere. In the 1950's the dam and lake were rebuilt by a new company, Lake Toxaway Estates, and the company is developing an exclusive mountain-lake residential community, with a new Toxaway Inn as well as houses and boathouses around the lake, making this again a vacation paradise.

As late as 1886 it was being written of Rutherford, one of the two oldest counties in the area, "Transportation is by wagon to the railroads of the adjacent counties, and thence to Charlotte, Wilmington, and Charleston." That of course applied to cotton and grain. The livestock went on the hoof. By 1887 Rutherfordton had its railroad. When the Carolina Central Railroad reached that town, a dream of thirty years was realized. Chartered in 1855 as the Wilmington, Charlotte, and Rutherfordton Railroad, it received aid from the state and from most of the counties through which it passed. Rutherford County voted bonds to pay for several thousand dollars worth of stock. The work went slowly, but during the Civil War construction was completed to Cherryville. By 1880 it had reached Shelby, and by 1887 trains were operating to Rutherfordton.

General Wilder, who owned the Cloudland Hotel and most of Roan Mountain and had an interest in the Cranberry iron mines, in the 1880's promoted a railroad project to connect the rich coal fields of Southwest Virginia and Eastern Kentucky with the South by a railroad across the mountains from some point on the Ohio River. A similar promotion had been made in the 1830's by Charleston men. This railroad was finally completed in 1915. The Charleston, Cincinnati, and Chicago Railroad Company, commonly called the "Three C's", was chartered by a special act of the Tennessee legislature in 1887 and under the general laws of that state in 1889. The Rutherford Railway Construction Company, chartered by the General Assembly in 1833 to construct a road from Rutherfordton to

Pictured above in 1905 in Spruce Pine, N.C. during construction of Clinchfield Railroad: mules and wagons at the Clinchfield depot, hauling for MacArthur Brothers, contractors for the construction of the Clinchfield Railroad, which ended at Spruce Pine at the time of this picture. In the upper right-hand corner of this picture is a portion of the roof of the depot. Just beyond on the right are two warehouses. All materials and supplies for the job were shipped by rail to the end of the railroad at Spruce Pine until they could be hauled by wagon across the ridge. The warehouses stand where the lower street business houses were later. The four mule team in the foreground is across the location of what became the lower street. The back end of the wagon is about where Belk's Store now stands. As the camera is pointed it would today take in all the area up to and including the Presbyterian Church and Baker's Resturant of today. Hardly visible near the extreme upper left hand is the edge of the small boardinghouse built by Taylor Phillips, which became Topliff Hotel, which burned. Today's Mayland Market is on the graded-down site. Mr. and Mrs. Fred Sullins had a boarding house, barely visible. They charged 40 cents a day for room and board, including dinner to take on the job. Wages were $1.10 per day for 10 hours work. Roads were just rutted tracks. A 4-mule team could haul only about a ton and it took an expert to hitch up and drive the mules.

the South Carolina line or to Gastonia by way of Shelby, whichever would be the most practical, had started construction, as had the Rutherfordton, Marion, and Tennessee, chartered in 1881. The "Three C's" absorbed these lines, built the road from Camden to Rock Hill and on to Blacksburg. It was in operation by December 1888, and Rutherfordton was the northern terminus of the road from Camden, South Carolina, until the road between Rutherfordton and Marion was completed in 1890. In 1891 the company faced bankruptcy and the road was sold at auction. With the reorganization, four corporations were formed representing Virginia, Tennessee, North Carolina, and South Carolina. The North Carolina portion from Tennessee went forward gradually, reaching Spruce Pine in Mitchell County in 1902 from Erwin, Tennessee, and by 1905 it had reached Altapass. In 1908 the Carolina, Clinchfield, and Ohio purchased the road and pushed construction to Bostic, South Carolina, and then to Spartanburg by 1909. At that time there were only two buildings in Spruce Pine, on opposite sides of the Toe River. In 1915 the northern terminus was reached at Elkhorn, Kentucky. In 1924 a new company, the Clinchfield Railroad, leased the line for 999 years. The Clinchfield is unique in that it cuts through the mountain barriers. Three and one-half per cent of the entire mileage of 277 miles is inside the fifty-five tunnels one of which is 7,854 feet long. The road passes through a rugged mountain country for almost its total length. It was said to have been the most expensive railroad per mile to build, but it was of vital importance in opening the mountain country through which it passes.

When the Asheville and Spartanburg was completed to Asheville, most of Northwest North Carolina was still without railroads. In 1882 the Eastern Tennessee and Western North Carolina, a narrow gauge road, reached Cranberry in Mitchell County, where iron mines had been worked for half a century. In 1895 the Linville River Railroad was begun, from Cranberry to Pineola, where three brothers named Camp, of Chicago, were engaged in producing lumber and tan bark. Not until 1917 did this railroad reach Boone, Watauga's county seat. In 1887 the Northwestern North Carolina Railroad, which operated between Greensboro and Winston and Salem and was owned by the Richmond and Danville railroad, proposed to continue its line to Wilkesboro or to within a mile of the town if the county of Wilkes would buy $100,000 worth of stock. County bonds were approved by the voters and the road was completed by 1890. As there was no railroad in Watauga, Ashe, or Alleghany counties at that time, the new road to Wilkes County meant much to the people of the entire section. At the western terminus, now North Wilkesboro, not more than thirty people lived. The Winston Land and Improvement Company bought the two farms that comprised the area of the present town, and created the town, with streets, alleys, business buildings, a school, an opera house, a bank, and stores. Lots were sold at auction. In 1895 a tannery was started by C. C. Smoot and Sons, North Wilkesboro's first industry. Finally the Norfolk and Western obtained authority for its Virginia-Carolina Railway to construct a road in Ashe County to Jefferson and Elk Cross Roads (now Todd). The road was finished in 1914. An extension of the line was built privately by the Hassinger Lumber Company to transport logs from the Cowles Tract of timber land at the Ashe-Watauga county border to present-day Fleetwood, from whence the Norfolk and Western carried the logs to their destination, the Hassinger band mill in Virginia. After the timber had been cut the track was to have been removed, but a group of business men, chiefly members of the Moretz family, incorporated, bought the right-of-way, leased track and locomotives and extended the little branch to Deep Gap in Watauga County. The train carried, in addition to timber, grain, farm produce, and general merchandise for the company's store at Deep Gap and for the public. The entire railroad with its crew of two, George Burchett, engineer, and Raymond Luther, fireman, ran for six and one-half miles. From 1924 until the Norfolk and Western discontinued its service between Todd and West Jefferson during the depression, the little train carried on. The tracks were taken up in 1932. A number of similar railroads were built in the mountains, serving the needs of the localities until highways took their place.

For example Clay and Cherokee counties constructed their own railroad from Andrews to Hayesville for hauling lumber and pulpwood, the Hiwassee Railroad, popularly called the "Peavine." A line from Pigeon River connected the Cataloochee Valley with Canton. Livestock no longer had to be driven to market on the hoof, products of truck farmers could be marketed,

Aerial view of Spruce Pine in 1972, a town created by a railroad. Note the strip mines that mark the nearby mountains   HUGH MORTON PHOTO

a shrubbery and nursery business grew rapidly.

The narrow gauge Chester and Lenoir Railroad which reached Lenoir in 1884 later was made a standard gauge road and was extended to Edgemont at the present Caldwell-Avery county line. Consideration was given to building the East Tennessee and Western North Carolina road from Cranberry to connect with it, thus providing transportation from Johnson City, Tennessee, through Caldwell County and on to Chester, South Carolina, one of the many nebulous railroad projects of the period. Twice the Carolina and Northwestern tracks were washed out by floods, 1916 and 1940. After the 1916 flood they were reconstructed, but by 1940 the line was discontinued, as was the East Tennessee and Western North Carolina between Cranberry and Boone after the flood.

The 1916 flood was disastrous to all of the railroads in Western North Carolina between Marshall and Marion. The Southern Railroad suffered seventy-seven complete breaks between Statesville and Ridgecrest, and seven camps with from two hundred to seven hundred men each were established to rebuild the road. The Clinchfield between Marion and Altapass was destroyed and was out of operation for over a month. All highway bridges over the Catawba were washed out, and only one road into Asheville remained usable, the one from Greenville, South Carolina. In Burke County two ferries were installed until the bridges could be rebuilt.

There was pathos and humor, heartbreak and triumph in the songs of the railroad builders, the engineers and the convicts who so dauntlessly thrust the rails up the mountains, who dug the tunnels and built the bridges, who dragged the locomotive up the mountain so the tunnel could be worked at from both ends. All of this romance and travail John Ehle has graphically depicted in his novel *The Road*. The railroads were the entering wedge driven into the isolation of the mountains. About the railroad there grew up a folk lore and a balladry expressing the hopes and aspirations of the people. The Gospel Train became an image of fundamentalist thought. The "hell-bound train," an express train loaded with sinners and headed for hell on a downhill grade with no brakes and with greased rails, became a part of the folk tradition.

Forty or fifty years after the coming of the railroad it was largely replaced by the highways and the trucks, the interstate systems, the throughways, and the parkways. But about them there has grown up no folklore and tradition equal to the romance that the railroad inspired.

CHAPTER THIRTEEN

Agriculture

The *Handbook of the State of North Carolina* prepared by the Department of Agriculture (1893) furnished a description of mountain farms with its inventory of each county's resources and the use of its acreage. The counties still had most of their land covered with trees, many of which would fall to the woodman's axe when the railroad came. For instance, 7/8 of Graham, 5/6 of Macon, 3/4 of Madison, Mitchell, Polk, Rutherford, and Surry were still forested. Another way of saying this was that Macon County included 39,000 acres of "improved" and 164,000 acres of "unimproved" land, Madison County 69,000 "improved" and 164,000 "unimproved." Farmers were advised that if they would clear their timber they would be richly rewarded and that after they had cleared the land and had taken two or three crops off it should be "suffered to lie at rest" whereupon grass would begin to flourish and fine stock might be produced. The northwestern counties of Ashe, Alleghany, Watauga, Mitchell and Yancey were especially suited to stock raising, and with cultivated grasses "a deep rich lawn" would flourish to the summit of the mountains. Ashe County had already become significant in cattle production, using the Devon or Shorthorn breed which was ideally suited to milk and beef production and work oxen for farm use. Only Buncombe County had more horses than Ashe, and Haywood was third in number of both cattle and horses. Watauga County ranked fourth in cattle and fifth in horses for the area. On every farm were a few hogs and sheep, the hogs for meat and the sheep for wool. They were scarcely counted as wealth, being valued at less than one dollar per head.

Throughout the area at least three times as many acres were planted in corn as in the next ranking crop, wheat. Corn was important for household use for "pone" and for whiskey. It was the principal feed for horses and hogs. It could be planted in land that was full of stumps, and no expensive tools were needed for its cultivation. The school sessions were determined in mountain areas by "before and after fodder." Thomas W. Ferguson wrote in thinking back over those days, "the one-armed system of farming has been employed by ninety per cent of our farmers... to the impoverishment of their soils. We plowed up our hillsides planting to permanent pasture. We plowed up every foot of our bottom lands... planting them to corn and other depleting crops."

Other cereal grains, oats and rye, were of less importance. Polk and Rutherford counties were planting about one-fourth as many acres to cotton as to corn, and Burke had 752 acres in cotton in 1884. It was also experimenting with eight acres of rice.

Certain trees were of great importance to the farm family. Chestnuts were gathered for household use and to be traded for necessities, and live stock and turkeys were fattened on the nuts that fell to the ground. The trees were cut for fence rails and posts. They were considered preferable to oak for their durability. So plentiful were the chestnut trees that Margaret Morley observed farmers chopping down trees loaded with ripe chestnuts in order to pick the nuts. With the coming of railroads, new markets were found for the chestnut tree. Early in the twentieth century the chestnut tree blight was noticed. A fungus, it was brought to the United States with a shipment of Asiatic chestnut seedlings, and it attacked American trees, probably first on Long Island. Carried by wind, birds and insects, the blight spread southward along the eastern slope of the Appalachians to southern Alabama and Mississippi. Efforts to stop it were of no avail. Although at first it did not cross the Blue Ridge, by 1924 Ashe and Watauga counties reported a ten percent rate of infection, and by 1940 approximately eighty-five percent of the chestnut trees in the Great Smoky Mountains National Park were affected. By 1965 the loss was complete.

Maple sugar was a popular sweetening on mountain farm tables and was traded to local merchants for sale outside the

Agriculture / 271

Chestnut trees throughout the region died, a great economic loss
ASHEVILLE CHAMBER OF COMMERCE PHOTO

area. It is still being sold in small cakes as a delicacy at gift and craft shops. In the early spring when the sap started to run, the trees were tapped and small wooden spouts inserted, usually on the south side so the sun would strike them during the day and make the sap run faster. About fifty gallons of sap were required to make a gallon of syrup, and a tree would yield about a gallon or a gallon and a half of sap a day. Buckets were hung on the tapped trees, and every day during the sugar making process the sap was collected and taken to the big iron pot where it was boiled down. During this process the syrup had to be watched constantly to prevent scorching. The syrup was transferred to a smaller pot and boiled longer to crystalize into sugar. It was formed into small cakes for ease in handling. Sugar making was often a family diversion, an occasion for camping on high slopes where the sugar maple trees were growing. In the court house descriptions of acreages of land in the nineteenth century, a number of mountain-top tracts were designated as sugar

A sorghum mill extracts the juice, which is then boiled down in the iron pot

camps. Some of these passed through the hands of a land speculator, William Lenoir of Caldwell County. For each area that he purchased he drew a plat and wrote a history in a notebook. In Ashe County he purchased and then sold a tract to William Horton May 15, 1842, which he designated as Nathan Horton's Sugar Camp.

Widespread in the mountains was the making of sorghum molasses. In October the sorghum grower set up his mill to crush the juice from the stalks. His horse plodded around and around turning the mill until all the juice was extracted. The juice drained into large kettles or drums which were carried to the boiler, a huge iron pot in which the straw-colored juice was boiled down to the desired thickness so that "they" could be stored in crocks or jugs. Seven gallons of juice were boiled down to one gallon of molasses. Neighbors brought their own crocks and apples, corn meal, or potatoes to barter for "them." *Molasses* was usually used in the plural. The rich and nourishing molasses was a welcome addition to the monotonous winter diet of the mountain people.

Apple and cherry orchards grew wonderfully well in the mountains and were set out on most farms until they seemed native to the region. Apples were among the products carried by wagon to market in the rail centers, and many farms had among their various buildings apple houses where the fruit was preserved for family use and for sale later in the season.

Almost every farm had its springhouse for keeping milk, meat, and vegetables cool. Prevalent also were smokehouses for preserving meat.

Making whisky was an occupation of many mountaineers.

The distillery was as important as the blacksmith shop or the grist mill. Zebulon Baird Vance sold a distillery to Colonel William Lenoir. Many would take their jugs to the still which they called "the grocery." During the Civil War the United States Congress placed a tax on whiskey and required distillers to obtain licenses. After the restoration of the Union, efforts were made to collect the tax in Western North Carolina, and mountain people did not look with favor upon the "revenuers." Violations were frequent. True, most of the counties had their licensed distilleries: Wilkes having fourteen, Burke, Polk, and Surry, five each in 1884. Yet the illicit "stills" became legendary during the 1870's, and words such as "blockaders," for those who marketed the product illegally, and "moonshiners," for those who produced their product at night to escape detection by the "Feds" (revenue officers) became a part of the vernacular.

Randolph Abbott Shotwell spent some time at his brother's plantation in the valley of the Green River in Polk County, and he said that " . . . having nothing to do, and nothing to read, it was easy to fall into the habit of partaking . . . from the big brown jug, which is found in all dwellings in that region. Polk County at that time . . . seemed overspread with illicit distillers. Every secluded ravine, every impenetrable brake, was apt to have a sylvan satyr. . . . Many of these rusty 'stills,' as they are locally termed, might be concealed in a large barrel, and can, therefore, be quickly removed from place to place to avoid the revenue officers; though . . . it was deemed safest by the majority of the distillers to send a few gallons, and a sum of money to the Revenue Headquarters for the district. . . . Most of the Revenue men grew rich in a wonderfully short period."

On the occasion of a visit with a neighbor, Shotwell's host sent a Negro on horseback to "the still over the hill," with two bushels of shelled corn. The distiller sent back one gallon of whiskey, keeping one for toll.

Whiskey was made from a fermented solution containing corn meal, sprouted corn, rye meal, and sometimes molasses or sugar. First the corn was spread out and watered to sprout it, then carefully dried, and ground into malt and mixed with the other ingredients. The solution was cooked, producing a liquid called beer, which was then allowed to ferment, great care being exercised to prevent its becoming vinegar. Next the beer was "run" by being boiled. Attached to the cap of the still was a coil, a piece of copper tubing, the other end being

The "moonshiners" hid their stills, but the smoke often gave away their location

placed in a container. As the beer in the still boiled the steam condensed in the coil and passed on to the container. This product, called "singlings," was put back into the cleaned still and the process was repeated, called "doubling." The result was whiskey. Its alcoholic content, "proof," was determined by the size of the bubbles formed on the surface when a small sample was poured into a vial. After the "doubling" the liquid was allowed to flow from the condenser until the whiskey in the container was of the desired proof, 100 proof (50% alcohol), or 80 proof (40% alcohol).

When Carl A. Schenck, Vanderbilt's forester, tried to buy the holdings of the moonshiners in the Pisgah Forest, he found that they were the least likely to sell out of any of the residents: "These men in their own interests were most anxious to remain, because moonshining was possible only in the proximity of cold and remote mountain springs. . . . They had their liquor distilleries in the mountain coves, and shifted them from site to site to avoid discovery. They went about armed, keeping the others in awe and threatening death to any betrayer of their secret.... If the sheriff actually seized a still and took it home with him, he never fully destroyed it; he merely shot some holes through the copper kettle with his revolver and allowed the kettle to be stolen from his yard in the hope of seizing it a second time and getting a second reward from the federal government. Both the better element and the sheriff were afraid of the moonshiner."

Brandy too was distilled from the fruit that abounded in the Southern Highlands, and "cherry bounce," as well, had a fame that was widespread. Cherry Mountain was some miles from Rutherfordton and the same distance from Morganton, Marion, and Shelby, from all of which towns there were frequent parties in the month of June each year. The top of the mountain lies within a thermal belt, so the fruit is rarely killed by frost, and the enormous quantities of cherries attracted visitors from all the surrounding country. Sometimes as many as two or three hundred young men, women, and children — whole families — met in the orchards on the same day, especially on Thursdays and Saturdays. "The meeting on Cherry Mountain on the second Saturday in June ... was largely attended; persons from Shelby, Marion, Rutherfordton, and other points being present. A good deal of Amos Owen's "cherry bounce" was imbibed by the crowd," reported M. L. White, Owens' biographer. Amos Owens owned Cherry Mountain, where the cherry trees grew three feet in diameter. His poplar, chestnut, and sourwood trees produced excellent blossoms for honey. From honey, cherry juice, and whiskey Amos made the cherry bounce.

Amos served in the Confederate Army, after which he returned home and resumed his distilling without the required legal formalities. For over forty years he made whiskey, and during that time he served four years in prison, one for Ku Klux Klan activities and twice for moonshining. His biographer says that the judge, before passing sentence, chided: "Amos Owens, stand up, ... why will you persist in your lawless course? Look at me, I am sixty years of age, was never drunk, and have never incurred the woe pronounced against him that putteth the bottle to his neighbor's lips. What have you to say, why the sentence of the law should not be pronounced upon you?" Amos cocked one eye, cleared his throat, and with mock solemnity, said, "Well, Judge, you have missed a durned lot of fun if you hain't never made, drunk, nor sold licker."

Farmers were eagerly awaiting the railroads, and farm products changed as soon as transportation became available, even at a distance. When the narrow gauge Chester and Lenoir Railway reached Lenoir in 1884, Watauga County farmers began growing a surplus of cabbage and potatoes; as early as 1882 it was reported that "on the turnpike at any given point a covered wagon or so is seldom out of sight." In 1886, 800 crates of cabbage and 3,000 crates of apples were shipped from Lenoir. The following year during November and December the following were shipped: 1356 crates of apples, 1078 crates of cabbage, 364 crates of potatoes, 657 sacks of chestnuts. Thirty-two thousand feet of lumber were used to make the crates alone. It was reported that on one acre in Watauga County two hundred dollars worth of cabbage was raised.

The great new crop of the area was tobacco, the bright leaf variety. Surry County led with 2,136 acres planted in 1884, but mountainous Madison County was second with 1,626 acres, and Buncombe was third with 947 acres. Every county in Western North Carolina had at least one tobacco farm. Production per acre ranged from 200 pounds in Cherokee County to 503 in Madison County. Zeigler and Grosscup in 1882 estimated Madison County's yield as equal to $250,000 or $200 per acre. W. W. Rollins of that county had sixty tenant farmers engaged in growing tobacco. "It is in tobacco that the Madison County farmer has found his Eldorado," Zeigler and Grosscup wrote. Uncleared land could be purchased for three dollars per acre, and a tract of one and one-half acres when cleared could be planted, cultivated, and harvested by a man and two small boys for a harvest worth $900.

According to Nanny May Tilley the tobacco crop spread from Catawba County to Burke County in 1875 when J. K. Bobbitt planted the first crop. A warehouse was opened in Hickory in 1880 by the Hall Brothers, who distributed pamphlets explaining tobacco culture and the advantages of the tobacco crop. One was the small bulk, which would facilitate transportation. In Buncombe County experiments in tobacco production had begun earlier, perhaps as early as 1854, but not until 1878 did tobacco become an important crop. In 1880 Asheville had four tobacco warehouses that handled 7,000,000 pounds of the leaf, and Madison County had one warehouse. Alas, by the end of the century the crop had gone into eclipse in most of the counties. Some farmers who in the 1880's had twenty or thirty tobacco barns by 1896 had none. Various explanations have been offered. Tilley believed that the rank flavor of the mountain tobacco was unsuited to cigarettes, which had become very popular. The crop of the coastal plain was milder and in greater demand. Haywood County persisted in bright leaf tobacco culture until 1904, after which for a period of twenty years or so no more was planted.

Then in 1923 burley tobacco was introduced in Haywood by Thurmond Haynes, who sold his crop in Greeneville, Tennessee. By 1925 every county in Western North Carolina except Alleghany, Ashe, Avery, Polk, and Watauga was growing burley tobacco on a commercial basis. Again Madison County became the leader, planting 2,500 acres in 1925. In 1929 Ott Tester, a former resident of North Carolina, brought from Tennessee plants which he planted in Watauga County, producing 800 pounds per acre, which sold at 21.2¢ per pound. By 1958 Watauga County ranked sixth in burley production in Western North Carolina with a crop that sold for $1,040,000. A tobacco warehouse and auction was opened in Boone in 1939. The problem in establishing a tobacco warehouse was to persuade the tobacco companies to send buyers. The Boone experience will illustrate. The project started through the activities of local leaders. Mr. S. C. Eggers became discouraged at having to haul his tobacco to Greeneville, Tennessee, to sell it. One morning he began taking pledges from Boone citizens, and within three hours he had $35,000 promised for the construction of a tobacco warehouse. Then came a time of tension. A committee consisting of Blandord Dougherty, President of Appalachian State Teachers College, Harry Hamilton, E. F. Lovill, attorney, and Congressman Robert Doughton sought and obtained the promise of Will Reynolds of the Reynolds Tobacco Company to send buyers if the other tobacco companies would do so. After offering considerable resistance, Major Bullington of the American Tobacco Company reluctantly agreed to send buyers to Boone. The warehouse when completed was leased to the Hardy Brothers of Mullins, South Carolina.

Through the influence of Robert Doughton a warehouse was established in Ashe County and eventually a second one was added. In 1958 Ashe County produced 2,218,000 pounds of tabacco which sold for $1,426,000. Doughton's own county Alleghany has never produced as much tobacco as Ashe and Watauga. Buncombe and Madison counties were the leading

278 / Part III: A Developing Economy

A field of tobacco, the money crop of mountain farmers
ASHEVILLE CITIZEN-TIMES CO.

Tobacco is auctioned in large warehouses
ASHEVILLE CHAMBER OF COMMERCE PHOTO

burley producers. In 1965 there were four warehouses in Asheville. Ashe County was third in production of burley and Yancey ranked next, followed by Haywood and Watauga respectively. Since 1940, acreage allotments have been in effect. In 1961 the average allotment for farms growing burley was six-tenths of an acre, and the harvest was worth $15,000,000. Allotments ranged from one-tenth of an acre to several acres. By 1958

TOBACCO ALLOTMENT DATA FOR 1968

County	No. of farms	Acreage Allotment	Rank in state
Burley Tobacco			
Alleghany	540	218.73	9
Ashe	2,535	1,046.56	3
Avery	247	108.35	31
Buncombe	2,946	1,400.65	2
Burke	14	447	21
Caldwell	19	6.74	20
Cherokee	194	68.64	15
Clay	217	84.53	12
Graham	685	301.51	8
Haywood	1,917	947.22	5
Henderson	110	42.47	16
Jackson	285	107.85	10
McDowell	70	24.56	18
Macon	238	76.80	13
Madison	2,809	2,066.71	1
Mitchell	963	470.36	7
Polk	6	1.75	24
Rutherford	55	23.46	19
Surry	7	0.94	27
Swain	215	70.18	14
Transylvania	72	23.13	17
Watauga	1,663	727.75	6
Wilkes	8	1.83	23
Yancey	1,795	983.05	4

		Flue-Cured Tobacco		
County	No. of farms	Acreage	Poundage	Rank in state
Burke	1	.48	822	68
Caldwell	265	405.96	682,635	59
Surry	3,062	9,287.81	16,790,906	18
Wilkes	930	1,301.66	2,073,603	49

Source: "North Carolina Tobacco Report, 1967–1968," *Bulletin of the North Carolina Department of Agriculture* No. 191, May, 1968, pp. 22, 20.

several counties were producing more than 2,000 pounds per acre, Watauga County's 2,108 being the highest yield in Western North Carolina. In that year the highest prices were received in Buncombe and Madison counties, sixty-five cents per pound. In 1968 the yield in Watauga County was 2,626 pounds per acre. Burley is planted in a seed bed in early spring as is bright leaf tobacco, and the successive stages of work are similar for both varieties, but the curing is different. Plants are usually cut by whole stalks, allowed to wilt overnight, then staked in the field for two or three days for further wilting before being hung high in well-ventilated barns with the stalks head down to air cure. The latter part of November the leaves are stripped from the stalks, graded, and tied into "hands," several leaves together, and taken to market for auction. The money from the burley crop comes along just in time for taxes and extra winter expenses. Many of the farmers now work away from their farms and fit the chores connected with their tobacco crop into evening and Saturday work. Each of the counties in Western North Carolina in 1964 had hundreds of part-time farms, ranging from 128 in Clay County to 837 in Ashe County. From Buncombe's 2,471 farms, 1,080 farm operatives work off their farms one hundred or more days each year. Figures are similar for Wilkes and Ashe counties. Tobacco is well-suited to part-time farming.

Agricultural cooperatives had been organized by the Grange in the 1870's in some parts of the nation but not in Western North Carolina. Farm periodicals emphasized their benefits during the following decade. Wilkes County promoters discovered the value of these associations for agricultural development when in 1912 they organized the United Fruit Growers of Western North Carolina in the interest of growing apples commercially. In 1925 an editorial in the Winston-Salem *Journal* read: "Nowhere in Eastern America are finer apples to be found than in the Wilkes County thermal belt. In a given area lying along the sides and top of the Brushy Mountains there is a strange atmospheric condition which wards off frosts and guards the young buds of fruit trees from cold while in a premature stage." The "thermal belts" and "verdant zones" on mountain slopes are suited to fruit production because they enjoy longer frost-free growing seasons than areas higher up the slopes and lower in the valleys. A thermal belt results from the drainage of cold air down a slope into a valley where it further cools by radiation or losing its heat to space. Thus there is a belt through the Brushy Mountains, the South Mountains, and on south through the Blue Ridge in Polk, Rutherford, and Henderson counties where above freezing weather exists between sub-freezing temperatures on both higher and lower elevations on the hillsides.

One problem of apple culture is storage until the price is good. The Brushy Mountain Fruit Cooperative Corporation, organized in 1931, and the Fruit Growers' Association, organized in 1936, were aided by the Carolina Refrigeration Cooperative Association which constructed storage facilities for apples and meat. Encouraged by the county agents, similar cooperatives were organized throughout Western North Carolina. While most of them were short lived, they led the way to specialized crops that were particularly adapted to the soil and climatic conditions.

Henderson County in 1960 led the state in the production of apples, with 200,000 bearing trees and about 10,000 new ones coming into production each year. In 1962 the crop was valued at $2,800,000. The county had fourteen packing houses and three processing plants, the newest of which was constructed by the Western North Carolina Apple Packing Cooperative. More than 1,500 people worked in harvesting and processing the crop. Apple trees will grow on soil unsuited to truck farming, another of Henderson County's specialities. Each year Hendersonville holds a five-day North Carolina Apple Festival, ending with a King Apple Parade on Labor Day. A queen and her court are elected and visiting queens from other festivals participate in the activities, which include folk music, square dancing, tours of apple orchards, and a coronation ball. North Carolina has 762 commercial apple orchards (ones with 100 or more trees) of which 622 are in the mountain counties. Haywood and Mitchell counties also have extensive commercial apple orchards.

Polk and Rutherford Counties are producers of peaches. Except in occasional years when late spring freezes ruin the crop, the mountain area produces almost one-fourth as many peaches as the sand hill counties of the piedmont.

The Extension Division of North Carolina State University operates the Mountain Horticultural Crops Research Station

282 / Part III: A Developing Economy

Burley tobacco is staked in the field to start the wilting process before hanging it in the barns to air-cure. Note the ever-present church

ASHEVILLE CHAMBER OF COMMERCE PHOTO

Apples grow well on the mountains. An orchard in bloom is a magnificent sight

ASHEVILLE CHAMBER OF COMMERCE PHOTO

in Henderson County. A staff of six scientists experiment with crops that will help all farmers in Western North Carolina to diversify their acreage. Such scientific studies are the culmination of efforts by federal, state, and local organizations to aid farmers in their methods of production and marketing.

At first the farmers' organizations had little influence in Western North Carolina. They did not have much appeal to subsistence farmers. Their warehouse movement and cooperative idea, as mentioned above, were taken up where commercial farming was begun. In Buncombe County the Farmers' Federation was organized in 1921 by a group of farmers under the leadership of James G. K. McClure to purchase and distribute farm supplies and market products grown commercially. One warehouse was built, then another, until by 1928 there were eight warehouses operating in four counties. Sixteen trucks were acquired for wholesale and retail delivery service, thus relieving farmers of the necessity of doing their own trucking. When the Grange was revived in the South about 1930 a new interest in commercial farming developed. At the demands of some of the more progressive farmers, county boards of commissioners provided the matching funds necessary to employ the county agents of the Extension Service, and the men chosen for those positions came to be among the most important figures in their respective counties. County "farm bureaus" sprang up to work with the county agents, but as the members were largely the commercial farmers, the "hoe farmers" were scarcely influenced by the organization movement of the 1920's. The depression of the 1930's was not felt as much by the self-sufficient rural people of Western North Carolina as it was in industrial areas. The income of the former had always been very low, and their homes and farms lacked the conveniences of an urban or suburban society, but the farms were almost completely owner operated, and food and fuel were as readily available as they had ever been.

By 1920 51.2% of the population of the United States had moved to urban areas, and since that time rural population has diminished until in 1969 the farm population was just 5.2% of the total. Although Western North Carolina remained comparatively rural, the trend was felt in the out-migration which between 1950 and 1960 amounted to 33% of the people in Swain County and over 20% in ten other counties. As late as 1960 only twelve of the twenty-four counties had areas classified by the census bureau as urban. Much of the rural acreage was being retired from farming. In 1959 43% of the land in the twenty-four counties was included in farms while in 1964 only about 35% was included. At the same time farm size was increasing, the average acreage in 1954 being 62 while in 1964 it was 80. The number of farms in Western North Carolina decreased from 52,161 in 1954 to 42,607 in 1959 and 29,955 in 1964. From 1954 when the area had 9,317 farms of less than ten acres, to 1964, the number of such farms had dwindled to 2,575; farms of 1,000 or more acres increased from 80 in the area in 1954 to 96 in 1964.

With these changes farming had become more specialized and dairying increased, especially near the cities and towns. Buncombe County was second in the state in dairying in 1954, and Henderson, Haywood, and Ashe counties ranked high. By 1964 the leading producers of dairy products ranked in the following order: Buncombe, Henderson, Alleghany, Haywood, Macon, Madison, Ashe, Yancey, and Surry. Alleghany has risen to third rank. Cheese making had been experimented with in Ashe County beginning in 1915 at Grassy Creek. The Dairy Extension Service of the North Carolina Department of Agriculture was promoting the establishment of cheese factories in several counties in the western part of the state. A number of the factories were opened in Ashe County and considerable enthusiasm developed there before World War One and poor roads for transportation of milk and cheese combined to bring an end to the experiment. Eventually the Kraft-Phoenix Creamery established a large plant in West Jefferson, buying from Ashe County farmers about 1,500,000 pounds of milk per month in the spring, summer, and fall, and 75,000 pounds per month in winter, for manufacture into cheese. Carnation, Pet, and Coble dairies also bought milk from the farms in Ashe County.

Ashe County leads the state in the production of fine beef cattle, the quality of which was improved when the State Board of Agriculture purchased several fine pure-bred bulls which were leased to responsible breeders of beef cattle. Haywood is a close rival to Ashe in the production of high grade beef cattle. It has been known for the quality of its herds since the introduction of Durham or Shorthorn cattle in the 1880's. Robert Plott introduced Angus cattle and T. Lenoir Gwyn established a fine

Pure-bred livestock fatten on the lush grass of the mountain balds in Ashe and Alleghany Counties — scene along the Blue Ridge Parkway

HUGH MORTON PHOTO

breeding herd of registered Herefords, these two herds forming a foundation for the excellence of Haywood County's beef cattle. Later Guernseys were brought in from Wisconsin by by H. O. Osborne to establish records in the production of milk and butter fat.

The North Carolina Department of Agriculture operates two veterinary diagnostic laboratories in Western North Carolina, one at Murphy and the other at Waynesville, to aid in the area's livestock production. Since 1908 the Mountain Research Station has been operated jointly by the North Carolina Department of Agriculture and the North Carolina State University Experiment Station, first at Swannanoa in Buncombe County and since 1944 on a 354 acre tract in Haywood County. Research is conducted in dairying, with a modern milking parlour, a lounging barn, a forty-stanchion conventional barn, a calf barn, a dry-cow barn, and silos. Poultry research is carried on with automatic incubators, a modern egg-cooling room, a broiler house, a laying house, a breeding house, and a 3 1/2 acre poultry range. Efforts are made to find superior lines for broiler and egg production, and nutritional studies are carried on. Burley tobacco research is provided with three curing barns and a tobacco grading and pack house.

Dean W. Colvard, a native of Ashe County with degrees from Berea College and two universities, worked with the Extension Service in Western North Carolina. With W. B. Austin, a member of the State Board of Agriculture, he established the Upper Mountain State Farm Experiment Station in Ashe County. Colvard, now Chancellor of the University of North Carolina at Charlotte, served as first superintendent of the station in Ashe County.

Since 1910 poultry and eggs have come to be an important item of farm production, with Wilkes County leading all others in the region, ranking second in the state in 1954. In 1919 a

LEADING POULTRY PRODUCING COUNTIES IN WESTERN NORTH CAROLINA

	1954	1964
Wilkes	$4,108,000	$19,537,019
Buncombe	1,620,000	2,748,675
Clay	686,000	1,885,894
Surry	642,000	4,708,043
Henderson	491,000	517,082
Caldwell	482,000	1,551,102
Rutherford	435,000	700,223
Cherokee	420,000	1,654,281
Macon	404,000	816,222
Watauga		994,263
Haywood		902,917
Ashe		1,397,120

Source: County and City Data Book, 1965.

World War One veteran T. O. Minton began producing baby chicks by incubator and established Champion Poultry Farm, which became the largest one in the entire South, marketing both fryers and eggs. Other Wilkes County men became commercial producers, and the North Carolina Mutual Hatchery Association was organized. In 1954 Wilkes County's poultry and poultry products brought a return of $4,108,000. In that year Lovette's Holly Farms Poultry Company, one of the largest of its kind in the world, was organized. In 1960 it paid out to poultry growers about $15,000,000. It has a national and an international market.

There is a trend toward diversification of crops and emphasis on truck farming, but corn is still the principal field crop in Western North Carolina. Although the acreage has steadily diminished, the production per acre has increased remarkably. In 1925 Transylvania County produced an average of 25 bushels per acre, the highest yield in the region, and Burke County produced only 13 bushels, the lowest yield; in 1960 Watauga County had the highest rate of production, 65 bushels per acre, Transylvania County produced 59.1 bushels per acre, and Burke 49 bushels. Rutherford County was lowest in the region with 40 bushels.

Rural electrification, which brought new conveniences to the entire area resulted from the creation of the Tennessee Valley Authority (TVA). Most of the activities of the TVA, which included social planning, educational experimentation, and relocation of families, did not greatly affect Western North Carolina. The Rural Electrification Authority of the federal government, formed in 1935, granted loans to rural cooperatives to furnish electric power to parts of the lower South. The state was stimulated to create the North Carolina Rural Electrification Authority to encourage the building of rural power lines. By 1951 85% of the farms in the state were supplied with electric power, and by 1961 the figure had increased to 97%. The areas not being served by the Duke Power Company, the Nantahala Power Company, and the Carolina Power Company,

288 / Part III: A Developing Economy

Shocks in the field. Corn is grown on practically all mountain farms
ASHEVILLE CHAMBER OF COMMERCE PHOTO

or by locally owned establishments were provided with power purchased from the TVA by the cooperatives, which are owned by the consumers of the power. There are four TVA lakes in Western North Carolina: Hiwassee built in the late 1930's and three built during World War Two to step up power supply — Fontana, Appalachia, and Chatuge. Chatuge and Appalachia are on the Hiwassee River farther down than the Hiwassee Dam; Fontana is on the Little Tennessee between Graham and Swain counties. Santeetlah and Tapoco on the Cheoah River in Graham County were constructed earlier by the Tallassee Power Company, now Tapoco, Incorporated. The lakes were designed chiefly for hydroelectric power, but flood control and recreational use were also projected.

Not all mountain residents appreciate the TVA for two reasons: vast acreages once under private development, in many cases owned by householders, were purchased at prices which the sellers found inadequate to purchase similar land elsewhere; and the production of power necessitates the drawdown of water in the lakes which sometimes curtails their recreational and aesthetic value. Nevertheless the TVA has participated in hundreds of demonstration projects such as farm and woodland management, fire prevention activities, reforestation, and forest products conferences. The TVA makes payments in lieu of taxes, which are transferred to the counties where its properties are located. Leaders in those counties frequently raise the objection to this practice that the same land under private development would be subject to much higher taxes and thus bear a greater share of the counties' fixed expenses. The impact of the TVA in the development of land and forest resources has not been as great as might have been expected, and residents of the counties concerned have mixed emotions concerning the project. Electric power is now available to all, but people feel that they have paid dearly for its use in giving up land that in most cases had been owned by their families for generations. They especially resent the fact that land in their counties today is selling for many times what they were paid for theirs. Regional planning agencies complain that the TVA has not exercised the wide scale influence envisioned for it — to improve all aspects of the life of the region.

Community land and water development is receiving increased attention in Western North Carolina. A district is organized for a designed watershed. Aid is sought from such services as the Soil Conservation Service, Agricultural Extension Service, Agricultural Stabilization and Conservation Service, county schools, county boards of commissioners, vocational agriculture teachers, the Soil and Water Conservation Committee, Farmers Home Administration, North Carolina Division of Forestry, the North Carolina Wildlife Resources Commission, utilities companies, lumber and pulpwood industries. More and more land is passing out of the hands of farmers and into the possession of promoters of various kinds. The fact that 2,598,000 acres in Western North Carolina were included in farms in 1959 and only 2,321,000 in 1964 illustrates the changing nature of land use in the mountains. The 272,000 acres had been diverted to other uses, such as golf courses, resorts, and industrial plants with accompanying suburban development providing homes for those who had migrated from farms to live near their work.

Many farm families supplement their incomes by work related to the increasing year-round recreation development in the mountains: the Great Smoky Mountain National Park, the Blue Ridge Parkway, ski slopes, lakes, camp sites, hunting and fishing sites, youth camps, and cottage and room rental. This kind of development offers the greatest promise of well-being to much of the area beyond the Blue Ridge. It is the culmination of more than a century of effort to bring the poor in health, the summer resident, the tourist, the retired couple, to the mountains, and the more recent effort to attract and develop industry and to provide for participation in active sports.

In 1970 in the coves and in the hills there are still those who scratch out a meager existence on their little farms. Their "cash money" comes from their fraction of an acre of tobacco allotment. Many farmers are prosperous. They use business methods, planned agriculture, scientific farming, the advice of county agents, the help of the United States Department of Agriculture and the extension services of North Carolina State University. They have tractors, planters, balers — modern machinery. They use the best fertilizers and contour plowing. They use every means possible to prevent erosion. Many make a business of breeding and raising beef cattle for the market, white-face Herefords and Black Angus. Others are highly successful producers of thousands of chickens and eggs. These commercial farmers are prosperous, highly respected and influential members of their communities. Their future is promising. The subsistence farmers need means to supplement their incomes. Local, state, and national agencies are working and planning to provide a better life for the people of the mountains. Great progress has been made. Consolidated schools and technical training are increasing the economic competence of the children of the mountain people.

CHAPTER FOURTEEN

Timber!

As settlers pushed into Western North Carolina, they found almost unbroken forest except on some of the mountain tops characterized as "balds," where there was only grass or shrubbery. Naturalists have estimated that in the mountains of North Carolina were as many as one hundred kinds of trees. In the highest forests, above four thousand feet in altitude, were black spruce and balsam. The oaks predominated in altitudes up to twenty-five hundred feet, and with them were mixed the shortleaf pine, the hickory, the black gum, and the red maple. Between twenty-five hundred and thirty-five hundred feet the oaks decreased and the yellow poplar, hemlock, birch, beech, ash, black walnut, and cherry predominated. Under the trees shrubs, principally rhododendron and mountain laurel, formed a dense growth. People told of walnut trees with a diameter of eight feet, and of wild cherry trees reaching a height of sixty feet to the first limb and with a diameter of four feet, as well as hickory, maple, ash, and yellow locust of prodigious size. Throughout the forests were countless numbers of the lordly and productive chestnut trees which furnished not only wood but food for man and beast. Although the forest was thought of as an obstacle to home building, it was the chief resource of the people. In a small way the early settlers were all lumbermen. Their principal tool was the axe, with which they marked their trails and chopped the trees for logs to build their cabins and for fuel. They girdled, cut, and burned the trees they wanted to get rid of. They were as apt to build their rail fences of choice black walnut as of pine or oak if the walnut was handier. They burned the woodlands so their livestock would have better pasturage.

Primitive cabins gave way as soon as possible to more commodious double log houses, to which additional rooms were added from time to time, and a collection of log buildings served various purposes: as barns, corn cribs, spring houses, smoke houses. Porches were added to the houses, and in many cases weatherboarding was applied to the exterior and sawed paneling to the interior. The simplest way to make boards for this purpose was to select a tall straight tree near an open space in the woods, and to cut it with a cross-cut saw. The tree was then sawed into lengths of from three to four feet and each was split into boards of the desired thickness, by use of a froe, a long blade made of iron or steel. The froe was driven into the end of the length of wood with a maul or mallet. Much longer and smoother boards could be made by sawing them, but the process was slow. The log was mounted on a scaffold, and two men with a long saw, one man above the log and one under it, would take a slice from each side of the log until a square was formed. Then one end was marked into the desired widths, one-fourth being allowed for the kerf, the saw incision. Two men could saw about one hundred feet of lumber in a day. For making furniture or coffins this method was used. The lumber was sometimes sawed at combination saw and grist mills. As late as 1884 Alleghany County had nine of these mills and Buncombe County had fourteen. The two were operated by water power from the same dam, and frequently stores and carpenter shops were adjuncts, as at Alexander's mill on the French Broad. The water power was produced by mountain streams, small but steady, which filled the millponds. Such ponds, covering about an acre of land, had dams of log cribwork covered with rough boards. One sawmill had a millrace several hundred feet long which carried the water to the wheel. The wheel had pockets into which the water flowed from the race, turning an eccentric which had been attached to the wheel. The eccentric pushed up and down, operating a vertical frame in which a saw was affixed. The log and saw were put in place and the water did the work of cutting the smooth boards. Another water driven sawmill had a wooden shaft attached to the water wheel. At the end of the shaft was a crank assembly. The crank was attached to a long saw with the teeth all pointing downward. The log

A better log house ASHEVILLE CITIZEN–TIMES CO.

to be sawed was placed on a carriage with flanged wheels, which could be pushed or pulled on wooden rails. The men would push the carriage and log up against the saw, which went up and down, cutting the boards. Two men could cut about one thousand feet of lumber per day by this method.

Steam sawmills were being introduced in Western North Carolina in the 1880's. Dr. J. B. Weaver had one in Asheville and both Noah Spainhour and R. L. McGhinnis owned steam mills in Lenoir, as did Edwards and Edwards in Hendersonville. Mitchell County had three, owned respectively by A. Job, and Baker and Buchanan of Elk Park, and J. B. Surles of Bakersville.

The sleds so often used on hillside farms and on rough trails, the wagons, and many of the tools were made of wood. On the trails it was sometimes necessary to rough-lock the sleds to keep them from getting out of control. To do this, hickory saplings or log chains were wrapped around the runners to create friction. Wagons too were rough-locked by fouling the wheels so they could not turn, the vehicle being slid down the steep hill without accident.

Small home tanneries provided the leather for shoes, saddles, and harnesses. Almost every community had a tannery, and most county seats had at least one saddle and harness maker.

The bark and wood of the chestnut yielded tannin, used in tanning leather. John T. Staton of Saluda, in Polk County, typified the village shoemaker. He was also a blacksmith, and when anybody died he made the coffin to bury him. Later tanneries offered employment to numbers of people.

In the 1880's the supply of timber in Maine, Michigan, and other Northern forests diminished and lumbermen from those areas came to the Southern Appalachians, scouring the area for choice timber. There were still tracts of virgin forest in areas where no roads had been built and where the inhabitants were few. Such an area was the Pink Bed Valley at the headwaters of the South Fork of the Mills River, a tributary of the French Broad. Randolph Shotwell and a companion hunted in the Pink Beds in 1870. They spent a night with G. W. (Wash) Holden, who owned a fine bottom land on Hominy Creek, with farm, sawmill, and store. Mr. Holden escorted them to the Pink Beds, a trip of seven or eight miles of continual climbing followed by a descent into a valley by a slippery rock path, to the Hunters' Cabin. Erected for the use of hunters and cattle herders, it was a mere log hut, with a slab floor and a gigantic chimney, near the middle of the Pink Beds, a valley "two or three miles wide and twelve miles long surrounded by lofty mountains." Shotwell said the valley was fairly carpeted with a species of wild flowers of pinkish hue, above which grew immense beds of whortleberries studded with laurel blossoms and sweet-scented honeysuckle. Probably the pink blossoms were kalmia or mountain laurel; the "laurel" was rhododendron, and the "honeysuckle" was wild azalea. Shotwell described the forest timber which covered most of the valley as "lofty and vigorous beyond anything I have seen in Western North Carolina. A single trunk of a monster pine, I recollect as above five feet through at the distance of thirty feet from the stump." In 1896 the first forestry school was established in the Pink Beds. The name "Pink Beds" was given by the pioneers to the tract that still bears the name. Before settlers came, cattle were allowed to graze there in summers, the owners being farmers along the French Broad. In this secluded area the cattle would not stray far nor damage cultivated fields, and fences were not needed. When fall came the cattle were removed on the hoof, and most were sold in South Carolina and Georgia. In the

A timber sled used in skidding logs and for other hauling purposes on steep hillsides
ASHEVILLE CHAMBER OF COMMERCE PHOTO

winters when the cattle were gone, the deer came down from the ridges and the farmers again made their way to the Pink Beds, this time to hunt. Often bears were killed there too. No families lived there, and only a few rude cabins for shelter for hunters and drovers had been built. Later a few settlers did move into the area, the most prominent being Hiram King, who built a two-story frame house and operated a water-powered saw and grist mill.

The Pink Beds from the Blue Ridge Parkway   U.S. FOREST SERVICE PHOTO

Hiram King House in the Pink Beds — restored

The lumbermen purchased large tracts of standing trees to be cut later, owners sometimes retaining their land, at other times selling outright. The price of land shot up: one five thousand acre tract of land that had been offered for sale at $750 in 1879 brought $10,000 from the Carolina Spruce Company in 1911. Such land sales promised employment for mountain men as woodsmen. They were needed to fell and trim the trees and to work as mill crews. One of the first markets was for railroad ties. Then after the railroads were in operation, lumber could be shipped to cities in regions where the supply had been exhausted. Sawmills began to multiply rapidly and steam saws became common. Generally no thought was given to a future crop, and the forests were damaged irreparably. One of the most difficult parts of lumbering was to get the logs from the mountainsides to the sawmills. In some places narrow-gauge railroads were built and equipped with Shay locomotives and McGiffert log loaders. The railroad line was laid beside a stream, gradually ascending the ridge. Where the terrain became steep, the track was laid back and forth across the hillsides, the trains alternately going backward and forward to ascend the grades. Sometimes splash dams were constructed of logs to accumulate sufficient water to float the logs down the mountain streams. When such a dam was opened the large flow of water thus released carried the logs to the mill. A boom was built in the Catawba River near Hickory by some owners of a band sawmill. They bought logs in the mountains and had them delivered by water to their boom, until it was broken by a flood and their logs floated down to the Atlantic Ocean. The men learned to fasten their boom securely at the riverbanks so that it would not break when the water rose.

Early in the twentieth century a survey of the area between the Blue Ridge and the Unaka Mountains by H. B. Ayers and W. W. Ashe of the U. S. Geological Survey and the U. S. Division of Forestry estimated that ten billion board feet of log timber had been destroyed in land clearing, five billion board feet had been used locally in the construction of farm buildings and fences, and only three billion board feet had reached a market. An additional drain of about 1,272,000 cords of small timber went into fuel each year. The residual stand of merchantable timber was being culled by loggers who took only the more valuable trees.* Severe erosion of hillside farms, evidence of fires on eighty per cent of the forested areas, and widespread damage from open range grazing of livestock were reported. One

---

* Rebecca Cushman, "Seed of Fire," book-length typescript, tells of an interview with Granville Calhoun who had represented the Whiting Lumber Company in Swain County. The company, chartered in Delaware, was officially named the Graham County Land and Transport Company. Calhoun told Miss Cushman about lumbering on Hazel Creek, now a part of the Great Smoky Mountains National Park, and the influence of the lumbermen on the Hazel Creek community in which he had grown up.

authority wrote, "Present conditions in the commercial and industrial world and in the Southern Alleghanies point to the rapid destruction of the virgin woods."

Asheville and the surrounding area provided a market for much lumber because of the prodigious growth following the completion of the railroads to the town. During the 1880's country estates were being built near Asheville on a grand scale. Senator Vance selected a small plateau on the North Fork of the Swannanoa River and built a house in the style of an English manor, of wood sawed nearby at the Burnett Mill. The rooms were paneled in native woods: the library in wild cherry, the dining room in black walnut and oak, and the living room in curly poplar. The Burnetts knew of only one curly poplar tree standing. It was five feet in diameter, and was growing four miles above the wagon road. They cut the tree in fourteen foot lengths and skidded it, one end on a sled drawn by a team of oxen, down to the upper end of the wagon road. The house was begun in 1880 and finished in 1886, although the landscaping of the grounds was not complete until 1890. The estate contained fifteen hundred wooded acres. Materials such as mantels, windows, and decorations were ordered from New York and were hauled the eight miles from Black Mountain in wagons, often ox-drawn. Senator Vance named the place Gombroon.

In 1878 Richmond Pearson, son of Chief Justice Richmond Pearson, inherited a large tract of land high on the west bank of the French Broad River. He named it Richmond Hill after his father's home and law school in Yadkin County. Ten years later the Richmond Hill house was built on a fine site overlooking Asheville. Although the exterior of the frame house was not remarkable for its beauty, the interior was fine. The walls of the rooms on the first floor were paneled, the entrance hall in oak, the library in walnut, the dining room in cherry, and the drawing room walls were hung in pink silk damask. Pearson served as a member of the United States House of Representatives and then as United States Minister to Persia, Greece, and Montenegro. He was an avid collector, and the house is a repository of paintings and art works from various parts of the world.

George Washington Vanderbilt, grandson of Commodore Cornelius and youngest son of William H. Vanderbilt, was in

Biltmore House, Vanderbilt mansion
ASHEVILLE CHAMBER OF COMMERCE PHOTO

his early twenties when his father died and he inherited the bulk of his fortune. Earlier, on his twenty-first birthday his father had doubled the $1,000,000 left the boy by the old Commodore. He had built up a large library of his own on the second floor of the family's Fifth Avenue mansion, and he spent much of his time in second-hand bookstores adding to his treasures. He had a wide knowledge of modern French literature, was thoroughly acquainted with the paintings in the family art gallery and with the distinguishing characteristics of their artists, and was a nightly visitor at the opera.

In the late 1880's George Vanderbilt purchased fifty-odd farms and some ten country places heretofore owned by impoverished Southern landed aristocracy, and as might be expected, the house and grounds that he developed were an exquisite work of art. Richard Morris Hunt, the New York architect who had designed the Fifth Avenue mansions of the Vanderbilts, was chosen to make the plans. Hunt had studied at the Ecole des Beaux Arts, and many of the mansions that he designed were in the style of the French chateaux, as Biltmore House, Vanderbilt's mansion, was to be. Frederick Law Olmsted, known as

Great stairway in Biltmore House

ASHEVILLE CHAMBER OF COMMERCE PHOTO

the first and greatest of American landscape architects, moved to the Biltmore grounds to create the most beautiful and elaborate country estate in America.

The site selected gave the mansion a superb setting and a breath-taking view. Indiana limestone was used for the house, and a three-mile extension of the railroad was built to carry materials to the location. Hundreds of craftsmen were brought from Europe and from other parts of the United States to cut the limestone and to do the elaborate carvings. A thousand workers were employed for five years in building the mansion, during which time Vanderbilt traveled widely in Europe acquiring paintings, tapestries, statuary, porcelain, and antiques for his 250-room house, which was opened at a Christmas party in 1895. The banquet hall seventy-two feet by forty feet with a seventy-five foot ceiling was designed for a magnificent set of tapestries. The library, which has twenty-thousand volumes, is enriched with a ceiling painted by Pellegrini for an Italian palace. Vanderbilt was still a bachelor. In 1898 he brought his bride to Biltmore. The former Edith Stuyvesant Dresser, she was a member of the distinguished New York family of Stuyvesants, and she had lived during her girlhood with an aunt in Paris, where Vanderbilt met her. She soon endeared herself to everyone on the estate and to the mountain people nearby.

When Vanderbilt planned his estate, there was a little railroad station called Asheville Junction on the banks of the Swannanoa. The post office was called Best, and the village consisted of a few ramshackle houses. Part of the land was below water level. Vanderbilt decided to change Best into a model village. Olmsted planned the village, but first more than 40,000 cubic feet of earth had to be used to fill in the part that was below water level and often flooded in the spring. Buildings first erected were the Estate Office, All Souls Episcopal Church, a new railway station, and the Plaza Building, which housed eight stores, and had five apartments on the second floor. The church was of Norman French architecture, but the houses were of English stucco and timber style. The aim was to make Biltmore resemble an English village. The houses were eagerly sought after, and they were rented for from eight to twenty-five dollars a month. Workers on the estate kept up the streets and the grounds, and the rent paid for all the services. The village was incorporated in 1903 and had a mayor and commissioners. Upon Mr. Vanderbilt's death in 1914 the village was sold to George Stephens. In 1929 it was taken into the city of Asheville. A hospital and dispensary, now incorporated as Biltmore Hospital, was founded by Vanderbilt. His daughter, Mrs. John Francis Amherst Cecil, continues to aid the institution.

When Vanderbilt bought the fifty farms the forests had been exploited until there were none left on the Asheville market. The trees had been killed by incessant forest fires set by the owners to improve the pasture in the woods. Most of the lands in the bottoms along the Swannanoa and French Broad rivers had been abandoned and were covered with sedgegrass. Olmsted planned a model farm, an arboretum, a game preserve, and an example of managed forestry, the first in the United States. The well-to-do young Gifford Pinchot was employed as forester. He had turned down offers to go into his maternal grandfather's office with the practical certainty of a fortune because he chose to study forestry, principally at the French Forest School at Nancy in Lorraine (his paternal grandfather was French). He had just recently returned to America when George Vanderbilt and Frederick Olmsted decided to put forestry into practice on Biltmore Estate. As Pinchot's father and Olmsted were old friends, the young man was invited to take charge of the forest. Millions of acres of land east of the Mississippi were as devastated as those at Biltmore. Reclamation of these North Carolina forests could serve as an object lesson to the nation. When Pinchot began his work at Biltmore, the destructive logging at the hands of the former owners had "been done with an eye single to immediate returns and wholly without regard for the safety of the forests, and fires had been permitted to burn unchecked. There had been much injudicious clearing of upper slopes, which, after a few years of unprofitable cultivation, were generally abandoned to erosion." Pinchot made a study of the 7280 acres, describing every bit of the forest, using squares of from five to seven acres, and then divided the forest into compartments, for each of which he mapped a plan for improvement cuttings. He planned to harvest all of the old trees that were going back, giving the young growth room and light to develop. He had to train native lumbermen to fell timber where it would do the least harm to the young growth, an idea that was contrary to their usual practice of cutting out of the way all of the young growth that would interfere with cheap and easy logging. Each tree to be cut was marked by Pinchot. The cutting began near Biltmore House, and because the wood there was very poor it was simply sawed into cordwood length and left for another gang to split into cordwood and unsalable brush. The wood was then hauled to the railroad to be shipped. A sawmill was soon acquired by Biltmore Forest, and a little later, as the crews moved into more heavily forested areas, they lumbered for saw logs. Drays or "go-devils" (sleds) were used to skid the logs to the roads, where they were loaded on wagons and hauled to the mill, a small portable circular one with a fifty-two inch saw and a twenty-horsepower steam engine. The smaller pieces of the logs were made into shingles.

One of Pinchot's responsibilities was to prepare a Biltmore Forest exhibit for the Chicago World's Fair. Olmsted was in

A monarch of the forest   ASHEVILLE CITIZEN-TIMES CO.

charge of the magnificent landscaping of the fair grounds. The value of managed forestry was to be sold to the public, the first exhibit of its kind ever made in the United States. It showed by enlarged photographs what the forest had been like and what had been done to improve it. The division into compartments and the plan for each compartment were shown by maps. A pamphlet written by Pinchot was distributed free of charge to visitors to the fair and to newspapers, and much friendly comment was received. Pinchot wrote, "The attempt to treat Biltmore Forest systematically derives a certain interest from the fact that it is the first practical application of forest management in the United States." He listed seventy varieties of trees found on Biltmore Estate, with both common and scientific names. An account of expenditures and receipts from the lumber showed a profit, despite the expense of building roads from the sawmill to the rollways, necessitating a road gang to keep the roads in order.

After the World's Fair exhibit was completed, Vanderbilt sent Pinchot to look for land higher in the mountains for his game preserve. Under consideration was the Pink Beds, a tract of 20,000 acres, part of which Vanderbilt purchased. Parts of the tract were by that time owned and occupied by farmers. Pinchot recommended the purchase and then made several trips to look over 80,000 acres adjacent to the Pink Beds, a region of steep slopes, sharp ridges, and narrow valleys, with a high percentage of mature timber. Vanderbilt purchased the land and named it Pisgah Forest. Located in Buncombe, Transylvania, Henderson, and Haywood counties, it was rich in virgin forests because of inaccessibility, and Vanderbilt hoped to practice forestry there at a profit. As the yellow poplar trees on Big Creek, directly under Mount Pisgah, were mature and going down-hill, Pinchot recommend cutting them and sawing the lumber at the mill in Biltmore Forest on the bank of the French Broad River.

About this time Pinchot became restless and decided to open an office as a forestry consultant in New York. His replacement as Vanderbilt's forester was Carl A. Schenck, a young German who had just completed a course under Sir Dietrich Brandis, a distinguished German forester who "might be called the 'Grandfather of American forestry,' although he never visited the United States." Olmsted, Pinchot, and other Americans interested in forestry were greatly influenced by Brandis.

Schenck arrived at Biltmore in 1895 and remained in the United States until 1914, although he never gave up his German citizenship. He had much to learn because the theories he had been taught did not coincide with conditions in Biltmore and Pisgah Forests. During his first months at Biltmore he lived with the Olmsteds in their summer residence. They helped him with the English language and with the affairs of the estate. Schenck's first responsibility was lumbering and marketing the yellow poplar trees in Big Cove Creek, which resulted disastrously. He had a splash dam constructed to his regret. It proved impractical.

Bad for the lover of nature was the destruction wrought by the logs as they swept down the stream. Laurels framing the bank of Big Creek were devastated, and the moss covering the rocks was washed away. The beauty of Big Creek was destroyed, the fertility of the cove was reduced by the acceleration of drainage, and a loss of thousands of dollars was incurred. The lower part of the Mills River through which Schenck's logs must pass to reach the French Broad and continue to the sawmill was lined with small farms, and many of the logs washed ashore onto the fields. The owners were furious and lawsuits resulted. Vanderbilt had to pay damages to the farmers to get his logs. Schenck was convinced that the building of permanent roads into forests of marketable trees was the only satisfactory means for transportation of logs, and many roads were built during his regime as forester.

Another of Schenck's disappointments resulted from his effort to restore old fields to forestry by producing seedling trees. He hoped to grow the seedlings by planting acorns and hickory nuts, five bushels to the acre, in shallow furrows made with a bull-tongue plow and covered with dirt of another furrow. Hundreds of bushels were planted with no success. Rodents ate most of the seeds. Sedgegrass crowded out the few that grew.

Forestry apprentices had come to Biltmore to work under Pinchot and Schenck, engaging in nursery work and in constructing trout ponds and a fish hatchery. They worked without renumeration so eager were they to learn forestry. In addition, rangers were employed, four at Biltmore Forest and three at Pisgah Forest. They were responsible for the progress of roads, nurseries, logging, wood cutting, and for prevention of forest fires and of trespass. Both Pinchot and Schenck had many dealings with the mountain people because Vanderbilt's purchases were in the higher altitudes, on the ridges and slopes, to which access was necessary through the many interior holdings, usually of small farmers in the narrow valleys. Pinchot wrote of the owners: "They regarded this country as their country, their common. And that was not surprising, for they needed everything usable in it — pasture, fish, game — to supplement the very meager living they were able to scratch from the soil of their little clearings, which often were no clearings at all, but mere 'deadenings,' filled with the whitened skeletons of trees killed by girdling."

"By immemorial custom and by law, the cattle and the long-legged hogs ran free over ridge and slope and bottom. You had to fence them out, not to fence them in. These people dwelt and slept mostly in one-room cabins. . . . An open fireplace was cookstove and furnace, with a kettle hanging from a crane." Glass was rare, and windows were closed by solid board shutters. Homespun was the common wear.

One of Schenck's most valuable apprentices was Overton Price, whose mother was a Westfeldt and who lived at Rugby Grange, one of the better-kept old Southern estates of the area.

He knew the language of the mountain people, the country, and the native trees. Later Price studied in Germany and returned home to become Pinchot's secretary. In 1900 Pinchot founded the Society of American Foresters, with fifteen members, four of them Biltmoreans, of whom Price was one. His treatise, "Practical Forestry in the Southern Appalachians," for the *Yearbook of the Department of Agriculture* in 1900 was prophetic of the importance the outside world would soon attach to the mountain area. He placed the emphasis on sound business measures and practical forestry and on producing repeated crops of merchantable lumber. Three considerations were pointed out: not only is the timber valuable, especially black walnut, cherry, hickory, white oak, and poplar; but the forests control the drainage basins of the rivers; moreover, the Southern Appalachians have a great future as a health and recreation resort because there is no equivalent great forest region within easy reach of so large a number of people.

Because of the number of young men who wanted to learn forestry and the absence of a forestry school in the United States, Schenck started one in 1897, and in 1898 he published a school catalogue. He advertised the curriculum as a one-year course in practical forest management with emphasis on field work. A school room was built in the Pink Beds for summer use, but in winter the lectures were given at Biltmore Forest. Those who finished the course found ready employment.

Schenck in 1908 sent out invitations to foresters all over the nation to come to a forest fair in Biltmore Forest. The invitations were in the form of a fifty-six page booklet in which his plantings in each of sixty-three tracts were described. The cost was listed as were the successes and failures of each plantation or tract. Tracts were labeled and numbered, and persons attending were shown these sixty-three extensive efforts at scientific forestry. This fair was to be a visual demonstration. Schenck's booklet was informative, inspiring, and humorous. A sample excerpt indicates the extent of his efforts and those of the Biltmore foresters and illustrates how these efforts provided guide lines for continued practical forestry: "Tip No. 2. The plantation marked No. 2, of Long Ridge, covers forty-five acres of steep slopes which were cleared some sixty years ago; abandoned for farming some thirty years ago; covered in 1895 with sedge-grass, and cut by deeply eroded gullies on the side facing the East. In 1895 Mr. Vanderbilt desired the entire hill to be planted in hardwoods. It was my wish to show him (and to all America) that forest planting could be done ... at an expense of $5.00 an acre." On this plantation he sowed bushels of chestnuts and hickory nuts and set out on the north slope 11,000 yearling chestnut oaks, ailanthus, black cherries, and hickories. On the west slope where the sedge was heavy he planted some 20,000 Douglas firs, sugar maples, white and black walnuts, black cherries, and white oaks. The cost of planting and work was $241.06. Some of these plantings did well; others did not. He did additional plantings in 1898, 1899, and 1900, after which time the plantation did well. He stated that Long Ridge, which had been a nasty scar on a hillside, was now flourishing, and added, "Nowadays it is a joy for me to crawl through this plantation! I feel like the Lord on the Seventh Day of creation when I am crawling."

Each of Schenck's sixty-three "Tips" dealt with similar efforts and eventual successes. Many foresters came to his forest fair, and from it they learned valuable lessons about conservation and successful forestry. The whole tenor of the pamphlet indicates Schenck's love for his trees and his work. This fair must have been one of the finest actual demonstrations of forestry ever presented to interested foresters.

In April 1909 Vanderbilt discharged Carl Schenck as forester, and forestry at Biltmore came to an end for almost forty years. Although the Biltmore Forest School had no endowment or support from public funds, it was self-supporting from tuition fees, and Schenck was financially independent. His decision was to operate the school on a field study basis, using land owned by lumber companies in North Carolina, in the Adirondacks, in Michigan, and in Oregon for working fields. In addition he took his students to Europe for two to three month periods to show them the results of sustained-yield European forestry. And so the forestry school continued to operate until 1914. Meanwhile several forestry schools had been established by American universities, and state boards of forestry were on the increase. Under Schenck's influence Governor William W. Kitchen of North Carolina issued a proclamation in 1909 placing all woodlands situated above contour line two thousand feet under increased fire protection. Schenck's contribution to the state and the nation was to emphasize the importance of privately owned forests, properly managed and protected to enable them to continue producing merchantable timber. The private lumber companies regarded him as a friend. Reuben Robertson of the Champion Fibre Company offered Schenck its Sunburst village for the forestry school headquarters. Sunburst was a model village built to house woodworkers, the buildings of which were not being used. Schenck accepted the offer, and he and his forestry school surveyed the whole territory near Canton.

The Champion Coated Paper Company was an Ohio concern incorporated about 1896 by Peter G. Thomson who had obtained from the Champion International Paper Company of Massachusetts a license to make paper, coating it on both sides at one operation. Great profits were made, but Thomson owned no forests, and he was buying wood from his competitors in Ohio. He needed a supply of spruce for making pulp. The spruce forests in the Smoky and Balsam mountains were the finest in the United States. In 1905 the Champion Fibre Company was organized, and from 1906 to 1908 it built its plant at Canton, North Carolina. Thomson borrowed over $3,000,000 during the panic of 1907 to complete the paper and pulp mill. Long known as the Ford of Pigeon and its post office known as Pigeon River, the place had only a few houses when the Western North Carolina Railroad reached it. The name Canton was bestowed by the General Assembly in 1894. The town had been the terminus of the railroad for two years and had developed accordingly. By 1906 it had about four hundred people, but after the Champion Paper Company went into operation it attracted workers and their families and by 1916 there were around six thousand people living in Canton and two thousand more in the surrounding area. Mr. Reuben Robertson, Thomson's son-in-law, was sent to Canton on a fifty-day assignment to make the plant a successful one, and he remained for the rest of his life, more than fifty years. Tanning was a sideline to the chief purpose of the company, paper making, yet the tannic acid made there paid for the wood. A process developed by Oma Carr, a chemical engineer, was applied to chestnut chips to make pulp after the tannic acid had been removed from them. The wood was reduced to small chips and subjected to treatment in boiling chemicals which dissolved the resinous material in the wood, leaving only the fibre. After washing, screening, and bleaching, it was formed in a sheet on a revolving cylinder covered with wire cloth, passed between rollers to wring out the water, then heated over steam cylinders for drying. Wound on reels in continous rolls as it appeared from the machine, it resembled cardboard or blotter. This product was shipped to Hamilton, Ohio, to be coated. At first, chestnut wood was essential to the plant for production of tannic acid, and Robertson said that the company came to North Carolina first for the spruce and second for the many chestnut trees. The chestnut blight which appeared about 1920 was of cataclysmic importance to the industry.

Spruce was difficult to obtain because it grew only in the highest altitudes, and after Schenck's survey revealed the great extent of pine forests available a process was developed to make a bleached kraft out of pine. Champion made the first white paper of pine.

The company purchased lands, often tracts with nothing ready for immediate harvest, but with "good forest reproduction on them." It also purchased wood from the farmers and from the national forests. The contracts with farmers contained a clause stating that they could be cancelled if the wood was not handled in accordance with sustained yield principles. It was essential for the company that the forests be maintained for perpetual yield.

By 1916 the Champion Fibre Company employed over one thousand men and was worth ten million dollars. Fifteen carloads of products left Canton daily. In addition the farmers had a cash crop and the lumbermen a market for their waste products. Supplies such as coal, lime, alkali, and sulphur were supplied from Tennessee and Virginia.

After the days of the Forestry School at Biltmore, no forestry program was carried on there until 1946, when the Champion Paper and Fibre Company (the name had been changed) made a contract with the estate to cut mature trees and do scientific thinning in certain areas. Max Dillingham, forester in charge, was a joint employee of the estate and the company. Natural reseeding was carried on from seed trees in natural regeneration. Of the 12,000 acres then in the estate, about 8,500 were in forest land. Suitable trees were cut for sawwood and were sawed at the sawmill on the estate and sold through a broker. Some forty employees worked on the operation, under contract, using their own equipment. All trees were marked before cutting, and all brush and limbs were scattered evenly over the forest floor. Champion built and maintained its own roads. Firewood was cut for the estate greenhouses and sawdust was used in the barns, so there was no waste.

The Champion Paper and Fibre Company has had enlightened policies concerning the preservation of forests and the use of the "sustained-yield" principle in its harvesting of and purchases of timber and wood. It has made progress in solving its problems of air and stream pollution. *Report No. 5, Pollution Survey of the French Broad River Basin* made by the State Stream Sanitation Committee (1957) criticized the company for discharging industrial waste into Pigeon River. The company spent $3,000,000 in 1962 and 1963 to develop a primary treatment system. Afterwards it began work on a secondary treatment system.

Mr. Vanderbilt in the early 1900's sold the timber rights in Pisgah Forest to the Carr Lumber Company for twelve dollars per acre, the contract to extend over a twenty-year period. During the twenty years the Vanderbilt estate netted about $870,000. Vanderbilt held that "private ownership of any resource necessary to the general welfare carries with it the moral obligation of faithful stewardship to the public." He said: "I have stuck to forestry from the beginning and I shall not forsake it now. For me to impair the future usefulness of Pisgah Forest in order to somewhat increase present revenues, would be bad business policy. But apart from that, it would be bad citizenship. As I see it, no man is a good citizen who destroys for selfish ends a growing forest." Vanderbilt might have received a much higher price for the timber if he had waived restrictions as to methods of cutting under this sale, but he required that the methods of practical forestry be followed. Overton Price wrote: "Pisgah Forest, its mountainous slopes clothed in an unbroken mantle of protective tree growth, is his monument. He transformed it by nearly a quarter of a century's efficient fire protection from a forest characterized by scanty young growth, thin humus covering, and impoverished soil, as the result of an injury it had received in former years from excessive grazing and recurrent fires, to one whose silvicultural condition is probably unequalled in the Southern Appalachians."

Although managed forestry was first applied in America at Biltmore Forest, the United States Government had shown an interest in forest conservation for many years. In 1876 the Division of Forestry had been established in the Department of Agriculture to gather statistics and disseminate information on forestry. Proposals that the United States retain in the public domain the timberlands that were still owned publicly were made but not acted upon until 1891 when the Forest Reserve Act was passed and President Harrison, on the advice of Arnold Hague of the U. S. Geological Service, set aside the Yellowstone Park Timberland Reserve of over a million and a quarter acres. This was the first U. S. Forest Reservation. The act did not provide for the practice of forestry or for protection of the forests. It merely withheld the land from sale or homesteading. President Cleveland added 21,279,840 acres to the Forest Reserves. Subsequent legislation outlined the duties and responbilities of those administering the reserves. Theodore Roosevelt became President of the United States in 1901, and upon the advice of Hoke Smith, Secretary of the Interior, Gifford Pinchot, and F. H. Newell, author of the act of 1891 providing for the reserves, he transformed forestry and irrigation into issues of national consequence and won for them a high degree of public acceptance. In his Annual Message, December 2, 1901, he wrote: "The fundamental idea of forestry is the perpetuation of forests by use. Forest protection is not an end in itself; it is a means to increase and sustain the resources of our country and the industries which depend upon them." At that time the Division of Forestry in the Department of Agriculture was renamed the Bureau of Forestry with Gifford Pinchot as its head. In 1905 the Forest Reserves were transferred to the Department of Agriculture's Bureau of Forestry, and renamed the United States Forest Service. The Forest Reserves were renamed National Forests.

So far, none of the legislation applied to the hardwood forests of the Southern Appalachians, where there was no land in the public domain. Efforts had been made to get the federal government to preserve portions of these forests. In 1885 Dr. Henry O. Marcy, a Boston physician, read before the American Academy of Medicine in New York, a paper concerning the advisability of securing a large reservation of the higher ranges of the mountains of North Carolina as a national park for the benefit of invalids. He said its advantages "would be of value incalculable to millions yet unborn." Other proposals for a national forest in the Appalachians were made, and after Theodore Roosevelt visited Asheville in 1902 there was a movement in

Congress to have the United States *purchase* lands in the Appalachians for parks and reserves. Destructive floods had occurred in the streams draining the Appalachians. These could be brought under control if the slopes were properly forested. A fundamental difference developed between the operation of the National Forests and the National Parks. In the latter the virgin forest is preserved; while in the former, controlled lumbering is practiced. The efforts to establish a national park are discussed elsewhere. Here the emphasis will be on National Forests, which were provided for by the Weeks Law in 1911. By the year 1910, the Forest Reserves had been increased to 25,605,700 acres, all west of the Mississippi River. The forests were yielding a revenue, one-fourth of the gross of which was distributed to the states in which the forests were located, while the nation appropriated $3,908,240.32 for operation. It seemed logical that Congress could appropriate money to purchase forest lands east of the Mississippi. Mr. James S. Whipple, Forest Commissioner of New York, explained: "Without forests we can have but little water. A study of this natural reservoir proves the importance and imperative necessity of preserving our forests. Let us examine it: The trees are part of it; the leaves on the trees are part of it; the twigs, old logs, limbs, and fallen limbs are part of it. All of these catch, delay, and hold back the raindrops as they fall. If you will observe the conditions of the forest floor you will notice that between the trees there are little basins in the ground, caused by the roots of the trees holding up the soil. These basins catch and hold the rain. Then underneath it all, formed from decaying leaves, twigs, limbs, and logs for a thousand years, is a black mold called humus. Thus humus has greater power to take up and hold moisture than any other known vegetable or animal matter. . . . [All of these are] parts of this perfect reservoir, built on nature's plan, detaining, holding, and keeping back the water, allowing it to soak into the ground to feed the little springs, thence the creeks, and keep the water flowing slowly from the hills all the year round.

"On the other hand, when the forest is cut away, the basins are broken down, all obstructions to the flow of water are removed, the humus is destroyed, and nature's reservoir is swept away, allowing the water to run quickly into the larger streams, causing destructive floods. Many times great damage and sometimes unhealthful conditions follow. When the storm is over, the flood subsides, the water is soon gone, and dry creek-beds appear." Federal purchase of forests in the Appalachians had been endorsed by three Presidents but had been opposed by Senators from the Northwest and by some Southern Senators who were adherents of strict states rights.

The Weeks Act, passed on the fifteenth of February, 1911, authorized the Secretary of Agriculture to recommend for purchase lands he believed necessary for the regulation of the flow of navigable streams at prices fixed by the National Forest Reservation Commission. The seller of a tract was allowed to reserve the timber and mineral rights, but all cutting of timber and all mining must be done under the rules and regulations established by the commission. The act provided that after the purchase of tracts small areas that were included which could be used for agriculture without injury to the forest or the stream flow and not needed for public purposes were to be offered for sale as homesteads in tracts not to exceed eighty acres, and jurisdiction over such land would revert to the state in which it lay. An amendment later substituted the exchange of land for actual purchase. The terms of the exchange are based on need of a national forest for a particular tract which is privately owned, and desire of an individual to acquire a tract not essential to the national forest. These exchanges are not on an acre for acre basis, and a farmer might receive a forty-acre tract in exchange for a much smaller one. Thus small individuals holdings not originally sold to the government have been acquired.

Since 1897 timber sales have been permitted in forest reservations, now National Forests, to residents of adjacent areas; this practice has been important. Residents in the mountains are permitted to engage in lumbering in the National Forests. To illustrate, a farmer who owns a sawmill and who desires to increase his income during the months that are unproductive on the farm may apply to a ranger for permission to cut certain trees that are overmature (no longer growing rapidly enough to make it worthwhile to save them) to make way for vigorous young stock. The farmer may know of such a group of trees. The ranger measures the trees to determine their stumpage value, based on the difference between their sale value and the cost of producing it less a proper allowance for profit and risk. If the amount due the government is less than $500 the ranger is not required to advertise the timber for sale, and a contract may be drawn up. Amounts involving a payment of over $500 must be advertised. The purchaser may pay cash, or he may arrange to make payments as he markets the lumber. The plan encourages conservation as the farmer wishes to be able to continue purchasing timber from the National Forest.

Under the Weeks Act National Forests were created in the Appalachian region of North Carolina, the Pisgah in 1916 and the Nantahala in 1920. The headquarters are in Asheville. The purchase of Vanderbilt's holdings in Pisgah Forest was approved in 1914 after his death although he had favored the sale. Mrs. Vanderbilt asked five dollars per acre, which was less than the average price of other tracts already acquired. Her feeling in the matter was expressed in a letter to the commission: "I wish earnestly to make such disposition of Pisgah Forest as will maintain in the fullest and most permanent way its national value as an object lesson in forestry, as well as its wonderful beauty and charm; and I realize that its ownership by the Nation will alone make its preservation permanent and certain. Accordingly I have decided to make as large a contribution as I can, in order to help bring this result about." It must be remembered that Vanderbilt had already realized twelve dollars per acre for the timber rights sold to the Carr Lumber Company.

The Weeks Act was passed under the power of the United States to preserve the navigability of streams and their watersheds. A subsequent act, more far-reaching, provided for the purchase of land for the practice of forestry, even where navigability of streams was not in jeopardy. Purchases of additional tracts were made and continued to be made until in 1966 there were 878,000 acres of land in national forests in the twenty-four counties of Western North Carolina. Of this, 480,000 is in the Pisgah National Forest, the balance in the Nantahala National Forest. A much greater percentage of land is in commercial forests, most of which are being managed today in accordance with the example furnished by the Forest Service. A survey conducted in 1966 showed that 14% of all land in the twenty-four counties is in National Forests, while 71.5% of all land is in commercial forests. In 1967 Macon County had the largest acreage of national forests, 148,016; Transylvania was second with 87,466. The other four leaders were Haywood, 67,454; Burke, 47,409; Buncombe, 31,874; Swain, 16,148.

In 1916 President Wilson proclaimed the creation of the Pisgah National Game Preserve, the first concrete wildlife management program for Western North Carolina.

Recognition of the multiple-use principle already practiced was achieved in the "Multiple-Use Sustained Yield Act" of

1960. The act named the basic renewable resources (water, recreation, wood, forage, and wildlife) for which the Forest Service is responsible. Once acquired, the National Forests have been utilized in as many ways as possible to provide for the recreational needs of the American people. The Forest Service almost at once set aside the Pink Beds as a site for a federal deer propagation program. Fawns were caught and reared there and then transferred to begin herds in North Carolina and other states. Trout were also propagated for restocking mountain streams.

In 1961, the fiftieth anniversary of the Weeks Law, Secretary of Agriculture Orville Freeman gave instructions to designate the Pink Beds "The Cradle of Forestry in America." Consequently a visitor center has been created near the site of Schenck's School of Forestry. It contains displays illustrating the multiple use of forests. Visitors may then follow nearby trails for a view of the region as it was during Schenck's regime.

The Pisgah and Nantahala National Forests are administered by four staff members and numerous associates at the Asheville headquarters, heading the four facets of modern forestry: water, timber, wildlife, and recreation. In the Nantahala National Forest ten rivers rise: the Nantahala, Cheoah, Tuckaseigee, Hiwassee, Valley, Cullasaja, Little Tennessee, Chattooga, Whitewater, and Toxaway. They feed large river systems, the Tennessee and the Savannah. The area receives as much as seventy inches of rainfall per year, and in some places it reaches one hundred or more inches. Near Franklin, at the headwaters of the Little Tennessee River, is the 5400 acre Coweeta Hydrological Laboratory, the only study area of its kind in the Eastern United States. There the soil is as deep as thirty inches, and observations are made of the effects of timber cutting, logging, fire, woods grazing, and land clearing on the flow and quality of the water and the silt content of streams. The aim is to develop methods of forest management to obtain better and more abundant water supplies. At Bent Creek Experimental Forest near Asheville, studies have shown that forest soil stripped of its trees absorbs less than one-fifth of an inch of rain in an hour, while properly managed forest land absorbs up to four inches of rainfall in an hour.

Nantahala National Forest contains 650 million boardfeet of saw timber and 400,000 cords of merchantable pulpwood. In 1956 the income from the sale of timber was $317,000. Twenty-five per cent of all income from the sale of forest products is

Deer preserve   ASHEVILLE CITIZEN-TIMES CO.

paid to the state to be used for schools and roads in the counties in which the forest is located. An additional ten per cent is appropriated to the Forest Service for improvement of roads and trails in the forest. The timber operators who purchase timber in the Nantahala National Forest had in 1956 an annual payroll of $696,000, and year-round employment was provided for five hundred people. As the volume of forest products increases the above figures also increase.

In 1937 the State of North Carolina and the United States Forest Service signed a cooperative wildlife agreement, which has been revised from time to time. The purpose is to protect wildlife, to plant fish in the streams throughout the forests, and to regulate fishing and hunting, and a license for either must be obtained from the state. State game, fish, and sanitary laws apply except in special game-management areas inside the forest, which in the Nantahala Forest are Fires Creek area north of Hayesville, Wayah Wildlife Management area west of Franklin, Standing Indian area at the head of the Nantahala River, and the Santeetlah area northwest of Robbinsville. In these the number of hunters and the hunting periods for wild boar, bear, and deer are restricted to maintain a sustained game production.

Timber! / 317

A mountain angler on Lake Logan near Waynesville HUGH MORTON PHOTO

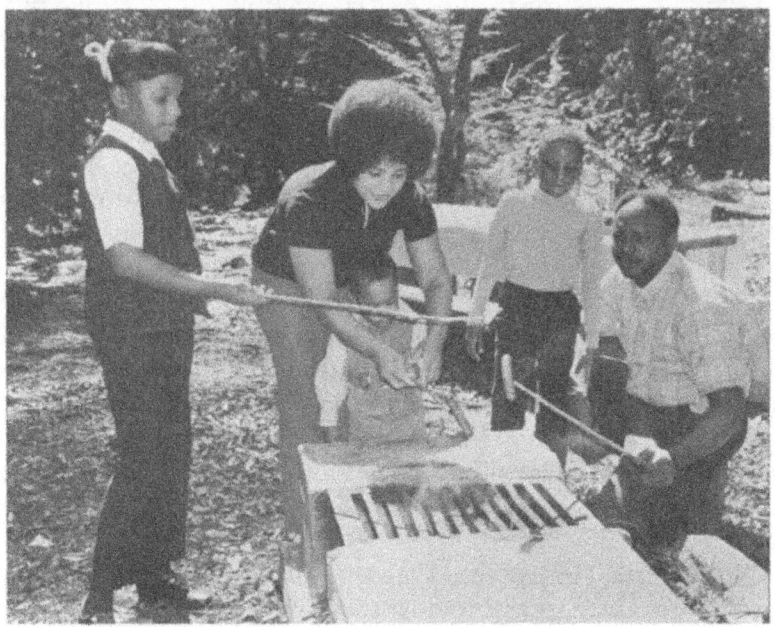

A cook-out in a camp ground of the Pisgah National Forest
U.S. FOREST SERVICE PHOTO

318 / Part III: A Developing Economy

Hiker on a trail in a national forest   U.S. FOREST SERVICE PHOTO

Special fees are charged by the state to hunt and fish in the Cooperative Wildlife Management areas. Twenty-three hundred persons per year are permitted to hunt bear and wild boar with dogs in North Carolina. Applicants pay the required fee and engage in a public drawing for the right to hunt. Hunt fees are refunded to those who lose out in the drawing.

There are 1200 miles of trout streams in the National Forests in North Carolina, constituting fifty per cent of the trout streams in the state, and brook, rainbow, and brown trout are present there. The Pisgah Forest Fish Hatchery in Transylvania County twelve miles from Brevard furnished nine- to ten- inch trout for the streams and lakes of the Great Smoky Mountains National Park, the Cherokee Indian Reservation, the Pisgah and Nantahala National Forests, and public trout waters in eight counties of Western North Carolina, and eggs are shipped to fish hatcheries in other states of the Appalachian area. A laboratory trains hatchery personnel.

Forest fire control has been so effective in the National Forests that the average loss in the Nantahala is now one-third

Timber! / 319

of one per cent. Towers and observatories at high points, with observers always on the alert and with telephone and radio service and roads and trails for the purpose, enable the fire fighting crews to put out most of the fires within the first hour after they start.

For those who like to camp or to hike, there are twenty-nine recreation areas, twenty of which have camping facilities and well-marked trails. In some areas the United States Forest Service rents sites on an annual basis for families wishing to build their own cabins. Typical of the camp sites is the Jack Rabbit Recreation Area on Chatuge Lake in Clay County, where camping, picnicking, boating, and water skiing are possible. The North Carolina Wildlife Commission and the United States Forest Service provided a boat launching ramp. Said to resemble a Swiss Alpine lake, Chatuge has been called the crown jewel in TVA's system of beautiful lakes. Each of the one hundred camping sites has a table, a tent platform, and a fireplace. Fifteen miles away is the Fires Creek Wildlife Management Area, where campers may fish and hunt during the legal

The Linville Gorge Wilderness Area

ASHEVILLE CHAMBER OF COMMERCE PHOTO

Inviting trail in the Linville Gorge Wilderness Area

U.S. FOREST SERVICE PHOTO

season. Twenty-six miles of developed trails lead to the rim of the mountains.

In 1937 the 2000-mile Appalachian Trail for foot travel was completed. Extending from Maine to Georgia, in North Carolina it winds over Roan Mountain, follows the boundary between the Pisgah National Forest and the Cherokee National Forest (in Tennessee), through the Great Smoky Mountains National Park, and into the Nantahala and Chattahoochee (Georgia) National Forests.

Three areas of unusual beauty are preserved within the National Forests. They are Roan Mountain, Linville Gorge Wilderness, and Joyce Kilmer Memorial Forest. The first and second have been known by tourists for generations. Roan Mountain, on the North Carolina-Tennessee line, is in late

Timber! / 321

Joyce Kilmer Memorial Forest in Graham County — marker
ASHEVILLE CHAMBER OF COMMERCE PHOTO

Vista of Joyce Kilmer Memorial Forest from Snowbird Mountain Lodge
U.S. FOREST SERVICE PHOTO

June blanketed with blooming purple rhododendron, with here and there beautiful stands of fir and spruce trees. Cloudland Hotel closed about 1917, and in 1940 the United States Forest Service purchased the area. Five thousand acres are managed for recreational use, although no camping facilities are provided. The Linville Gorge Wilderness has been admired by visitors since it was visited by the French botanist Andre Michaux in 1802. No road has ever been built along this stretch of the Linville River because its banks are so rugged, with Linville Mountain on its right and Jonas Ridge on its left. The latter is unique in its strange rock formations that are visible for miles — Hawksbill, Table Rock, and the Chimneys. Travelers on foot and on horseback have for years gone to Wiseman's View on Linville Mountain for the panorama of the gorge and Jonas Ridge. Along the riverbank and throughout the gorge are an abundance of wild flowers and shrubs of great variety. Camping is permitted in the Linville Gorge Wilderness but no facilities are furnished. However, about five miles from Wiseman's View, at Linville Falls, a campground is provided.

In Graham County in the Nantahala National Forest is a 3800 acre tract of virgin wilderness with trees hundreds of years old, some measuring twenty feet around the base and more than a hundred feet high, and a great variety of shrubs. It is designated the Joyce Kilmer Memorial Forest in honor of the poet-soldier who lost his life in France in World War One, whose poem "Trees" is loved by the American public.

The trees are here for all to admire and enjoy. They enable both travelers and residents, the city pent and the people of the wooded hills, to get close to the heart of nature — to feel like nature's noblemen. Let it be the resolve of all who live in or come to the mountains that when a tree is cut a tree must be planted.

CHAPTER FIFTEEN

From Indian Trails to Broad Highways

In 1879 there began in North Carolina a movement that was to make possible the most far-reaching reform in the history of the state. This was initiated by the Mecklenburg Road Law. Prior to that time all road work had been done by the free-labor system called the "labor tax" under which every able-bodied man was obligated to give a certain number of days' work per year for the upkeep of roads. The new law applied to three counties, Mecklenburg, Forsyth, and Stokes, but it was available to any county by action of the county commissioners if requested by a petition of a specified number of voters. It provided for a combination of free-labor and tax support for construction of roads. The law was repealed two years later and then was re-enacted. A new principle had entered the minds of the legislators and of the people of the state.

Since 1867 various experiments with road building had been tried. First, the township justices had been made responsible for administering the state road laws and appointing road supervisors for their districts. The constitution as amended in 1875 assigned road control to the county commissioners, who were chosen by the township justices appointed by the legislature. However, in 1880 the General Assembly in special session restored the township trustees' responsibility for roads. In 1887 the "chain-gang law" authorized the counties to assign to road work convicts with sentences of less than ten years. Meanwhile the practice of requiring every able-bodied man to work on the public roads continued. The roads remained as bad as before.

Two professors at the state university, State Geologist J. A. Holmes and William Cain, a civil engineer, in a report to Governor Thomas M. Holt in 1893, wrote: "The problem of better public roads, especially in the midland and western counties, perhaps outranks in importance all other industrial questions now before the people of the State." Holmes and Cain recommended that all public roads be constructed and kept in repair as far as possible by men employed and trained for the work. They emphasized that railroads could in no way substitute for roads. "Every citizen should be within easy reach, over a good public highway, of the railroad, the county seat, and the nearest market town."

It was the contention of the two professors that the state lost $10,519,000 annually because of bad roads in the middle and western counties. The figures were broken down as follows: "Loss on account of the cost of feeding, and loss of time by the 134,000 country mules and horses in the middle and western counties, during four weeks of impassable roads: $1,600,000; "Loss, on account of bad roads, of the time and maintenance of 210,000 country horses and mules, 105,000 wagons and harness, and wages of 105,000 teamsters, during one month: $3,948,000; "Loss on account of bad roads, of the services and expense of feeding 25,000 town horses, and services of 12,000 teamsters, and wear and tear on 12,500 wagons and harness, all of which could be saved by having good roads and streets: $4,531,000; "Wasted in working public roads in taxes and labor: $440,000; Total: $10,519,000." They maintained that the state could save this amount annually by installing a system of good macadamized roads.

Rural Free Delivery (RFD) which was experimental with a law passed by Congress in 1893 was impractical in Western North Carolina because of the poor roads, although by 1898 it had become a permanent feature of the postal service. In 1899 a Good Roads Association of Asheville was organized, the first in the state. The private macadam roads on the Vanderbilt estate had demonstrated what might be done with public roads. The association under the leadership of Dr. C. P. Ambler built one mile of macadam road from Asheville to Biltmore and campaigned for better roads in Buncombe County. It cooperated with neighboring counties in holding meetings, and a similar association was formed in Hendersonville. In 1902 a North Carolina Good Roads Association was formed to work

From Indian Trails to Broad Highways / 325

Post offices were usually in stores or homes   ASHEVILLE CITIZEN-TIMES CO.

out a formula to help the counties acquire better roads through federal support, extended use of convicts, instruction in road building, and a course in road building to be offered at State College of Agriculture and Mechanic Arts and at the state university.

Meanwhile some efforts were made by individuals or corporations to attract the tourist trade to areas not served by railroads, requiring them to invest private capital for roads. Mr. S. T. Kelsey, one of the founders of Highlands in Macon County, was employed to make a survey for a projected railroad that was to follow the Blue Ridge through the Carolinas and Virginia. He was impressed with the scenic possibilities of the area which became Linville. Kelsey interested his friend Donald MacRae of Wilmington, who in turn sent his son Hugh to look over the valley. A corporation was formed to purchase land and lay out a resort village. As the location was remote and travel would be difficult, the company constructed the Yonahlossee road in 1890 and 1891 along the southern slope of Grandfather Mountain from Linville to Blowing Rock with a branch road leading to the top of the mountain. The main road was twenty miles long and from ten to fourteen feet wide, and the cost of building was about $10,000. Kelsey surveyed and supervised the construction of the project, employing local workmen. Joe Lee Hartley, who worked on the two-year project, described the task: "We had bush crews and log crews, shovel and mattock crews. There were some 300 men working on the road. . . . I walked five miles to work for 300 days. When we got the road about half way done, up there around the side of the Grandfather, we had a shack under the rocks."

In their 1893 report Holmes and Cain called the road "an excellent one for summer travel . . . through one of the most beautiful and interesting portions of the mountain region of North Carolina."

The Good Roads movement grew in popularity and a Southern Appalachian Good Roads Association was organized in 1909. Two years later the Southern Railway and the Atlantic Coastline Railway entered the campaign. Their officials believed that good roads would encourage production and result in more balanced marketing. A Good Roads Train was operated in the mountains by the Southern Railway in 1911. It contained three coaches, one of which contained working models and road building equipment, with explanations of how to build and maintain good roads, and one a stereopticon and screen showing good and bad roads. Railway officials and experts from the United States Office of Public Roads gave lectures in Marshall, Asheville, Waynesville, Sylva, Hendersonville, Lake Toxaway, Brevard, Rutherfordton, Marion, Morganton, North Wilkesboro, and Mount Airy.

The automobile had come into use on North Carolina roads and streets, and a license fee of five dollars per auto was

Copy of photo made by Donald McRae of the Linville-Blowing Rock hack on the Yonahlossee Road at Wilson Creek in the 1890's   HUGH MORTON PHOTO

imposed in 1909, of which three dollars was returned to the county in which it was collected.

In 1911 the General Assembly authorized construction of the Central Highway to extend from Morehead City to the Tennessee line, to follow the railroad. Work lagged and the road was not completed until 1921. The plan was to improve roads already constructed, making them thirty feet wide from ditch to ditch and with no grade over four and one-half percent. Buncombe County already had a good road from Swannanoa Gap on the east to the county line on the west, a combination of macadam in some places and sand clay in others. Sand clay roads were cheaper to build than macadam and a county could build more miles with its money. Sand clay roads required constant attention, but they could be kept up by just a few men. When the Central Highway Committee attempted to inspect the entire route in 1912, its members had to begin the tour in Haywood County, Madison County's roads not being in condition for travel even in midsummer.

A scenic highway to be known as the "Crest of the Blue Ridge Highway" was being surveyed in 1911, from Marion, Virginia, to Talullah Falls, Georgia, where it would connect with a good road to Atlanta. It was to enter North Carolina in Ashe County via Beaver Creek and Elk Cross Roads, where there was a good dirt road as far as Boone. The next thirty-five miles, to Linville via Blowing Rock, would utilize the Yonahlossee road. From Linville to Linville Falls the road was under construction, although there was not yet any surfacing material and it would get very heavy in winter. Tourists would be expected to stop at Linville Falls to see the gorge and the falls. From that point the road would proceed close to the summit of the Blue Ridge on an entirely new route with beautiful scenery. The highest point on the highway would be Stepps Gap, approximately 5,500 feet, only 1,200 less than Mount Mitchell. Thence it would pass through the heart of the Black Mountains where there had never been any roads. The road was to lead through Asheville to Hendersonville and Brevard, then pass the resorts of Lake Toxaway, Lake Sapphire, and Fairfield Lake to Highlands, and on to Talullah Falls. At Asheville the proposed road was to coincide with one already constructed to the top of Sunset Mountain. This five mile macadam road had been constructed by Dr. E. W. Grove as an exclusive automobile route, there being a separate road to the summit for carriages.

The scheme for the scenic road originated with Dr. Joseph Hyde Pratt, State Geologist, and the survey was made under the auspices of the North Carolina Geological and Economic Survey by students of the University of North Carolina during their summer vacation. T. F. Hickerson, a member of the party, reported that they spent ten days "very pleasantly at Dr. C. P. Ambler's summer home before starting the survey at Bull Gap, ten miles east of Asheville. There were no wagon roads between Bull Gap and Stepps Gap near Mt. Mitchell, . . . there were scarcely any trails that could be traveled in safety with a horse." The section surveyed averaged 5,000 feet in altitude. The camp equipment, including seven tents, ten folding cots, clothes and two double blankets for each person, a stove and cooking equipment, tablewear, and rations, had to be packed on mules or portaged a distance of about seven miles over the steep and rough trails.

In 1912 a portion of the road between Linville and Altapass was constructed under the direction of Dr. Pratt, with one hundred men. The Appalachian Highway Company had been chartered to build the road, and people along the route were giving the right-of-way and were encouraged to buy stock. The portion between Altapass and Pineola was completed before work was stopped because of World War One. The surface was of sand, clay, and gravel. A toll road, it was expected to entice more tourists to the area, to have them stay longer and visit the inns along the scenic route.

Locke Craig, an Asheville man, became governor of North Carolina in 1913. He designated two days in November of that year as "Good Roads Days." These were declared state holidays on which every able-bodied citizen was asked to strike a few blows for progress. They were part of a series of Good Roads Days in different states. Governor Craig went to his home county and, donning overalls, worked as a common laborer with the other citizens.

The first new road in North Carolina to be built by state convicts was a seven mile stretch over Hickory Nut Gap of a road which was projected to run from Asheville to Charlotte. The General Assembly had provided for the upkeep of the road after its completion, although it was to be turned over to Buncombe, Henderson, and Rutherford counties for administration. The county commissioners of each county were to appoint a commissioner to have charge of upkeep and maintenance of the road. Sol Gallert of Rutherford County had prepared the bill authorizing state aid, and R. R. Williams of Buncombe County presented it. The bill required that five thousand dollars be raised locally for dynamite and tools. The Coxe Estate in Asheville gave one thousand, the town of Edneyville voted a bond issue and gave fifteen hundred, and private citizens subscribed $5,761.60. Gallert said, "I look to see the time when these hills will be the playground of America, the road lined with homes of summer visitors and the hills and valleys dotted with the homes of our mountain people." He estimated that the people of Rutherford and Buncombe counties had up to that time expended $500,000 in turnpike tolls "in the eternal damnation of their souls through cursing at being stuck axle deep in the mud, broken poles, and having to lead their horses up a wretched road they were paying the privilege of driving over."

Governor Craig when he opened the road officially on November seventh, 1915, declared, "I believe the most favored spot on earth is here in the glorious mountains of North Carolina. It is a land, an inheritance for us, with its marvelous climate, pure water, its brooks and streams and rivers, where we have no flies or very few of them, because a fly cannot live on these rocks; no malaria and no diseases save those we can ourselves get rid of."

The state university began in 1914 holding annual good roads institutes at Chapel Hill, with lectures, conferences, and exchange of experiences. Only three of the counties of Western North Carolina were represented at the first institute — Madison, McDowell, and Rutherford. Many arguments as to how to raise money for the needed roads arose at the institutes. Practically all were agreed that the chain gang must continue, but equipment and materials were costly, and gradually the idea that bonds should be sold came up for debate. The question was who should issue the bonds, county or township, both practices being in use from place to place. In 1913 the General Assembly passed several laws permitting specific townships to sell bonds for road building, and one general law was passed which authorized townships to sell bonds upon receipt of a petition of voters by the county commissioners. With the responsibility left to local initiative, the building of roads was to continue to produce a hodge-podge of good roads near the county seats and very bad ones in outlying portions of each county. Governor Craig appointed a State Highway Commission in 1915, and the legislature appropriated $10,000 as its budget, to be used in advising the counties about road building.

A breakthrough in federal aid for highways came in 1916 with an act to be administered by the United States Department of Agriculture. In order to participate, a state had to have an organization to raise half the funds to construct and maintain Federal Aid Roads. The next year the State Highway Commission was authorized to serve in this respect. Counties' responsibility for roads was still emphasized, and they were to furnish most of the state's half of the necessary funds for the new roads. The General Assembly now authorized expenditure of automobile license fees as a maintenance fund for a state highway system. Eighty-seven of the state's one hundred counties set up projects, and by January 1920 sixty-seven miles of road were completed in spite of the interruption caused by

Hub-deep

A casualty of travel on mud roads

World War One. The objective was a system of roads from county-seat to county-seat.

Roadbuilding in the mountains presented problems, but the railroads helped. During the winter of 1919–1920 District Engineer H. E. Noell was assigned the construction of a road over the mountain that had given the railroad builders so much trouble, from Old Fort to Ridgecrest. The old road was passable only in dry weather. It wound around the mountain as the railroad did. At times the Noell party had to take a train from Old Fort to Ridgecrest and work downhill toward Old Fort. Later Noell was assigned construction and maintenance work in Yancey, Mitchell, Avery, Burke, McDowell, Henderson, Polk, Rutherford, and Cleveland counties. His headquarters were in Marion, and to reach Avery County he had to travel eighty-five miles via Morganton, Lenoir, Blowing Rock, and Linville. On one occasion a team of two large horses was hitched

Fording the Swannanoa

to his old Ford car to pull him out of the mud, and when they could pull no more an extra team was added. To work in the northern part of Avery County he had to travel from Marion on the Clinchfield Railroad to Johnson City, spend the night, and catch the East Tennessee and Western North Carolina train (the narrow gauge line known as "Tweetsie") to Cranberry, travel over the project perhaps by horseback, return to Cranberry for the night, back to Johnson City for the next night, take the Clinchfield to work in Yancey and Mitchell Counties, where he used car or horseback, then to Marion by train.

Until that time in most of the highway construction in Western North Carolina Asheville had been the hub, and the outlying areas in the mountains that had no railroads were still dependent on turnpikes. As late as 1915 Watauga County marketed its produce by covered wagon down the Blowing Rock-Lenoir Turnpike, a toll road which Watauga County residents had the right to use free of toll. For other travelers on the turnpike a three-horse wagon cost sixty cents, and a car, seventy-five cents. Mrs. Gwyn Barlow, who kept the toll gate, said, "After they'd haul the mountain produce to Lenoir, they'd fill their wagons with supplies for the mountain stores. Often the wagons mired up hub deep." North Wilkesboro was another gateway to the so-called "Lost Provinces" of North Carolina: Watauga, Ashe, and Alleghany counties. The railroad into Ashe from Abingdon, Virginia, had been built by the Norfolk and Western only to tap the lumber resources of the county and did not connect with any other North Carolina point. Ashe County had closer relationships with Virginia than with other points in North Carolina.

When Cameron Morrison of Charlotte ran for governor in 1920 he spoke at Wilkesboro, promising support for roads throughout the state. The "Lost Provinces" were unwilling to support any movement for internal improvements unless they would benefit, and Morrison was campaigning on a program of good roads, a state system with county upkeep. Later he devoted half of his inaugural address to the subject.

The 1921 session of the General Assembly established the state highway system. Men from Northwestern North Carolina played a prominent part in the legislation, with support from both Democrats and Republicans. Chairman of the House Committee on Roads was Thomas C. (Tam) Bowie of Ashe County, and Rufus A. Doughton of Alleghany County was the leader of Democratic support for the bill. Newspapers called him the "Grand Old Man of North Carolina Politics." Both Bowie and Doughton had served in the legislature for a long time and were from the "Lost Provinces." D. D. Dougherty of the Appalachian Training School in Boone was the intermediary to secure Republican support for the measure because Frank Linney, State Chairman of the Republican Party, lived in Boone.

A public hearing was held on the Doughton-Connor Bill (Bowie's name was added later), and twenty speakers were heard, one of whom was Dr. Mary Martin Sloop of Crossnore School, whose speech was acknowledged by the Greensboro *Daily News* as the best speech of the evening. She had long

Road scene near Webster

Family travel

engaged in mission work and knew "the horrors of the red clay road."

In the House Bowie made the opening speech. Mr. Blaine Coffey (Republican) read a telegram from Frank Linney asking him to vote for the bill. In recognition of the priority of the needs of Western North Carolina, Miss Exum Clement of Buncombe County, the only woman member of the House, was invited to preside at the third reading and passage of the Doughton-Conner-Bowie Bill, which passed 102 to 14. The Senate approved thirty-two to six, and a new era was about to begin.

The act differed from Governor Morrison's proposal to continue county responsibility for roads. The law was amended many times by subsequent General Assemblies. The state assumed control of 5,500 miles of hard-surfaced and other dependable highways running to all county seats and to all principal towns, state parks, and principal state institutions and linking up with state highways of adjoining states and with national highways into national forest reserves by the most practicable routes. Special emphasis was placed on the development of agriculture, and the commercial and natural resources of the state. The law permitted the state to assume control of the state highways, to repair, construct, reconstruct, and maintain said highways at the expense of the entire state and to relieve the counties, cities, and towns of the state of this burden. The law of 1921 authorized a bond issue of $50,000,000, a one cent a gallon tax on gasoline to retire the bonds, and an increase in the price of automobile licenses. A new highway commission was provided for with at least three Republican members in a total of ten in addition to the chairman. Each commissioner was to represent a highway district. Governor Morrison appointed Rufus A. Doughton of Sparta, John C. McBee of Bakersville, and J. D. Stikeleather of Asheville as members for the western districts.

In addition to mapping out and beginning construction of new road proposals, a number of roads already begun were completed rapidly under direction of the commissioner. Among these was the Central Highway, which in Western North Carolina passed through Morganton, Marion, Asheville, and Marshall, first designated as State Route 10 and later as U. S. 70 Highway.

Mountain terrain challenged the highway commission and the engineers. Surveyors often had to use ropes and ladders, and roads were built "over rocky mountains, under rocky mountains, and around rocky mountains." Sometimes a route chosen was not the most direct and least expensive one. J. G. Stikeleather of the Ninth Division in routing Highway US 64 between Franklin and Highlands decided on an expensive scenic route along the Cullasaja River. Federal aid was denied for the more expensive route, but the state built it.

Frank Page, Chairman of the State Highway Commission, reported in 1924 an appraisal of the 1921 law. "It does not have to be argued to them [the people] that roads have a civilizing influence, that through these means of communication the "Lost Provinces" of the northwest, beyond their impenetrable mountains and two days' journey from the capital of their state, have been brought within seven hours of respectable speed. . . . The whole state is knit together in this net of highways."

By 1927, $115,000,000 in bonds for road building had been authorized, and road building continued. Four years later the state assumed responsibility for maintenance of all of the secondary roads. The counties gave up equipment and prisoners and the state established thirty prison camps for highway workers under command of the State Highway Commission. Only one county in Western North Carolina, Buncombe, had been operating chain gangs during the nineteen-twenties. However, eleven of these counties had leased their convicts to other counties that used chain gangs. Prior to 1931 the State Highway Commission hired convicts from the counties for work on state highways and assigned convicts from the state prison to such work. North Carolina's laws had given the judge the option of sentencing a convicted man to the county roads or to the state prison, in case the sentence was for a term of less than ten years.

Highway construction continued during the 1920's and 1930's with exciting new links being dedicated. For instance, in 1926 a new highway from Cowee Mountain Gap to Franklin was opened with a barbecue attended by hundreds of people from Macon and neighboring counties. Before the road was built most people in Macon County did their trading in Georgia or South Carolina, traveling via the Talullah Falls (Georgia) Railway. Persons wishing to go to Raleigh would take the train to Franklin, travel to Cornelia, Georgia, and change to the Southern Railroad to Greenville and Spartanburg, South Carolina, and then back into North Carolina. Travel by mail hack from Franklin was on a dirt road requiring seven hours between Franklin and Dillsboro. The hack left Franklin at four o'clock A.M. At Dillsboro the traveler took a train to Murphy or Asheville. Most persons in Franklin read newspapers published in Georgia or South Carolina because they arrived sooner than the North Carolina papers.

From Indian Trails to Broad Highways / 337

Chimney Rock, a natural phenomenon on the Hickory Nut Gorge Road
ASHEVILLE CITIZEN-TIMES CO.

Work on the projected "Crest of the Blue Ridge Highway" had been halted when the United States entered World War One and was not resumed after the war. During 1933 a plan was made to connect the Shenandoah National Park with the Great Smoky Mountains National Park by a parkway along the crest of the mountains. Harley Jolley who wrote the history of the Blue Ridge Parkway gave Robert L. Doughton, resident of Alleghany County and member of the United States House of Representatives, much of the credit for the plan. At first the intention was to make the road self-liquidating by imposing

Civilian Conservation Corps worked on the Blue Ridge Parkway. The young men were given a chance to better their education. Note that in the 1930's the CCC was integrated   U.S. FOREST SERVICE PHOTO

tolls on the users; however, North Carolina had the objective of removing all tolls from its highways, ferries, and bridges, and Governor J. C. B. Ehringhaus was opposed to a toll road. A sum of $4,000,000 from the funds allotted under the National Recovery Act was set aside for the building of the road as a "make work" project. (It is estimated that when complete the Blue Ridge Parkway will have cost $96,000,000.)

A spirited rivalry concerning the route developed between North Carolina and Tennessee. Boosters in Tennessee wanted the parkway to cross through the northwest part of North Carolina into Tennessee and pass through the mountainous area to enter the Great Smoky Mountain National Park from the north. North Carolina's promoters, many of them residents of Asheville, wished the road to be confined to Virginia and North Carolina, to enter the park from the southeast. Secretary of the Interior Ickes finally, after a two year delay, chose a route that led directly south from Roanoke to the North Carolina line following the crest of the Blue Ridge to a point near Mount Mitchell, thence toward Asheville and by Waynesville to the park. The states of Virginia and North Carolina purchased

CCC men learned to use power tools.   U.S. FOREST SERVICE PHOTO

the right of way and a scenic easement of four hundred feet on each side of the projected road at a cost of about $2,000,000 each and presented the land to the federal government.

Actual construction of the road was awarded to private contractors, but they were expected to employ as much local help as possible. Work such as planting and stabilizing the construction slopes, controlling erosion, and building fences was done by men in CCC camps established along the route and by emergency relief crews of men who lived nearby. Three utility areas and ten recreational areas were constructed in North Carolina. Much of the land through which the parkway passed was far from improved roads, and living conditions there had always been primitive. The opportunity to earn thirty cents an hour was new to this isolated population. Governor Ehringhaus asked Secretary Ickes to give priority to areas where need for employment was greatest and where

A mountain wonderland HUGH MORTON PHOTO

the most scenic areas were located, and Ickes agreed, so the work was carried on piecemeal. Negotiations for the right to build the portion through the Cherokee Indian lands were the subject of controversy for five years. Eventually the state paid the Cherokees a price agreeable to them and agreed to build a state road for them from Soco Gap to the village of Cherokee, and the right of way was obtained. After World War II that stretch of the road was completed. The portion that will run along the southeast side of Grandfather Mountain, now under construction, remains the last unfinished link in the original project. Congress assigned the Blue Ridge Parkway to the National Park Service for maintenance and management. Designed for non-commerical use, the parkway offers an opportunity for quiet, leisurely driving and enjoyment of natural scenery which annually attracts millions of tourists. In 1970 it was used by 12,789,724 persons, and it had become one of North Carolina's most important tourist assets.

In spite of the state take-over of secondary roads in 1931, their condition had not been much improved when Kerr Scott became governor in 1949. The new chief executive was a farmer who had known the problem of the dirt road all his life, and he asked the legislature to approve a secondary road bond issue of $200,000,000 and a one-cent-a-gallon increase in the gasoline tax to retire the bonds. The state constitution required that a proposal for a bond issue of that size must be approved by a referendum, and opponents believed that the voters would turn down the issue. But the people did not reject a proposal that would get them out of the mud. Cities and counties with good railway connections voted overwhelmingly against the bond issue but rural counties won the election.

Additional highway legislation was made essential during the Scott administration by the increasing number of times per week the rural folk visited their nearby towns following the improvement of secondary roads. The constantly increasing number of motor cars and trucks caused city streets to be incapable of handling the traffic. The Powell Bill, so called because State Senator Junius K. Powell's signature led on the bill as it was introduced, provided state funds for municipalities. Appropriations are based on population and non-state highway system street mileage within each city and town.

Congress in 1954 provided for an Urban Planning Assistance Program to finance overall economic development of counties and towns, and subsequently the General Assembly passed the legislation necessary for state participation. These two acts led to area-wide studies to develop municipal thoroughfare plans, and several cities and towns in Western North Carolina engaged in long-range community planning which included traffic handling. Among the first to do so were Asheville, Morganton, Brevard, Mt. Airy, and Marion. The State Department of Conservation and Development created a community planning division to cooperate with smaller municipalities in developing their plans.

Scott, near the end of his four years in office, summarized his success in road building: " . . . when I leave the governorship less than a month from now, North Carolina will have more than doubled the mileage of paved roads it had four years ago. New hard-surfaced roads will total 14,810 miles. That's 179 more than the 14,631 miles paved in North Carolina in all the years previous to 1949. . . ."

VOTE ON THE ROAD BOND ISSUE, 1949

County	For	Against
Surry	5,479	965
Watauga	5,344	269
Ashe	4,575	243
Caldwell	3,097	1,620
Wilkes	8,397	407
Alleghany	1,496	322
Burke	4,484	1,586
Rutherford	2,740	3,229
McDowell	2,157	737
Polk	1,588	323
Yancey	4,351	54
Jackson	3,794	393
Madison	3,738	262
Cherokee	3,449	296
Mitchell	2,788	85
Macon	2,374	546
Avery	2,039	251
Clay	1,291	52
Swain	1,820	155
Graham	1,402	111
Henderson	1,722	2,130
Haywood	5,097	933
Transylvania	1,748	762
Buncombe	5,658	8,529

Source: Waynick, *North Carolina Roads*, p. 59.

In 1931 when the state assumed jurisdiction over the secondary roads there were 54,000 miles of such roads in the state. In 1961 the length had been increased to 58,000 miles, of which approximately forty-five per cent were paved. Yet the western counties had only twenty-eight percent of their roads paved. Roads are added to the state highway system by the Highway Commission after petitions have been presented by the citizens, if the said road meets the requirements set up by the commission. Such addition is made on the basis of priority rating.

Governor Dan Moore in 1965 asked the General Assembly to approve a $300,000,000 bond issue for a highway program. It did. As required by the state constitution the bond issue had to be adopted by referendum, and the issue received the overwhelming approval of the people of the state, 245,194 of the 320,000 votes cast. Working for the road bond program was the Governor's Committee for Better Roads, only four members of which were from the twenty-four counties of Western North Carolina. The governor no doubt knew that these counties would favor the proposal.

The bill as passed by the legislature divided the funds into three parts: for primary roads, secondary roads, and cities and towns. Funds for secondary roads were to be allocated on the basis of the number of unpaved roads in each county. The State Highway Commission had in 1961 set up a fifteen-year plan for road construction contracted for on a basis of competitive bidding. No longer were highways to be built by prisoners or free labor, although prison camps remained and inmates were employed for highway maintenance and improvement.

After 1916 the United States furnished funds for highway building but not for maintenance. Most of this money was acquired by a four-cent-a-gallon gasoline tax. The funds were available for primary, secondary, and urban roads, to be matched by the state with equal funds. Roads in Western North Carolina that were continuous through several states were designated as United States Highways: 70 (the old Central Highway); 64, which from Morganton dipped southward through Rutherford, Henderson, Transylvania, Macon, Clay, and Cherokee counties; 19 and 23, which passed through northward from Asheville to the Tennessee line and westward from Asheville; 25 along the old Buncombe Turnpike; 74 from Charlotte, which terminated at Asheville on the west; 421, 321, and 221, all of which met in Boone, 221 connecting with Ashe and Alleghany on the way to Virginia; and 21, which passed through Surry County. These were primary roads and were frequently improved and sometimes shortened in mileage. Yet many of their miles were narrow, hilly, curving, and slow.

Almost half of the federal aid funds now are being allocated to the interstate highways, a new series of national and defense roads on which the United States has been working since 1941. It was originally hoped that the system would be completed by 1972. The roads are four-lane divided highways for the cost of which the federal government pays ninety per cent. When completed they will serve several counties in Western North Carolina. The most important of them for this area is Interstate 40, which begins in Greensboro and passes through Burke, McDowell, Buncombe, and Haywood counties. It will eventually reach Los Angeles, and it is to be connected with Atlanta by

Interstate 26, with which Interstate 77 has a link through Surry County on a route through West Virginia, Virginia, and North Carolina. Interstate 77 connects with Interstate 40.

The Appalachian Region Development Act passed by Congress in 1965 was described by Governor Moore as "the most successful program yet devised to help people help themselves." The priorities were established by the states participating, and Governor Sanford named twenty-nine counties in Western North Carolina to take part. The states initiated their own programs. The plan was one of fund-matching, and in North Carolina the emphasis was placed chiefly on roads, four lane corridors to swing out from the Interstate 26 and 40 interchange at Asheville to provide new and improved access to the market areas of Atlanta, Chattanooga,

ROADS IN WESTERN NORTH CAROLINA, 1961

	Paved Mileage	Unpaved Mileage	Total Mileage
Alleghany	44.8	345.1	389.9
Ashe	94.0	581.4	675.4
Avery	52.7	188.9	241.6
Buncombe	420.3	539.0	959.3
Burke	260.5	367.1	627.6
Caldwell	188.1	358.3	546.4
Cherokee	102.7	350.0	452.7
Clay	58.2	143.9	202.1
Graham	45.0	124.7	169.7
Haywood	146.7	287.7	434.4
Henderson	180.1	468.2	648.3
Jackson	83.0	349.4	432.4
McDowell	182.4	251.5	433.9
Macon	111.7	423.5	535.2
Madison	102.9	405.1	509.0
Mitchell	62.5	200.7	263.2
Polk	114.0	250.4	364.4
Rutherford	370.7	549.7	920.4
Surry	238.0	619.3	857.3
Swain	74.3	109.0	183.3
Transylvania	91.7	217.9	309.6
Watauga	87.6	364.7	452.3
Wilkes	234.0	859.9	1,093.9
Yancey	76.4	200.8	272.2

Source: North Carolina State Highway Commission, *Secondary Roads Maintenance Improvement Construction,* January 1, 1962.

and Cincinnati. Progress has been slow. By June 1968 two by-passes had been constructed, one around Waynesville and the other around Weaverville. Counties not touched by the interstate system are Alleghany, Ashe, Wilkes, Watauga, Avery, Mitchell, Yancey, Madison, Cherokee, Clay, Jackson, Graham, Transylvania, Swain, and Rutherford. The Appalachian highways if built as planned will serve Cherokee, Graham, Swain, Clay, Macon, Jackson, and Madison.

The fifteen-year plan of the State Highway Commission (1961) classified its trunk and feeder roads on a basis of first, second, and third priorities. Alleghany, Ashe, Watauga, Avery, Mitchell, and Yancey counties were placed on second and third priority lists, with no immediate plans for widening or straightening many of their roads in the near future.

Although the section has a long way to go before its road problems have been solved, anyone would probably agree with John Harden, historian of North Carolina roads: "Hardly any instrument of organized society is so vital to the people as the highway. It is the link between country and town, the route to the marketplace, the way of knowledge and education, the artery of commerce, the call of adventure, the measure of civilization."

In North Carolina, the "Good Roads State," roads have been all of these things. In fact, Western North Carolina owes practically all of its progress since 1921 to its roads and its schools. But the mountain region has always been discriminated against by the legislature because lawmakers from the east have dominated the state government. Money begets money, and improved mountain highways will pay tenfold dividends from the vast numbers of tourists who will come to this region of beauty and recreation.

CHAPTER SIXTEEN

Business and Industry

"Reader... fix your mind on a Southern 'gentleman'...." Observe the routine of his daily life. See him rise in the morning from a Northern bed, and clothe himself in Northern apparel; see him walk across the floor on a Northern carpet, and perform his ablutions out of a Northern ewer and basin...." So Hinton R. Helper follows this Southern gentleman through a day in which everything he uses is of Northern manufacture. Helper's diatribe against the South (1857) for allowing the North to do all of the South's manufacturing could not have been directed against Western North Carolina where most of the furniture and textiles were of home or local manufacture. For example, as early as 1820 cabinet makers in the part of Wilkes County that became Caldwell County had establishments that made furniture for people on order, serving a wide area. One employed six men. And for a number of years before the Civil War some German cabinet makers had a factory in Asheville and produced from mountain woods fine work which they carted around Western North Carolina and the neighboring states to sell. It brought a high price from the well-to-do customers along their routes.

If mountain people did change to "store-bought" household goods after the railroads came, they later reversed to partial self-sufficiency as may be perceived from this parody on Helper from the *Asheville Citizen* in 1963, concerning Haywood County: "Mr. Average citizen in Haywood finds products of his native county on every hand. As he awakes in the morning, flips on the light — that . . . is made in one of the largest hydro-electric plants in the East; lifts his head from a foam rubber pillow; shifts his weight to the edge of a companion product, foam mattress; slips his feet into a pair of Haywood slippers; pulls back the drapes made in Haywood. His pajamas were no doubt made on looms with vital hard rubber parts made in Haywood. He finishes dressing, getting garments from drawers of furniture made in his native county. In the dining room he sits down at a breakfast suite made not too far up the street from his home. He makes a few hurried notes in his memo pad — paper Haywood made — and obliges the wife by writing another note for the milkman to leave more milk in plastic coated cartons, all made in Haywood. Now into his $25 shoes — soles made in Haywood, he is on his way to work. . . . Between the house and garage his chest swells as he surveys the thick carpet of grass on his lawn — result of Haywood made fertilizer. The car hums. The fan belt turns the water pump circulating water through the radiator hose — both items Haywood made. . . . He is greeted at the office by his auditor who hands him an encouraging profit and loss sheet for study. Needless to say the finer paper is also Haywood made. The burley in his cigarette could have come from one of the 1,800 farms producing burley in the county. At lunch, a hot roast beef sandwich followed by apple pie with ice cream reminds him that these products are perhaps part of the $7 million farm income for the county. As Mr. Average Citizen retires for the night, he gets to thinking of how Haywood-made products played important roles in his life throughout the day. Drifting off into deep natural, restful sleep, he is heard to mumble: 'Haywood — the State's Best Balanced County. Yes, sir, and about the most self-contained.' "

The history of economic enterprise in Western North Carolina falls into four categories: individual enterprise, investment of outside capital in the area, large-scale locally-owned businesses, and consolidation of locally-owned industries by outside companies which are often holding companies and operate in a number of states.

The one form of business that all in Western North Carolina became accustomed to was the general store. Such stores were distributed throughout the counties. In the nineteenth century supplies for the most remote stores came from wholesalers who were retailers as well. The supply merchant sent wagons pulled by oxen and loaded with mountain produce to one of the nearest large towns. The wagons returned with merchandise to sell or trade at retail and also to provide rural merchants with their stocks. Fred O. Scroggs of Hayesville has the account books, in beautiful penmanship, of Nelson Strange, his great-grand-father, who was a merchant at Brasstown and Hayesville, Clay County. His invoices show that he sent wagons to Gainesville, Athens, and Augusta, Georgia, and to Maryville, Tennessee. Nelson Strange had six slaves whom he freed when they grew older. He paid a local blacksmith $67.50 to make one of the wagons for the long journeys. Among the items sold that were on the account book in the year 1860 were these: coffee, vials of oil, vials of drops, vials of peppermint, candles, castor oil, snuff, tobacco, nails, sets of plates, calico, skein silk and ribbons, vials of Godfrey's syrup, pens and envelopes, turpentine, preserve dishes, flannel, wool, worsted, brush and blacking, borax, coffee mills, plow lines, pen stocks, sugar, sets of knives, cigars, silk handkerchiefs, tumblers, brimstone (sulphur used to preserve fruit), sheepskin, fry pan and spoon, bridle and bit, 600 fish hooks, spelling books, shirts, pepper, rice, court plaster, soap, paper of tacks, paper of needles, cinnamon, roping, pair of combs, bell, suspenders, cravats, and powder and shot (by the pound). A shoemaker made shoes on order in the store.

Among the items traded by the people to the merchants, none were more important than crude botanicals used for drugs. The catalogue of G. W. F. Harper of Caldwell County for 1876 offered for sale the botanicals that he had taken in trade, which he described as "crude medicinal herbs, roots, barks, seeds, flowers, etc. Goods neatly and compactly pressed in bales of 200 to 500 pounds each, and forwarded in prime order. . . ." The produce book of the G. W. F. Harper store for the same year shows that in September, October, and November, the largest sums paid to individual customers totaled respectively $59.60, $44.28, and $143.18. The items included the following: burdock, mint, hellebore, flax seed, butterfly, beeswax, butter, beth root or purple trillium, blood root, lob seal, Indian turnip, catnip, may apple, skull cap, lion's tongue, feathers, dried fruit, eggs, bitter root, boneset, seneca, star root, angelica, ginseng, sassafras bark, lady slippers. The most valuable item was ginseng, for which the store paid one dollar per pound.

Collecting medicinal herbs ASHEVILLE CITIZEN-TIMES CO.

Calvin Josiah Cowles of Elkville and later of Wilkesboro, Wilkes County, developed a thriving root and herb business in that county in mid-nineteenth century. He traveled annually to Philadelphia, Boston, and Washington, D. C., to do business with northern merchants. Later Arthur Cowles moved the root and herb business to Gap Creek in Ashe County.* J. D. Cameron's *Handbook of North Carolina* for 1893 claimed that North Carolina provided the largest supply and the greatest variety of herbs for botanic medicines gathered in the United States. At that time the Messrs. Wallace of Statesville gathered herbs from the entire state, employing three hundred agents in contracting for them and collecting them, chiefly in the mountains. "On the Atlantic slope of the Blue Ridge," Cameron wrote, "there are said to grow no less than 2,500 varieties of plants used in the Materia Medica. . . . The yearly business of the Wallace firm reaches nearly 2,000,000 pounds in leaves, bark, and roots." At that time ginseng had advanced from one dollar to between two to three dollars per pound.

This field of business still survives. In 1970 the Wilcox Drug Company of Boone is the largest crude botanical drug company in the South, sending out trucks to buying depots and stores

---

* Calvin Cowles' store records contain accounts of customers in northern cities. One for 1857 included sales of skins: bear, mink, otter, oppossum, muskrat, raccoon, gray fox, rabbit, mole, and pole cat.

to collect the herbs. It cleans, processes, and ships crude botanical drugs: cherry bark, ginseng, passion flower, witch hazel bark and leaves, and deer tongue. One million pounds of these herbs are shipped each year. Associated with the drug company is the Appalachian Evergreen Company which ships holly, hemlock, and galax leaves to all parts of the world. More than 2000 people derive part of their income from the sale of these products. Other crude drug firms in operation in 1970 are the Blue Ridge Drug Company in West Jefferson and the Greer Drug and Chemical Company in Lenoir.

Except in Asheville there were few stores other than general stores in Western North Carolina in the nineteenth century. A few county seats boasted a hardware dealer, a fertilizer store, and a drug store; a few businesses were specializing in farm implements, and there were nurserymen in four places.

Investment in land for speculation has characterized the history of Western North Carolina from the beginning, when tracts larger than could possibly be developed were acquired. In 1796 a Philadelphia financier, Tench Coxe, purchased for himself and associates more than 500,000 acres in Buncombe, Rutherford, and Mecklenburg counties. As the counties were divided so were the lands originally belonging to Coxe and his associates who were called the Speculation Land Company.* In 1819, 399,090 acres of the land were deeded to Augustus Sackett of New York, and the company became the New York Speculation Land Company. Sackett advertised land for sale and employed James Dyer Justice as his agent. Men in succeeding generations of the Justice family represented the company until 1920 when G. W. Justice and Judge Fred McBrayer bought the remaining land, approximately 10,000 acres. Throughout the hundred years as land had been sold the mineral rights had been retained by the company, an item of importance when gold was being mined in Rutherford County.

From time to time other companies were organized for the purpose of buying and selling Western North Carolina lands.

---

* Tench Coxe probably never visited his lands, but another Tench Coxe was admitted to the bar in Buncombe County between 1804–1812. Coxe created artificial towns and advertised them. Papers of G. W. Justice contain much of Coxe's advertising.

Such was a company of Pennsylvanians that acquired 130,000 acres in six separate tracts which they advertised in the North. The Baltimore *Commercial*, June 3, 1876, contained this description: "This part of the State is the land of corn and cattle, clear streams, speckled trout, bouyant spirits, 'stalwart men and bonnie lasses.' The mountains of Western North Carolina are fine grazing lands to their very tops. . . . This beautiful western country . . . as a summer resort is justly admitted to be the Switzerland of America."

An example of individuals who dealt in land on a large scale was Calvin J. Cowles of Wilkes County who owned at one time 14,000 acres in Western North Carolina chiefly in Wilkes, Alexander, Ashe, and Caldwell counties and advertised his land resources around the nation. The Cowles papers in the Southern Historical Collection at Chapel Hill contain many details of his land business.

Mining was promoted by S. C. Kerr, State Geologist, who devoted extensive study to the mineral potential of Western North Carolina, and outside capital was attracted for extracting the deposits. Nothing like the gold fever, which had called large numbers of people to Burke, McDowell, and Rutherford counties from 1829 to 1833 and produced gold estimated at from $6,000,000 to $16,000,000 worth of the metal, occurred again, but mining was an important enterprise in the area in the last quarter of the nineteenth century.

The North Carolina State Exposition in Raleigh in 1884 exhibited minerals and the *Authorized Visitors Guide* listed the state's mines by counties. The following counties had iron mines: Alleghany, 3; Ashe, 4; Cherokee, 6; Mitchell, 2; Watauga, 2; and Yancey, 1. There were gold mines in Ashe, 1; Burke, 7; Caldwell, 5; Clay, 5; Cherokee, 4; Jackson, 3; Macon, 11; McDowell, 5; Polk, 6; Rutherford, 4; Watauga, 2; Yancey, 1. Copper was mined in Alleghany, 1; Ashe, 8; Haywood, 1; Jackson, 9; Madison, 1; and Watauga, 3. The mica mines were Ashe, 2; Haywood, 2; Jackson, 3; Macon, 4; Madison, 1; Mitchell, 11; Watauga, 2; Yancey, 10. There were also scattered sulphur, silver, lead, corundum, and asbestos mines.

The Cranberry iron mines in Mitchell County had been worked since the early 1820's and were the most famous ones in the state. The East Tennessee and Western North Carolina Railroad was built from Johnson City to Cranberry to facilitate the transfer of the raw ore to the North.

Mitchell and Yancey counties produced most of the mica used in the United States. L. M. Warlick appealed to Thomas Settle, Congressman, to prevent the placing of mica on the free list of the tariff law that was being considered in 1893. He pointed out that the chief competitor was India where miners worked for from five to seven cents a day while in North Carolina they earned from seventy-five cents to one dollar per day. A mica mine in Mitchell County, the "Clarissey", was three hundred feet deep and the mica at that depth was said to be as fine grade as that taken from the top. A half interest in the mine sold about 1883 for $10,000. Another mine near the Clarissey had, up to 1886, produced $10,000 worth of mica. Zeigler and Grosscup believed mica to yield more money than any other metal in Western North Carolina in the 1880's. The Ray mines near Burnsville in Yancey County were considered the best in the area, but both Mitchell and Yancey were mining large quantities to be used for stove fronts and mica washers.

Mica continues to be extracted. For example the Deneen Mica Company, Inc., employs forty-five people and ships its product all over the nation and to foreign countries for use in roofing, oil well drilling, and other fields. The Spruce Pine Mica Company, which employs about sixty persons, produces much mica for electronic equipment. However it imports practically all the raw mica used from Brazil and India, certain African countries, Australia, and Argentina, because local production of fine mica is so small. The raw mica must be split to a thickness sometimes of 1/2 thousandth of an inch, without scratching. Workers in Spruce Pine for several generations have engaged in this painstaking work. Mica furnished by this company was used for some of the parts in Telstar and for the Apollo satellite program.

Feldspar, a byproduct of the mica mines, was for years piled up as waste, but as time passed it became more valuable than mica. The Feldspar Corporation, which has its principal office in Spruce Pine, has plants in three other locations, two outside the state, all completely mechanized. The Spruce Pine plant employs 170 persons and produces feldspar, sand, and mica. It is the largest producer of its kind in the world. Each plant maintains a research laboratory. It is claimed that a fully automatic

Mica mining from an open pit near Spruce Pine   NATIONAL PARK SERVICE

filter plant to eliminate stream pollution returns the copious amount of water used in the process of froth flotation to the river free of contaminants.

The Ore Knob copper mine in the southeastern part of Ashe County had been worked since the middle of the nineteenth century, but a well-planned and systematic operation was established after the Civil War and the mine became one of the best-known in the state. A fall in the price of copper caused the owners to shut it down in the 1880's. Efforts to reoperate the mine were made unsuccessfully from time to time. During the 1950's the mine reopened but it closed in 1962. The copper ore reached by the present shafts was exhausted.

From Mitchell to Cherokee counties there are extensive deposits of kaolin. In Jackson County near Dillsboro and Sylva extensive works were established in the 1880's to refine the material before sending it to New Jersey to be made into porcelain and pottery products. The Harris Clay Company, founded by Charles J. Harris in 1888, is in operation today, the single producer in North Carolina, having bought out its competitors. In 1960 the Harris family sold the company to C. P. Edwards, III, but it is still under the name Harris Clay Company. It employs

103 workers, owns hundreds of acres of land in Mitchell County from which it will extract kaolin, and sells to General Electric for the making of electric porcelain, to the Syracuse China Company, and the Shenango Pottery Company.

Electric power for the mountain area was at first provided by individual promoters. Asheville had a steam plant that produced electric current for street lights and for the street railways. Hydroelectric power in Asheville was first furnished when William Trotter Weaver of Buncombe County saw the potential of the French Broad River, acquired a location five miles from the city and developed it. A granite dam was built and power was produced for Asheville businesses and industries. Mark Killian, who had a flour mill and a wagon works, built the first water power electric plant for Waynesville about 1903. Then in 1905 J. B. Sloan and others in Waynesville erected a power plant on the Pigeon River that furnished power to the community for twenty-five years. These two examples could be repeated in various county seats in the annals of the early twentieth century. Electricity was essential to the growing educational institutions. The first electricity provided for Cullowhee Normal and Industrial School was made (1909) by use of a gasoline engine. A few years later a local corn-and-wheat mill at the river was purchased and a new electric generator was installed, which provided all of the electric power used on the campus until 1939. At Appalachian Training School in 1915 a dam of heavy timber, ten feet high, was built on the South Fork of New River and a power house was erected on the bank, to produce electricity for the school and later for the town. Boone's electrical needs are still supplied by the university-owned New River Power and Light Company.

In time municipal power plants were created in Elk Park, Avery County; Bryson City, Swain County; Franklin and Highlands, Macon County; and Andrews, Cherokee County.* On the Broad River in 1926 Dr. Lucius B. Morse and associates created Lake Lure by a dam across the Rocky Broad River

---

* Most county seat towns built power plants for electric lights. Elkin built a municipal plant in 1926, with a dam on Elkin Creek. It was sold to the Southern Public Utilities Company which also moved into North Wilkesboro and Mount Airy.

and built a power house for the resort, as years earlier the dam that created Lake Kanuga had been used to furnish power for the summer residential community.

The next stage in the development of electrical power came when the Duke Power and the Carolina Power and Light companies absorbed existing companies and built huge dams and power plants in Western North Carolina. The Carolina Power and Light Company built a plant on the French Broad, and on the Pigeon River they built one of the largest power plants in the state. Duke Power Company created Lake James in 1916–1923 from the North Fork of the Catawba and the Linville rivers and from smaller tributaries of the two. It covers 6510 acres and has a shoreline of approximately 150 miles. In 1963 another plant was added which is eleven percent hydroelectric, 89 percent of its power being generated by steam. The Tallassee Power Company built the Cheoah and Santeetlah plants for industrial power to be used in Tennessee. Then came the Tennessee Valley Authority (TVA) and also the North Carolina Rural Electrification Authority (REA) to stimulate the building of rural power lines. The Nantahala Power and Light Company built Nantahala Lake in Clay and Macon counties in 1942, with a shoreline of thirty miles and an area of 1605 acres. The dam is used for generation of electricity.

The topography, the volume and the even flow of streams, the physical settings for power sites, and the abundant rainfall evenly distributed throughout the year make the mountain region ideal as a source of water-generated electric power. The mountain streams are capable of developing tremendous amounts of cheap and abundant water power, one of the area's chief assets. North Carolina ranks first among the Southern states in potential power.

Western North Carolina's first cotton mill, the Elkin Manufacturing Company, has been mentioned. Surprisingly it was spared by Stoneman's raiders in 1865. In Buncombe County John Cairns, a native of Scotland, came to Reems Creek in 1868 and started a woolen mill. It had sixteen looms and 812 spindles. Farmers brought their wool to the mill and exchanged it for material to clothe their families. Three types of cloth were made: jeans, a rough weave; a hard finished material for suits;

and a soft material for women's dresses, skirts, and coats. The mill operated until 1914 when it was converted to a grist mill and made flour and meal until 1954. In 1869 J. F. and W. A. Moore started the Green Hill cotton mill at Mt. Airy, with twenty-one looms and 1000 spindles. It could produce 700 yards of sheeting and 250 pounds of warp in a day. In 1877 at Elkin two new mills were started in 1877. The Gwynville Woolen and Flouring Mills with 240 spindles was put into operation by L. L. Gwyn and Alexander Chatham. It could produce 100 pounds of wool rolls and 100 pounds of spun yarn per day. The Elkin Valley Mills with two looms and 240 spindles was started for woolen manufacture. It also had a flour mill attached.

The Gwynville Mills has grown into the Chatham Manufacturing Company, one of the very large woolen mills, a leading producer of blankets, upholstery material, woolen suitings and apparel fabrics. Chatham purchased Gwyn's interest in 1890. Alexander Chatham was succeeded by Hugh, Thurmond, and Hugh Gywn Chatham, II. Mrs. Hugh Gwyn Chatham II was a Morehead, and in 1957 Chatham acquired the Leaksville Woolen Mills, the oldest continuous woolen mill in the South, founded by John Morehead in 1853. The Chatham plant covers 120 acres, has 500,000 square feet of floor space, and employs 2500 people. When Chatham prospers, Elkin prospers.

Mt. Airy has nineteen textile, hosiery, or apparel firms among its fifty-seven manufacturers. Surry County has become an industrial center, with textiles its leading product.

In the 1880's a number of villages had individuals who did wool-carding, to relieve home weavers of that step in the home manufacture of textiles: Weaverville, Robbinsville, Waynesville and Pigeon Valley, Flat Rock, and Dysartville (McDowell County).

Before the Civil War a group of four enterprising men, Samuel Patterson, Edmund Jones, James C. Harper, and James Harper, of Caldwell County started a cotton factory in the village of Patterson. It supplied warp for home looms in the area and was powered by the waters of the Yadkin River until it was burned in 1865 by Stoneman's cavalry. In 1872 it was replaced by a second mill, this time with eighteen looms, 960 spindles, and a capacity to produce 600 yards of sheeting per day, 250 pounds of cotton yarn, and 150 pounds of wool yarn, its three products. A second cotton mill was founded in 1883 by P. G. Moore and N. H. Guy. Within a few years a number of thriving mills were in operation in Caldwell County: the Lenoir Cotton Mill (1901); the Hudson Cotton Manufacturing Company (1904); Dudley Shoals Cotton Mill at Granite Falls (1906); Falls Manufacturing Company (1915–1916); Southern Manufacturing Company (1922–1923); the last three founded by D. H. Warlick; Whitnel Cotton Mill (1907), established by J. O. White and J. L. Nelson for whom the community of Whitnel was named; the Moore Mill at Valmead; the Steele Cotton Mill (1918); by T. H. Broyhill and R. L. Steele; the Caldwell Cotton Mill at Hudson by R. L. Gwyn.

Meanwhile in Rutherford County Simpson Bobo Tanner and Raleigh Rutherford Haynes, with a number of associates, built cotton mills along the Second Broad River. In 1887 Tanner and J. S. Spencer of Charlotte and others including Haynes organized the company and built the Henrietta Mills of which Tanner served as general manager. In 1892 Haynes built the Florence Mill in Forest City, of which he was president until he resigned to give his full attention to the Cliffside Mills in 1901. Meanwhile in 1896 the Caroleen Mill, of which Haynes was a large stockholder, was built. Later S. B. Tanner and his son K. S. Tanner built the Spindale group of mills and the town of Spindale. The establishment of mills in Rutherford County gave the farmers a sale for their cotton, the employees a livelihood, and so benefited the merchants and the economy of the county in general. Forest City, in lower Rutherford County, grew into a very attractive city. It was earlier called Burnt Chimney for a chimney which survived a fire at the small crossroads community. A village had started there, was incorporated in 1877, was largely destroyed by fire in 1886, and was rebuilt. The name was changed by law in 1887 to Forest City. Three years later a cotton mill was constructed but it failed in 1895. In 1897 the Florence Mill with 12,200 spindles gave new life to the town, a mill village housed workers from other parts of the county, and the name Forest City became more appropriate. Banks, newspapers, civic clubs and service organizations co-operated in making Forest City a model city.

Haynes had a railroad built to connect the mills at Avondale and Cliffside with the main line from Charlotte and Wilmington. The presence of railroads was essential to the development of the textile mills in Rutherford County.

From 1900 to 1930 there was a new type of growth for the textile industry in the South, a great migration of Northern industries because of Southern encouragement, low production costs, nearby raw materials, and non-union cheap labor. The South profited greatly from this influx but the workers were often exploited. In 1927 the average annual earnings in North Carolina were $691 compared with $966 in Massachusetts, $1053 in Rhode Island, and $1029 in New Hampshire. Southern workers survived not because of the low cost of living but because of their low standard of living. Except for rent, living costs were higher in the South than in the North. Women and children worked in the mills sixty-six and even seventy-two hours per week. Longer hours and lower pay gave Southern mill owners an advantage over Northern ones. The usual age for beginning work was fourteen.

While most of the mountain people owned the land on which they lived, it was necessary for them to leave their homes in order to work in the mills. The companies built cheap houses, often poorly constructed and cold, unpainted, high on stilts above the ground, for the mill villages. Stores were operated by the companies, often charging exorbitant prices but offering credit.

In 1910 Carroll Baldwin of Baltimore built a plant and mill village near Marion because of available labor and railway transportation. A good many Marion citizens bought stock in the company, but a controlling interest was retained by the Baldwin family, and following World War One conditions became very bad. Miss Sally Baldwin who had inherited the control lived in Baltimore and knew nothing of conditions at the mill. Workers labored in two twelve-hour shifts, sixty-six hours per week, in unsanitary surroundings. Tubercular employees spat on the floor. The dust-covered floor was swept while the workers were on the job, but it was never scrubbed. Workers' diet consisted of corn meal, bread, greens, salt back, very few fresh vegetables, no fruit, little fresh meat or milk. The incidence of pellagra was high. There was a song,

> I'm going to starve.
> Everybody will,
> Cause you can't make a livin'
> In a cotton mill."

In 1929 the stretch-out system was instituted; workers had almost no rest periods. Twenty minutes were added to the twelve-hour day. Workers were earning from $5 to $13 a week. They decided to strike. Employees at the nearby Clinchfield Mill joined the Baldwin strikers. They were helped to form a union and a charter was granted by the United Textile Workers (UTW). As the local had no welfare funds to tide the strikers over the period of unemployment, aid was sent from several organizations outside Marion. Money sent from Northern states was used to buy food. During the strike the workers turned to mountain activities, carving and whittling, building furniture; they had a string band with twelve pieces with a number of two and three piece combinations and soloists. They composed songs about their suffering; old tunes with new words covered every phase of the strike.

Many workers were removed from their homes because they had participated. The strike lasted from July till September when an agreement was reached. Hours were to be reduced and wages were to be increased as the company saw fit. There was to be no discrimination against strike leaders. Those who had been discharged were to be reinstated. The Baldwin company was faithless. Another strike resulted. Six strikers were shot, four in the back. Those accused as killers of the strikers were acquitted on December 21, "so they could go home for Christmas," according to one member of the jury. Several union leaders were convicted on charges brought against them by the mill. Alfred Hoffman, an organizer of craft unions who came in after the strike had begun, was fined $1000 and sentenced to jail for thirty days for his activities in Marion. Labor conditions have improved, but wages are still less than in the North.

Marion has other textile mills, the Clinchfield Manufacturing Company, the Cross Cotton Mills, the Washington Mills, five hosiery mills, two knitting mills, and at nearby Sevier, the American Thread Company. Marion is served by the Southern and Clinchfield railroads.

Valdese has an unusual history. It was an experiment in colonization by a European colony planted near the close of the nineteenth century. It was developed by a group of Waldenses who had for centuries refused to accept the dogmas of the Catholic Church and instead worshipped as they believed the early Christians had. Migrating to an area of narrow valleys and steep mountains in the Cottian Alps in Savoy, now Italy, they were able to eke out a living in spite of persecutions in 1476, 1555, and 1686. In the seige of 1686, made by the Duke of Savoy at the command of King Louis XIV of France, many Waldenses were massacred. Little groups that managed to escape to Switzerland procured financial aid from King William III of England. Using guerilla tactics and weapons purchased with money from England, they were able to regain possession of their valleys. Persecution did not end until 1848 when they were granted full religious liberties and freedom of conscience by the King of Savoy. The population increased so rapidly that the small area that had long been their home was unable to support them, and groups began to migrate to the Western Hemisphere, going to Uruguay, Brazil, Argentina, Missouri, and Utah. Thus it was that Marvin F. Scaife, president of the Morganton Land and Improvement Company, who learned about the crowded conditions in the Waldensian valleys, offered to sell the Waldenses 100,000 acres of land in the mountains of North Carolina for $50,000, to be paid over a twenty year period. The two farmers who were sent to decide whether to accept the offer rejected the 100,000 acres offered to them, and they were taken to examine various sites until they selected a ten thousand acre tract between Morganton and Connelly Springs, about which they were not enthusiastic because of the poor soil of sand, clay, and rock. Twenty-nine Waldenses and their pastor Doctor Charles Albert Tron arrived in Burke County in 1893. A corporation was formed with a board of directors consisting of six Waldenses and three American members of the Morganton Land and Improvement Company. A loan from the land company enabled the Waldenses to purchase simple tools to clear the land and put in a crop. Dr. Tron returned to Italy and briefed others on conditions in the new colony. Eight Waldenses from Utah and 128 additional settlers from Italy arrived near the end of 1893. Extreme hardships and poverty marked the first year in North Carolina. In the spring a hosiery mill was arranged for, to be operated by John Meier, superintendent of the Oats Hosiery Mill in Charlotte, in a two-story barn constructed by the Waldenses. All employees were to be Waldenses unless the demand exceeded the supply of workers. In 1894 Dr. Tron arrived from Italy and arranged to return 5000 less desirable of the 10,000 acres contracted for and a reduction of the debt from $25,000 to $15,627.33. This included the cost of sawmill, livestock, tools, and other items. After rude homes, a store, and two schools had been provided, a surplus of lumber was available for sale. Times continued to be critical and in

1894, after the experience of about eighteen months, the corporation was dissolved and the Morganton Land and Improvement Company agreed to take back the land and resell it in tracts of from forty to eighty acres to individual Waldenses at five percent interest. The transaction left a debt of $1,500, which Dr. Tron personally paid. In order to pay for their land Waldensian young people found paying jobs. When Meier moved his hosiery mill to Newton and then to South Carolina, a number of workers went with the mill and sent back their meager earnings, learning the trade and at the same time helping to save their fathers' lands.

The stones that had to be gathered to make the lands suitable for farming furnished material for warm, sturdy buildings. The stone church was finished in 1897 at a cost of about $6,000, workmen having contributed their labor at a pay rate of five cents per hour. In 1901 John and Francis Garrou, Waldenses, started the Waldensian Hosiery Mill, encouraged by W. C. Erwin and A. M. Ingold of the First National Bank of Morganton. By 1939 this mill employed 475 persons. In 1914 a cotton mill, the Valdese Manufacturing Company, was started by John Louis Garrou. By 1937 it employed 200 persons. In 1913 another hosiery mill was opened, followed in 1915 by the Waldensian Bakery, which by 1940 had 140 employees and thirty-five trucks and was one of the great bakeries of the Carolinas. In 1927 several small hoisery mills were incorporated as the Alba-Waldensian Hosiery Mills. By 1938 Valdese was known as the "fastest growing town in North Carolina."

Notable in the economy of Western North Carolina is the furniture industry. Furniture factories were established in the foothill towns because of their nearness to the supply of forest products and because of the labor supply. A number of companies bought forest tracts and on them have begun practices of conservation and scientific forestry. Unusual is the fact that until recent years virtually all of the furniture factories were owned by Western Carolinians. Lenoir is the center of the industry in the area.

Caldwell County has a tradition of furniture making. In 1878 Henry Reichert advertised the opening of a furniture factory at Powelltown near Lenoir in which he would produce "furniture of every description at the lowest prices and on the best terms for cash or barter." He also offered coffins for sale. In 1889 the Lenoir Furniture Factory was organized, the first one in the town. It was owned by G. F. Harper, J. M. Bernhardt, and C. L. Bernhardt.

Meanwhile in 1889 A. W. Britt and a group of associates from Ohio moved to Asheville, purchased a small furniture factory known as the Avery and Erwin Company, and a lumber mill, both of which they operated until 1895. Hard times during the depression of the 1890's struck their project, it was reorganized as the Skyland Furniture Company, and in 1898 it went bankrupt.

The furniture industry during the 1890's was attempted in a strip of eighteen counties reaching from Alamance to Haywood, with a number of efforts being made in Marion. In 1896 Thomas Wrenn founded the Catawba Furniture Company with sixty-five workers in partnership with Henry W. Fraser, a former textile manufacturer. The Marion Furniture Company was organized by D. R. Raper who sold stock to the town's people in public sales.

In Lenoir in 1907 Dr. A. A. Kent, F. H. Coffey, and others established the Kent-Coffey Manufacturing Company to make dressers, chiffoniers, and wash stands. The largest furniture organization in Caldwell County began in 1905 as the Kent Furniture and Coffin Company, with T. H. Broyhill, Dr. A. A. Kent, and associates as owners. Broyhill bought his share of the stock by furnishing lumber from his sawmill. In 1912 Broyhill bought the stock of the other owners and the name became the Lenoir Furniture Company, then the Broyhill Furniture Company. In 1919 Broyhill was joined by his brother J. E. Broyhill and the firm grew to occupy six plants and to be the fourth of the big five in the furniture industry in the nation, and is probably the largest family-held furniture enterprise in the world. Other prosperous furniture manufacturers are Caldwell Furniture Company (1909), Lexington Mirror Company (1912), Fairfield Chair Company (1921), Hibriten Chair Company (1930), Spainhour Furniture Company (1943), Hammary Manufacturing Company (1943), Kincaid Furniture Company (1946), Blowing Rock Furniture Industries (1946). In 1964 the Kent-Coffey, Spainhour, and Blowing Rock companies were purchased by Magnavox, starting the break with the home-ownership tradition. Employment in Caldwell County furniture plants exceeded 5000 in 1966.

Lenoir and Caldwell County had a population of 54,723 in 1967. There were in 1960 seventy industrial plants with an industrial employment of 11,152. Broyhill had four plants in Caldwell County. There were twenty-four furniture factories with seventeen related industries. The largest furniture companies were Broyhill, Flair, Fairfield, and Caldwell. Other major industries are the Alba-Waldensian Hosiery Mills, the American Efird Mills at Whitnel, the Burlington Industries at Rhodhiss, Blue Bell, Polk Manufacturing Company, and Hemlock Manufacturing Company.

Drexel Enterprises in Burke County is the third largest furniture industry in the United States. Most of the Drexel plants are in Western North Carolina. Others are in High Point and in Kingstree, South Carolina. Western North Carolina leads the world in the production of case goods. In 1903 Samuel Huffman founded Drexal Furniture Company. He was succeeded by his son Robert. The company has nine plants with over 5000 employees and is the largest producer of bedroom and dining room furniture. In 1961 Drexal acquired the Southern Desk Company and in 1963 Heritage Furniture Company, the best upholstering firm in the South. The 1931 sales of $2,000,000 have increased twenty times. Drexel has now been acquired by the Champion Paper and Fibre Company.

The Henredon Furniture Industries of Morganton, Grand Rapids, and Spruce Pine make beautiful and expensive furniture. Net sales in 1961 were $11,405,750 and in 1968, $24,375,265. Net earning in 1968 were $3,889,864. Property, plant, and equipment are valued at $20,228,759. The three enterprising founders of the company were T. Henry Wilson, Ralph Edwards, and Donnell Van Noppen.

Burke County with the towns of Morganton, Valdese, Hildebran, Icard, and Glen Alpine is one of the region's oldest and most prosperous counties. In addition to furniture, textiles, and hosiery, there are Union Carbide and machine and iron works. In 1950 the population was 46,341, in 1960, 52,701 and by 1970 it had reached 60,364. Morganton in 1960 had 12,000 people, and in that year 12,513 persons were employed in the county.

Brevard, the home of Olin-Mathieson and of a DuPont photographic plant, has grown and prospered as these industries have prospered. In 1915 Harry H. Straus made endless belts for cigarette machines. In 1934 he began to use the fiber of seed flax, a plant grown for use in linseed oil. In 1936 he built a factory to use flax fibers for cigarette paper. Since the majority of cigarettes are manufactured in North Carolina and since Western North Carolina rivers have waters with low mineral content, Brevard was an ideal place for manufacturing cigarette paper. Frenchmen were brought over to teach the workers. Mountain people learned so rapidly that in six months the Frenchmen were gone. September 2, 1939, the first cigarette paper was produced at Ecusta. In 1949 Olin built a cellophane plant at Pisgah Forest. Olin-Mathieson was formed in 1954 from the union of Olin Industries and the Mathieson Chemical Corporation. This corporation controls also the Winchester-Western Arms Company and the Squibb Pharmaceutical Company. It produces cigarette paper, cellophane, chemicals, metals, packaging, pharmaceuticals, sporting arms and ammunition. Its annual sales exceed $700,000,000. At Ecusta and Pisgah Forest lightweight printing paper, cigarette paper, endless belts, cigarette filters, and cellophane packaging are manufactured. In 1966, 3000 people were employed compared to 350 in 1939. In 1939 the population of Brevard was 3000, in 1967 it was 5000, and in the Brevard trading area there were 8500. In 1965 Olin-Mathieson had a payroll in Brevard of $18,000,000.

In 1964 the DuPont company established at Brevard a photographic products plant to make medical x-ray films. It had previously built there in 1958 a plant to make silicon for electronic devices. In 1967 the DuPont plant put $4,500,000 into the Transylvania County economy, and its payroll and purchases were $5,167,644. The company spent $39,000,000 in 1967 to increase its facilities.

American Enka, an American branch of a Dutch corporation, was established near Asheville in 1928. Its growth is one of the success stories of American industry. In 1930 the company produced 6,000,000 pounds of viscose process rayon yarn. Soon thereafter it developed high-tenacity rayon yarn for automobile tires. In 1940 Enka produced 23,000,000 pounds, provided jobs for 3000, and had an annual payroll of $5,000,000. In 1948 a new plant was built at Lowland, Tennessee, with an original capacity of 20,000,000 pounds of filament rayon. This production has quintupled and Enka entered the nylon market, first with nylon staple fiber and later with the more popular filament yarn. Enka was the first United States producer

Enka Corporation, 1965

of fine denier nylon 6. In 1958 there was a large expansion at Enka, North Carolina, which doubled the capacity of fine filament nylon. In 1962 the company began to produce heavy denier yarns for the carpet, tire, automotive, and home furnishing industries. The North Carolina plant production of this yarn has increased from 2,000,000 to 45,000,000 pounds a year. In 1965 another plant was built at Lowland, Tennessee, and the two plants now produce 65,000,000 pounds a year. In 1957 rayon staple fiber production was begun and a complete line of viscose rayon products was manufactured for use in apparel, home furnishings, carpets, industrial fabrics, and for blending with natural and manmade fibers. Now 100,000,000 pounds of these fibers are produced annually. In 1958 Enka acquired the Rex Corporation and William Brand and Company, manufacturers of wire and cable. In 1955 a new research center was built. An addition was made in 1963. Enka in 1966 had over $215,000,000 invested in plants, annual sales of $201,332,000, paid $57,607,000 in salaries, wages, and fringe benefits. Production increased from 6,000,000 pounds in 1930 to 375,000,000 pounds in 1966, of rayon, nylon, and polyester fibers. Enka ranks (1966) 324th in sales among the 500 largest United States corporations,

259th in invested capital, and 327th in net profits. In 1965 there were 9000 employees on the payrolls of the entire corporation. Then a $90,000,000 plant expansion created more than a thousand new jobs.

Prior to the real state "bust" Asheville grew rapidly. From 1930–1960 the rate of growth declined. The growth rate of Western North Carolina also declined. From 1930–1960 Asheville had a net out-migration of 10,000 and the Western North Carolina region a net of 71,000. In Asheville since 1960 tremendous progress has occurred. Migration trends have changed and Asheville had a net in-migration of 5000, but for the region as a whole out-migration is still continuing at a reduced rate. In 1965 it was predicted that Asheville would have a population of 69,100 by 1970 and 147,500 by 1980 and the metropolitan area 196,100.

In 1960–1964 only four counties — Haywood, Transylvania, Henderson, and Buncombe — had wages above the state average and only Haywood and Transylvania were above the national average. Seventeen of the region's counties increased at a rate above the nation as a whole; but in only five counties did the dollar value of the increase surpass that of the nation. In 1960 the average weekly earning in manufacturing was $73.78, eighteen percent below that of the nation. Areas which have a majority of manufacturing employment in capital-intensive industry — industry which uses more capital relative to labor — receive higher than average wages.

AVERAGE ANNUAL WEEKLY EARNINGS 1964

U.S.	$102.97	Graham	77.51	Mitchell	60.21
Ashe	64.38	Haywood	123.31	Polk	68.28
Avery	58.50	Henderson	83.76	Rutherford	75.63
Buncombe	85.11	Jackson	70.39	Swain	60.79
Burke	76.28	McDowell	75.40	Transylvania	108.99
Cherokee	59.83	Macon	64.96	Watauga	65.34
Clay	56.92	Madison	67.69	Yancey	73.37

In Asheville fifty percent of the manufacturing work force are employed in above-average wage industries, but wages have been seventeen per-cent below the national average because productivity was lower. Many industries have recently come; the workers lacked experience. While the value per man hour productivity was for the United States $7.08, for Asheville it was $5.70, and for Western North Carolina other than Asheville,

$4.66. It is important to attract industry that has a potential for high wages. The handicap of inexperienced workers will soon be overcome if the state and communities will supply technical training for such industries.

North Wilkesboro is the leading commercial center of Northwestern North Carolina. It has prosperous furniture factories, cotton mills, hosiery mills. The first industries in the county were the North Wilkesboro Brick Company, the C. C. Smoot and Sons Tannery, and the Wilkesboro Manufacturing Company, which made building materials. These developed during the 1890's. Forest Furniture (1901), Oak Furniture (1903), which employed 300 men when it burned in 1954, Meadows Mill Company (1908), which builds grist mills, Home Chair Company of Ronda (1919), American Furniture (1927), Carolina Mirror (1936), Peerless Hosiery, a Durham corporation, Blue Ridge Shoe Company (1960), and the Holly Farms Poultry Company are the county's largest industries.

Mount Airy, the northern gateway to the Blue Ridge Mountains and the leading urban area in Surry County, has a population of 7200, a contiguous population of 25,000, and a retail shopping area of 50,000. It has fifty-seven manufacturers employing over 9000 workers with a payroll of about $42,000,000. In addition to the nineteen textile, hosiery, or apparel firms, Mt. Airy has eight furniture or allied industries, and nine concrete or granite companies are located in or near the city. The world's largest open-faced granite quarry, covering eighty acres, has long been famous. Industrial growth in Mount Airy has shown an increase of 2300 new jobs in the last five years.

Boone is the only urban community in Watauga, Avery, Ashe, and Alleghany counties. The leading industries have been encouraged to come into the area by community leaders. The International Resistance Company (now TRW), Shadowline, the Blue Ridge Shoe Company, and the Vermont-American Tool Company are the chief employers. Some locally-owned concerns have been in existence for many years. The North State Canning Company makes and cans kraut, utilizing one of the successful farm products. A similar operation in Ashe County is Beaver Creek Foods, Incorporated, which cans green beans, providing employment and a market for the beans grown in the area. There are twenty-six plants processing food and tobacco products in Western North Carolina employing more than twenty persons each.

Most vital to the economy of Watauga County is Appalachian State University which has over six hundred employees and an annual payroll of more than $2,000,000. More important are the thousands of young people who have earned their education at the school, enabling them to serve the area, the state, and neighboring states where they are recognized as excellently prepared teachers.

A shot in the arm to Watauga County has come from the enterprises of the late Grover Robbins and his brothers Harry and Spencer Robbins. In 1957 they started Tweetsie Railroad, a popular tourist attraction. Next they developed Hound Ears, and a few years later they acquired control of the Beech Mountain project which was already under development. An airport has been constructed, and the 5600 foot gondola-equipped ski slope, one of their seven ski slopes, is the highest in Eastern America. There will be four golf courses and four thousand homesites. There is a construction payroll of $1,000,000. The Robbins Brothers after acquiring Beech Mountain created the Carolina Caribbean Corporation. It operates Beech Mountain; The Reef in the Virgin Islands; Land Harbors of America, a deluxe camping site; and numerous other real estate developments. Its tourist attraction, The Land of Oz, is highly successful.

Fourteen of the counties have populations of under 20,000. Thirteen have fewer than fifty persons per square mile. Jackson County is one of these and will illustrate the importance of attracting industries. Western Carolina University at Cullowhee has in addition to its faculty hundreds of other employees. Next to the university the backbone of the economy of Jackson County is the Mead Corporation. Mead's paperboard mill began operations in Sylva in 1928 when chestnut wood was still available. It came to Western North Carolina because of available lumber, and it pioneered paperboard production from chestnut chips. In 1966 its payroll in Sylva was $2,200,000 for 258 employees. The company's headquarters are in Dayton, Ohio, and in 1967 it had a total of 21,000 employees and sales of $633,092,360. Also important in Jackson County are knitwear, blanket, and quilting plants of the Harn Corporation. Jackson is one of fifteen counties in our study having fewer than five manufacturing industries each that employ one hundred or more persons. There is not a single county that has not at least one such industry. Ten counties had fewer than 1000 employed in manufacturing, and each of ten had combined annual payrolls of less than Jackson County's $3,665,000 in 1963. In 1947 three counties had fewer than one hundred each employed in manufacturing; in 1963 Alleghany had 1,118, Madison had 639, and Watauga 896 so engaged. Clay County lost 23% of its population by out-migration between 1950 and 1960, and in 1963 it had ninety fewer employed in manufacturing than in 1947. Other counties experiencing out-migration of more than sixteen per cent during the decade 1950–1960 were McDowell, Rutherford, Wilkes, Watauga, Yancey, Ashe, Avery, Alleghany, Cherokee, Macon, Madison, Mitchell. Out-migration has been discussed before. Because of its incidence the following counties have a larger percentage of people over sixty-five than all but four other counties in the state: Alleghany, Ashe, Buncombe, Cherokee, Clay, Henderson, Macon, and Polk. Many of the ambitious young potential leaders have been drained out of their home counties because of lack of economic opportunity. In only three of the counties is the rate of natural increase in the population as large as that of the state as a whole. An encouraging observation is that while in most of the counties the number of manufacturing establishments remained nearly the same in 1963 as in 1954, the number of persons employed increased materially: Alleghany County 509 to 1118, Ashe 540 to 1917, Avery 336 to 484, Buncombe 11,071 to 16,450, Burke 8,291 to 12,345, Caldwell 9041 to 11,550, Madison 154 to 639, Swain 362 to 665, and Watauga 172 to 896. These figures indicate that the increase of the gross national product of the United States has been reflected in this area. Economists estimate that for every one hundred new factory jobs there are seventy-five other jobs created in real estate, finance, insurance, utilities, transportation, communications, and local government (especially schools).

It is possible for Western North Carolina to continue industrial expansion and to develop new products, and every effort is being made by the planning organizations to utilize the opportunities and services offered by the state and federal government for the purpose. Another excellent prospect for the area is in the development of its recreational and tourist facilities, and in this respect Western North Carolina has a positive advantage.

As late as 1937 the livelihood of the Eastern Cherokees was earned chiefly by growing a variety of crops on small plots: making sorghum from cane, filling their cellars with food for the cold winters, picking wild huckleberries and strawberries for market. Over 5000 acres of forest were being held as a common property. Any member of the tribe was permitted to market an assigned number of trees, for which he paid a percentage into the common fund. Simply furnished mountain cabins were the homes of the majority of the families, but there were those who lived in sparsely settled mountain sections in smaller cabins; while in the valley were many modern homes.

Since World War Two the Eastern Cherokees have been changing from an agrarian to an industrialized people. Hundreds are employed by White Shield of Carolina, manufacturers of quilted goods; Cherokee, Inc., makers of one hundred forty Indian arts and crafts products; and the Vassar Corporation, which makes hair nets and other accessories for women's hair. In 1963 a group of professional and business people organized Cherokee Area Industries, Inc., to stimulate industrial and commercial growth. They purchased land for development of an industrial park. The first company to lease a portion of the park was Mountain Maid Company, employing thirty-five people. In 1955 the Qualla Arts and Crafts Mutual, Inc., was created, continuing a reservation crafts program begun in the 1930's. This cooperative markets items made by the Indians in their homes, the profits being divided among the members.

CHAPTER SEVENTEEN

In Pursuit of Pleasure

Before the coming of the railroads and roads into the mountains the usual visitor made his way laboriously to a hotel or boarding house in a scenic spot, and there he stayed for the duration of his vacation. Such a hotel was completed at Blowing Rock in 1885. It had an ideal location at the crest of the Blue Ridge. Fascinating nature trails were about the only diversion offered the guests after they arrived. The trip up the mountain from the railway station in Lenoir was made by hack or surry that met the train, and on days when the weather was fine the ride could be exciting. Blowing Rock was then deemed to be the ideal tourist attraction in Northwest North Carolina. It was still a straggling village two miles long approached by the turnpike from Lenoir. From the turnpike one could see Jonas Ridge, Hawksbill, Table Rock, Pilot Mountain, Grandfather Mountain. Blowing Rock's 4200 foot elevation provided an ideal summer climate. There were post offices in the village and at Green Park at the top of the ridge. From the "rock" itself one could often look down on a sea of mist, see the clouds rise and then see the peaks emerge from the snowy billows: the Roan, the Grandfather, the Bald, the Yellow, and the Black Mountains. The beetling crag, the Blowing Rock, is a great spur that hangs over the "Globe" or valley of the John's River. It catches the currents of air sent up from the depths. These currents will blow back hats, handkerchiefs, and light objects thrown from the rock. The Green Park Hotel near the Blowing Rock was built between the springs of the New River which flows into the Ohio and

Hugh Morton on one of the crags of Grandfather Mountain
PHOTO COURTESY OF HUGH MORTON

the Yadkin which flows into the Atlantic. The Green Park was quite modern in 1896 with fireplaces in all of the rooms and hot and cold baths. The Blowing Rock Hotel one and one-half miles north of the Green Park had nine hundred feet of piazzas, a telegraph, a livery stable, and a ball room. The village of Blowing Rock also had the Watauga Hotel, the Brady House, and the Stewart House.

With the completion of the Yonahlossee Turnpike to Linville along the side of Grandfather Mountain, guests at Blowing Rock could ride to Linville by a hack operated regularly by the Linville Improvement Company. There at Eseeola Lodge they might tarry a few days. Linville had a nine hole golf course, and Grandfather Mountain invited exploration. Grandfather is the most rugged and picturesque mountain in Western North Carolina. Its craggy peaks when seen at a distance have the rough features of a Grant Wood type of American pioneer or grandfather. The mountain had been a landmark for the pioneers. Daniel Boone hunted on its slopes. Scientists have claimed that it is one of the oldest rock formations in the world. Some geologists have asserted that it is two billion years old. To climb to the top of its peaks has always been a challenge to rugged tourists. The Linville Improvement Company had vision when it built a road to the crest of Grandfather Mountain. The turnpike that ran to Linville continued to Cranberry, a station on the East Tennessee and Western North Carolina Railroad.

The highest mountain in Eastern America is Mount Mitchell, one of the Black Mountains. Above five thousand feet it bore spruce trees. About 1912 its spruce was purchased and lumbered, also the spruce at the head of Cane River. Lumbering and fire destroyed most of these rare spruce forests. All was soon gone except near the top of Mount Mitchell.

In 1914 George T. Winston pleaded with the people of the state to preserve the forest on Mount Mitchell:

> From out of the primal sea I rose on high
> Above the clouds I kissed the sunlit sky,
> My rock the oldest in the rock-built earth;
> When I was born, it was the great world's birth.
> Long million years my crumbling sides did yield,
> To rain and frost and wind, a fertile field

For widening Piedmont plane and ocean shore.
Now nature kind assails my life no more;
At last in verdure soft and warm I'm clad,
Mid sapphire skies my emerald peaks are glad,
But hark! What frightened terror, new and dire!
"Tis human greed for gold! "Tis axe and fire!
O mighty State, prevent this deed of shame,
This great dishonor keep from thy great name.

Under Governor Locke Craig North Carolina purchased twenty acres near the top for a state park the first to be established. An association was formed to erect a monument to Dr. Elisha Mitchell, geologist who lost his life on the mountain. General Julian S. Carr of Durham, capitalist and philanthropist, was the leader of the movement. In 1917 Governor Bickett employed a forest warden to protect the park from fire, to advise tourists, to repair trails, and to look after the state's interests. In 1919 nature lovers noted that there were black bears, deer, wolves, panthers, "boomers," "rough grouse," and snow birds on Mt. Mitchell. Interesting trees were the Frazer balsam, yellow birch, mountain ash, service (called locally "sarvis"), red spruce, red cherry, hemlock, maple, oak, and white pine. Among the shrubs observed were the rose rhododendron, the handsomest of the species, the great rhododendron, mountain laurel, blueberries, currants, gooseberries, red raspberries, hobble bush, and hackberry. Flowers and herbs mentioned by naturalists were wood sorrel, trillium, clintonia, woodland aster, sharp-leafed wood aster, yellow meadow lily, St. John's wort, boneset, meadow-parsnip, grass of Parnassus, Oswego tea, saxafrage, purple turtlehead, trumpet weed, black cohosh, Indian pipe, Indian turnip, galax, tweyblade, and many kinds of fern.

A lumbering railroad had been built to get the logs down the mountain, and when lumbering activities ceased, the Mount Mitchell Railroad was put into operation to the "Top of Eastern America." It ran from the Mt. Mitchell station on the Western North Carolina Railroad to the summit of the peak. A 1917 advertising brochure described it: "Switchbacks cunningly constructed by an unexcelled feat of engineering, make the ascent gentle and pleasant.... Mount Mitchell Railroad zigzags [up] the mountainside, spans mountain gorges and ravines and climbs almost to the tip of the majestic monarch of them all...." Other high mountains that made up the scene as the passengers rode up the mountain were Mt. Celo 6357 feet, the Black

In Pursuit of Pleasure / 375

The Blowing Rock ASHEVILLE CHAMBER OF COMMERCE PHOTO

Mt. Mitchell Excursion Train ASHEVILLE CITIZEN-TIMES CO.

376 / *Part III: A Developing Economy*

Mt. Mitchell Motorway   ASHEVILLE CITIZEN–TIMES CO.

Trillium, one of the most beloved of mountain flowers
                                               ASHEVILLE CITIZEN–TIMES CO.

Brothers 6620–6690 feet, and Balsam Cone 6645 feet. Train fare was $2.50 for the round trip.

The route of the Mount Mitchell Railroad passed through Montreat, the Presbyterian Assembly's summer home. The passengers rode up the mountain in the morning, took lunch at Camp Alice at the station near the peak, then went on foot to the top, where Elisha Mitchell is buried. Camp Alice had a large dining hall, and there were cottages and a tent colony for those who wanted to spend the night to watch the sunrise.

After a brief trial the railroad proved to be impractical, and a cinder-surfaced road was built for about twenty miles from the town of Black Mountain to Camp Alice on Mount Mitchell, with a rise in elevation from 2700 to about 6700 feet. The opening of the Mount Mitchell Motor Road was celebrated by a large party, guests of the Mount Mitchell Development Company officials. They assembled at Black Mountain, went to a reception on the mountain, had dinner there and returned for a reception at Blue Ridge. This was a one-way toll road for automobiles, with the cars traveling up the mountain until a certain hour in the morning, allowing them time for the ascent before the downward traffic began in the afternoon. Among the strict printed regulations was the one that "no colored person will be admitted over the road except those going as drivers, nurses or attendants, accompanied by employers." The speed limit on the road was fifteen miles per hour.

At last in 1940 a free road was opened to Mt. Mitchell. The route left highway U. S. 70 near Marion on state route 104, thence to Buck Creek Gap intersection with the Blue Ridge Parkway, then to the intersection with the former Mt. Mitchell toll road. From that point the former toll road had been widened and was being offered free under the supervision of the Pisgah National Forest, the state, and the Blue Ridge Parkway.

The Brevard, Cashiers, Highlands area has been called "the land of waterfalls." The natural beauty of the area is enhanced by dozens of rippling streams and cascading waterfalls: Looking Glass Falls, Connestee Falls, Dry Falls, Bridal Veil Falls are a few. Outstanding is Whiteside Mountain, said to be the highest granite cliff in Eastern America. Lake Toxaway, Cashiers, Highlands, High Hampton are beautiful resort areas, a paradise for vacationers and summer residents. A number of prominent South Carolinians built summer homes in Cashiers Valley before the Civil War. One of the best known estates was High Hampton, the home of Wade Hampton, and another was that of Captain S. P. Ravenel of Charleston.

Charles Jenks came to the area in 1872 to operate the corundum mines in Macon County, North Carolina, and Rabun County, Georgia. The mines closed in 1873 and Jenks went to Highlands to regain his health. While he was there he was associated with two men who came from Kansas in 1875 to plant a town, Captain S. T. Kelsey and C. C. Hutchinson. They purchased land from J. W. Dobson. Kelsey was a builder of towns. At Highlands he built roads, erected buildings, advertised the resort. In 1890 the population was about 350. As a summer resort it was peopled chiefly by people from South Carolina. In 1887 Jenks and a group of New York and Massachusetts electrical and mechanical engineers formed the Western North Carolina Mining and Improvement Company. They purchased four hundred acres on the top of Hogback Mountain, later called Mount Toxaway. Jenks built a clubhouse for the company at the top and a wagon road leading to it. Subsequently he purchased for the company 2300 acres of woodland and trout streams along Horsepasture River and the Panthertown head of the Tuckaseigee River. The company was renamed the Sapphire Valley Company.

The key to the mountain region is Asheville in the lovely valley of the French Broad. It is set in an amphitheater of hills and affords splendid views of Mt. Pisgah and the mountain-rimmed horizon. Just east of Asheville the peaceful Swannanoa unites with the French Broad. The elevation is 2250 feet and the climate is mild and dry. From Asheville the valley runs eighteen miles north and south. It is known as the Asheville Plateau. At the North Carolina-Tennessee border, twenty-five miles northwest of Asheville, a high ridge blocks the northern end of the valley. Thirty miles south the Blue Ridge Mountains form an escarpment. The tallest peak near Asheville is Mt. Pisgah. The French Broad influences the wind directions, which are generally from the northwest except in September when they are from the southeast. The annual precipitation is thirty-eight inches, quite low for North Carolina. The growing season consists of a freeze-free period of 195 days. Floods occur at about twelve year intervals. Snowfall has varied from .7 inch in 1931–1932 to 40.6 inches in 1959–1960. The mean annual temperature is 56°.

In 1793 Asheville was just a trading post called Morristown. Incorporated in 1797 it was renamed Asheville for Samuel Ashe of New Hanover County. It was still a sleepy little village with a population of 2610 at the coming of the Western North Carolina Railroad (1880), but it had had a varied history. A year earlier the first telegraph line had been built into the town and a public library had been opened. "Judge" Edward Aston, mayor of Asheville, had publicized the town as a health resort by letter-writing and by mailing out thousands of circulars throughout the nation and European countries telling of Asheville's advantages as a resort for those who suffered from lung trouble. The location seemed designed for man's happiness, with grand and majestic views. After 1880 capitalists and health seekers poured in. The Swannanoa Hotel was opened. A four story brick building with "fire plugs on every floor," it had Asheville's first bathroom. George Willis Pack stayed there and had the bathroom built, walled in, and lined with zinc. Famous visitors were Zeb Vance, Bill Nye, and James Whitcomb Riley. On a balcony overlooking the street a band played a concert every afternoon, and each night there was dancing in the ballroom. The Swannanoa rivaled the older Eagle Hotel which also had a band. Excursion trains ran from Salisbury to Asheville on Saturdays carrying young people to the dances.

Asheville became a mecca for those suffering from tuberculosis, and prominent doctors recommended it; others came and established sanitariums. Its health assets were "a healthful climate, pure air, good water, unsurpassed scenery and congenial people." By 1890 its population had quadrupled to 10,000.

Dr. Gatchell, a native of Wisconsin who wrote the circular that "Judge" Aston mailed out in such quantities, established the first sanitarium for consumptives in Asheville. In 1875 Dr. J. W. Gleitsmann, a German by birth, came to Asheville from Baltimore and established the Mountain Sanitarium for Pulmonary Diseases. He wrote and read before the American Public Health Association a paper "Western North Carolina As a Health Resort." The paper was circulated widely — about 64,000 copies. Mr. Fred A. Hall came to Asheville in 1883 with tuberculosis. He recovered and became a prominent citizen.

380 / Part III: A Developing Economy

Lower Falls on Cullasaja River NATIONAL PARK SERVICE PHOTO

Looking down North Mills River from Kramer's Vista near Bent Creek Gap
U.S. FOREST SERVICE PHOTO

In Pursuit of Pleasure / 381

Looking Glass Rock, Pisgah National Forest U.S. FOREST SERVICE PHOTO

Sliding Rock Falls, Pisgah National Forest U.S. FOREST SERVICE PHOTO

Swannanoa Hotel Asheville ASHEVILLE CITIZEN-TIMES CO.

His case history and recovery were written of and published in the *Boston Medical Journal*. As a result many others came seeking health.

Asheville became first a summer resort. Soon thereafter many visitors came for the winter because of the clear air and the mild climate. In 1885 the city authorities began to clean up sanitary conditions which were detrimental to the city as a health resort. A new city code was adopted in 1887, in which were these provisions: "[The commissioners may] lay a tax ... [annually] on all dogs, and on swine, horses and cattle running at large within the town ... ; [they] shall possess the power to prohibit cattle, horses, or hogs from running at large in said town." A sanitary chief and a sanitary inspector were appointed. All citizens became increasingly conscious of Asheville's natural advantages as a health resort and did everything possible to promote this phase of the city's life. Soon other sanitariums were established. Among them was the Winyah Sanitarium started by Dr. Karl von Ruch. Many cases of tuberculosis were treated in hotels and boarding houses as well as in sanitariums. So widely and favorably known did the Asheville area become for its beneficent climate and for diseases of the throat and lungs that the United States Government shortly after World War One built at Oteen a hospital for the treatment of veterans of the armed services who had contracted tuberculosis. Many who came to Asheville for visits and cures remained and became enthusiastic residents. They built homes, invested money, began

Kenilworth Hotel   ASHEVILLE CITIZEN-TIMES CO.

industries, and thus contributed to the city's growth. Following World War One about three thousand persons were treated annually for tuberculosis. Residing in the city were perhaps an equal number of newcomers who were not under the care of physicians. Each of these persons spent freely in the city. It was estimated that the tubercular patients spent three million dollars annually.

In the 1920's governmental agencies began to realize that good public health was a social obligation. Federal, state, and local governments built hospitals and sanitariums. As a result Asheville and other popular health resorts were less frequented. By 1928 most of the sanitariums around the city were forced to close and the number of patients from other places became neglible. Although Asheville then ceased to be a health resort, it became a most popular retreat for tourists and retired persons. This was true, to a degree, of all parts of Western North Carolina. Chambers of Commerce, privately owned resorts, and organizations all over the mountains published handbooks, pamphlets, brochures which stressed the scenic beauty, the recreational facilities, the invigorating climate, the pure water, and the beautiful streams of the region. Organizations were formed to promote the tourist season — the summer months. To a great degree the economy of the region came to depend upon the number of tourists and summer visitors. Even more important than the tourists are the thousands of people who have built summer homes, second homes, or vacation homes in this delightful land.

Asheville is said to have had more and better hotels than any city of the same size in the United States. The Battery Park mentioned earlier attracted numbers of very wealthy visitors. Kenilworth Inn, a big rambling hotel was built in 1891. The Southern Railroad and George W. Vanderbilt owned stock in the company. It was then one of the finest hotels in the South and had 250 rooms. Fire destroyed it in 1909 and the rebuilding was started in 1913 at a cost of $1,240,000. Of English design, it was a show place advertised as "the Healthiest and Most Delightful Resort in America." With beautifully landscaped grounds it stood on a hill overlooking Asheville and the Biltmore Estate. It became a sanitarium in 1930 under Dr. William Ray Griffin and Dr. Mark A. Griffin and was used for patients with mental and nervous disorders.

Grove Park Inn, built by E. W. Grove, wealthy drug manufacturer, in 1914 on the western slopes of Sunset Mountain was the epitome of elegance and comfort. At least five Presidents have stayed there, and it has housed a full complement of wealthy visitors. This hotel is still serving as a convention center of strong appeal. During the 1920's Grove had the gracious Battery Park hotel razed and the hill lowered. A new Battery Park rose on the site, one that was in keeping with the technology of that decade. A block away the George Vanderbilt Hotel and a new convention hall attracted large gatherings.

In addition to the hotels, Asheville had more than one hundred boarding houses, among which was one at 81 Charlotte Street built about 1870 for Fanny Patton. It was closed in 1960. Burned once, it was rebuilt. It and the Patton House next door were the first Asheville houses to have running water. Aunt Charlotte, who belonged to the household, was highly indignant and wanted to know if Thomas (Captain Patton) hadn't taken leave of his senses "bringing the privy in the house." There was a fireplace in every room. There were wardrobes but no closets. An old Negro servant named Margaret but called "Cookie" was asked by a northern lady if she remembered the Civil War. She answered: "Course I does; that was when them Yankees came down here and took all us folks had."

Extravagant praise for Asheville is to be found in the advertising brochures which have been broadcast since 1880. Hinton A. Helper wrote one titled "Nature's Trundle Bed of Recuperation for Tourist and Health Seeker," in which he claimed: "The climate is not excelled by any in the world. The soil is rich and the lands productive.... The timber lands are the best in the South. The mineral wealth is inexhaustible. The manufacturing facilities are unsurpassed." One bulletin recounted the economic growth from 1880 to 1890. Its author stated that in 1880 the assessed valuation was $904,428, while in 1890 it was $4,956,000. In 1889 $819,000 worth of real estate was sold and 184 buildings were erected. The C. E. Graham cotton mill employed 250 and the Asheville Furniture Company had ninety employees. A brochure of 1899 designed to attract industry cited the different business establishments: one large tobacco factory, two ice factories, three planing mills, twenty-six carriage and wagon makers, the largest cotton factory in the South, two laundries, machine shops, foundries, a roller flour mill, the largest tannery in Western North Carolina, the largest bottling company in the state, three greenhouses, two daily and four weekly newspapers, one cornet band, two literary clubs, a lumber business, four tobacco warehouses, two military companies, the Asheville Club, social and golf clubs. An Asheville guide of 1904 praised the Kenilworth Inn, Theobald's Cafe, Candy Kitchen, and Ice Cream Parlor. Mentioned favorably were Clarence Worrall's Art Institute and Bon Marche, which it called an outstanding store. A new auditorium was built on the site of one burned in 1903 and a new library was built on Pack Square. The Biltmore Estate was open to the public on Tuesdays, Thursdays, and Saturdays. A Brochure described "Zealandia," the residence of Mr. Philip S. Henry of London. It had been so-named by Captain J. Evans Brown who lived in New Zealand. Praised also was the Mineral Springs Hotel run by Mrs. R. Cathey at Skyland, North Carolina. The population by 1900 had climbed to 14,694, and in the metropolitan area were 27,000 people. There were ten miles of brick paving, one and one-half miles of stone paving, one and one-half miles of macadam, seven miles of brick sidewalks, twenty miles of sewerage, fourteen miles of electric railway, and the assessed valuation was $6,000,000.

A *Road and Tour Book* of Western North Carolina for 1916 indicated further growth: thirty-eight miles of paved streets, population of 34,000, seventy-five miles of sidewalks, 125 miles of macadam roads, an assessed property valuation of $15,000,000, a public library of 13,000 volumes, a municipal swimming pool, six banks, three hospitals, forty churches, 250,000 visitors annually.

The most extravagant promotional publication to that date was *Azure Lure* published in 1924. The assessed valuation of Asheville property was $80,000,000 and the population of 50,000 enjoyed sixty-four miles of paved streets. The booklet emphasized the availability of water power, with 117,500 developed horse power and 1,067,000 horsepower undeveloped. Western North Carolina had fifteen golf courses, a small number indeed, but golf in 1924 was in somewhat the same position that skiing occupies today.

One of the cataclysmic events in the history of twentieth-century Western North Carolina was the "boom and bust" in Asheville. First came the highly-inflated Florida real estate boom in the 1920's. Many fortunes were made — on paper; then the boom collapsed. Before its collapse, high-powered real estate promoters moved to Asheville and Hendersonville and generated the enthusiasm that caused the runaway inflation in real estate that resulted in the boom and the bust. In 1925 Thomas Wolfe visited Asheville and wrote to Aline Bernstein that he had just returned from "Boom Town" where everyone was talking about the progress and prosperity of Asheville. He had drunk their corn whiskey and listened to their glowing talk of how they would soon be millionaires, of how Asheville would have 100,000 people by 1930. Yet, by 1926 Wolfe was writing his sister regretting that while his mother had lost money in Florida real estate he was consoling her with the idea that Asheville would have a certain assured growth. He aptly added that a few near-swindlers and near-thieves would clean up but that the admiring boobs would lose their shirts and that Asheville would never be the national capital.

In *You Can't Go Home Again* he described Asheville as being no longer a small town. Its streets were teeming with life. The look on people's faces was frightening: madness, frenzy, the eyes glistening with excitement. People were intoxicated by speculation in real estate — the idea of getting rich quickly, suddenly, overnight. Real estate men were everywhere. Everyone bought real estate — barbers, lawyers, grocers, bootblacks, janitors. The rule was to buy, always to buy. Whatever one bought and at whatever price, he felt he could sell it the next day at a great profit. All of this buying was "on time," always "on time," and the profits were paper profits — the millionaires, paper millionaires.

In November 1930 the roof fell in. In the *New York Times*

"New" Battery Park Hotel, 1920's   ASHEVILLE CITIZEN-TIMES CO.

appeared a report from the *Asheville Citizen*, November 20, 1930, describing the closing of eight banks in Western North Carolina, most of them in or near Asheville and Hendersonville. These failures resulted from the closing of the Central Bank and Trust Company, Asheville's largest financial institution with combined assets of its banking and trust departments of $52,645,191.43. Coincident with its failure, three Hendersonville banks closed: the First Bank and Trust Company, the American Bank and Trust Company, and the Citizens' National Bank. Also closing were the Biltmore Oteen Bank, the Bank of Leicester and the Clay County Bank. On the same day the *Raleigh News and Observer* listed twenty-seven state banks that had closed in 1930 in Western North Carolina. The depression enveloped the nation, but in Asheville it was a gigantic bust. John Mitchell, Chief State Bank Examiner, blamed the closing of the Western North Carolina banks on the real estate boom. The banks had lent money on real estate at inflated values to such an extent that they could not meet the demands of their depositors. Catastrophic for Asheville was the failure of the Central Bank and Trust Company. For seventeen years it had been perhaps the most progressive financial institution in Western North

388 / *Part III: A Developing Economy*

Carolina and it had done much to aid the region.

Jonathan Daniels in *Tar Heels: A Portrait of North Carolina* (New York, 1947) attributed the origin of the boom to George W. Vanderbilt and E. W. Grove. He felt that they had corrupted the people of Asheville and raised false hopes. His accusations and implications are unjust. Vanderbilt may have been a feudal lord but he aided Western North Carolina. So did Grove. Wolfe regretted that Grove tore down the picturesque old Battery Park Hotel and replaced it with a modern building of brick, concrete, and steel. Most people have thought that his Grove Park Inn was magnificently picturesque. Vanderbilt's estate and contributions antedated the twentieth century. Grove Park Inn was built in 1912. The bank failure, the collapse, the bust did not come until 1930. Even then it was not a completely local affair. The stock market crash had occurred in October, 1929, the depression was becoming accelerated, twenty-seven other Western North Carolina banks had already failed in 1930. Probably all of these failures happened because of the failure of Caldwell and Company in Nashville, a gigantic Southern financial institution. As a result of the failure of the Central Bank and Trust Company, its president was sentenced to prison and later Asheville's mayor committed suicide.

During the 1890's Warm Springs (in Madison County), which had been a health resort since 1779, was renamed Hot Springs, and a remarkable hotel was built there, the Mountain Park. It was a handsome rambling structure, in every room of which the sun shone. It had a large lobby, spacious parlors, one-fourth mile of verandas. It had elevators, steam heat, toilets, fireplaces, an orchestra, a music hall, billiard parlors, bowling alleys, a golf course, tennis courts, and riding horses. Nearby were the famed springs, which contained many mineral elements. There was a spring house for drinking water and a bath house in which baths were built in the springs themselves. During the years when health-seekers believed in the efficacy of mineral waters, Hot Springs was one of the most popular resorts in Western North Carolina. Thousands came who were not ill. They came because of the good food, the dances, the pleasant company, and the recreational attractions of the hotel.

After the United States entered World War One as many as twenty-eight hundred German prisoners were interned in the hotel. They had been members of crews of German ships caught in American or allied ports and waters at the time of the entry of the United States in the war. They gave band concerts and enjoyed their stay in the beautiful surroundings. On one occasion when it was rumored that they were to be transferred, some of them poisoned the drinking water hoping to be made ill to prevent their being removed. They used too much poison and some of the prisoners died.

After medical opinion developed that the benefits derived from the waters of the springs resulted from hydro-therapy, and that the treatment could be given in any medical institution, the decline in numbers who came to Hot Springs resulted in closing the famous hotel.

Near Hot Springs is Lover's Leap about which there is the legend of the Indian maiden Mist-on-the-Mountain, the daughter of Lone Wolf. She loved an Indian brave named Magwa. Another brave, the jealous Tall Pine, killed Magwa and the maiden leaped off the cliff. About that time Tall Pine was killed by a panther. Not far away is Douglas Lake, made by one of the TVA dams. And some seven miles away is Paint Rock, famous in Indian legends and a landmark on the first wagon road through the mountains. On the cliffs are strange markings, now almost indecipherable, which gave the rock its name. Formerly a ferry was used to carry people across the river to connect with the railroad.

Hot Springs, the town, has a beautiful location. It is completely surrounded by mountains, is on an attractive river, and Spring Creek flows through the town. It should attract many tourists, but since the closing of the hotel it has withered on the vine, had few tourists, and ceased to grow. Nearby above Spring Creek is a camping and recreation area operated by the National Park Service in Pisgah National Forest. Here picnicking, camping, swimming are enjoyed.

Western North Carolina's attraction for tourists was enhanced by the building of the Blue Ridge Parkway. It has been the scenic route for millions of visitors from Northeastern United States to this region, and these guests have been an inestimable boon to the economy of the region. The travelers have fanned out to adjacent resorts. Today's tourists are from diverse elements

390 / *Part III: A Developing Economy*

Lovers Leap, French Broad River, near Hot Springs

of the population. Many of the earlier generation of tourists were well-to-do middle-aged people who stayed one, two, or three weeks at a resort hotel or "took the water" at a mineral spring. They sought rest and relaxation. Often they were society's elite. Those in this group still come but they are a small minority. Now the worker with a weekend or a week's vacation comes and brings his family, or a number of men and families come for a weekend of golf, or skiing. In some of the older resort towns as in Blowing Rock the two groups clash. The long-time, established summer residents resent the intrusion or invasion by the tourists. They close their facilities to them. Linville and Blowing Rock golf courses have become virtual private clubs and have limited play by non-members. But the local businesses cater to all who come. Every effort is being made to get those who come to stay longer. Tourists are given the most courteous attention, and amusements with family appeal are provided. Tweetsie Railroad between Boone and Blowing Rock and Ghost Town at Maggie Valley have appeal for all members of the family, although they were designed for the children. *Horn in the West* and *Unto These Hills* interest the whole family. Beech Mountain has chair lifts, fishing, riding, hiking, in addition to skiing and golf. It features a Disney Land type of amusement park, the Land of Oz, to which people ride by chair lifts.

Doughton Park on the Blue Ridge Parkway contains six thousand acres, a lodge, picnic area, camp ground, twenty miles of trails, scenic Wildcat Rocks and precipitous bluffs. Nearby is the Brinegar Cabin where one can see hand-weaving demonstrations from May to October. The park was named for Congressman Robert Doughton from Alleghany County. At Blowing Rock the denim manufacturer, Moses Cone, had enjoyed a summer mansion located on Flat Top Mountain in an estate with 3750 acres and two beautiful man-made lakes. He died in 1908, and his will specified that after the death of Mrs. Cone the estate would become the property of the State of North Carolina. A few years after Mrs. Cone's death in 1947 the state transferred the estate to the federal government to be used as part of the Blue Ridge Parkway. The mansion is used as a museum and sales center for mountain handicrafts of the Southern Highlands Handicraft Guild. The woven coverlet given to Miss Frances Goodrich which awakened her interest

Tweetsie Railroad, tourist attraction

ASHEVILLE CHAMBER OF COMMERCE PHOTO

392 / Part III: A Developing Economy

Brinegar Cabin on Blue Ridge Parkway before restoration

NATIONAL PARK SERVICE PHOTO

Brinegar Cabin after restoration

NATIONAL PARK SERVICE PHOTO

in hand weaving and started the revival of weaving in North Carolina is on display there. More than twenty miles of unpaved roads on the estate are reserved for pedestrian, horseback, and carriage use.

Nearby, also on the Blue Ridge Parkway, is the 4000 acre Julian Price Memorial Park. Price was formerly president of the Jefferson Standard Life Insurance Company. The park has some of the most attractive camp sites in Western North Carolina, and it offers fishing to campers.

Cataloochi at Maggie Valley and Blowing Rock Ski Lodge (now Appalachian Ski Mountain) near Blowing Rock were the first of the North Carolina ski resorts. Another is Hound Ears in the Shull's Mills and Foscoe area of Watauga County on the side of a mountain, the pinnacle of which resembles the hanging ears of a hound dog. Each year sees new ski slopes put into use, and around them residential communities develop.

Between two of the peaks of Grandfather Mountain Hugh Morton, descendant of Hugh McRae, has built a mile high swinging pedestrian bridge and at one end is a reception center large enough to house a small convention. Each year since 1956 there has been a gathering of the Scottish clans from a wide area, and Highland Games are held on the mountainside on a weekend in July. Events on Saturday consist of highland dancing, piping, track and field events. On Sunday after a worship service and lunch the champions put on an exhibition, followed by a "Highland Shoot," an archery tournament. Kilts and bonnets are worn for the weekend making it a colorful occasion. Thirteen clans, the Burns club of Charlotte, and the Saint Andrews Societies of Charleston, Savannah, New York State, and Washington, D. C. are the sponsors.

Since 1926 on the fourth Sunday in June has been held the "Singing on the Mountain" on the slopes of Grandfather. For twenty-three consecutive years there was no rain on this date, and mountain folk considered the fact almost miraculous and attributed it to the beneficence of God. The annual sing is looked forward to and visited by thousands of religious people and about as many who are just curious. Some thirty thousand were present in 1957. On the day of the singing people travel to Grandfather as they did to camp meetings a few decades ago. "Grandfather Mountain is a symbol of the eternity of the hills." People gather to hear the words of many preachers and to sing the songs that they love. The singing is also a social event. Whole

One of the first ski slopes, Appalachian Ski Mountain

ASHEVILLE CHAMBER OF COMMERCE PHOTO

Chalet above the slopes

Chairlift at Beech Mountain

Bagpipers on Grandfather Mountain at Highland Games

HUGH MORTON PHOTO

On the Parade Grounds at the Highland Games

HUGH MORTON PHOTO

396 / Part III: A Developing Economy

Singing on the Mountain   HUGH MORTON PHOTO

Ground breaking for final link of Blue Ridge Parkway by Governor Dan Moore and Assistant-Director of the National Park Service   HUGH MORTON PHOTO

In Pursuit of Pleasure / 397

An overlook on the Blue Ridge Parkway

families, old friends, and kin, separated by mountain ranges and hours of travel gather there to visit and to share their picnic food with each other. This event, the largest mountain sing in the Southern highlands, uplifts all who attend. Uncle Joe Hartley who helped to build the Yonahlossee Turnpike in 1891 started the Grandfather singing in 1924 when 125 members of a Sunday school had a picnic on the slope of the mountain. After the picnic they had some "beautiful singing."

Few people who enjoy the 507,159 acres, the 1200 species of plants, the 130 species of trees, the 52 species of fur bearing animals, the great natural beauty, the hiking, driving, camping facilities of the Great Smoky Mountains National Park realize the tremendous and long-continued efforts by many enthusiasts

398 / Part III: A Developing Economy

View to the south from Clingman's Dome parking area, Great Smokies
HUGH MORTON PHOTO

before the park became a reality. The first campaign was by a dedicated band of Asheville people and their supporters. October 29, 1885, in an address before the American Academy of Medicine, Dr. Henry O. Marcy, of Boston, advocated securing "a large reservation of the higher ranges as a park." By 1892 destruction of the forests was a cause of concern and Charles S. Sargent with an editorial in *Garden and Forest* was the first to present in print a plan for a national forest. A year earlier (1891) Joseph A. Holmes, state geologist of North Carolina, had suggested to Gifford Pinchot a great national forest for the Southern Appalachians. The Biltmore Forest experiment no doubt influenced both Holmes and Pinchot. In 1893 the North Carolina General Assembly passed a resolution in favor of establishing such a park. It was presented to the House by Congressman John S. Henderson in 1894, but Congress was not yet concerned.

"The first organized association for national legislation to set up a federal park in the Southern Appalachian Mountains was begun by Dr. Chase P. Ambler of Asheville . . . in 1899." He presented the idea to his friend from Ohio, Judge William R. Day. Day suggested that an Asheville organization be formed which, assisted by the Asheville Board of Trade, would work for a national park. Ambler, George H. Smathers, and Senator Jeter C. Pritchard sought to interest the Southern press, doctors, lawyers and other groups to get them to address petitions to Pritchard asking him to use his influence to have a Congressional committee appointed. It was agreed that twenty to forty thousand acres could be bought for one dollar an acre, and that immediate action was imperative to preserve the forests, the game, and the fish because lumbermen were destroying the forests and tanneries were killing the fish.

In 1899 the Asheville Board of Trade organized a Parks and Forestry Committee which obtained the aid of newspapers of North Carolina and neighboring states in giving publicity to the movement. It was soon realized by George Vanderbilt and others that there was a need to include parts of North Carolina, Tennessee, and adjacent states in a great eastern national park. Therefore letters were sent to governors, senators, representatives, and influential people in North Carolina, South Carolina, Georgia, Tennessee, and Virginia asking them to assemble in Asheville November 11, 1899, to organize an association for the promotion of a national park and forest reserve. Forty-two of those statesmen, editors, and industrialists came and organized the Appalachian National Park Association with the object of obtaining a national park in the Southern Appalachian Mountains. Efforts of the press, Congressmen, and interested citizens were exerted toward that end. Five thousand booklets telling the story of the movement were printed. January 4, 1900, Senator Jeter Pritchard introduced in the Senate the petition from the Appalachian National Park Association. Reasons for urging Congressional action were the natural beauty of the region, the superb forests, the necessity of preserving the headwaters of many mountain rivers, the healthfulness of the climate, and the central location for the East, the South, and the Midwest. Much support came from scientists and those interested in forestry. Needless to say, the efforts failed. The nation was not sufficiently educated to the idea of this national park.

After the passage of the Weeks Law in 1911 the Forest Service established a Smoky Mountain purchase unit and began obtaining options for the purchase of land belonging to the Little River Lumber Company, but the purchases were not completed because of World War One. The publication of the now famous books by Horace Kephart and Margaret Morley created favorable opinion for preservation of the forests in the Smoky Mountains. Meanwhile Hugh McRae offered to sell the Grandfather Mountain area to the federal government for a park. A bill introduced in 1917 for its purchase failed to pass. Between 1922 and 1923 other bills were introduced, proposing purchases in various locations. There were at that time nineteen national parks and not one was in Eastern United States, where two-thirds of the population lived.

The successful park movement grew out of the efforts in Knoxville of Mrs. Willis P. Davis. In 1924 Dr. Herbert Work, Secretary of the Interior, appointed a committee to study the establishment of one or more national parks in the Southern Appalachians. A southern Appalachian National Park committee and commissions in Tennessee and North Carolina were created to promote the park and to have a part in selecting its site. Harlan P. Kelsey, a member of the Southern Appalachain Committee, and E. C. Brooks, President of North Carolina State College, were active workers. In 1925 Congress authorized the Secretary of the Interior to ascertain boundaries for three parks: the Shenandoah, the Mammoth Cave, and the Great Smoky Mountain, and to receive offers of land and money for their creation. Congress appropriated no money for the projects. Then the work of the North Carolina and Tennessee commissions began in earnest. State Senator Mark Squires of Lenoir, chairman of the North Carolina commission, and Colonel David C. Chapman of the Tennessee commission deserve credit for selling the idea of the park to their respective states. The Tennessee legislature voted $273,557 to purchase the 76,507 acres from the Little River Lumber Company, and the Knoxville Chamber of Commerce guaranteed one-third of the price.

Proponents of the Grandfather Mountain-Linville area and lumbermen in North Carolina opposed the location of the park in the Smokies. The latter called forth the wrath of Horace Kephart: "Why should this last stand of splendid, irreplaceable trees be sacrificed to the greedy maw of the sawmill? Why should future generations be robbed of all chance to see with their own eyes what a real forest, a real wildwood, a real unimproved work of God is like . . . ? If cut . . . it would be a drop in the bucket. . . . Let these few old trees stand! . . . There is no use talking about conserving the Smoky forest by turning it into a national forest after the lumbermen get through with it. . . . The only question is: Shall the Smoky Mountains be made into a national park or a desert?"

By 1926 only $500,000 had been raised in North Carolina, and most of that had come from the area near the park. Statewide support had not been given. On April 22, 1926, a bill for the creation of two national parks became law. North Carolina and Tennessee authorized bond issues to meet the states' obligations for the Great Smoky Mountains National Park. Additional funds were needed, and John D. Rockefeller, Jr., established the Laura Spellman Rockefeller Fund of $5,000,000 to make the park possible. North Carolina and Tennessee acquired 158,799.21 acres and deeded the tract to the federal government on February 6, 1930. Effective work in developing the park began in 1931, and on September 2, 1940, President Roosevelt dedicated it. Eighteen million dollars, it was estimated, were needed for further development.

After man's exodus when the land for the park was purchased in 1926, there remained ghost communities along the Little Tennessee and Tuckaseigee rivers and on Hazel Creek, which rises deep in the Smokies and runs for twenty miles to Fontana Lake. It is fed by eight large streams and receives the flow from the watershed of what was once the largest virgin forest in Western North Carolina. Once the forest was alive with game, the streams with fish. Around 1850 settlers came to Hazel Creek and built log cabins. The slopes were excellent for cattle and sheep, and hogs fattened on the forest mast. People lived off the land, with an abundance of game. Granville Calhoun, pioneer, entrepreneur, railroad builder, miner, jack-of-all-trades, lived through the entire cycle of human "development" of Hazel Creek. His family were among the early settlers. The first employment for people on Hazel Creek was offered when the Johnson and Harris Lumber Company cut timber and floated the logs down to their mill. A series of dams built across the creek held the logs until the water was high enough to float them. In 1909 W. M. Ritter built a logging railroad and set up a large double hand-mill which employed four hundred men. Each side of the mill turned out one million board feet a month. From 1911 to 1928 Ritter cut 210,000,000 board feet from this one creek and was called the "hardwood king of the world." In 1890 copper was discovered on Sugar Fork Creek and the Adams Mining Company mined copper from 1900 to 1905. In 1926 when the states of Tennessee and North Carolina bought all of the land from the people and turned it into the Great Smoky Mountains National Park, owners were reluctant to sell. A fair price was paid for the mountain and forest land, but what the sellers received was insufficient for them to buy equivalent property near towns like Bryson City. They took their money and began sorrowfully to look for new homes. For them a way of life was gone forever. Hundreds had to leave their snug mountain retreats, but only death will take from them their memories of the "good old days." John Wikle wrote in the *Asheville Citizen* "The bear goes unharmed and the deer play undisturbed; where bare-footed children once hoed corn, now bears wild blackberries. Where once stood a great sawmill there is only a mass of vines and trees; there is only a ghost hid in the trees where once people lived." Hazel Creek now looks as it did in 1850 when the first man came. The people who once lived and reveled in a virgin paradise are now the poorer inhabitants of nearby towns. But the park will regain and retain the primeval beauty of the region.

The holdings of the lumber companies were acquired without difficulty except for the 92,800 acres owned by the Champion Fibre Company, almost one-fifth of the national park. This company owned the core of the virgin timber, the slopes of New Found Gap, part of Clingman's Dome, all of Mount Le Conte, the Chimney Tops, the Three Forks, Greenbrier Wilderness, and Mount Guyot. Reuben Robertson, president of the company, argued that the spruce on the company's holdings was essential to its continued operation. Eventually Champion agreed to sell all of its land in the park for $3,000,000. The company began buying its spruce in Canada, shipping it to Canton at less expense than if it had built a railroad to the crest of the Smokies to get out the timber.

Eventually the federal government bought additional land. In 1933 President Roosevelt allocated $1,550,000 from Civilian Conservation Corps funds for land purchase, and by 1935 the

400,000 acres set by Congress as a requirement had been met. The two states had contributed $4,095,696, the United States $3,503,766, and the Rockefeller Memorial Fund $5,065,000. Another gift of John D. Rockefeller, Jr., of $100,000 made it possible for the National Park Service to purchase 1000 acres in the Linville Falls area. The Linville Gorge had already been purchased by the Forest Service as part of the Pisgah National Forest. The combined falls and gorge are now certain to be preserved for posterity as a "wild area." Camping facilities have been provided at the falls. Together the falls and the gorge provide one of the most breathtaking experiences possible for weekend visitors or one-day picnickers. The Blue Ridge Parkway's last link is now being built the length of Grandfather Mountain along a route between the crest and the former Yonahlossee Turnpike, now Highway 221, creating a strip of national park where many hoped to locate the national park of the Southern Highlands.

Millions of people come to the Great Smoky Mountains National Park each year. They hike along its winding mountain trails, pitch their camps in its forests, and view some of the most luxuriant plant life in Eastern America. "More than 650 miles of horse and foot trails wind along crystal clear streams and waterfalls, past giant trees, ... through the wild beauty of spring flowers or autumn colors, and into high mountain meadows." The park offers guided nature walks along many of the trails. There are also many self-guided nature trails. The famous Appalachian Trail enters the park at Davenport Gap and traverses it for seventy-one miles, leaving it near Fontana Dam. One can hike the seventy-one miles in six to eight days, sleeping in trailside shelters. The park has some six hundred miles of streams that add beauty and can be fished for rainbow and brook trout. It can be lovely during any of the four seasons but it is probably the most beautiful during the latter half of October when there are clear days and cool nights and the coloring of the leaves presents a panorama of almost unbelievable colors.

Many social and residential communities have been created, some of them organized as private clubs, others because of common interests. Among such communities near Hendersonville are Pleasant Estates, the Highland Lake Club, with clubhouse and cottages open to the public, and Laurel Park; several clubs in

Tryon; Hound Ears Club and Lodge; and the Carolina Caribbean Club at Beech Mountain. In addition, several communities and real estate developments have club-like restrictions; among these are Linville and Little Switzerland. A prototype of these, a club that was successful for several years was Kanuga, near Hendersonville. In the first decade of this century George Stephens of Asheville organized it after studying similar clubs in the Adirondacks, on Long Island, and in Wisconsin. A group of Charlotte businessmen bought the tract of one thousand acres and divided it into lots fifty feet by two hundred. Each of the two hundred carefully screened members received a lot, which he could not sell without the permission of Stephens and the trustees. Dues were a sum of $150 for ten years. The cost of the houses built by the members was restricted to a minimum of $400 and a maximum of $2500. Running water was piped from springs on the mountain, and a dam provided a lake and a source of power for electricity. The resort opened in 1909 and was used for only six years. The flood of 1916 washed out the lake and destroyed the buildings. In 1927 the Episcopal Church bought the site for a summer conference ground.

Little Switzerland was started by Judge Heriot Clarkson about 1910. The original purchase was for eleven thousand acres. A company was formed; inns, camps, and homes were planned. It was to be an attractive and exclusive colony with no lots smaller than one acre. A water system was installed and lots were sold to interesting and distinguished people. The altitude of Little Switzerland is 3478 feet and it has a beautiful setting and magnificent views. The Switzerland Inn, owned by Mrs. Ida Clarkson, was run in connection with six cottages and a Swiss chalet. Twelve miles of scenic roads, two beautiful waterfalls, flowers and mountain shrubbery, and unsurpassed scenery have been the chief attractions. When the Blue Ridge Parkway was planned to traverse the crest of the Blue Ridge it had to pass through Little Switzerland property. Judge Clarkson objected, saying it would take three miles of the company property two hundred feet wide. Nevertheless the parkway was built to bisect the property and it has added beauty and distinction to Little Switzerland. This unique development runs for five miles along the parkway and extends one-half mile in width. There are many attractive homes on the spacious lots. Geneva Hall is the community center and nearby are camps Glen Laurel and As You Like It.

Soon after World War One, camps for boys and girls were established throughout the mountains. At first these were rugged, designed to allow the campers to experience primitive conditions. Often they were operated by local people who had no experience or training for the work. No standards for sanitation and healthful conditions had been established. But within a few years the Southern Camping Association and the American Camping Association were organized, and they carried on regular inspection of member camps. Their seals of approval were sought by camp operators and were looked for by parents in selecting camps. In addition to the many excellent privately owned camps there are a number of boy and girl scout camps.

One of Transylvania County's eighteen camp communities is more than a camp. It is the Brevard Music Center, started as the Transylvania Music Camp by James Christian Pfohl in 1944. An annual music festival has been held since 1946. Now the Transylvania Music Camp is the summer home of the Brevard Music Center. It has 250 student campers, more than 165 faculty and staff members. Nine regularly performing musical groups present five concerts weekly during the summer. Improvements at the center include an additional forty acres, twenty-seven new buildings, and a new auditorium built of redwood and stone. The Music Center attracts outstanding young musicians, and there is a faculty member for every two students.

Tryon, an "unspoiled paradise," has an exquisite setting. Lofty mountains rear their peaks four to five miles away. About them Mrs. Ella W. Peattie wrote the poem "These Be the Mountains That Comfort Me." The mountains provide shelter from the cold north winds. The mean temperature for January, the coldest month, is 43°, the mean summer temperature 74°. Nearby are the charming Pacolet Valley, the crystal-clear Pacolet River, and 175 acre Lake Lanier. Sydney Lanier lived near Tryon for several years before his death in 1881. In 1896 Tryon was visited by the vice-president of the Southern Railway Company who helped to popularize the town. William Gillette, actor and playwright, built an attractive home, now the Thousand Pines Inn. Other prominent people came for the winter and many built homes. They formed the Tryon Riding and Hunt Club, the Tryon Country Club, and made the area a fashionable riding and hunting country. An annual steeple chase and a horse and hounds show are held. There are also an annual spring festival and a tilting tournament. Attractive hotels are the Mimosa, Oak Hall, Oakwood, Edgewood, Thousand Pines, and Pinecrest. Two of them are open all year, the others only in winter. Prominent visitors have been John Burroughs, Fanny Hurst, Edward Waldo Emerson, Admiral Robert W. Peary, the Reverend Charles G. Sewell. Tryon is an artists' colony, and it has been for half a century a handicraft center.

The Western North Carolina Associated Communities (WNCAC) grew from a drive that began in Asheville. In May 1946 the Asheville Chamber of Commerce invited public officials, leaders of civic organizations, and leading citizens from twenty-three western countries to attend a dinner meeting and discuss coordination and cooperation among the communities on regional matters. No organization developed from that meeting, perhaps because "personal acquaintance and confidence ... could not be stretched this far." Just about a month later, some eighteen people, all from communities west of Asheville, met together at Dillsboro in Jackson County in a meeting to explore promotion of tourist business, roads, and other matters of mutual interest. At this second meeting the Western North Carolina Associated Communities (WNCAC) was organized. Eleven counties were represented, plus Western Carolina College, the Cherokee Indian Reservation, and Fontana Village resort area. A projects committee recommended seven particular jobs to be launched by the WNCAC: 1. To develop the North Carolina side of the Smoky Mountains National Park; 2. To establish a museum for preservation of historical materials of the mountain region; 3. To attempt to secure more adequate accommodations for tourists; 4. To assist in the completion of the Bryson City-Fontana Road; 5. To initiate a historical outdoor drama; 6. To work toward the completion of the Blue Ridge Parkway; 7. To encourage the organization of a Chamber of Commerce in each community of the WNCAC region. The organization of the Cherokee Historical Association and the production of the drama *Unto These Hills* are accomplishments of WNCAC. The play, poignantly concerned chiefly with the removal of the Cherokees, provides seasonal incomes for one hundred seventy persons and attracts tourists to the area. The organizers of WNCAC began talking about such a drama in 1946, and in 1950 the first performance was given. The inspiration came from "The Lost Colony," the symphonic drama by Paul

Green which has been performed on Roanoke Island throughout the summer each year since 1937. As the purpose of WNCAC was to present a drama concerning the Cherokee Indians, the cooperation of a local committee from Cherokee was essential. Kermit Hunter was asked to write the drama. Then the Cherokee Historical Association was formed to build a theater and produce the play. On March 24, 1948, the historical association was incorporated as a non-profit organization; officers were Harry E. Buchanan of Hendersonville, chairman, Percy Ferebee, vice-chairman, Mrs. Molly Arneach of Cherokee, secretary, and Joe Jennings, treasurer. Funds were recruited by pledges from people and organizations of eleven counties, the drama was written, and the Mountainside Theater with access roads was built. Contributions were made by Indian Service employees and the Eastern Band of Cherokees, traders at Cherokee, and the Catholic Church. A total of $29,286.75 was raised, to which the North Carolina General Assembly was persuaded to contribute $35,000 in 1949. Veterans who were engaged in building trades classes at Cherokee High School contributed much labor, and many others worked throughout the year 1949. From the first performance on July 1, 1950, the drama was a success.

Then the Cherokee Historical Association turned its attention to the Tsali Institute, a non-profit organization for the historical and anthropological study of the Cherokee Indians. It built a full size Indian village of about the year 1750, Oconaluftee, toward which the North Carolina General Assembly appropriated $25,000. Mud huts and primitive cabins in which Indians engage in native crafts exemplify the life of the Cherokees. The Museum of the Cherokee Indian is another product of the Association. It brings together artifacts that trace the complete history of the Indian, especially the Cherokees.

New developments for the Eastern Cherokees are the various governmental service agencies such as a twenty-five bed hospital, a forestry division, an agricultural and soil conservation service, a water and sewer facility, the Neighborhood Youth Corps of the United States Department of Labor, and a community action program under the Office of Economic Opportunity.

The Boundary Tree Enterprise, tribally owned, includes a lodge and motel and a building housing the showroom of the Qualla Arts and Crafts Mutual. Most of the motels, craft shops, restaurants, and filling stations are owned and operated by Cherokees.

"Chiefing" — *Cherokee Indian wearing a Plains Indian war bonnet to attract tourists*

Friends of the band have deplored the resort to "chiefing" which has been practiced by some of the men and boys. They wear the feather headdress of the Sioux Indians of the Great Plains during the tourist season and stand in front of gift shops in Cherokee to attract customers. They charge twenty-five to fifty cents to allow the curious to take their pictures and then entice the people into the shops where the handcrafted products such as baskets, pottery, and beadwork are sold.

The United States Department of the Interior estimates that five million tourists visit Cherokee annually. Their purchases and the services they require are an obvious boost to the economy of the Cherokees and the region. The reservation has been called by the Department of the Interior the model Indian reservation of the country. It is a unique example of cooperation by the federal government, state government, associated communities and a particular community.

Two years after the opening of *Unto These Hills*, some of the leading citizens of Boone including Mrs. J. B. Stallings, Mrs. Leo Pritchett, Stanley Harris, D. J. Whitener and Mrs. Charles Cannon of Concord organized the Southern Appalachian Historical Association. This organization engaged Kermit Hunter to write an outdoor drama *Horn in the West*. The "Horn" was the call of the west, of the untamed wilderness and of freedom. It is the story of the westward movement and the struggle of a group of colonists for independence and freedom from oppression, unjust taxes, and legal injustice. It involves the movement of the people across the mountains and their clash with the Indians. Daniel Boone is a heroic character in the play, but his deeds were not performed by the real Daniel Boone as he was in Kentucky at the time the drama is supposed to have taken place. The play is gripping, picturesque, exciting. It is great entertainment. It has verisimilitude: that is, although the narrative is fiction events could have happened as they are created for the audience. The setting for the drama is a unique outdoor theater that seats 2400 people.

Kermit Hunter explained the nature of his outdoor dramas as art forms of three types: folk art built upon the manners, customs, beliefs, and ideals of an earlier America; commercial art, to provide dividends (tourists spend an average of $15 per day per person); fine art, to portray scenes, characters, and ideas based on fundamental and timeless truths and to give the audience inspiration. *Horn in the West* is produced in the Daniel Boone Theater on a tract of land purchased by the town of Boone. Two other attractions are to be found there. One is the Daniel Boone Native Garden, created by the Garden Club of North Carolina to preserve and permit people to enjoy the native shrubs, flowers, and trees of the area. The other is the Tatum House, the actual log house occupied by generations of the Tatum family and described by Charles Dudley Warner in *On Horseback*. It was moved to these grounds and is furnished authentically as a museum of rural life of the nineteenth century.

The Zebulon B. Vance birthplace in the Reems Creek area of Buncombe County is a historic site administered by the State Department of Archives and History. The site includes the dwelling house and six farm buildings. One other log building will be added. The restoration includes the original chimney, two original fireplaces, paneling, flooring, rafters and foundation rock taken from the old house. The dwelling contains many pieces of furniture, weaving, tools, pots, artifacts used by pioneers in the eighteenth century. The Vance house was built not long after the Revolution, but it is associated with Zebulon B. Vance, the state's Civil War Governor, Senator, soldier and orator who attained "more honors than any other man in the State's history." There is also a visitor-center-museum which has an exhibit room, a lecture room, an administrative office, and rest rooms.

In McDowell County the Carson House is being restored as a museum of history to "illustrate life in the Upper Catawba Valley a hundred fifty to a hundred years ago." Built about 1810, the house served as the first court house when the county was created in 1843, as a stage coach stop and a fashionable inn, and during the Civil War as a "small exclusive school for girls."

"As eastern America searches desperately for recreational outlets for its tens of millions, Appalachia becomes infinitely more important as a preserve for people than as a site for new industries."

Among the cherished heritages of mountain people are the folk tales, the ballads, and the folk dances. Greater effort should be made to preserve and to popularize these.

Tourist facilities are far different from what they were fifty years ago. The highway and the automobile have been responsible for the change. Formerly tourists were content to stay in rustic, fairly crude inns, lodges, hotels. Now people drive as far and as fast as they wish, and they will drive to where the most luxurious and attractive hotels and motels are to be found. The prices are much higher, of course, but people are willing to spend money freely for pleasure and luxuries. Far more "first class" motels are needed.

The 1950's and 1960's have been years of the most rapid tourist development. An area endowed with supernal beauty and a delightfully cool summer climate had to be developed and advertised. Some attractions there were, but many were added, including winter sports. Roan Mountain in rhododendron time, the Moses Cone Estate, Mount Mitchell, Grandfather

Zebulon Baird Vance birthplace before restoration

ASHEVILLE CITIZEN-TIMES CO.

Vance Birthplace after restoration   ASHEVILLE CHAMBER OF COMMERCE PHOTO

Mountain, Linville Falls, Wiseman's View, and the Great Smokies should be on the itinerary of most travelers to the mountains. The Kerr Scott Dam and Reservoir, a federal construction, provides flood control of the Yadkin and its tributaries and recreational facilities. It is one of several projected dams for the Yadkin River system. Two new state parks are being developed, Pilot Mountain in Surry County and Stone Mountain in Wilkes County.

The present trend is toward larger and more exclusive resorts. The Robbins brothers were highly successful in developing Hound Ears. It appears that they are even more successful with Beech Mountain. The Morton-McRae family who own Grandfather Mountain have developed Invershiel, a residential community in Scottish style. They have built a beautiful new golf course and lake at the foot of Grandfather Mountain. Around the lake and golf course they are selling home sites. Dr. Thomas Brigham and Mr. and Mrs. George McRae who helped start the Beech Mountain project are now developing Sugar Mountain. A group of Winston-Salem men and the L. A. Reynolds Construction Company have developed Seven Devils, a resort and residential area with ski slopes, a lake, homesites, golf and tennis. Roaring Gap, in Alleghany County, a resort chiefly of people from Winston-Salem has been enjoyed for many years. Nearby the High Meadows Golf Club and Ski Slope have been added recently. Today the area from Tryon to Franklin is a "golden strip" filled with summer and retirement homes and resorts. Skiing and other winter sports have been introduced. Many of the homes are luxurious and are owned chiefly by people from elsewhere. In Jackson County, for example, 2500 of 8000 property owners are from outside the state. Among the fine inns in that area are High Hampton, Sapphire Valley, and Highlands Inn.

In 1960 the total expenditures of all travelers in North Carolina were estimated at $408,000,000. Out-of-state travelers spent $245,000,000, North Carolina people $163,000,000. There was an increase in travel expenditures over 1959 of 4.5%, over 1948 of 167%. Including local trade engaged in by travelers the amount spent in 1960 was $810,000,000. From these figures one can readily see that "the travel business in North Carolina is a vast industry. . . . The travel dollar flows into a wide range of industries." The travel industry in the mountain region in 1960 brought in $58,800,000. This was 14.4% of the state total and

Richard Nixon at the Roan Mountain Rhododendron Festival, 1958
HUGH MORTON PHOTO

10.4% of retail trade and service receipts. The total receipts of businesses that serve travelers, including local trade, was $102,800,000. Western North Carolina's travel business is invaluable and extensive, but the region that contains the Blue Ridge Parkway and the Great Smoky Mountains National Park should have a greater share of the state's travel business. The roads from the North and Midwest passing through North Carolina must be improved. More broad highways and interstate routes are needed. Northwestern North Carolina does not have more than a few miles of four lane highways.

Two Winston-Salem *Journal* editorials stressed the position of Western North Carolina: "We need to tell the rest of the world about all that this area offers, and we need to tell our own people (like motel staffers, service station attendants, waitresses). We need more popular entertainment. We must convince wives that they should accompany their husbands on business trips here, and we must persuade them — and all visitors — to stay longer.... The fact remains that... recreational open space is fast becoming the most precious commodity in America. All that remains is some determination of how best to use this land for the good of all of us."

SOURCES

Much of the information consisted of oral history from lengthy interviews (some of the elderly persons are now deceased):

D. Hiden Ramsey, Asheville
Bascom Lamar Lunsford, Turkey Creek
James Larkin Pearson, North Wilkesboro
Dr. Benjamin Washburn, Rutherfordton
Dr. Alfred Mordecai, Greensboro and Blowing Rock
Granville Calhoun, Bryson City
John McLeod, Mars Hill
W. Ernest Bird, Cullowhee
Willis Weatherford, Blue Ridge
J. Walter Moore, Hayesville
Mrs. Maude Gentry Long, Hot Springs
Worth Morgan, Forest City
Leroy Sossamon, Bryson City
Mrs. Marian Ingram, Robbinsville
Mrs. Lillian Thomasson, Bryson City
Miss Cordelia Camp, Asheville
Mrs. Mary Jane McCrary, Brevard
Mrs. Nancy Alexander, Lenoir
Patton Phillips, Graham County
Gordon Winkler, Boone
S. C. Eggers, Boone
Miss Myra Champion, Asheville
Mrs. Carrie Winkler, Boone
James Patton, Chapel Hill
Clark Medford, Waynesville
Cratis Williams, Boone
George M. Stephens, Asheville
Dr. Edward W. Phifer, Morganton
Robert Conway, Dept. of Archives and History

W. H. Plemmons, Boone, formerly of Asheville
Mrs. Janice Whitener, Boone
James Stroup, Spruce Pine
Rush Wray, Burnsville
Daniel Boone, VI, Burnsville
Thomas W. Ferguson, Ferguson
Mrs. Annie Winkler, North Wilkesboro
John Wikle, Bryson City
Lynn Gault, Brasstown
W. B. Stephen, Pigeon Forge
Woody Brothers, Spruce Pine
Edith J. Cornell, Boone
Mrs. Lexine Baird, Mars Hill
Harley Jolley, Mars Hill
Fred O. Scroggs, Hayesville
Robbins Brothers, Watauga County
Mrs. A. P. Kephart, authority on camping
Rufus Morgan, Franklin
Jason Deyton, Spruce Pine
John Foster West, Wilkes County and Boone
Miss Doris Sparks, historian of Patterson School
Mrs. Elizabeth McKibben Williams, Waynesville
John O. Goodwin, Blowing Rock
Jack Guy, Beech Creek
Richard Chase, Beech Creek
Don Lineberger, Brevard
Mrs. Daisy Feagan, Columbus
Weimar Jones, Franklin
Col. Paul Rockwell, Asheville
Alonzo Shields, Murphy

The administrative staffs of the Rutherford County Hospital, Grace Hospital at Morganton, Western Carolina Center, officials of Enka, Mead, and other companies, the National Park Service, and the U.S. Forest Service were interviewed. Questionnaires were sent to twenty-four school superintendents concerning integration. Visits were made to these schools: John C. Campbell Folkschool, Crossnore, Penland, Western Carolina University, Caldwell Community College, Warren Wilson College, and Tuscola High School.

PRIMARY SOURCES, PUBLISHED AND UNPUBLISHED

Bannerman, Arthur M., "The Historical Background of Warren Wilson College," *The Owl and the Spade*, XXI (Oct., 1944).

Barringer, O. L., "An Automobile Trip to Blowing Rock," *Country Life* (June, 1910).

Battle, William James, "A Mountain Tramp from Black Mountain to Highlands and to Blowing Rock," *UNC Magazine 1886–1889*, VIII, Nos. 2 and 4.

Battle, William, *Memories of an Old-Time Tar Heel* (Chapel Hill, 1945).

Branson, Levi, *North Carolina Business Directory* (Raleigh, 1884).

Butler, Marguerite, "A Dream Come True," *Mountain Life and Work*, VII, No. 3.

Campbell, Robert F., *Mission Work Among the Mountain Whites in Asheville Presbytery* (Asheville, 1898).

Chataigne's North Carolina Directory and Gazetteer (Raleigh, 1884).

Cilley, Clinton A., Diary, 1875–1885, Southern Historical Collection, UNC Library, Chapel Hill.

Cowles, Calvin Josiah, Papers, Southern Historical Collection, UNC Library, Chapel Hill.

Cozens, S. D., "An Orderly Entrance Into Town," *Fifteenth Pennsylvania Cavalry* (Phila., 1906).

Davis, Rebecca Harding, "By-Paths in the Mountains," *Harper's New Monthly Magazine* (1880).

Doak, Henry Melvil, *The Wagonauts Abroad* (Nashville, 1892).

Erwin, W. C., "Catawba Valley and Highlands," Pamphlet in the W. C. Erwin Collection, Southern Historical Collection, UNC Library, Chapel Hill (see also the Erwin Papers in this file).

Ferguson, Thomas W., *Home on the Yadkin* (Winston-Salem, 1957).

Ford, Willis, "Penland Goes to the Fair," *Mountain Life and Work*, IX (3), 19–21.

Guyot, Arnold, "Notes on the Geography of the Mountain District of Western North Carolina," *North Carolina Historical Review*, XV, 251–318.

Hamiltom, J. G. de Roulhac, ed., *The Papers of Randolph Abbott Shotwell* (Raleigh, 1931).

Harper, G. F. W., "Produce Book, 1877–1878," Southern Historical Collection UNC Library, Chapel Hill.
Harper, James C., Diary, Southern Historical Collection, UNC Library, Chapel Hill.
Hodges, Luther, *Addresses and Papers*, James Patton, ed. (Raleigh, 1962)
James, William, "On a Certain Blindness in Human Beings," *Essays on Faith and Morals* (New York, 1896).
Kephart, Horace, "Land of the Eastern Wilderness," *World's Work* (April, 1926), 617–32.
King, Edward, "The Great South. Among the Mountains of Western North Carolina," *Scribner's Monthly* (March, 1874).
Lenoir, William, Papers, # 426. Southern Historical Collection, UNC Library, Chapel Hill.
McClure, James, "Ten Years of the Farmers' Federation," *Mountain Life and Work*, VII (April, 1930), 23–25.
Madison, Bobert Lee, "Experiences of a Pedagogue in the Carolina Highlands," series of articles, *Asheville Citizen-Times* (April 23–August 13, 1938).
Mason, Henry McGilbert, "Memoir of a Southern Appalachian Mountaineer," typescript.
Merrimon, A. S., "The A. S. Merrimon Journal," *North Carolina Historical Review*, VIII, 300–330.
Mordecai, Alfred, "James Edwin Brooks, M.D." *North Carolina Medical Journal* (June, 1958).
"Notes from the John C. Campbell Folk School," *Mountain Life and Work* (Jan., 1928).
Pinchot, Gifford, *Biltmore Forest, An Account of Its Treatment and the Results of the First Year's Work* (Chicago, 1893). Booklet distributed at the World's Fair.
Pinchot, Gifford, *Breaking New Ground* (New York, 1947).
Schenck, Carl Alvin, *The Biltmore Story* (St. Paul, 1955).
Schenck, Carl Alvin, *The Forest Fair in Biltmore Forest* (Asheville, 1908).
Schenck, David, Diary, Vol. 8, "Jottings on the Circuits," typed from the originals given by Paul W. Schenck, Southern Historical Collection, UNC Library, Chapel Hill.
Settle, Thomas, Papers, Southern Historical Collection, UNC Library, Chapel Hill.
Seven Months a Prisoner: or Thirty-six Days in the Woods (Indianapolis, 1868).
Simpson, George L., *Western North Carolina Associated Communities* (Cherokee, 1956).
Sloop, Mary M., and Le Gette Blythe, *Miracle in the Hills* (New York, 1953).
Smith, H. P., *Some Results of Mission Work in the Mountains of North Carolina* (Asheville, 1898).
The War of the Rebellion: A Compilation of the Official Records of the Union and Confederate Armies (Washington, D.C., 1897).

Warner, Charles Dudley, *On Horseback: a Tour in Virginia, North Carolina, and Tennessee* (Boston, 1888).
Washburn, Benjamin E., *As I Recall* (New York, 1960).
_ _ _ _ _ *A Country Doctor in the South Mountains* (Asheville, 1955).
_ _ _ _ _ *A History of the North Carolina State Board of Health, 1877–1925* (Raleigh, 1966).
_ _ _ _ _ *Rutherford County and Its Hospital* (Spindale, 1960).
Washington, Lawrence D., *Confessions of a Schoolmaster* (San Antonio, 1939).
West, John Foster, "Folklore of a Mountain Childhood," *North Carolina Folklore*, XVI (November, 1968), No. 3, 166–169.
Western North Carolina Land Company (Philadelphia, 1874), also 1876 and 1883 editions).
Wiley, Calvin H., Papers, Southern Historical Collection, UNC Library, Chapel Hill.
Zeigler, Wilbur G., and Ben S. Grosscup, *The Heart of the Alleghanies or Western North Carolina* (Raleigh, 1883).

OFFICIAL REPORTS, DOCUMENTS, AND GOVERNMENT PUBLICATIONS

Acts Relating to the Western North Carolina Railroad (n/d) a bound reprint of all acts, 1852–1880.
The Applachian Trail, Forest Service, U.S. Department of Agriculture. This is one of hundreds of brochures published by the U.S. Forest Service concerning the facilities and opportunities offered the public in the the National forests, which may be obtained from the Asheville office of the service.
Ayres, H. B. and W. W. Ashe, *Southern Appalachian Forests.* (Washington, 1905). U.S. Geological Survey, Professional Paper No. 37.
Biennial Reports of the State Superintendent of Public Instruction, 1887–1888 to the present. All of these were searched for data concerning the public schools.
Cameron, J. D., *Handbook of the State of North Carolina* (Raleigh, 1893).
"Cherokee Indian Agency," U.S. Department of the Interior, mimeographed.
Clark, Walter, ed., *Histories of the Several Regiments and Battalions from North Carolina in the Great War 1861–1865* (Raleigh, 1927) 5 vols.
Clark, Walter, Ed., *North Carolina State Records.*
Connor, R. D. W., *North Carolina Handbook,* (Raleigh, 1913).
County and City Data Book, various issues by the U.S. Census.
Documents of the Sessions of the North Carolina General Assembly, 1871, 1872, 1879. Investigations of fraud and corruption.
Educational Publications of the State Superintendent of Public Instruction, Valuable source of data throughout the entire period.
First Biennial Report of the Commissioners to Build the Western Insane Asylum of North Carolina at Morganton, N.C. (Raleigh, 1876).

418 / Sources

Holmes, J. A., and William Cain, *North Carolina Geological Survey* (Raleigh, 1893).
Laws and Resolutions of the State of North Carolina Passed by the General Assembly at Its Session of 1876–1877 (Raleigh, 1877).
North Carolina Agricultural Statistics: Tobacco, Featuring County Estimates, 1925–1968 (Raleigh, 1968).
North Carolina *Constitution.*
North Carolina Board of Health, *Biennial Reports.*
North Carolina Board of Higher Education in North Carolina, *Reports.*
North Carolina Department of Water and Air Resources, annual reports.
North Carolina Geological Survey, *Mineral Industry of North Carolina* (Raleigh, 1901ff. Economic Papers nos. 4, 6–9, 11, 14, 15, 23, 34, 49, 55, 60).
North Carolina Tobacco Reports, 1967–1968, Bulletin of the N.C. Dept. of Agriculture, No. 191 (May, 1968).
Page, Roger J., *The Code of the City of Asheville* (Asheville, 1887).
Parker, John M., III, *Residual Kaolin Deposits of the Spruce Pine District* (Bulletin No. 8, N.C. Dept. of Conservation and Development 1946).
Pickett, George, "Report," N. C. Department of Air and Water Resources at Governor Moore's Conference in Asheville, 1968.
The Power Situation in North Carolina, N. C. Dept. of Conservation and Development, 1924.
Pratt, Joseph Hyde, *Good Roads Days*. (Ec. Paper No. 35, Raleigh, 1914).
_____ *Proceedings of the Annual Convention of the North Carolina Good Roads Association* (Charlotte 1912).
_____ *Proceedings of the Good Roads Institute* (Raleigh, 1914).
_____ and Miss H. M. Berry, *Geological and Economic Survey*, Economic Paper No. 44 (Raleigh, 1917).
Public Education in North Carolina, a Report by the Educational Commission (1920).
Report of the Board of Directors, State School for the Deaf and Dumb, Morganton, 1895.
A Report from Western North Carolina University: Story of Twenty Years Progress (Cullowhee, 1969).
State of North Carolina Wildlife Commission, *Official Regulations.*
Trees, The Yearbook of Agriculture, U.S. Department of Agriculture (Washington, D.C., 1949).
Weather and Climate. Bulletin No. 396, Experiment Station (Raleigh)

MASTERS' THESES AND DOCTORAL DISSERTATIONS

Allen, Roscoe J., "A History and Development of Education in Wilkes County North Carolina," thesis, University of Tennessee, 1952.
Bowlick, C. A., "A Study of the Cranberry Ore Belt," thesis, Appalachian State University, hereinafter cited as ASU.

Cotton, W. D., "Appalachian North Carolina, a Political Study...," doctoral dissertation, UNC, Chapel Hill, 1954.
Gardner, Anne Cofield, "Social Organization and Community Solidarity in Painttown," thesis, UNC, Chapel Hill.
Hartman, Vladimir E., "A Cultural Study of a Mountain Community in Western North Carolina," doctoral dissertation, UNC, Chapel Hill, 1957.
Holcombe, David, "The Western North Carolina Railroad," thesis, Wake Forest University.
Jolley, Harley, "The Blue Ridge Parkway: Origins and Early Development," doctoral dissertation, Florida State University, 1964, recently expanded and published by the University of Tennessee Press.
Jones, Perry, "The European Wild Boar in North Carolina," thesis, ASU, 1959.
Kuhlman, Clarence E., "Municipally Owned Electric Utilities in North Carolina," doctoral dissertation, UNC, Chapel Hill, 1941.
Penley, Larry, "A Baptist People and the Events Leading to the Formation of the Three Forks Association," thesis, ASU.
Perritt, Lytton Gladstone, "Growth and Development of Electric Power in the Carolinas," doctoral dissertation, UNC, Chapel Hill.
Plemmons, William H., "The City of Asheville," thesis, Duke University.
Schaff, W. R., "The Growth and Development of Education in Caldwell County," thesis, UNC, Chapel Hill, 1926.
Sparks, Doris, "The History of Patterson School, Caldwell County," thesis, ASU, 1951.
Thomas, David Nolan, "The Early History of the North Carolina Furniture Industry, 1880–1921, doctoral dissertation, UNC, Chapel Hill, 1964.
Ward, Francis Ehl, "The East Tennessee and Western North Carolina Railroad," thesis, ASU.
Williams, Cratis, "The Southern Mountaineer in Fiction," doctoral dissertation, New York University, Ann Arbor Microfilm.
Wooten, Samuel R., "A History of Richmond Hill Law School," thesis, ASU, 1963.

PERIODICALS

Abrams, Amos, "Frank Proffitt: A Legend A-Borning," *North Carolina Folklore*, XIV (Nov., 1966), No. 2, p. 19.
Argow, Keith, "The Cradle of Forestry in America," *Journal of Forestry*, LXII (1964), reprinted from *American Forests* (May, 1954).
Armstrong Anne W., "The Southern Mountaineers," *The Yale Review* (Spring, 1935).
Ashe, W. W., "Creation of the Eastern National Forests," *American Forestry* (Sept., 1922), 521–25.
Ashe W W., "Linville Gorge, A State Park for North Carolina," *Parks and Recreation* (Jan.–Feb., 1923), 235–90.

"Ballads and Songs of Western North Carolina," *Journal of American Folklore*, XII (April, May, June, 1909), 238.
Bell, Marshall, "Hon. Cope Elias, a Memorial Sketch," Report of the Thirteenth Annual Meeting of the North Carolina Bar Assn., 60–62. The bar association reports contain obituaries of deceased lawyers.
Burnett, Edward Condy, "The Hog Drivers' Play Song and Some of Its Relatives," *Agricultural History*, XXXIII, 161.
Canby, Henry Seidel, "Top of Smoky," *Harpers*, (March, 1916), pp. 580–583.
"Backwinds of the Blue Ridge," *Blackwood's Magazine* (Dec., 1912).
"An American Backwater," *Blackwoods Magazine* (Sept., 1911), pp. 355–66.
Buckley, S. B., "Mountains of North Carolina and Tennessee," *American Journal of Science and Arts*, XXVII (March, 1859).
Carter, L. L. "Appalachian Highlands," *Travel Magazine* (Sept., 1909).
Chapman, Marston, "American Speech as Practiced in the Southern Highlands," *New York Century Magazine*, CXVII (1929), 617–623.
Connor, R. D. W., "The Peabody Educational Fund," *South Atlantic Quarterly*, V, 169–181.
Cope, James, "Mountaineers of Western North Carolina," *Mountain Life and Work*, I (Oct., 1925), No. 3, 9–11.
Eaton, Allen, "The Mountain Handicrafts," *Mountain Life and Work*, VI, No. 2, 22–30.
French Broad River Basin Pollution Survey Report, State Stream Sanitation Committee, N. C. State Board of Health, 1957.
Fuller, Raymond, "All-time American Stock," *Mentor*, XVI (7), 15–16.
Griffith, Robert W., "Industrial Development of Western North Carolina," *The Southern Tourist* (March, 1926).
Guild, Curtis, Jr., "The Appalachian Forests," *American Forestry*, XVI (1910), 69.
Gwaltney, W. R., "Capture of Fort Hamby," *The Statesville Landmark* (6, 19, 1903).
Harmon, George D., "The North Carolina Cherokees and the New Echota Treaty of 1835," *North Carolina Historical Review*, VI (July, 1929), 237–253.
Hatcher, J. Wesley, "Glimpses of Apalachian America's Basic Conditions of Living," *Mountain Life and Work*, XIV (Jan., 1939).
Holliman, Harvey, "A Factory in the Sky," *Mountain Life and Work*, X, 29. Traces Enka from the start to 1940.
Huffman, Alfred, "The Mountaineer in Industry," *Mountain Life and Work*, V (Jan., 1930), 5–7.
Hunter, Kermit, "The Outdoor Historical Drama," *North Carolina Historical Review*, XXX, 218–222.
Kennedy, Philip Houston, "Present Status of Ballad Collecting and Geographical Ballad Distribution in North Carolina," *North Carolina Folklore*, XIII, 1–2, 67–82.

Kirke, Edmund, "On the French Broad," *Lippincotts Magazine* (Dec., 1840).
Knight, Edgar W., "Education in the Southern Mountains," *School and Society* (July 29, 1922), 13 pages.
Loehr, Rodney C., "Saving the Kerf: the Introduction of the Bandsaw," *Agricultural History*, XXIII (July, 1949), 168–172.
Maunder, Elwood R. and Elwood Demmon, "Trailblazing in the Southern Paper Industry," *Forest History*, V (1961) 6–12.
Mooney, James, "Folklore of the Carolina Mountains," *Journal of American Folklore* (April–June, 1889).
Moser, Joan, "Traditional Music of the Southern Appalachians: Traditional Fiddle Tunes," *North Carolina Folklore*, XII (Dec., 1964), No. 2, p. 2.
Myers, John, "The Mountaineer in Industry," *Mountain Life and Work*, VI (July, 1930), 7–11.
North Carolina Medical Journal. All volumes were examined for data concerning the western counties.
Phifer, Edward W., "Saga of a Burke County Family," *North Carolina Historical Review*, XXXIX, three installments.
―――― "Slavery in Microcosm: Burke County, North Carolina," *Journal of Southern History*, XXVIII, 137–165.
"Picturesque America on the French Broad River," *Appleton's Journal* (1870–71).
Pinchot, Gifford, "How Forestry Began in the United States," *Agricultural History*, XI (Jan., 1937), 255–265.
"Pisgah Forest Purchased," *American Forests*, XX (1914), 425–429. Pratt, H. H., "Southern Appalachian Forest Reserve," *Elisah Mitchell Scientific Society Journal* (December, 1905), 156–64.
Price Overton W., "George Washington Vanderbilt, Pioneer in Forestry," *American Forests*, XX (1914), 419–425.
―――― "Practical Forestry in Southern Appalachians," *Yearbook of the U.S. Dept. of Agriculture* (1900).
Rambo, M. G., "The 'Submerged Tenth' Among the Southern Mountaineers," *Methodist Review* (July, 1905), 565–75.
Randolph, H. S., "The Asheville Farm School," *Mountain Life and Work* (October, 1932), 16–20.
Reece, W. Todd, "Mores of Mountain Music," *North Carolina Folklore*, VIII (Dec., 1968), No. 2, 36–37.
Schantz, O. M., "Beyond the Haze in the High Smokies," *Country Life in America* (Aug., 1926), 60–61.
Sharp, Paul F., "The Tree-Farming Movement: Its Origin and Development," *Agricultural History*, XXXIII (April, 1949), 41–45.
Sheppard, Muriel E., "Forgotten Valley," *South Atlantic Quarterly*, XXXIII (1934), 63–82.
Shurtleff, A. A., "A visit to the Proposed National Park Areas in the Southern Appalachians," *Landscape Architecture*, (Jan., 1926), 67–73.
Smiley, David L., "Educational Attitudes of North Carolina Baptists," *North Carolina Historical Review*, XXXV (1958), 316–27.

Smith, Charles Dennis, "The Appalachian Park Movement, 1885–1901," *North Carolina Historical Review*, XXXVII, 58–65.
Smith, J. R., "Farming Appalachia," *The American Review of Reviews* (March, 1916), 329–36.
Street, Julia Montgomery, "Mountain Dulcimer," *North Carolina Folklore*, XIV (Nov., 1966), No. 2, 27.
Tieran, Frances Fisher (Christian Reid), "The Mountain Regions of North Carolina," *Appleton's Journal*, (March, 1877).
Watkins, Floyd C., "Thomas Wolfe," *South Atlantic Quarterly*, I (1951).
Wilds, J. T., "The Mountain Whites of the South," *Missionary Review* (Dec., 1895).
Woolson, Constance Fenimore, "The French Broad," *Harper's New Monthly Magazine* (April, 1875).

GENERAL WORKS, REGIONAL, COUNTY, AND LOCAL HISTORIES

Alexander, Nancy, *Here Will I Dwell* (Lenoir, 1956), A History of Caldwell County.
Allen, W. C., *History of Haywood County* (Waynesville, 1908).
Allen, Martha N., *Asheville and Land of the Sky* (Charlotte, 1960).
Alley, Felix A., *Random Thoughts and Musings of a Mountaineer* (Salisbury).
Anderson, Robert Campbell, *The Story of Montreat from Its Beginning, 1897–1947* (Montreat, 1947).
Annual Eastern National Park to Park Guide (Asheville).
Arthur, John Preston, *Western North Carolina: A History from 1730–1913* (Raleigh, 1914).
Awle, Wm. Cicero, *Centennial of Haywood County and Its County Seat* (Waynesville, 1908).
Baker, Gladys, *The County Agent* (Chicago, 1939).
Barrett, John, *North Carolina As a Civil War Battleground* (Raleigh, 1960).
_____ *The Civil War in North Carolina* (Chapel Hill, 1963).
Biltmore House and Gardens, pamphlet published by the Biltmore Company.
Biographical Directory of the American Congress (Washington, D.C.   ).
Biographical History of North Carolina (Greensboro,   ).
Bird, William Ernest, "Geographic and Historical Backgrounds of the Cullowhee Area," paper read to the joint meeting of the North Carolina Literary and Historical Association and the Western North Carolina Historical Association, Cullowhee, July 22, 1960.
_____ *The History of Western Carolina College: The Progress of an Idea* (Chapel Hill, 1963).
Black Mountain College: The Visual Arts As Practiced at Black Mountain College. Program of an exhibit with historical sketch, Carroll Rice Museum (1966).
Blythe, LeGette, *Mountain Doctor* (New York, 1964).

Boswell, Martha Gash, "Notes on Transylvania Railroad," *Transylvania Souvenir Program, 1861–1961* (Brevard, 1961).
———— "Brevard's First Boom," *Ibid.*
Boyd, C. R. *Resources of Southwest Virginia* (New York, 1881).
Brooks, James E., *Green Leaf and Gold* (Raleigh, 1962).
Brown, Cecil Kenneth, *The State Highway System of North Carolina, Its Evolution and Present Status* (Chapel Hill, 1931).
————, *A State Movement in Railroad Development* (Chapel Hill, 1928).
Brown, Frank C., *Collection of North Carolina Folklore*, gen. ed., Norman I. White (Durham, 1952), 7 vols.
Brown, Hugo Victor, *A History of the Education of Negroes* (Raleigh, 1961).
Brown, O Lester, *Blanford Barnard Dougherty: A Man to Match His Mountains* (Boone, 1963).
Buckingham, James S., *Slave States of America* (London, 1842).
Burkhead, L. S., *A Centennial History of Methodism in North Carolina* (Raleigh, 1876).
Camp, Cordelia, *David Lowry Swain: Governor and University President.* (Asheville, 1963).
————, *Governor Vance: A Life for Young People* (Asheville, 1961).
————, "Handicrafts in Western North Carolina Highlands," typescript.
———— *A Thought at Midnight* (Asheville, 1969). The Asheville Teachers College.
Campbell, John C., *The Southern Highlander and His Homeland* (New York, 1921).
Campbell, Olive Dame, and Cecil Sharp, *English Folk Songs from the Southern Appalachians* (New York and London, 1917).
————, *Southern Highland Schools Maintained by Denominational and Independent Agencies* (New York, 1921).
Carolina and Northwestern Railway, People's Own Line (Richmond, 1877).
Cathey, Cornelius O., *Agriculture in North Carolina Before the Civil War* (Raleigh, 1967).
Centennial History of Clay County, North Carolina, 1861–1961 (Hayesville, 1961).
Chase, Richard, *Grandfather Tales: American-English Folk Tales* (Boston, 1948).
The Cherokee Indian, Qualla Indian Reservation. Booklet.
Chunn, Ida, *Descriptive Guidebook to North Carolina Mountains* (New York, 1881).
Clark, Elmer T., *Methodism in Western North Carolina* (Lake Junaluska, 1966).
Cohen, John, "Introduction to Styles in Old-Time Music," *New Lost City Ramblers Song Book* (New York, 1964).
Connor, R. D. W., *Rebuilding an Ancient Commonwealth* (Chapel Hill, 1930).
Cooper, Horton, *History of Avery County* (Newland, 1963).
Co-operative Study of the City of Asheville — Buncombe County, North Carolina State Board of Health Conference (Jan. 30–Feb. 5, 1963).

Corbitt, David Leroy, *The Formation of the North Carolina Counties 1663–1943* (Raleigh, 1950).
Crabtree, Beth G., *North Carolina Governors, 1585–1958* (Raleigh, 1958).
Craig, D. I., *A History of the Development of the Presbyterian Church in North Carolina and of Synodical Home Missions* (Richmond, 1907).
Cranford, Fred, *The Waldenses of Burke County* (Morganton, 1969).
Croffert, W. A., *The Vanderbilts* (New York, 1886).
Crouch, John, *Historical Sketches of Wilkes County* (Wilkesboro, 1902).
Cushman, Rebecca, *Swing Your Mountain Gal* (Boston and New York, 1934).
———— "Seed of Fire," book-length typescript, many photographs. North Carolina Collection, UNC Library, Chapel Hill.
Dabney, Charles William, *Universal Education in the South* (Chapel Hill, 1936).
Daniels, Jonathan, *Tar Heels* (New York, 1947).
Davidson, Donald, *The Tennessee* (New York, 1948).
Davidson, John Mitchell, "Sketch of the Davidson Family," typescript in North Carolina Room, Pack Memorial Library, Asheville.
Davidson, Theodore F., "Reminiscences and Traditions of Western North Carolina," paper read before the Pen and Plate Club of Asheville.
De Long, Mrs. Roy J., "Food Preservation in Early Transylvania County," Transylvania County Centennial Historical Program (Brevard, 1961).
Dorland-Bell Schools Bulletin.
Drane, Brent S., *Chestnut and the Chestnut Blight* (Raleigh).
Dugger, Shepherd M., *The War Trails of the Blue Ridge* (Banner Elk, 1932).
————, *The Balsam Groves of Grandfather Mountain* (Philadelphia, 1909).
Dykeman, Wilma, *Prophet of Plenty* (Knoxville, 1966).
———— and James Stokely, *Seeds of Southern Change: The Life of Will Alexander* (New York, 1962).
Eaton, Allen, *Handicrafts of the Southern Highlands* (New York, 1937).
Edmonds, Helen G., *The Negro and Fusion Politics in North Carolina, 1894–1901* (Chapel Hill, 1951).
Ehle, John, *The Road* (New York, 1967).
Electric Power in a Finer Carolina, Carolina Power and Light Co. pamphlet.
Feasibility Study, Continuing Education Center (for ASU) (Helen, Georgia, 1969).
Fiftieth Anniversary Rededication and Open House of Grace Hospital, Morganton, May 13, 1956, contains historical sketch.
Fiske, John, *Old Virginia and Her Neighbors* (Boston, 1897).
Fletcher, Arthur, *A History of Ashe County* (Jefferson, 1963).
Fletcher, J. L., *A History of the Ashe, North Carolina, and New River, Virginia, Baptist Associations* (Raleigh, 1935).
The Floods of 1916. Southern Railway Co. (1917).
Freel, Mrs. C. S., "Fort Butler and the Cherokee Departure for the Indian Territory." Address.

Sources / 425

Freel, Margaret, *Our Heritage: The People of Cherokee County, North Carolina.*
Frome, Michael, *Strangers in High Places* (Garden City, New York, 1966).
Gibson, Henry H., *American Forest Trees*, ed. by H. Maxwell (Chicago, 1913).
Glea Alpine Springs, (advertising pamphlet, 1879).
Gray, Idyl Dial, *Azure Lure: A Romance of the Mountains* (Asheville, 1924).
Griffin, Clarence W., *History of Old Tryon and Rutherford Counties, 1730–1936* (Asheville, 1937).
_ _ _ _ _, *History of Rutherford County, 1937–1951* (Asheville, 1957).
_ _ _ _ _, *Western North Carolina Sketches* (Forest City, 1941).
Gulick, John, *Cherokees at the Crossroads* (Chapel Hill, 1960).
Hale, P. M., *In the Coal and Iron Counties of North Carolina* (Raleigh, 1883).
_ _ _ _ _, *Woods and Timbers of North Carolina* (Raleigh, 1890).
Harden, John, *North Carolina Roads and their Builders*, II (Raleigh, 1966).
Hayes, Johnson, *The Land of Wilkes* (Wilkesboro, 1962).
Helper, Hinton Rowan, *The Impending Crisis of the South* (New York, 1857).
Henderson, Archibald, *The Conquest of the Old Southwest* (New York, 1920).
Henredon Furniture Industries, Inc., *Annual Report*, (1968).
Henry, Mellinger E., *Folk-Songs from the Southern Highlands* (New York, 1938).
Herring, Harriet L., *Passing of the Mill Village: Revolution in a Southern Institution* (Chapel Hill, 1949).
Hickerson, Thomas Felix, *Echoes of Happy Valley: Letters and Diaries, Family Life in the South, Civil War History* (Chapel Hill, 1962).
_ _ _ _ _, *Happy Valley* (Durham, 1940).
Hobbs, Samuel H., Jr., *North Carolina Economic and Social* (Chapel Hill, 1930).
Holder, Rose Howell, *McIver of North Carolina* (Chapel Hill, 1957).
Hollingsworth, Jesse G., *History of Surry County, or Annals of Northwest North Carolina* (Greensboro, 1935).
Holmes, J. S., *Mount Mitchell and Mount Mitchell State Park* (1919).
Housley, Jay, *Brief History of Tapoco and the Great Smoky Country* (Tapoco Lodge, n/d).
Hoyle, Bernadette, *Tar Heel Writers I Know* (Winston-Salem, 1956).
Illick, Joseph S., *Tree Habits: How to Know the Hardwoods* (Washington, D.C., 1924).
Illustrated Guidebook of the Western North Carolina Railroad (n/d).
Jackson, George Pullen, *Another Sheaf of White Spirituals* (Gainesville, Florida, 1952).
_ _ _ _ _, *White Spirituals of the South Uplands* (Chapel Hill, 1933).
_ _ _ _ _, *Spiritual Folk Songs of Early America* (New York, 1937).
Jefferys, Grady, *Crossties Through Carolina* (Raleigh, 1969).
Jenkins, Mark, *Historical Sketch of Calvary Episcopal Church* (Fletcher, 1958).
Johnson, Gerald W., *The Making of a Southern Industrialist* (Chapel Hill, 1952).
Johnson, Monte, "The Presbyterian," *Religion in the Appalachian Mountains* (Berea, 1955).

Judson College Catalogue, 1890–1891.

Kephart, Horace, *National Park in the Great Smoky Mountains* (Asheville, 1925).

_____, *Our Southern Highlanders* (New York, 1922).

Kerr, W. C., *Western North Carolina* (Raleigh, 1883).

King, Edward, *The Great South* (Hartford, 1875).

Knight, Edgar W., *Public School Education in North Carolina* (Durham, 1916).

Koch, Frederick H., *Smoky Mountain Road* (Chapel Hill, 1939).

Leach, MacEdward, *The Ballad Book* (New York, 1933).

Lefler, Hugh T. and Albert Ray Newsome, *North Carolina: The History of a Southern State* (Chapel Hill, 1954).

Lewis, Charles Lee, *Philander Priestly Claxton: Crusader for Public Education* (Knoxville, 1948).

Lomax, Alan, *The Folk Songs of North America* (New York, 1960).

Long, W. Ray, *An Historical Sketch of Linville* (n/d).

Lovvorn, R. L., *Health and Health Services in the Southern Appalachians* (Raleigh, 1959).

McCrary, Mary Jane, *The Goodly Heritage* (Brevard, 1959).

_____, "Transylvania County, 1861–1961" *Transylvania County Centennial Historical Souvenir Program* (Brevard, 1961).

McLeod, John, *From These Stones* (Mars Hill, 1965).

McNelley, Pat, ed., *The First Forty Years: John C. Campbell Folkschool* (Brasstown, 1966).

Malone, Dumas, *Edwin A. Alderman, a Biography* (New York, 1946).

Manpower Education in Western North Carolina (Washington, D.C. 1968).

Mead, Martha N., *Asheville in the Land of the Sky* (Richmond, 1942).

Mead Corporation, *Progress Report for Employees: Forty Years of Progress in Sylva, North Carolina*, (Typescript, n/d).

Medford, W. Clark, *Land of the Sky* (Waynesville,   ).

_____, *Mountain People, Mountain Times* (Waynesville, 1963).

Miller, Leonard P., *Education in Buncombe County* (Asheville, 1965).

Milling, Chapman J., *Red Carolinians* (Chapel Hill, 1940).

Montreat-Anderson College Catalogue, 1913 through 1966, shows the history year by year.

Moore, Hight C., *Patton: Southern Highlander. A Biography of Reverend Robert Logan Patton* (n/d).

Morgan, Lucy, and LeGette Blythe, *Gift From the Hills* (New York, 1958).

Morley, Margaret, *The Carolina Mountains* (Boston and New York, 1913).

Noble, M. C. S., *A History of the Public School of North Carolina* (Chapel Hill, 1930).

Mount Mitchell Railroad (Asheville, 1918).

Mountain Research Station. Pamphlet distributed at the station.

Niles, John J., *Songs of the Hill Folk: Twelve Ballads from Kentucky, Virginia, and North Carolina* (1934).

North Carolina Good Roads Association, *Road Maps and Tour Book* (1916).

Nowell, Elizabeth, *The Letters of Thomas Wolfe* (New York, 1956).

Nowell, Elizabeth, *Thomas Wolfe* (New York, 1960).

Orr, Oliver H., Jr., *Charles Brantley Aycock* (Chapel Hill, 1961).
Pace, Herbert E., *Fifty Years Ago Around Saluda* (Saluda, 1957).
Parker, Haywood, *Folklore of the North Carolina Mountaineer* (Asheville, 1906).
Parris, John A., *My Mountains, My People* (Asheville, 1957).
_____, *Roaming the Mountains* (Asheville, 1955).
Patton, Sadie Smathers, "Madison County," unpublished typescript.
_____, "Mills River Baptist Church: the History of the First Hundred years," typescript.
_____, "Pages from the History of the Speculation Lands in Western North Carolina," typescript in North Carolina Collection, UNC Library, Chapel Hill.
_____, *Sketches of Polk County History* (Hendersonville, 1950).
_____, *The Story of Henderson County* (Asheville, 1947).
Pearson, James Larkin, *Fifty Acres and Other Poems* (Wilkesboro, 1933).
Pearson, Thomas, *Richmond Hill Museum* (Asheville, 1959).
The 1916 Pictorial History of Haywood County, special industrial and resort edition of the *Carolina Mountaineer* and the *Canton Observer*. Reprint.
Plyler, Alva W., "The Early Circuit Riders of Western North Carolina," address before the Western North Carolina Conference Historical Society (Asheville, Nov. 14, 1917).
Pomeroy, Kenneth B., and James G. Yoho, *North Carolina Lands* (Washington, D.C.,   ).
Population and Economic Analysis of the Asheville Metropolitan Area and the Western North Carolina Region That It Serves (Asheville, 1966).
Powell, William S. *Higher Education in North Carolina* (Raleigh, 1964).
Preslaw, Charles J. ed., *A History of Catawba County* (Salisbury, 1954).
Price, Charles L., "The Railroad Schemes of George W. Swepson," *East Carolina College Publications in History*, I (1964), 32–50.
Price, R. M., *Holston Methodism* (Nashville, 1908).
Pringle, George H., *Inventory of Assets of Jackson County*, Jackson County Chamber of Commerce, (n/d).
Proceedings of the North Carolina Teachers Assembly, Haywood White Sulphur Springs, June 16–July 1, 1884.
Putnam, John F., *The Plucked Dulcimer of the Southern Mountains* (Berea, 1957).
Richmond and Danville Railroad, *Excursion Guide to Virginia and North Carolina Health Resorts* (1883).
Richmond and Danville Railroad, *Summer Resort* (1884).
Richardson, Frank, *From Sunrise to Sunset* (Bristol, 1910).
Roberts, Bruce, *The Face of North Carolina* (Charlotte, 1960).
Robertson, Archie, *Slow Train to Yesterday* (Boston, 1945).
Sage, Frances and Margaretta Williamson, *Rural Children in Selected Counties in North Carolina* (Washington, D.C., 1918).
Sawyer, Harriet Adams, *Souvenir of Asheville or Skyland* (St. Louis, 1892).
Scarborough, Dorothy, *A Songcatcher in the Southern Mountains* (New York, 1937).

Scheer, Julian, *Tweetsie, The Blue Ridge Stemwinder* (Charlotte, 1958).
Sharpe, William, *A New Geography of North Carolina*, 3 vols. (Raleigh, 1954).
———, *A Complete Guide to the Mountains of North Carolina* (Raleigh, 1953).
Sill, James B., *Historical Sketches: Diocese of Western North Carolina* (Asheville, 1955).
Small, John K., *Flora of the Southeastern United States*, 2nd ed. (New York, 1913).
Smathers, G. H., *The History of Land Titles in Western North Carolina*, (1938).
Smith, A. D., *Western North Carolina Historical and Biographical* (Charlotte, 1890).
Smith, R. P., *Experiences in Mountain Mission Work* (Richmond, 1931).
Smith, Harvey L., *Society and Health in a Mountain Community* (Chapel Hill, 1961).
Sondley, F. A., "Colonel Allen Turner Davidson," address, 1922.
———, *History of Buncombe County*, 2 vols., (Asheville, 1930).
South, Stanley, *Indians of North Carolina* (Raleigh, 1959).
Southern Railway, *Flood of July, 1916: How the Southern Railway Met an Emergency* (1917).
Spencer, Cornelia Phillips, *The Last Ninety Days of the War in North Carolina* (New York, 1866).
Spilman, Bernard W., *Ridgecrest — Past, Present, Future* (Ridgecrest, 1928).
Stephens, Eleanor B. *What We Can Do* (Asheville, 1962).
Stevens, William, *Anvil of Adversity* (New York, 1968).
Stillwell, E. H., *Notes on the History of Western North Carolina Part I: A Handbook and Syllabus* (Cullowhee, 1927).
Strange, Robert, *Eoneguski, or The Cherokee Chief* (1839).
Taliaferro, Hardin E., "Fisher River Sketches," *Harper's New Monthly Magazine* (1859); reproduced, 1955.
Thomasson, Lillian Franklin, *Swain County, Early History and Educational Development* (Bryson City, 1965).
Tiernan, Frances Fisher (Christian Reid), *The Land of the Sky* (New York, 1876).
Tilley, Nannie Lee, *The Bright Leaf Tobacco Industry, 1860–1926* (Chapel Hill, 1948).
Tindall, George B., *The Emergence of the New South* (Baton Rouge, 1967).
Toynbee, Arnold J. *The Study of History* (New York and London, 1947).
Van Noppen, Ina W., *Stoneman's Last Raid* (Boone, 1961).
Walser, Richard, *The Enigma of Thomas Wolfe* (Cambridge,   ).
———, *Nematodes in My Garden of Verse: A Little Book of Tar Heel Poems* (Winston-Salem, 1959).
———, *North Carolina Poetry* (Richmond, 1951).
———, *Poets of North Carolina* (Richmond, 1963).
Warren Wilson College Catalogue, 1969–70.

Watts, George B., *The Waldenses in the New World* (Durham, 1941).
Way, William W., Jr., *The Clinchfield Railroad* (Chapel Hill, 1931).
Waynick, Capus, *North Carolina Roads and Their Builders*, I (Raleigh, 1949).
Weatherford, W. D., *Life and Religion in Southern Appalachia* (New York, 1962).
Western North Carolina Regional Planning Commission Report (1961).
White, M. L., *The History of Amos Owens of Cherry Mountain* (Polkville, 1901).
Whitener, Daniel J., *A History of Watauga County* (Boone, 1949).
Wilburn, Hiram C., *Cherokee Landmarks Around the Great Smokies* (Asheville, 1966).
Wiley, Calvin, *North Carolina Reader*, No. III (New York, 1868).
Wilgus, D. K., *Anglo-American Folksong Scholarship Since 1898* (New Brusnwick, 1959).
Wilson, Mary Moretz, "Nineteenth Century Education in Watauga County," typescript.
_____, "The Deep Gap Tie and Lumber Company," typescript.
Wolfe, Tom, "The Last American Hero," *The Kandy-Kolored Tangerine Flake Streamline Baby* (New York, 1963).
Wolfe, Thomas *You Can't Go Home Again* (New York, 1934).
_____, *The Hills Beyond* (New York, 1941).
Woodward, Van, *Origins of the New South* (Baton Rouge, 1951).
Yates, Bowling C., "Culture Study of the Pink Beds, Cradle of Forestry in America," address to the Western North Carolina Historical Assn., (July 24, 1964).

INDEX

Aaron Seminary, 158
Abernethy, Rev., Laban, 91, 154
Abrams, Dr. Amos, 231
Alderman, Edwin A., 133, 166, 167, 171, 174, 179
Alexander's Inn, 39
Alexander, James Mitchell, 39
Alexander, Nancy, 220
Alexander Schools, 157
Allanstand Industries, 186, 226
Alleghany County, 3, 20, 48, 73, 92, 98, 119, 136, 142, 166, 169, 277, 279, 284, 285, 292, 333, 337, 344
Allen High School, 151, 158–159
Allen Industrial Home, see Allen High School
Allen, Maria, 112
Allen, Wilson, 42, 44
Anderson, Dr. R. C., 162
Anderson, W.W., 245
Andrews, 266
Anesthesia, use of, 106
Appalachian Regional Commission, 119
Appalachian Regional Development program, 147
Appalachian School, 163, 164, 187
Appalachian State Normal School, see Appalachian State University
Appalachian State University, 140, 145, 146, 147, 179–183, 218, 220, 277, 354, 368
Appalachian Training School, see Appalachian State University
Apple culture, 280–281
Arden, 84, 87, 163, 193, 195, 198
Arthur, John Preston, 220
Asbury, Bishop Francis, 75, 77
Ashe County, 2, 3, 8, 20, 48, 73, 84, 93, 96, 104, 108, 113, 119, 137, 140, 142, 177, 194, 220, 245, 253, 266, 269, 270, 272, 277, 279, 280, 284, 285, 286, 333, 342, 344, 353
Asheville, 8, 10, 16, 34, 35, 36, 37, 58, 70, 83, 84, 85, 87, 88, 91, 92, 100, 106, 109, 111, 115, 117, 118, 126, 127, 141, 142, 143, 144, 148, 151, 158, 159, 167, 177, 181, 196, 198, 204, 208–209, 211, 214, 220, 222, 225, 239, 241, 253, 254, 255, 268, 276, 279, 326, 328, 366, 378–388
Asheville-Biltmore College, see UNC at Asheville
Asheville-Biltmore Technical Institute, 113
Asheville Farm School, 159, 160
Asheville Female College, 37, 158
Asheville Male Academy, 57
Asheville Normal and Associated Schools, 159
Asheville Normal and Collegiate Institute, 159–161
Associate Reformed Presbyterian Church, 87
Avery, Major Alphonso Calhoun, 11, 32, 33, 88, 91
Avery County, 3, 20, 47, 113, 129, 137, 138, 139, 142, 148, 149, 158, 193, 220, 229, 277, 279, 331, 332, 342, 344
Avery County High School, 139
Avery, Isaac, 28, 89
Avery, William Waightstill, 28, 32, 91
Aycock, Charles Brantley, 93, 132, 136, 179

Ayers, H.B. and W.W. Ashe, report, 297

Bader, William, 193
Bailey, Judge John L., 88, 91, 92
Bakersville, 44, 47, 90, 293
Ballads, 226–230
Balsam Mountains, 1, 7, 53
Banner Elk, 8, 139, 162
Baptist, 32, 37, 71, 72–74
Baptist, Free Will, 37, 73, 87
Baptist, Missionary, 73
Baptist, Primitive, 73
Battery Park Hotel, 58, 259
Beaucatcher Mountain, 36
Beaver Creek, 85
Bechtler's Mint, 57
Beech Creek, 195
Bell, Croydon and Thelma Harrington, 220
Bellevue, 32
Belvedere, 32
Ben Lippen, 87
Benners, I. N., 127
Berry, S.V., 85
Bethel Baptist Assn., 73
Biltmore, 187, 298–301, 302, 307
Biltmore Forest, 302, 306
Biltmore Junior College, see UNC at Asheville
Biltmore Village, 85
Bingham, Major Harvey, 8, 14
Bird, Dean William Ernest, 52, 220
Blackburn, Edmund Spencer, 98
Black Mountain, 37, 87, 169, 298
Black Mountain College, 115
Black Mountain Range, 1, 40, 41
Blake, Fanny, 83
Blalock, Keith, 8
Bledsoe, George, 222
Blount, John Gray, 4
Blowing Rock, 10, 85, 110, 179, 197, 326, 331, 373, 375
Blowing Rock Assembly, 87
Blowing Rock-Lenoir Turnpike, 372
Blue Ridge Assembly, 87
Blue Ridge Hearthside Crafts Assn., 193, 194
Blue Ridge Parkway, 119, 337–340, 389
Blythe, Legette, 221
Board of Health, State, 104, 106, 107, 116
Board of Water and Air Resources, 115
Bonclarken, 87
Boner, John Henry, 218
"Boom and Bust," Asheville, 386–388
Boon, Samuel, McDaniel, and Thomas, 42
Boone, 47–48, 167, 195, 267, 277, 367–368
Bostian, L. E., 82
Bowie, Thomas C. (Tam), 93, 333
Bowman, Jacob M., 45
Brasstown, 198
Brevard, 51, 83, 84, 155, 158, 262, 263, 326, 328, 363–365, 377–378
Brevard College, 154, 158
Brevard Epworth School, see Brevard College
Brevard Institute, see Brevard College
Briar Creek Baptist Assn., 74
Brinegar Cabin, 188, 391, 392

430

Brittain's Cave, 186
Broad River, 57
Brooker, W. L., 141
Brooks, E.C., 218
Brooks, Dr. J. E., 110–111
Broughton Hospital, 103, 114
Brown, Davis P., 198
Brown, E.D., 82
Brown, Frank C., 229
Brown, James, 14
Brown, Lawrence, 100–101
Brown Mountain Lights, 245
Brown, O. Lester, 220
Brown Seminary, 158
Brown, Brigadier General Simeon, 9
Broyhill, James T., 94, 99
Brushy Mountain Baptist Assn., 74
Bryan, T. Conn, 221
Bryan's Hotel, 47
Bryson City, 57, 130, 218
Buck Hotel, 35
Buell, Hillhouse, 84
Buncombe County, 2, 4, 14, 20, 28, 36, 37, 73, 77, 78, 79, 80, 89, 98, 100, 101, 109, 113, 117, 126, 129, 136, 140, 143, 144, 147, 162, 163, 182, 185, 197, 220, 232, 254, 276, 277, 279, 280, 283, 284, 286, 292, 304, 314, 329, 334, 342, 343, 344, 365–366
Buncombe County Health Department, 115
Buncombe Hotel, 35
Buncombe Turnpike, 39
Burchett, George, 266
Burger Mountain, 87
Burke County, 4, 11, 16, 18, 20, 25, 30, 32, 33, 77, 84, 90, 91, 98, 113, 142, 144, 153, 177, 220, 268, 273, 276, 279, 287, 314, 331, 342, 343, 344
Burnett, Frances Hodgson, 307
Burnett, Fred M., 62, 298
Burnsville, 16, 40, 42, 90, 157, 185
Burt, Lucy, 164
Buxton, Jarvis, 84, 85
Bynum, John Gray, 32
Bynum, J.S., 32

Caesar's Head, 90
Cain, William, 324, 326
Cairns, John, Jr., 207
Caldwell County, 3, 14, 18, 20, 45, 88, 93, 113, 135, 136, 142, 153, 163, 220, 272, 279, 342, 344, 346
Caldwell Community College, 113
Caldwell, Tod R., 16, 90
Calfee, John E., 159
Calloway, Elijah, 93
Calloway, James, 93
Camp, Cordelia, 221
Campbell, John C., 68, 213
Campbell, Olive Dame, 192, 213, 225, 226, 227
Campbell, Robert F., 80, 81
Camp Meetings, 77
Camps, summer, 405
Candler, Coke, 100
Cannon, Dr. Gaine, 104
Canton, 116, 118, 119, 252, 261, 266, 308
Carolina Power and Light Co., 355
Carroll, Ruth and Latrobe, 230
Carson House, 34, 410, 411

Carson, Col. John, 28
Carson, Col. Joseph McDowell, 58
Carson, Samuel P., 28
Carter, H. B., 36
Carter, Sol W., hotel, 40, 42
Cashiers, 377
Cataloochee, 90, 266
Catawba River, 90, 268
Cathcart, William, 4
Cathey, Mrs. George, 189
Catholic churches, 37, 85, 87
Cattle, 284–286
Civilian Conservation Corps, 338, 339
Cecil, Mrs. John F. A., 301
Central Bank and Trust Co., 142
Champion Paper and Fibre Co., 116, 119, 308–310
Chappell, Fred, 214
Charleston, see Bryson City
Chase, Richard, 195–196, 220, 244
Chatham Manufacturing Co., 94
Chatham, Richard Thurmond, 94
Chatuge Lake, 319
Chautauqua, teachers', 168–169
Cheoah Range, 1
Cherokee, town of, 53, 340
Cherokee County, 3, 15, 20, 56, 74, 80, 90, 96, 113, 127, 136, 142, 151, 182, 220, 276, 279, 286, 342, 344
Cherokee Historical Association and related activities, 408
Cherokee Indians, 4, 21, 22, 53, 57, 89–90, 144–145, 175, 209, 340, 370
Chestnut trees, 270–271
Chimney Rock, 57, 337
Christmont, 87
Christ School, 84, 163
Church of God, 87
Church, Harrison, 8
Cilley, Col. Clinton A., 89
Civil War, 6–12
Classes, social, 6, 70
Claxton, Philander P., 167, 168
Clay County, 3, 15, 20, 54, 56, 77, 80, 104, 129, 137, 142, 151, 158, 173, 177, 178, 279, 280, 286, 319, 342, 344, 348
Clay, Harry, 101
Clement, Miss Exum, 334
Clinchfield Railroad, 264–265
Clingman, Thomas Lanier, 35, 90
Clingman's Dome, 1
Cloudland Hotel, 45, 47, 254, 263
Cloyd, Uriah, 153
Clyde, 118
College of the City of Asheville, see UNC at Asheville
Columbus, 58, 138
Colvard, Dean W., 286
Cone Mansion, 391
Cone, Moses H., 179
Connor, R.D.W., 5
Conservation and Development, Dept. of, 118
Conservation, state agencies, 188
Conservative Party, see Democratic Party
Constitutional Convention of 1868, 123
Cooper, Horton, 220, 221
Cooperatives, 280–281, 283
Corn production, 287–288
Cotton manufacturing, 355–361

432 / Index

Counties, formation of, 2–3
Court week, 27–28
Cowee Mountains, 1, 53
Cowles, Arthur, 349
Cowles, Calvin Josiah, 349, 351
Cowles, Charles Holden, 98
Coxe, Frank, 58
Crab Tree Orphan's Home, 81
Cradle of Forestry, 315
Craig, Gov. Locke, 92, 93, 132, 181, 329
Craigmont, 87
Cranberry, 47, 185, 246, 263, 265, 267, 351, 352
Credle, Ellis, 219
Crest of the Blue Ridge Highway, 328–329
Crossnore School, 138, 192, 195, 221
Cullowhee, 174, 175, 176, 178, 179, 180, 181
Curry, J. L. M., 128, 171
Cushman, Rebecca, 215, 297

Dargan, Olive Tilford, 216, 247
Davenport College, 76, 153–154
Davenport, William, 153
Davidson, Allen Turner, 90, 92
Davidson County (now Tennessee), 2
Davidson, Theodore F., 91, 92
Davis, E. Mac, 81
Davis, Rebecca Harding, 37, 208–210
Deaf, School for the, 96, 131, 132
Deer Preserve, Pisgah National Forest, 316
Democratic Party, 15, 16, 30, 89, 90, 92, 93, 94, 95, 96, 97, 98, 99, 100, 123, 132, 333
Dillsboro, 197, 336, 353
Diphtheria, 105
Disciples of Christ, 37, 87
Distillers, illicit, 18, 272–275
Dixon, George F., 121
Dobson, 10
Doctors' fees, 104
Dorland — Bell School, 159, 160
Dougherty, Blanford B., 140, 179, 180, 181, 277
Dougherty, Dauphin Disco, 179, 181, 333
Doughton Park, 391–392
Doughton, Robert, 92, 277, 337
Doughton, Rufus, 92, 333, 335
Douglas, Clementine, 189–192
Dramas, outdoor, 390, 406, 409
Ducktown Branch of the Western North Carolina Railroad, 169
Dugger, Shepherd, 211
Duke Power Co., 355
Dula, Tom, 70, 228–229
DuPont Co., 364–365
Dyes, for cloth, 66
Dykeman, Wilma (Stokeley), 213–214

Eagle Hotel, 35
Eagle Mills School, 158
East La Porte, 53
East La Porte Male and Female Academy, 152
Ecusta Paper Corporation, 118
Edgewood Academy, 131
Eggers, S.C., 277
Ehle, John, 148, 214, 268
Electrification, rural, 287–289
Elias, Don, 100–101
Elias, Kope, 51, 56, 91–92, 175
Elkin, 49, 94

Elkin Baptist Association, 74
Ellis, Dan, 8
Enka Corporation, 92, 364–366
Episcopal Church, 11, 32, 37, 82–85, 87
Equalization Board, 142
Equalizing Fund, 131, 139, 140
Ervin, Joseph William, 98
Ervin, Samuel James, Jr., 98
Erwin, Alfred, 32
Erwin, Major E. A. M., 34
Erwin, W.C., 30
Etowah Institute, 158
Evangelical activity, 69, 71
Evangelical and Reformed Church, 87

Fairfield Lake, 328
Fairview College, 158
Family life, mountain, 62
Fancy Gap, 1
Farmer, Col. H. T., 35
Farmers' Alliance, 95, 96, 97, 173, 175
Feldspar, 352–353
Fiddlers' conventions, 224–225
Fields-of-the-wood, 87
Fishback, Col. John, 194
Fisher's River Baptist Assn., 73
Fiske, John, 5
Flat Rock, 35, 83, 87, 218, 220, 254
Fleming, Sam, 28
Fletcher, Arthur L., 220
Flowers, Col. C. W., 14
Folk, Col. George, 47, 88, 91
Fontana, 288
Ford Foundation, 112
Fort Hamby, 12–14
Fourteenth North Carolina Battalion, "One-Eyed Battalion," 8
Frances, Michael, 90
Franklin, 53, 56, 57, 92, 129, 167, 173, 175, 315, 336
Franklin Family, 33
Freel, Margaret, 74, 220
French Broad Baptist Assn., 73, 74
Fruitland Institute, 157
Fullwood, William, 19
Furniture Industry, 361–363
Fusion Period, 94, 97

Gaither, Col. Burgess S., 32, 33, 90
Gault, Lynn, 198
General Education Board, 133
Gillem, Brigadier General Alvan C., 9, 11, 12
Glade Valley School, 161
Glen Alpine, 33
Glen Alpine Academy, 153
Globe Academy, 153
Goodrich, Frances, 186–187
Good Roads Associations, 324
Goodwin Guild Weavers, 192–193
Goodwin, John O., 190–191
Gordon, Charles, 4
Graham, Dr. Thomas Alexander, 168
Graham County, 3, 20, 22, 56, 57, 80, 104, 136, 142, 144, 172, 178, 279, 288, 322, 342, 344
Granite Falls, 135, 245
Granny women, 66, 103, 105
Great Smokes, see Smokies
Grandfather Home, 162

Grandfather Mountain, 1, 393, 397
Grange, 95, 280
Gray, Idyl Dial, 211
Great Smoky Mountains National Park, 119, 212, 270, 337, 397–403
Green, Rev. J. B., 14
Green, Lewis W., 222
Green River Plantation, 58, 111
Greene County (now Tennessee), 2
Greer, Dr. I. G., 231
Gudger, Hezekiah A., 91
Gudger, Jack, 51
Gudger, J. H., 35
Gudger, James M., 32, 33, 36, 42, 91
Guy, Jack, 195
Gwin, James, 10, 11
Gwinville Mills, 356

Hall, Dave, 101
Hamilton, Harry, 277
Hamilton, J. G. deR., 17
Hampton, Wade, 53
Hancock, Mary, 220
Hankle, James Stuart, 83
Hannum, Alberta Pierson, 22
Happy Valley, 88
Harper, Ella, 20
Harper, G. W. F., 348
Harper, James, 153
Harper, James C., 93, 153
Harris Clay Company, 353–354
Hartley, Joe Lee, 326
Hawkins County (now Tennessee), 2
Hayes, J. F., 262–263
Hayes, Judge Johnson J., 72, 74, 220
Hayesville, 54, 56, 86, 92, 129, 138, 151, 173, 348
Hayesville College, 158
Haynes, Thurmond, 277
Haywood Agricultural Society, 52
Haywood County, 2, 20, 40, 52, 75, 80, 92, 113, 118, 126, 127, 136, 142, 143, 157, 158, 178, 182, 220, 252, 269, 277, 279, 284, 285, 286, 304, 314, 326, 342, 343, 344, 346–347, 366, 367
Haywood Institute, 157
Haywood White Sulphur Springs, 51, 52, 169, 261
Helper, Hinton R., 346
Henderson and Brevard Railway, 262
Henderson County, 2, 20, 34, 80, 96, 113, 142, 177, 220, 229, 279, 281, 283, 284, 286, 304, 329, 331, 342, 344, 365–366
Hendersonville, 8, 35, 74, 84, 87, 106, 137, 143, 156, 177, 262, 281, 324, 326, 328
Hickerson, T. F., 220, 328
Hickory Nut Gap, 254
Hicks, John O., 151
Hicksville High School, also Hicksville Academy, 151
Hicks, Rev. William, 158
Highlands, 53, 325, 328, 378
Hill-Burton Act, 112
Hinsley, Jay, 101
Higher Education, Board of, 145
High Hampton, 53
Hinton Rural Life Center, 86
Hiwassee, 225
Hiwassee Railroad, 266

Hobbs, S. H., 5
Hoey, Clyde, 98, 180
Hofecker, Glen, 193
Holden, G. W. (Wash), 294
Holden, Gov. Wm. H., 15, 16
Holmes, J. A., 324, 326
Holshouser, Governor James, 100
Holston Methodist Conference, 75, 76, 77
Hominy Academy, 37
Hominy Creek, 37, 92, 117
Hookworm disease, 107
Hookworm eradication campaign, 107–109
Hoppeldt, Dr. J. M., 32
Horse Trading, 68
Hospitals, establishment of, 109–115, 139, 154, 162
Horton, Nathan, 272
Horton, William, 272
Hot Springs, 40, 83, 118, 160, 226, 260 388–389
Hughson, Rev. Walter, 112
Hunt, Richard Morris, 299
Hunter, Kermit, 219
Hunting, 42–44, 51, 62, 64

Jackson County, 3, 20, 52, 53, 75, 80, 92, 104, 113, 136, 142, 143, 144, 173, 174, 177, 178, 263, 279, 342, 344, 353, 368
Jackson, George Pullen, 231–232
Jacocks, Dr. W. P., 107
James, William, 59
Jarvis, Governor Thomas Jordan, 126, 251, 258
Jefferson, 48, 49, 85, 93, 98, 266
Job., A., 293
John C. Campbell Folk School, 164, 192, 165
Johnson, Thomas G., 36
John's River, 89
Johnstone, F. W., 83
Jolley, Harley, 221, 337
Jones, Edmund, 91
Jones, E. W., 153
Joyce Kilmer Memorial Forest, 320–321, 322
Joyner, J. Y., 133, 135, 136, 171
Judaculla Rock, 53, 55
Judson College, 74, 156–157
Justice, G. W., 350
Justice, James Dyer, 350

Kanuga Lake, Episcopal Assembly, 87
Kaolin, 353–354
Keener, Ulrich, 75
Kelsey, S. T., 325, 326
Kephart, Horace, 211–214
King, Edward, 59
King, Hiram, 295–296
Kirby, Col. Isaac M., 10
Kirk, Col. George, 9, 16, 30, 91
Kirk-Holden War, 16
Knight, Edgar W., 137
Ku Klux Klan, 15, 16, 17, 275

Lake Junaluska, 86, 118, 143
Lake Sapphire, 328
Lake Toxaway, 263, 328
Land Law of 1777, 4
Language, mountain, 68
Lanier, Sydney, 210–211
Lankford, B. D., 51

434 / Index

Laurel Fork, 129
Laurel Hill, 129
Laurel Springs, 92
Lawyers, 101–102
Lees-McRae College, 162
Lees, Mrs. S. P., 162
Leicester Academy, 37
Lenoir, 10, 11, 76, 88, 89, 93, 94, 107, 113, 153, 158, 199, 267, 276, 293, 331
Lenoir Rhyne College, 113
Lenoir, W. A., 153
Lenoir, William, 272, 273
Lenski, Lois, 219
Lewis Fork Creek, 13
Linney, Frank, 333
Linney, James Polk, 14
Linney, Romulus, 222
Linney, Romulus Z., 89
Linville, 326, 331, 373
Linville Falls, 33, 328
Linville Gorge, 33, 34, 319
Literary Fund, 123
Literary Fund, new, 134
Littlefield, Milton, 16, 256
Little Switzerland, 87
Little Tennessee River, 57
Littlewood, Mrs. John, 194
Log cabin, building of, 59, 61
Lomax, Alan, 231
Love's Trading Post, 53
Lovette's Holly Farms Poultry Co., 287
Lovill, Captain Edward F., 179, 277
Lunsford, Bascom Lamar, 231, 240, 242, 244
Luther, Raymond, 266
Lutheran Church, 85
Lutheridge, 87
Lynn, 210

McBee, John C., 335
McBrayer, Judge Fred, 350
McBrayer, Dr. Lewis Burgin, 110
McCarthy, W.C., 154
McCoy, George, 162
McDowell County, 2, 3, 16, 18, 20, 33, 98, 113, 140, 299, 330, 331, 342, 343, 344
McGhinnis, B.L., 293
McIver, Charles Duncan, 133, 166, 167, 171, 174, 179
McLeod, John, 220
McLoud, C.M., 36
McRae, Donald and Hugh, 326
McRae, Elizabeth, 162
Madison County, 2, 8, 14, 20, 51, 73, 74, 80, 81, 91, 96, 98, 99, 100, 136, 142, 144, 172, 177, 220, 269, 276, 277, 279, 280, 284, 320, 330, 342, 344
Madison, Robert Lee, 173–180
Marion, 33, 34, 40, 70, 265, 267, 275, 326, 332
Marshall, 14, 16, 51, 118, 129, 193, 326
Mars Hill College, 74, 93, 113, 128, 156, 157
Mars Hill, town of, 188, 157, 199, 220
Martin, General James G., 12, 85
Martin, Muriel, 192
Mast, Mrs. Finley, 188
Mead Corporation, 368
Mead, Martha Norburn, 222
Measles, 106
Medical Society, State, 103, 104, 107
Medford, Clark, 220

Medford, Wid, 169
Medicinal herbs, 66, 105, 348–350
Meiggs and Freeman Line, 53
Men, mountain, 62–65
Mental Health, Department of, 113
Merrimon, Augustus S., 14, 15, 90
Methodist church, 71, 75–78
Methodist circuits, 75, 76
Methodist districts, 75, 77, 86
Methodist Episcopal, African, 37
Methodist Episcopal (northern), 32, 37, 76
Methodist Episcopal, South, 32, 37, 76–78, 86
Methodist Episcopal Zion, 32, 37
Methodist Protestant, 32, 37, 75–76, 78
Mica, 352
Miller, Helen Topping, 222
Miller, Col. John K., 9
Miller, Robert Johnson, 84
Miller, William, 34
Mills, 61, 63, 292, 293
Mills River, 51, 294
Mining, 351–354
Minton, T.O., 287
Missionary Baptist, 73
Mitchell County, 3, 8, 20, 44, 45, 73, 79, 80, 82, 96, 104, 127, 137, 142, 149, 177, 193, 269, 279, 331, 332, 342, 344, 352, 353, 354
Mitchell, Dr. Elisha, 44
Mitchell Institute, 157
Montanic Institute, 37, 129
Montezuma, 158
Montlove, 83
Montreat, 85–86
Montreat-Anderson College, 86, 162
Moody, B. H., 197
Moore, Charles Augustus, 92
Moore, Governor Daniel Killian, 92, 99, 101, 115, 343
Moore, Frederick, 92
Moore, Hight C., 218
Moore, Robert L., 156
Moore, Mr. and Mrs. Walter, 86
Moore, Walter E., 52, 92, 175
Moore, Col. William, 92
Moravian Falls, 93
Moravian Falls Academy, 153
Mordecai, Dr. Alfred, 110, 111
Morgan, Lucy, 164, 188, 189, 221
Morgan, Dr. and Mrs. Ralph, 197
Morgan, Dr. Rufus, 164, 187, 188
Morganton, 7, 11, 25, 30, 33, 76, 83, 84, 88, 89, 90, 98, 103, 112, 114, 131, 132, 153, 208, 245, 253, 255, 275, 326, 331
Morganton Academy, 153
Morley, Margaret, 215–216, 270
Morris, B. T., 34
Morrison, Governor Cameron, 183, 333
Moser, Artus, 233, 241
Moser, Joan, 236
Moses, Edward P., 173–174, 178
Mount Airy, 1, 10, 326, 367
Mount Mitchell, 1, 40–41, 373–374, 375–377
Mountain Baptist Assn., 72–73
Munday, Alexander, 54
Murchison's Black Mountain land, 42
Murphy, 56, 87, 90, 92, 157, 164, 258, 285
Murphy Branch of the W.N.C. Railroad, 261
Macon County, 2, 20, 53, 80, 113, 135, 136, 142, 167, 177, 178, 198, 269, 279, 284, 286,

314, 325, 336, 342, 344
Murphy Institute, 157

Nantahala Gorge, 56
Nantahala National Forest, 314, 315, 316
Nantahala Range, 1, 54
National Forests, 310–316
Neighborhood Youth Corps, 149–150
Nelson, D. B., 175
New Echota, Treaty of, 21
New Found Mountains, 1
Newland, William, 179, 180
New River, 93
Newspapers, 32, 37, 47, 53, 117, 129, 245, 346
Newton, George, 79
Noble, M. C. S., 171, 179
Nolichucky River, 45, 117, 118
Normal Schools, 166
Norris, Dr. amd Mrs. Henry, 111
North Carolina Fund, 149
North Carolina Methodist Conference, 76
North Carolina State Board of Health, 115
North Wilkesboro, 177, 266, 326, 333, 367
Nursing education, 111–113
Nye, Stuart, 198

Oberlin Home and School, 158
Oconaluftee River, 21, 90, 199
O'Henry (William Sydney Porter), 211
Old Fort, 30, 34, 214, 253, 257, 331
Olin Mathieson, 168, 363–364
Olmsted, Frederick Law, 299, 302
"Omie Wise," ballad, 70
Ore Knob Copper Mine, 353
Osborne, H. O., 285
Our Lady of the Hills, 87
Out-Migration, 366, 369
Owens, Amos, 275

Pace, C. M., 34
Page, Frank, 336
Palmer, Col. William J., 9, 11
Parris, John, 215
Patterson, town of, 90
Patterson Mill, 10
Patterson, Rufus Lenoir, 88
Patterson, Samuel, 163
Patterson School, 163
Patton, Robert Logan, 152–153
Patton, Sadie Smathers, 220
Peabody Fund, 128–129, 166, 167, 168
Peabody, George, 128
Peabody Schools, 128–129
Pearson, Cam, 32
Pearson, James Larkin, 216–217
Pearson, Judge Richmond, 88, 91, 298
Pearson, Richmond, son of the judge, 98–99, 298
Pease, Mr. and Mrs. Louis M., 158–159
Pell, Rev. R. P., 80, 82
Penland, 163
Penland House, 45
Penland Pottery, 198
Penland School, 164, 189, 192, 194, 197, 221
Phifer, Dr. Edw. M., 18–19, 112, 220
Phillips, Aunt Susan, 187
Pigeon River, 117, 118, 129, 255
Pilot Mountain, 49
Pinchot, Gifford, 302–304

Pineola, 265
Pink Beds, 294
Pisgah, 129
Pisgah Forest, 262, 304
Pisgah Forest Pottery, 198
Pisgah National Forest, 314, 315, 317
Pisgah Range, 1
Plemmons, Levi, 36
Plumtree, 139
Polk County, 3, 16, 18, 20, 33, 57, 58, 96, 136, 138, 142, 168, 261, 269, 270, 273, 277, 279, 281, 331, 342, 344
Poole, Maria, 221
Populist Party (People's Party), 94, 96, 97, 132
Poultry and eggs, 286–287
Powell, William S., 221
Power, electric, 354–355
Power plants, municipal, 354–355
Presbyterian church, 32, 37, 71, 78–82
Presbyterian, U.S., 79
Presbyterian, U.S.A., 37
Presbyteries, 79, 80
Presnell, Ed., 197
Price, Overton, 305, 306, 310
Pritchard, Jeter C., 91, 98, 99
Pritchard, Richard M., 99
Proffitt, Frank, 197, 223, 224, 231
Purdom, Ed., 197

Quaker Meadows, 19, 32
Qualla Boundary, 21, 57
Qualla Reservation, 22
Quilting, 66

Radical, see Republican
Ravenscroft, Bishop John Stark, 83, 84
Ravenscroft School, 84–85
Ray, G. D., 40
Read, Opie Percival, 221
Reagan House, 39
Reagan, Dr. James A., 109, 154
Reconstruction, 17, 30, 90, 94, 95
Reed, J. H., 36
Reem's Creek, 259, 355
Reid, Christian (Frances Fisher Tiernan), 211, 212
Republican Party, 15, 16, 90, 94, 95, 96, 97, 98, 99, 100, 101, 123, 132, 333
Reynolds, Robert Rice, 98
Richland Institute, 158
Richmond Hill Law School, 88
Riddle, Dr. J. B., 112
Riddle, Dr. J. Iverson, 113
Ridgecrest, 86, 253, 267, 331
Roan Mountain, 1, 45, 47, 129, 320
Robbins Brothers, Carolina Caribbean Corp. 368
Robbinsville, 56, 57, 81, 90, 172, 173, 316
Robertson, Reuben, 308
Rockefeller, John D., Jr., 133
Rockefeller Sanitary Commission, 107
Rogers, David, 178
Rutherford College, 91, 154
Rutherford County, 2, 16, 17, 18, 21, 33, 57, 98, 111, 113, 127, 142, 151, 161, 263, 264, 269, 270, 279, 281, 286, 287, 329, 330, 331, 342, 344
Round Hill Academy, 157
Round Knob, 169, 170

436 / Index

Rutherford, Griffith, 4
Rutherfordton, 1, 21, 57, 76, 84, 111, 254, 263, 265, 275, 326

Saluda, 261
Saluda Gap, 8, 35, 57
Sanford, Governor Terry, 145, 149
Sanitation Committee, State, 117
Scarlet fever, 106
Schreiber, Virginia Bryan, 148
Schenck, Carl A., 274, 304–309
Schenck, Judge David, 22, 30–57 *passim*
School of Forestry, 306–308
Scott, Governor Kerr Scott, 143, 341
Scroggs, Fred O., 348
Sears, Dr. Barnas, 128
Sebartle, Patty, 148
Second Broad River, 57
Sevier, John, 4
Sharp, Cecil, 21, 165, 225, 226, 227, 232
Sharpe, Bill, 221
Sharpe, Wallace, 14
Sharpe, Col. Wash., 14
Shotwell, Randolph A., 17, 37, 273, 294
Shuford, Abel A., 87
Sieber, Henry Alexander, 218
Silva Institute, 157
Silvers, Frankie, 228
Silverstein, Joseph H., 262
Ski resorts, 393–394
Skiles, William West
Slagle, Thomas, 54
Sleds, 293, 295
Sloan, J.B., 354
Sloop, Dr. Eustice H., 109, 139
Sloop, Dr. Mary Martin, 109, 139, 200, 220, 333
Smallpox, 106
Smather's Inn, 39, 51
Smathers, John C., 39
Smiley, J. E., 129, 130
Smith, R. P., 66, 80
Smokies, Great, 53
Snowbird Mountains, 90
Snyder Memorial Academy, 81
Social and Residential Communities, 403–404, 412
Sondley, Foster, 220
South Carolina Methodist Conference, 76
Southern Education Board, 133
Southern Highland Handicraft Guild, 190, 192
Sossamon, Leroy, 218
South Hominy, 129
South Mountains, 21, 33, 57, 113
Spainhour, Noah, 293
Sparta, 48, 92, 161, 167, 168
Speculation, land, 350–351
Speculation Land Company, 57
Spruce Pine, 191, 264, 267
Stacy, Rev. A. G., 153
Stearns Schools, 138
Stekoa, 53
Stephen, W. B., 198
Stephens, George, 87, 301
Stikeleather, J.D., 335
Stone, Mr. and Mrs. George, 189
Stoneman, Major General George, 8–12, 83, 153
Stone Mountain Baptist Association, 74

Stone Mountain Pottery, 198
Stony Fork Baptist Association, 74
Strange, Robert, 207
Stream Sanitation Committee, State, 116
Street, Julia Montgomery, 221
Strike at the Baldwin Mill, 358–359
Stringfield, Major W. W., 52
Stroup, H. M., 197
Sullivan County (now Tennessee), 2
Sumner County (now Tennessee), 2
Surry County, 2, 20, 48, 72, 73, 76, 109, 136, 142, 269, 273, 276, 279, 284, 286, 342, 344
Sutton, Mrs. Orus, 198
Surles, J. B., 193
Swain County, 3, 20, 57, 75, 80, 104, 113, 130, 142, 279, 284, 314, 342, 344
Swain, Governor David Lowry, 89
Swannanoa, 160, 286
Swannanoa Gap, 7, 86, 257
Swan Ponds, 32
Swepson, George, 16, 256
Sylva, 53, 157, 174, 326, 353, 368

Table Rock Academy, 153
Taliaferro, Hardin E., 207–208
Tallassee Power Co., 355
Tanning, 262, 266, 293–294
Tait, S. C. W., 32
Tate, Robert, 4
Tate, Dr. W. C., 162
Tate, Samuel McDowell, 256
Tate, William, 4
Taylor, Rev. Fitch, 155
Taylor, Roy A., 100
Teacher qualifications, 177
Teacher salaries, 135, 136
Technical institutes, 145
Tenella (Mrs. Bayard Clark), 218
Tennessee County (now Tennessee), 2
Thermal Belt, 280
Thomas, Col. William Holland, his legion of Indians and Highlanders, 7, 12
Thomas Col. William Holland, 21, 57, 89–90
Thomasson, Lillian, 129, 220
Thomson, Peter G., 308
Tobacco, 51, 276–280
Todd, 246, 266
Toe River (Estatoe), 44, 117
Toms, Captain J. M., 34
Tourism, 371–397
Toynbee, Arnold, 18
Transylvania County, 3, 20, 51, 75, 77, 80, 83, 104, 113, 142, 155, 178, 279, 287, 304, 314, 342, 344, 363–365, 366–367
Trap Hill, 158
Travel expenditures, 412–413
Truett, George, 151, 152
Tryon, 189, 211, 220, 261, 405
Tryon County, 2, 20
Tuberculosis, 105, 110
Tuckaseigee River, 53, 71
Tucker, Glenn, 220,
Tucker, James M., 86
Tucker River, 117
Tufts, Edgar, 82, 139, 152
Tufts, Edgar Hall, 162
Turkey Creek Camp Ground at Leicester, 77
Tuscola High School, 143
Tuscola Institute, 158

Index / 437

Tusquitee Creek, 54
Tusquitee Range, 1
TVA, 287–289, 355
Typhoid, 104

Unakas, 1
Unicoi Mountains, 1
Union Grove Fiddlers' Convention, 225, 239, 240
Union League, 15
United Methodist Church, 78, 86
University of North Carolina at Asheville, 115, 147–148
Valdese, 245, 359–361
Valle Crucis, 83–84, 85, 90, 187
Valle Crucis School, 163
Valley River, 56
Valley Town, 90
Vance, Eleanor P., 187, 189
Vance, Dr. Robert B., 28
Vance, General R. B., 10
Vance, Zebulon Baird, 30, 70, 90, 95, 98, 126, 205–206, 258, 273, 298
Vance, Zebulon B., birthplace, 410–411
Vanderbilt, George Washington, 85, 298–307, 310
Vanderbilt, Mrs. George Washington, 187, 301
Van Noppen, Ina Woestemeyer, 221

Wages in industry, average, 366–367
Wainwright, Mary Taylor, 84
Wainwright, Rev. Richard, 84
Walker, Elmeda, 193
Walser, Richard, 218
WAMY, 149, 193
Warm Springs, see Hot Springs
Warner, Charles Dudley, 27, 47, 152
Warren Wilson College, 160
Washburn, Dr. Benjamin, 21, 105
Washburn, R. C., 56
Washington County, 2
Washington, Lawrence D., 130
Watauga Academy, see Appalachian State University
Watauga County, 3, 7, 8, 11, 14, 20, 45, 47, 48, 77, 79, 80, 82, 84, 85, 89, 113, 121, 136, 140, 142, 149, 152, 167, 177, 179, 193, 229, 246, 266, 269, 270, 276, 277, 279, 280, 286, 287, 332, 333, 342, 344
Watson, Arthel L. ("Doc"), 231
Watts, George R., 221
Waynesville, 51, 52, 54, 106, 118, 129, 169, 173, 261, 285, 317, 326, 338, 345, 354
Weatherford, Dr. Willis, 213–214
Weaver College, 37, 109, 154–155
Weaver, Dr. H. B., 109
Weaver, Dr. J. B., 293
Weaver, William Trotter, 354
Weaverville, 40, 222, 345
Weaverville College, see Weaver College
Weaving, 66–67
Webster, 52, 92, 101, 129, 173, 174, 334
Weir, Weldon, 100, 101

West, John Foster, 247
Western Baptist Association, 74
Western Carolina Center, 113, 114, 131
Western Carolina University, 145, 146, 147, 173–180, 183, 354, 368
Western Insane Asylum, see Broughton Hospital
Western North Carolina Associated Communities, 406–407
Western North Carolina Conference (Methodist), 78
Western North Carolina Correctional Center, 114
Western North Carolina Land Company, 41
Western North Carolina Railroad, 16, 30, 34, 51, 92, 126, 169, 174, 208, 214, 254, 255, 256, 258, 308
Western North Carolina Regional Planning Commission, 118
Western Union Academy, 151
West Jefferson, 252, 266, 284
West Liberty Baptist Association, 74
Westminster School, 161
Wetmore, Thomas C., 84
Whiteside Mountain, 53
White Sulphur Springs, Waynesville, see Haywood White Sulphur Springs
Whittier, 53
Wiggins Family, 57
Wilcox Drug Company, 349–350
Wildacres, 87
Wiley, Calvin, 37, 121, 207
Wilkes Community College, 113
Wilkesboro, 7, 10, 48, 74, 84, 92, 93, 98, 266
Wilkes County, 3, 4, 8, 12, 14, 20, 48, 72, 74, 76, 93, 96, 130, 135, 142, 143, 153, 158, 177, 220, 249, 266, 273, 279, 280, 286, 342, 344, 346
Williams, Dean Cratis Williams, 216, 231
Williams, Jonathan, 34, 219
Wilson, Major James W., 33, 251, 258
Wilson, Dell, 222
Wilson, John McKamie, Jr., 19
Wilson, "Big Tom," 42–44
Winston, Dr. George P., 180
Wiseman's View, 322
Wolfe, Thomas, 202–206
Wolfe, Tom, 249
Women, mountain, 65–67
Woodfin, Nicholas W., 8, 90
Woody, "Aunt Cumi," 187
Woody family, 197
Woolson, Constance Fenimore, 207
World Methodist Center, 86

Yadkin Baptist Association, 72
Yale, Charlotte, 187, 189
Yancey County, 2, 3, 8, 20, 41, 45, 73, 79, 104, 136, 137, 142, 144, 149, 193, 269, 279, 284, 331, 332, 342, 344, 352
Yancey Institute, 157
Yellow Fever, 106
York, Brantley, 154
Yount, John 214

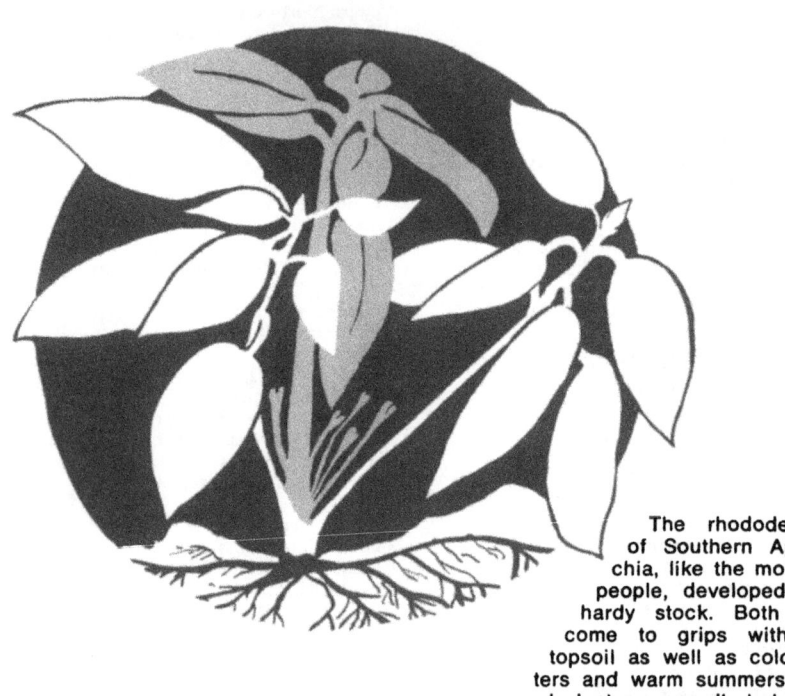

The rhododendron of Southern Appalachia, like the mountain people, developed from hardy stock. Both have come to grips with thin topsoil as well as cold winters and warm summers. Man and plant are proudly independent and evergreen.
Design by Sherry Waterworth
Dept. of Art
Appalachian State University

ABOUT THE AUTHORS

INA FAYE WOESTEMEYER VAN NOPPEN (1906-1980) and JOHN JAMES VAN NOPPEN III (1906-1975) were professors of History and English, respectively, at Appalachian State Teachers College from 1947 to 1972. Ina taught history and was one of the campus' earliest female professors with a doctorate. The Van Noppens co-wrote *Daniel Boone, Backwoodsman: The Green Woods Were His Portion* (1966) and *Western North Carolina Since the Civil War* (1973). Ina won the 1962 Thomas Wolfe Award from the Western North Carolina Historical Association for her *Stoneman's Last Raid*. In 1973, the couple also won the 1973 Thomas Wolfe Award.

www.ingramcontent.com/pod-product-compliance
Lightning Source LLC
Chambersburg PA
CBHW031306150426
43191CB00005B/104